Alexander

The LONDON
& POLITICAL

July 2013

ICS

C000156367

Interdisciplinary Perspectives
on Organization Studies

Titles of Related Interest

BOURGINE & WALLISER
Economics and Cognitive Science

DAVIS
Managing and Organizing Multinational Corporations

JÖNSSON
Accounting for Improvement

EDEN
Messing About in Problems

EILON
Management Assertions and Aversions

MORE
Organizations in the Communication Age

Related Journals

Accounting, Management & Information Technology

Accounting, Organizations and Society

Omega

Socio-Economic Planning Sciences

free specimen copies available on request

Interdisciplinary Perspectives on Organization Studies

Edited by

SIEGWART M. LINDENBERG
University of Groningen, Netherlands

HEIN SCHREUDER
University of Limburg, Netherlands

PERGAMON PRESS

OXFORD · NEW YORK · SEOUL · TOKYO

UK   Pergamon Press Ltd, Headington Hill Hall,
Oxford OX3 0BW, England

USA   Pergamon Press Inc., 660 White Plains Road,
Tarrytown, New York 10591-5153, USA

KOREA   Pergamon Press Korea, KPO Box 315, Seoul 110-603, Korea

JAPAN   Pergamon Press Japan, Tsunashima Building Annex,
3-20-12 Yushima, Bunkyo-ku, Tokyo 113, Japan

First edition 1993

Library of Congress Cataloging in Publication Data
Interdisciplinary perspectives on organization
studies / edited by Siegwart M. Lindenberg [and]
Hein Schreuder.
p.   cm.
1. Organizational sociology.   I. Lindenberg, S. (Siegwart), 1941–
II. Schreuder, H.
HM131.I542   1993
302.3′5—dc20   92–33026

ISBN 0–08–040814–1

Transferred to digital printing 2005.

Contents

Part III   Organizations and Environments

Part IV   Interorganizational Perspectives

Introduction

A FEW years ago, when Christopher Winship and Sherwin Rosen planned a special issue of the *American Journal of Sociology* on sociology and economics and issued calls for papers, they received so many papers on organizations and institutions related to organizations that they decided to focus the entire issue on this topic (cf. Winship and Rosen, 1988). Interests among economists and sociologists in what may be broadly called "organization studies" have strongly converged, and, perhaps for the first time in a hundred years, these substantive interests have also been accompanied by a convergence on theoretical issues. Exchanges across the disciplinary boundaries are just beginning to bear fruit. Despite these important developments, the exchanges have been quite limited and there has been too little groundwork done for these to succeed.

The Netherlands Institute for Advanced Study (NIAS) in Wassenaar, the Netherlands, offered the possibility to organize an interdisciplinary thematic group on organization studies in the year 1989/90. Sociologists, economists and psychologists were coming together to form a forum on organization studies. At the end of that year, a substantial conference was supposed to show the result. This conference did indeed take place and this book is based on it. A majority of the speakers had been part of the thematic group, at least for part of the time, or had been in discussion with the group during the year although they were not themselves present at NIAS. It is probably for the first time that such intensive interdisciplinary contact had taken place in this field. Of course, the disciplinary boundaries are still there and should be there but the book clearly shows the budding dialogue and the fact that results from the various disciplines are not just different but also relevant for what goes on in the other disciplines. In order to achieve this, many misconceptions had to be overcome and disciplinary languages had to be learned. In this respect, the article by Grandori on power versus efficiency is particularly instructive.

The book is organized into four parts: Integrative perspectives; decision-making, leadership, and innovation; organization and environments; and interorganizational perspectives. It is useful to highlight some of the results within each of these four parts.

Part I of the book deals with perspectives on organization studies that are integrative with regard to economics and sociology. Many of the themes discussed in this part return in other parts of the book. In his opening contribution, Williamson, an economist, expounds the instruments needed for a transaction cost analysis of organizations. The puzzle he originally addressed also created openings for sociology: if the market is such a marvel of adaptability why does a great deal of transactions take place within firms? His basic answer is that there are different forms of generic economic organization (market and hierarchy) and that, for each, adaptability in the face of disturbance is the major problem. For some transactions, the market context, for others hierarchy offers more adaptability. The cost-effective choice of one form or the other thus depends on adaptability features of the transactions. Within hierarchies, Williamson distinguished finer grained governance structures for different adaptability features of transactions. In this contribution, he does not get into these refinements but he adds two new features to the overall analysis. First of all, he adds a new generic form: the hybrid, between market and hierarchy. Secondly, he combines the analysis of organizational form with attention to the institutional environment, including reputational network effects. Changes in property rights, contract law, reputation effects and uncertainty over disturbances affect the comparative cost of governance for the three generic forms and thus influence the choice among them.

In the next paper, Schreuder, an economist, is more critical of the distinction between market and hierarchy. He argues that the distinction as it is used by Williamson obscures the fact that there are different coordination mechanisms in organizations and that all of them may operate in conjunction with market coordination by the price mechanism. Examples of the non-price coordination mechanisms are standardization of work processes, of outputs, of skills and of norms (all as suggested by Mintzberg). Many transactions will be executed under the regime of a bundle of coordination mechanisms geared to the transactional properties involved. The assumption of cost efficient choice of organizational form then explicitly includes communication costs as part of both transaction and production costs.

Williamson's analysis of organizations has many openings for the input from sociologists, and Schreuder suggests additional ones. However, both Williamson and Schreuder work within an efficiency framework, while many sociologists have argued that what is important in organizations is not efficiency but power. This difference has barred communication between economics and sociology of organizations in many cases. Grandori, an economist and sociologist, analyzes different variants of the concepts "power" and "efficiency" as used in the respective disciplines and she concludes that the opposition between "efficiency" and "power" perspectives is far too general to be useful. Where one is talking about dependency and ways of reducing it, the other may be talking about power and ways of increasing it. It turns out that in many instances the efficiency/power opposition is about kind and locus of efficiency. For example, cost efficiency with regard to organizational form neglects the possibility that the transaction partners may have conflicting interests concerning organizational form. Such a conflict can have direct consequences for the allocative efficiency within an organization, and who decides? Most economic studies of organizations are not concerned with allocative efficiency, and it is up to the sociologists to introduce it under the name of power. Grandori suggests various "translations" between the power and efficiency frameworks and sees especially two issues building common ground: fairness of organization forms, and the strategic modification of transaction parameters. Friedberg's paper in Part III is particularly interesting in this regard.

There is also a powerful efficiency framework within sociology, viz. Weber's conception of rational organization. Coleman, a sociologist, argues that Weber (and the many sociologists following his lead) made a serious mistake in equating rational organization with bureaucracy, implying that bureaucracy is more efficient than any other form of organization. Non-bureaucratic devices such as nepotism or shared ownership, argues Coleman, are used to increase efficiency where trust plays an important role. Once this is recognized, it also becomes apparent that organizations make use of social structures on the outside (like social capital in the form of kinship and friendship networks) in order to increase efficiency on the inside. Weber's view was that a rational organization protects itself against the influence of these outside structures. Coleman's analysis fits well with the gist of contributions in Part III. But there is also another twist to the outside/inside interaction in Coleman's paper. By and large, the allocation of property rights takes place outside the organization. However, changes in these rights change what is efficient inside the organization, so that the properties of rational organization become contingent on the constitutional allocation of rights. There is a clear connection of this line of reasoning with Williamson's idea about the influence of the institutional environment on the comparative governance costs.

Part II focuses on issues around decision-making, leadership, and innovation in organizations. Pool and Koopman, both psychologists, show that within their discipline Weber's model of rational organization does not hold sway. Here the language is different as well. One does not speak of governance structures, agency problems or hierarchies, but of typologies of decision-making, leadership and culture. Still, the issues are related. Integrating suggestions from the literature in their field, the authors suggest a typology of decision-making based on two dimensions: high versus low formalization and flexibility/decentralization versus control/centralization. In this way, they come up with four types or "models": the neo-rational model of centralized but informal decision-making; the bureaucratic model of centralization with high formalization; the arena model with decentralization but high formalization; and the open-end model with decentralization and low formalization. However, they go a step further than many of their colleagues by making explicit that such a classification contains theoretical claims that can be tested empirically. Are these two dimensions enough to capture the variety of decision-making strategies? Are the dimensions independent? By and large, their research corroborates the typology. But the authors point to the importance of linking this kind of research to other lines of inquiry. For example, they suggest to pay more attention to what precedes decision-making. In Williamson's language we would ask: what adaptability problems arise from the characteristics of the transactions? They also point to the importance of relating personal characteristics and skills to problems of decision-making, a topic touched upon in Part III in Lindenberg's paper. They also suggest research on how "paradigm shifts" on decision-making occur within organizations, a topic that leads us directly to the work on the management of meaning in the following paper.

Attention to decision-making becomes very important when there are thorough changes going on and routines have to be broken and newly assembled. In his paper on organizational innovation, Bouwen reiterates that organizations are not given realities but social constructions with ongoing negotiations among the parties involved. Pool and Koopman had found that the "open-end" model, in which this constructivist view is also held by the people involved, was indeed the most frequent type in their empirical research. For Williamson, a "relational team" in which consensus and commitment is fostered will indeed be the most efficient governance structure when the employees control a great deal of firm specific assets without their output being easily metered. Lindenberg points in addition to problems of self-discipline that are being dealt with by management of meaning techniques. Bouwen's study adds yet another factor: whenever organizational learning is important (as in thorough change processes), a one-sided (power, sales, expert) strategy will work much less than a two-sided strategy that also manages meaning and creates involvement.

A very related point is made by the sociologist Hofmaier, but now for a whole program. In Sweden, government, employers and unions are involved in a countrywide development of a dialogue approach to industrial governance. Hofmaier describes the theoretical background and the development of this approach. The difference with Williamson and Bouwen's points is that in Sweden the approach seems to have gone beyond a discussion of conditions (say asset specificity or organizational learning in times of restructuring) under which management of meaning is an efficiency-increasing tool. Rather, the symbolic significance of this tool has acquired its own dynamics which has drawn research in organization studies into the dialogue itself. It remains to be seen whether and how the insights developed outside this context will influence the further development. The fact that it seems important to the Swedes themselves that the dialogue takes place in the context of a market society may point to the possibility of such an outside influence.

Part III deals with the relation between organizations and their environment. In the by now classical contingency theory, this relationship was modeled in analogy to the actor model in economics: actors (organizations) and their constraints (environment). In the meantime a more interactionist view has taken hold of both economics and the sociology of institutions. It is by now much better accepted that people also choose their constraints (for example in constitutional political economy, the economics of self-discipline, and constitutional sociology à la Coleman). The papers in Part III are all more or less critical of classical contingency theory, but in very different ways and for very different reasons. And although all four authors are sociologists, they represent quite different views within that discipline.

Friedberg credits organizational economists with helping to overcome the view of "formal organizations" that are dominated by the technological context. However, in his collaboration with Crozier, Friedberg had gone a step further. "Concrete action systems" replace the old "formal organization". The major difference is that the rules of the game are not just constraints. They are also the result of strategic interaction and power processes among the participants. Organizational boundaries become thereby blurred and the emphasis shifts to processes of organizing. This shift cautions against an overemphasis on formalization and hierarchy and it changes the view on exchange relationships prevalent in sociology. From an organizing point of view, exchange is intimately intertwined with the strategic influence on the terms of exchange (a power game) which, interestingly enough, bears some resemblance to "private orderings", i.e. the creation of governance structures among the transacting parties which Williamson analyzed from an efficiency point of view. Only, the two authors stress different sides of the same coin. Williamson focuses on the activity that strategically influences the conditions of stability of the relation (given self-interest with guile), Friedberg pays mainly attention to activities that strategically influence the freedom of action (given the boundaries of the relation's stability). Friedberg's particular emphasis on freedom of action will draw attention to different aspects in the process of organizing.

The new emphasis on institutions among economists deals mainly with formal rules such as property rights. Sociologists have often stressed the importance of informal rules. Barnett and Carroll attempt to deal with both kinds of rules. They analyze one situation in which traditional contingency can be assumed (with formal rules) and another where it cannot be assumed (with informal rules). They use the context of population ecology to show that paying attention to one or the other has advantages and disadvantages. For example, the role assigned to legitimation ("taken for grantedness") of organizational form is mainly based on informal rules, and their part in the process means that they are not exogenous to the spread of a particular organizational form. The advantage is that a single process is seen to drive the early evolution of all organizational populations. The disadvantage is that the effect of rules on organizational populations cannot be modelled with statistical tools. Conversely, the latter is possible with formal rules that are (almost) exogenous to the form development, but the disadvantage is that many formal rules are designed by authorities to deal with specific problems, which renders many analyses very idiosyncratic. The authors believe that ideally one should find ways of comparing the impact of formal and informal rules.

Before organizational economics existed, economists viewed organizations as points for input and output, to be aggregated rather than studied as entities. Technological determinism could easily fasten to this view of organizations via production functions. The bureaucratic view of rational organization could lead to the same view of technology. The context in which classical contingency theory developed was thus one of a technological environment for organizations. In his paper, Berting argues that this technological determinism is very slow to vanish. It is still deeply rooted in Western civilization and it is maintained by a very inclusive view of technology which covers artifacts, control, and theory of application. And this inclusive view received additional support from recent developments that blur the distinction between science and technology. Study of societal and cultural aspects of technological development and of the opportunities that are provided by different technological options is thereby neglected. The issue Berting raises is currently also debated in connection with efficiency arguments about organizational form. If there are conditions that favor the technological development in a particular direction, it becomes subsequently efficient to choose this technology. Efficiency considerations were not involved in the early development (see Granovetter, 1990).

The bureaucratic view of organizations has yet another problematic relationship to the environment. It assumes that with the progressive disenchantment of the world, people also become progressively more socialized into beings that can smoothly function in hierarchies. The view can be found already in Weber and Mannheim and has been elaborated by Elias. Yet, as Lindenberg argues, there are good reasons and evidence to believe that the original trend toward more self-control training in the household has turned around with increasing prosperity. According to the bureaucratic model of organizations, people entering organizations are supposed to have a zone of indifference for which they sell the right to command to the employer. The employer commands them and they subsequently command themselves to do what the employer ordered. Yet, as people get progressively less self-command training at home, they are also less equipped to handle lack of direct control. Procrastination, impatience and addiction create problems in carrying out the employer's tasks. This happens at a time when due to increasing asset specificity and metering costs, many jobs become more autonomous, thus actually requiring more rather than less self-command capital. The governance structures must adjust to this change by functionally legitimated hierarchy, lateral control and a great deal of instruction on the purpose of organizational goals.

Part IV focuses on interorganizational perspectives. Organizations are embedded in networks and institutional bodies that are of profound influence on their functioning. The emphasis here is not on one organization and its environment but on the interrelations between organizations. There is organization to this interrelation and it also influences the environment for each individual organization. All four authors are sociologists and White and Burt discuss explicitly the distinguishing feature of their approach from economics. White argues that economists have mainly theorized about exchange markets while what is really important to Western economies are product markets. These markets are quite small and within it, producers have taken up a particular position on a schedule of terms of trade. What do firms inside such a market worry about? According to White's model, they are not concerned with supply and demand schedules, money supply or macro-institutional features. Rather, producers' concern is to hold on to distinctive positions in their markets. They are committed for substantial periods with physical and social capital, as they specialize with a view to maximum net return. Thus, the environment for each producer looks very different from that commonly assumed. It contains first of all other producers in that market and signals about their market share and cost-of-production schedule. Seen this way, there is much more social structure to markets than the textbook economic model could possibly assimilate.

The further step from White's market model is the interrelation between markets. While White does deal with them, it is especially Burt who elaborates on this aspect. If we begin with relatively small production markets, the question is how are these markets integrated? Burt distinguished two kinds of approaches to this question. First, one can look at attempts by producers to embed transactions in corporate ties of ownership, joint ventures and other strategic expansions of corporate hierarchies. Another way of looking at market integration is to study dependency relations between markets. Burt chooses the second approach for his own study of the American economy. He shows that profitability for a firm depends on its autonomy within a network of market relations. There are two main conclusions from his study. First, the American economy is internally structured by what he calls "market groups," each consisting of a set of core markets, a set of satellite markets and strong satellite dependence on the core. Thus, he adds an important intermediary structure to White's product markets. The second conclusion is that the market integration is mainly a dyadic phenomenon. This conclusion is a welcome one for the first approach mentioned by Burt (including transaction cost economics of organizations) which is oriented toward dyads without having proven that this does not obscure relevant structures. The next step, not yet supplied by Burt, would be to trace the consequences of market groups for the internal organization of each firm.

The first approach mentioned by Burt is demonstrated in the paper by Ziegler. He treats enterprises as corporate actors with interests that are structurally determined by their position in the market and by financial participations. From these interests and the given constraints, it is possible for Ziegler to account quite well for interlocking directorates among more than 100,000 pairs of companies. By distinguishing various types of common directorships, he could detect the differential purpose of interorganizational relations. Executives as formal agents seem to control and monitor strong interests. Loyal representatives (for example, former executives) are used for cooptation, interorganizational intelligence and for establishing reciprocal ties proscribed by law. In short, it was possible for Ziegler to get a good handle on the generation of corporate networks. To a large extent, this study emphasises the growing insight that constraints are more or less chosen and that organizations are not sitting ducks *vis-à-vis* a given environment.

The last contribution in this book changes perspective and deals with an issue that up until now concerned mainly inter-state relations but may also become important for (decentralized units of) large international corporations: interorganizational democracy. Lammers's main point is that it would be worth-while studying interorganizational democracy in analogy to intra-organizational democracy introduced as a classic theme by Michels. What Lammers' paper has in common with the other three of this group is that he adds a new level of organization studies: the organization of organizations. Quite clearly, this extension should be a challenge for all involved in organization studies.

We hope that these studies will prove useful for the further interdisciplinary integration of organization studies. We gratefully acknowledge permission by *Administrative Science Quarterly* to reprint the version of Oliver Williamson's paper that was published by *ASQ*. Professor Williamson had presented an earlier version at our conference. We would like to thank the Netherlands Institute for Advanced Study for their considerable support, especially the director Professor D. J. van de Kaa, and the organizing genius Rita Buis. All the other NIAS staff has been very helpful as well. We would also like to thank Paul Koopman, René van der Vlist and Reinhard Wippler who helped organize the thematic group. We gratefully acknowledge financial support for the conference from NIAS, from the Royal Netherlands Academy of Arts and Sciences (KNAW) and of the Netherlands Organization for Scientific Research (NWO). Cora Yfke Sikkema in Groningen helped much with the editing chores and Sammye Haigh of Pergamon Press helped patiently in getting this book published.

SIEGWART LINDENBERG
HEIN SCHREUDER

References

Granovetter, M. S. (1990) The old and the new economic sociology: a history and an agenda. In *Beyond the Marketplace*, pp. 89–112, R. Friedland and A. F. Robertson (eds.), New York: Aldine de Gruyter.

Winship, C. and Rosen, S. (1988) Organizations and Institutions: Sociological and Economic Approaches to the Analysis of Social Structure. Supplement to the *American Journal of Sociology*, Vol. 94.

PART I

Integrative Paradigms

Comparative Economic Organization: The Analysis of Discrete Structural Alternatives

OLIVER E. WILLIAMSON[1]

Although microeconomic organization is formidably complex and has long resisted systematic analysis, that has been changing as new modes of analysis have become available, as recognition of the importance of institutions to economic performance has grown, and as the limits of earlier modes of analysis have become evident. Information economics, game theory, agency theory, and population ecology have all made significant advances.

This paper approaches the study of economic organization from a comparative institutional point of view in which transaction-cost economizing is featured. Comparative economic organization never examines organization forms separately but always in relation to alternatives. Transaction-cost economics places the principal burden of analysis on comparisons of transaction costs—which, broadly, are the "costs of running the economic system" (Arrow, 1969, p. 48).

[1]The author is Transamerica Professor of Business, Economics, and Law at the University of California, Berkeley and Senior Research Scientist of the Institute for Policy Reform. The paper benefitted from presentations at workshops at the University of California, Berkeley, the University of California, Los Angeles/University of Southern California, the University of California, Irvine, the University of Michigan, and the Netherlands Institute for Advanced Study. Helpful comments from workshop participants and from Glenn Carroll, Melvin Eisenberg, Bengt Holmstrom, David Kreps, Gillian Hadfield, Scott Masten, Vai-Lam Mui, Richard Nelson, Dan Ostas, Michael Riordan, Roberta Romano, Richard Stewart, Jean Tirole, and Birger Wernerfelt as well as the referees, editor, and managing editor of this journal are gratefully acknowledged. A much shorter version was prepared for and presented as the opening address to the annual meeting of German Academic Business Economists at Frankfurt, Germany in June 1990. A German translation of that address has since been published in the papers and proceedings. The final version of this paper was produced while I was at Saarbrücken University as Distinguished U.S. Senior Scientist, Alexander von Humboldt-Stiftung, for which support I express appreciation.

Oliver E. Williamson

My purpose in this paper is to extend and refine the apparatus out of which transaction-cost economics works, thereby to respond to some of the leading criticisms. Four objections to prior work in this area are especially pertinent. One objection is that the two stages of the new institutional economics research agenda—the institutional environment and the institutions of governance—have developed in disjunct ways. The first of these paints on a very large historical canvas and emphasizes the institutional rules of the game: customs, laws, politics (North, 1986). The latter is much more microanalytic and focuses on the comparative efficacy with which alternative generic forms of governance—markets, hybrids, hierarchies—economize on transaction costs. Can this disjunction problem be overcome? Second, transaction-cost economics has been criticized because it deals with polar forms—markets and hierarchies—to the neglect of intermediate or hybrid forms. Although that objection has begun to be addressed by recent treatments of long-term contracting in which bilateral dependency conditions are supported by a variety of specialized governance features (hostages, arbitration, take-or-pay procurement clauses, tied sales, reciprocity, regulation, etc.), the abstract attributes that characterize alternative modes of governance have remained obscure. What are the key attributes and how do they vary among forms? This is responsive to the third objection, namely, that efforts to operationalize transaction-cost economics have given disproportionate attention to the abstract description of transactions as compared with the abstract description of governance. The dimensionalization of both is needed. Finally, there is the embeddedness problem: Transaction-cost economics purports to have general application but has been developed almost entirely with reference to Western capitalist economies (Hamilton and Biggart, 1988). Is a unified treatment of Western and non-Western, capitalist and noncapitalist economies really feasible? This paper attempts to address these objections by posing the problem of organization as one of discrete structural analysis.

Discrete Structural Analysis

The term discrete structural analysis was introduced into the study of comparative economic organization by Simon (1978, pp. 6–7), who observed that

> As economics expands beyond its central core of price theory, and its central concern with quantities of commodities and money, we observe in it ... [a] shift from a highly quantitative analysis, in which equilibration at the margin plays a central role, to a much more qualitative institutional analysis, in which discrete structural alternatives are compared ...

[S]uch analyses can often be carried out without elaborate mathematical apparatus or marginal calculation. In general, much cruder and simpler arguments will suffice to demonstrate an inequality between two quantities than are required to show the conditions under which these quantities are equated at the margin.

But what exactly is discrete structural analysis? Is it employed only because "there is at present no [satisfactory] way of characterizing organizations in terms of continuous variation over a spectrum" (Ward, 1967, p. 38)? Or is there a deeper rationale?

Of the variety of factors that support discrete structural analysis, I focus here on the following: (1) firms are not merely extensions of markets but employ different means, (2) discrete contract law differences provide crucial support for and serve to define each generic form of governance, and (3) marginal analysis is typically concerned with second-order refinements to the neglect of first-order economizing.

Different Means

Although the study of economic organization deals principally with markets and market mechanisms, it is haunted by a troublesome fact: a great deal of economic activity takes place within firms (Barnard, 1938; Chandler, 1962, 1977). Conceivably, however, no novel economizing issues are posed within firms, because technology is largely determinative—the firm is mainly defined by economies of scale and scope and is merely an instrument for transforming inputs into outputs according to the laws of technology—and because market mechanisms carry over into firms. I have taken exception with the technology view elsewhere (Williamson, 1975). Consider, therefore, the latter.

In parallel with von Clausewitz's (1980) views on war, I maintain that hierarchy is not merely a contractual act but is also a contractual instrument, a continuation of market relations by other means. The challenge to comparative contractual analysis is to discern and explicate the different means. As developed below, each viable form of governance—market, hybrid, and hierarchy—is defined by a syndrome of attributes that bear a supporting relation to one another. Many hypothetical forms of organization never arise, or quickly die out, because they combine inconsistent features.

Contract Law

The mapping of contract law onto economic organization has been examined elsewhere (Williamson, 1979, 1985). Although some of that is repeated here, there are two significant differences. First, I advance the hypothesis that each generic form of governance—market, hybrid, and hierarchy—needs to be supported by a different form of contract law. Second, the form of contract law that supports hierarchy is that of forbearance.

Classical Contract Law. Classical contract law applies to the ideal transaction in law and economics—"sharp in by clear agreement; sharp out by clear performance" (Macneil, 1974, p. 738)—in which the identity of the parties is irrelevant. "Thick" markets are ones in which individual buyers and sellers bear no dependency relation to each other. Instead, each party can go its own way at negligible cost to another. If contracts are renewed period by period, that is only because current suppliers are continuously meeting bids in the spot market. Such transactions are monetized in extreme degree; contract law is interpreted in a very legalistic way: more formal terms supercede less formal should disputes arise between formal and less formal features (e.g., written agreements versus oral amendments), and hard bargaining, to which the rules of contract law are strictly applied, characterizes these transactions. Classical contract law is congruent with and supports the autonomous market form of organization (Macneil, 1974, 1978).

Neoclassical Contract Law and Excuse Doctrine. Neoclassical contract law and excuse doctrine, which relieves parties from strict enforcement, apply to contracts in which the parties to the transaction maintain autonomy but are bilaterally dependent to a nontrivial degree. Identity plainly matters if premature termination or persistent maladaptation would place burdens on one or both parties. Perceptive parties reject classical contract law and move into a neoclassical contracting regime because this better facilitates continuity and promotes efficient adaptation.

As developed below, hybrid modes of contracting are supported by neoclassical contract law. The parties to such contracts maintain autonomy, but the contract is mediated by an elastic contracting mechanism. Public utility regulation, in which the relations between public utility forms and their customers are mediated by a regulatory agency, is one example (Goldberg, 1976; Williamson, 1976). Exchange agreements or reciprocal trading in which the parties experience (and respond similarly to) similar disturbances is another illustration (Williamson, 1983). Franchising is another way of preserving semi-autonomy, but added supports are needed (Klein, 1980; Hadfield, 1990). More generally, long-term, incomplete contracts require special adaptive mechanisms to effect realignment and restore efficiency when beset by unanticipated disturbances.

Disturbances are of three kinds: inconsequential, consequential, and highly consequential. Inconsequential disturbances are ones for which the deviation from efficiency is too small to recover the costs of adjustment. The net gains from realignment are negative for minor disturbances because (as discussed below) requests for adjustments need to be justified and are subject to review, the costs of which exceed the prospective gains.

Middle-range or consequential disturbances are ones to which neoclassical contract law applies. These are transactions for which Karl Llewellyn's concept of "contract as framework" is pertinent. Thus Llewellyn (1931, p. 737) refers to contract as "a framework highly adjustable, a framework which almost never accurately indicates real working relations, but which affords a rough indication around which such relations vary, an occasional guide in cases of doubt, and a norm of ultimate appeal when the relations cease in fact to work." The thirty-two-year coal supply agreement between the Nevada Power Company and the Northwest Trading Company illustrates the elastic mechanisms employed by a neoclassical contract. That contract reads in part as follows:

> ... In the event an inequitable condition occurs which adversely affects one Party, it shall then be the joint and equal responsibility of both Parties to act promptly and in good faith to determine the action required to cure or adjust for the inequity and effectively to implement such action. Upon written claim of inequity served by one Party upon the other, the Parties shall act jointly to reach an agreement concerning the claimed inequity within sixty (60) days of the date of such written claim. An adjusted base coal price that differs from market price by more than ten percent (10%) shall constitute a hardship. The Party claiming inequity shall include in its claim such information and data as may be reasonably necessary to substantiate the claim and shall freely and without delay furnish such other information and data as the other Party reasonably may deem relevant and necessary. If the Parties cannot reach agreement within sixty (60) days the matter shall be submitted to arbitration.

By contrast with a classical contract, this contract (1) contemplates unanticipated disturbances for which adaptation is needed, (2) provides a tolerance zone (of ± 10%) within which misalignments will be absorbed, (3) requires information disclosure and substantiation if adaptation is proposed, and (4) provides for arbitration in the event voluntary agreement fails.

The forum to which this neoclassical contract refers disputes is (initially, at least) that of arbitration rather than the courts. Fuller (1963, pp. 11–12) described the procedural differences between arbitration and litigation:

[T]here are open to the arbitrator ... quick methods of education not open to the courts. An arbitrator will frequently interrupt the examination of witnesses with a request that the parties educate him to the point where he can understand the testimony being received. This education can proceed informally, with frequent interruptions by the arbitrator, and by informed persons on either side, when a point needs clarification. Sometimes there will be arguments across the table, occasionally even within each of the separate camps. The end result will usually be a clarification that will enable everyone to proceed more intelligently with the case.

Such adaptability notwithstanding, neoclassical contracts are not indefinitely elastic. As disturbances become highly consequential, neoclassical contracts experience real strain, because the autonomous ownership status of the parties continuously poses an incentive to defect. The general proposition here is that when the "lawful" gains to be had by insistence upon literal enforcement exceed the discounted value of continuing the exchange relationship, defection from the spirit of the contract can be anticipated.

When, in effect, arbitration gives way to litigation, accommodation can no longer be presumed. Instead, the contract reverts to a much more legalistic regime—although, even here, neoclassical contract law averts truly punitive consequences by permitting appeal to exceptions that qualify under some form of excuse doctrine. The legal system's commitment to the keeping of promises under neoclassical contract law is modest, as Macneil (1974, p. 731) explained:

> ... contract remedies are generally among the weakest of those the legal system can deliver. But a host of doctrines and techniques lies in the way even of those remedies: impossibility, frustration, mistake, manipulative interpretation, jury discretion, consideration, illegality, duress, undue influence, unconscionability, capacity, forfeiture and penalty rules, doctrines of substantial performance, severability, bankruptcy laws, statutes of frauds, to name some; almost any contract doctrine can and does serve to make the commitment of the legal system to promise keeping less than complete.

From an economic point of view, the tradeoff that needs to be faced in excusing contract performance is between stronger incentives and reduced opportunism. If the state realization in question was unforeseen and unforeseeable (different in degree and/or especially in kind from the range of normal business experience), if strict enforcement would have truly punitive consequences, and especially if the resulting "injustice" is supported by (lawful) opportunism, then excuse can be seen mainly as a way of mitigating opportunism, ideally without adverse impact on incentives. If, however, excuse is granted routinely whenever adversity occurs, then incentives to think through contracts, choose technologies judiciously, share risks efficiently, and avert adversity will be impaired. Excuse doctrine should therefore be used sparingly—which it evidently is (Farnsworth, 1968, p. 885; Buxbaum, 1985).

The relief afforded by excuse doctrine notwithstanding, neo-classical contracts deal with consequential disturbances only at great cost: arbitration is costly to administer and its adaptive range is limited. As consequential disturbances and, especially, as highly consequential disturbances become more frequent, the hybrid mode supported by arbitration and excuse doctrine incurs added costs and comes under added strain. Even more elastic and adaptive arrangements warrant consideration.

Forbearance. Internal organization, hierarchy, qualifies as a still more elastic and adaptive mode of organization. What type of contract law applies to internal organization? How does this have a bearing on contract performance?

Describing the firm as a "nexus of contracts" (Alchian and Demsetz, 1972; Jensen and Meckling, 1976; Fama, 1980) suggests that the firm is no different from the market in contractual respects. Alchian and Demsetz (1972, p. 777) originally took the position that the relation between a shopper and his grocer and that between an employer and employee was identical in contractual respects:

> The single consumer can assign his grocer to the task of obtaining whatever the customer can induce the grocer to provide at a price acceptable to both parties. That is precisely all that an employer can do to an employee. To speak of managing, directing, or assigning workers to various tasks is a deceptive way of noting that the employer continually is involved in renegotiation of contracts on terms that must be acceptable to both parties. . . . Long-term contracts between employer and employee are not the essence of the organization we call a firm.

That it has been instructive to view the firm as a nexus of contracts is evident from the numerous insights that this literature has generated. But to regard the corporation only as a nexus of contracts misses much of what is truly distinctive about this mode of governance. As developed below, bilateral adaptation effected through fiat is a distinguishing feature of internal organization. But wherein do the fiat differences between market and hierarchy arise? If, moreover, hierarchy enjoys an "advantage" with respect to fiat, why can't the market replicate this?

One explanation is that fiat has its origins in the employment contract (Barnard, 1938; Simon, 1951; Coase, 1952; Masten, 1988). Although there is a good deal to be said for that explanation, I propose a separate and complementary explanation: The implicit contract law of internal organization is that of forbearance. Thus, whereas courts routinely grant standing to firms should there be disputes over prices, the damages to be ascribed to delays, failures of quality, and the like, courts will refuse to hear disputes between one internal division and another over identical technical issues. Access to the courts being denied, the parties must resolve their differences internally. Accordingly, hierarchy is its own court of ultimate appeal.

What is known as the "business judgment rule" holds that "Absent bad faith or some other corrupt motive, directors are normally not liable to the corporation for mistakes of judgment, whether those mistakes are classified as mistakes of fact or mistakes of law" (Gilson, 1986, p. 741). Not only does that rule serve as "a quasi-jurisdictional barrier to prevent courts from exercising regulatory powers over the activities of corporate managers" (Manne, 1967, p. 271), but "The courts' abdication of regulatory authority through the business judgement rule may well be the most significant common law contribution to corporate governance" (Gilson, 1986, p. 741). The business judgment rule, which applies to the relation between shareholders and directors, can be interpreted as a particular manifestation of forbearance doctrine, which applies to the management of the firm more generally. To review alleged mistakes of judgment or to adjudicate internal disputes would sorely test the competence of courts and would undermine the efficacy of hierarchy.

Accordingly, the reason why the market is unable to replicate the firm with respect to fiat is that market transactions are defined by contract law of an altogether different kind. There is a logic to classical market contracting and there is a logic for forbearance law, and the choice of one regime precludes the other. Whether a transaction is organized as make or buy—internal procurement or market procurement, respectively—thus matters greatly in dispute-resolution respects: the courts will hear disputes of the one kind and will refuse to be drawn into the resolution of disputes of the other. Internal disputes between one division and another regarding the appropriate transfer prices, the damages to be ascribed to delays, failures of quality, and the like, are thus denied a court hearing.

To be sure, not all disputes within firms are technical. Personnel disputes are more complicated. Issues of worker safety, dignity, the limits of the "zone of acceptance," and the like sometimes pose societal spillover costs that are undervalued in the firm's private net benefit calculus. Underprovision of human and worker rights could ensue if the courts refused to consider issues of these kinds. Also, executive compensation agreements can sometimes be written in ways that make it difficult to draw a sharp line between personnel and technical issues. Even with personnel disputes, however, there is a presumption that such differences will be resolved internally. For example, unions may refuse to bring individual grievances to arbitration (Cox, 1958, p. 24):

> [G]iving the union control over all claims arising under the collective agreement comports so much better with the functional nature of a collective bargaining agreement. . . . Allowing an individual to carry a claim to arbitration whenever he is dissatisfied with the adjustment worked out by the company and the union . . . discourages the kind of day-to-day cooperation between company and union which is normally the mark of sound industrial relations—a relationship in which grievances are treated as problems to be solved and contracts are only guideposts in a dynamic human relationship. When . . . the individual's claim endangers group interests, the union's function is to resolve the competition by reaching an accommodation or striking a balance.

As compared with markets, internal incentives in hierarchies are flat or low-powered, which is to say that changes in effort expended have little or no immediate effect on compensation. That is mainly because the high-powered incentives of markets are unavoidably compromised by internal organization (Williamson, 1985, ch. 6; 1988). Also, however, hierarchy uses flat incentives because these elicit greater cooperation and because unwanted side effects are checked by added internal controls (see Williamson, 1988; Holmstrom, 1989). Not only, therefore, will workers and managers be more willing to accommodate, because their compensation is the same whether they "do this" or "do that," but an unwillingness to accommodate is interpreted not as an excess of zeal but as a predilection to behave in a noncooperative way. Long-term promotion prospects are damaged as a consequence. Defection from the spirit of the agreement in favor of litigiousness is quite perverse if neither immediate nor long-term gains are thereby realized. The combination of fiat with low-powered incentives is a manifestation of the syndrome condition of economic organization to which I referred earlier (and develop more fully below).

The underlying rationale for forbearance law is twofold: (1) parties to an internal dispute have deep knowledge—both about the circumstances surrounding a dispute as well as the efficiency properties of alternative solutions—that can be communicated to the court only at great cost, and (2) permitting internal disputes to be appealed to the court would undermine the efficacy and integrity of hierarchy. If fiat were merely advisory, in that internal disputes over net receipts could be pursued in the courts, the firm would be little more than an "inside contracting" system (Williamson, 1985, pp. 218–222). The application of forbearance doctrine to internal organization means that parties to an internal exchange can work out their differences themselves or appeal unresolved disputes to the hierarchy for a decision. But this exhausts their alternatives. When push comes to shove, "legalistic" arguments fail. Greater reliance on instrumental reasoning and mutual accommodation result. This argument contradicts Alchian and Demsetz's (1972, p. 777) claim that the firm "has no power of fiat, no authority, no disciplinary action any different in the slightest degree from ordinary market contracting." That is exactly wrong: firms can and do exercise fiat that markets cannot. Prior neglect of contract law differences and their ramifications explain the error.

First-Order Economizing

Although the need to get priorities straight is unarguable, first-order economizing—effective adaptation and the elimination of waste—has been neglected. Adaptation is especially crucial. As developed below, it is the central economic problem. But as Frank Knight (1941, p. 252) insisted, the elimination of waste is also important:

> ... men in general and within limits, wish to behave economically, to make their activities and their organization "efficient" rather than wasteful. This fact does deserve the utmost emphasis; and an adequate definition of the science of economics ... might well make it explicit that the main relevance of the discussion is found in its relation to social policy, assumed to be directed toward the end indicated, of increasing economic efficiency, of reducing waste.

Relatedly, but independently, Oskar Lange (1938, p. 109) held that "the real danger of socialism is that of the bureaucratization of economic life, and not the impossibility of coping with the problem of allocation of resources." Inasmuch, however, as Lange (1938, p. 109) believed that this argument belonged "in the field of sociology" he concluded that it "must be dispensed with here." Subsequent informed observers of socialism followed this lead, whereupon the problems of bureaucracy were, until recently, given scant attention. Instead, the study of socialism was preoccupied with technical features—marginal cost pricing, activity analysis, and the like—with respect to which a broadly sanguine consensus took shape (Bergson, 1948; Montias, 1976; Koopmans, 1977).

The natural interpretation of the organizational concerns expressed by Knight and Lange—or, at least, the interpretation that I propose here—is that economics was too preoccupied with issues of allocative efficiency, in which marginal analysis was featured, to the neglect of organizational efficiency, in which discrete structural alternatives were brought under scrutiny. Partly that is because the mathematics for dealing with clusters of attributes is only now beginning to be developed (Topkis, 1978; Milgrom and Roberts, 1990; Holmstrom and Milgrom, 1991). Even more basic, however, is the propensity to focus exclusively on market mechanisms to the neglect of discrete structural alternatives. The argument, for example, that all systems of honest trade are variants on the reputation-effect mechanisms of markets (Milgrom, North, and Weingast, 1990, p. 16) ignores the possibility that some ways of infusing contractual integrity (e.g. hierarchy) employ altogether different means. Market-favoring predispositions need to be disputed, lest the study of economic organization in all of its forms be needlessly and harmfully truncated.

Dimensionalizing Governance

What are the key attributes with respect to which governance structures differ? The discriminating alignment hypothesis to which transaction-cost economics owes much of its predictive content holds that transactions, which differ in their attributes, are aligned with governance structures, which differ in their costs and competencies, in a discriminating (mainly, transaction-cost-economizing) way. But whereas the dimensionalization of transactions received early and explicit attention, the dimensionalization of governance structures has been relatively slighted. What are the factors that are responsible for the aforementioned differential costs and competencies?

One of those key differences has been already indicated: market, hybrid, and hierarchy differ in contract law respects. Indeed, were it the case that the very same type of contract law were to be uniformly applied to all forms of governance, important distinctions between these three generic forms would be vitiated. But there is more to governance than contract law. Crucial differences in adaptability and in the use of incentive and control instruments are also germane.

Adaptation As the Central Economic Problem

Hayek (1945, p. 523) insistently argued that "economic problems arise always and only in consequence of change" and that this truth was obscured by those who held that "technological knowledge" is of foremost importance. He disputed the latter and urged that "the economic problem of society is mainly one of rapid adaptation in the particular circumstances of time and place" (Hayek, 1945, p. 524). Of special importance to Hayek was the proposition that the price system, as compared with central planning, is an extraordinarily efficient mechanism for communicating information and inducing change (Hayek, 1945, pp. 524–527).

Interestingly, Barnard (1938) also held that the main concern of organization was that of adaptation to changing circumstances, but his concern was with adaptation within internal organization. Confronted with a continuously fluctuating environment, the "survival of an organization depends upon the maintenance of an equilibrium of complex character... [This] calls for readjustment of processes internal to the organization. ... [whence] the center of our interest is the processes by which [adaptation] is accomplished" (Barnard, 1938, p. 6).

That is very curious. Both Hayek and Barnard hold that the central problem of economic organization is adaptation. But whereas Hayek locates this adaptive capacity in the market, it was the adaptive capacity of internal organization on which Barnard focused attention. If the "marvel of the market" (Hayek) is matched by the "marvel of internal organization" (Barnard), then wherein does one outperform the other?

The marvel to which Hayek (1945, p. 528) referred had spontaneous origins: "The price system is ... one of those formations which man has learned to use ... after he stumbled on it without understanding it." The importance of such spontaneous cooperation notwithstanding, it was Barnard's experience that intended cooperation was important and undervalued. The latter was defined as "that kind of cooperation among men that is conscious, deliberate, purposeful" (Barnard, 1938, p. 4) and was realized through formal organization, especially hierarchy.

I submit that adaptability is the central problem of economic organization and that both Hayek and Barnard are correct, because they are referring to adaptations of different kinds, both of which are needed in a high-performance system. The adaptations to which Hayek refers are those for which prices serve as sufficient statistics. Changes in the demand or supply of a commodity are reflected in price changes, in response to which "individual participants ... [are] able to take the right action" (Hayek, 1945, p. 527). I will refer to adaptations of this kind as adaptation (A), where (A) denotes autonomy. This is the neoclassical ideal in which consumers and producers respond independently to parametric price changes so as to maximize their utility and profits, respectively.

That would entirely suffice if all disturbances were of this kind. Some disturbances, however, require coordinated responses, lest the individual parts operate at cross-purposes or otherwise suboptimize. Failures of coordination may arise because autonomous parties read and react to signals differently, even though their purpose is to achieve a timely and compatible combined response. The "nonconvergent expectations" to which Malgren (1961) referred is an illustration. Although, in principle, convergent expectations could be realized by asking one party to read and interpret the signals for all, the lead party may behave strategically—by distorting information or disclosing it in an incomplete and selective fashion.

More generally, parties that bear a long-term bilateral dependency relation to one another must recognize that incomplete contracts require gapfilling and sometimes get out of alignment. Although it is always in the collective interest of autonomous parties to fill gaps, correct errors, and effect efficient realignments, it is also the case that the distribution of the resulting gains is indeterminate. Self-interested bargaining predictably obtains. Such bargaining is itself costly.

The main costs, however, are that transactions are maladapted to the environment during the bargaining interval. Also, the prospect of ex post bargaining invites ex ante prepositioning of an inefficient kind (Grossman and Hart, 1986).

Recourse to a different mechanism is suggested as the needs for coordinated investments and for uncontested (or less contested) coordinated realignments increase in frequency and consequentiality. Adaptations of these coordinated kinds will be referred to as adaptation (C), where (C) denotes cooperation. The conscious, deliberate, and purposeful efforts to craft adaptive internal co-ordinating mechanisms were those on which Barnard focused. Independent adaptations here would at best realize imperfect realignments and could operate at cross-purposes. Lest the aforementioned costs and delays associated with strategic bargaining be incurred, the relation is reconfigured by supplanting autonomy by hierarchy. The authority relation (fiat) had adaptive advantages over autonomy for transactions of a bilaterally (or multilaterally) dependent kind.

Instruments

Vertical and lateral integration are usefully thought of as organization forms of last resort, to be employed when all else fails. That is because markets are a "marvel" in adaptation (A) respects. Given a disturbance for which prices serve as sufficient statistics, individual buyers and suppliers can reposition autonomously. Appropriating, as they do, individual streams of net receipts, each party has a strong incentive to reduce costs and adapt efficiently. What I have referred to as high-powered incentives result when consequences are tightly linked to actions in this way (Williamson, 1988). Other autonomous traders have neither legitimate claims against the gains nor can they be held accountable for the losses. Accounting systems cannot be manipulated to share gains or subsidize losses.

Matters get more complicated when bilateral dependency intrudes. As discussed above, bilateral dependency introduces an opportunity to realize gains through hierarchy. As compared with the market, the use of formal organizazion to orchestrate coordinated adaptation to unanticipated disturbances enjoys adaptive advantages as the condition of bilateral dependency progressively builds up. But these adaptation (C) gains come at a cost. Not only can related divisions within the firm make plausible claims that they are causally responsible for the gains (in indeterminate degree), but divisions that report losses can make plausible claims that others are culpable. There are many ways, moreover, in which the headquarters can use the accounting system to effect strategic redistributions (through transfer pricing changes, overhead assignments, inventory conventions, etc.), whatever the preferences of the parties. The upshot is that internal organization degrades incentive intensity, and added bureaucratic costs result (Williamson, 1985, ch. 6; 1988).

These three features—adaptability of type A, adaptability of type C, and differential incentive intensity—do not exhaust the important differences between market and hierarchy. Also important are the differential reliance on administrative controls, and, as developed above, the different contract law regimes to which each is subject. Suffice it to observe here that (1) hierarchy is buttressed by the differential efficacy of administrative controls within firms, as compared with between firms, and (2) incentive intensity within firms is sometimes deliberately suppressed. Incentive intensity is not an objective but is merely an instrument. If added incentive intensity gets in the way of bilateral adaptability, then weaker incentive intensity supported by added administrative controls (monitoring and career rewards and penalties) can be optimal.

Markets and hierarchies are polar modes. As indicated at the outset, however, a major purpose of this paper is to locate hybrid modes—various forms of long-term contracting, reciprocal trading, regulation, franchising, and the like—in relation to these polar modes. Plainly, the neoclassical contract law of hybrid governance differs from both the classical contract law of markets and the forbearance contract law of hierarchies, being more elastic than the former but more legalistic than the latter. The added question is How do hybrids compare with respect to adaptability (types A and C), incentive intensity, and administrative control?

The hybrid mode displays intermediate values in all four features. It preserves ownership autonomy, which elicits strong incentives and encourages adaptation to type A disturbances (those to which one party can respond efficiently without consulting the other). Because there is bilateral dependency, however, long-term contracts are supported by added contractual safeguards and administrative apparatus (information disclosure, dispute-settlement machinery). These facilitate adaptations of type C but come at the cost of incentive attenuation. Concerns for "equity" intrude. Thus the Nevada Power Company–Northwest Trading Company coal contract, whose adaptation mechanics were set out above, begins with the following: "It is the intent of the Parties hereto that this agreement, as a whole and in all of its parts, shall be equitable to both Parties throughout its term." Such efforts unavoidably dampen incentive-intensity features.

One advantage of hierarchy over the hybrid with respect to bilateral adaptation is that internal contracts can be more incomplete. More importantly, adaptations to consequential disturbances are less costly within firms because (1) proposals to adapt require less documentation, (2) resolving internal disputes by fiat rather than arbitration saves resources and facilitates timely adaptation, (3) information that is deeply impacted can more easily be accessed and more accurately assessed, (4) internal dispute resolution enjoys the support of informal organization (Barnard, 1938; Scott, 1987), and (5) internal organization has access to additional incentive instruments—including especially career reward and joint profit sharing—that promote a team orientation. Furthermore, highly consequential disturbances that would occasion breakdown or costly litigation under the hybrid mode can be accommodated more easily. The advantages of hierarchy over hybrid in adaptation C respects are not, however, realized without cost. Weaker incentive intensity (greater bureaucratic costs) attend the move from hybrid to hierarchy, ceteris paribus.

TABLE 1   *Distinguishing Attributes of Market, Hybrid, and Hierarchy Governance Structures**

| | Governance structure | | |
Attributes	Market	Hybrid	Hierarchy
Instruments			
Incentive intensity	++	+	0
Administrative controls	0	+	++
Performance attributes			
Adaptation (A)	++	+	0
Adaptation (C)	0	+	++
Contract law	++	+	0

* ++ = strong; + = semi-strong; 0 = weak.

Summarizing, the hybrid mode is characterized by semi-strong incentives, an intermediate degree of administrative apparatus, displays semi-strong adaptations of both kinds, and works out of a semi-legalistic contract law regime. As compared with market and hierarchy, which are polar opposites, the hybrid mode is located between the two of these in all five attribute respects. Based on the foregoing, and denoting strong, semi-strong, and weak by ++, +, and 0, respectively, the instruments, adaptive attributes, and contract law features that distinguish markets, hybrids, and hierarchies are shown in Table 1.

Discriminating Alignment

Transaction-cost economics subscribes to Commons's view (1924, 1934) that the transaction is the basic unit of analysis. That important insight takes on operational significance upon identifying the critical dimensions with respect to which transactions differ. Without purporting to be exhaustive, these include the frequency with which transactions recur, the uncertainty to which transactions are subject, and the type and degree of asset specificity involved in supplying the good or service in question (Williamson, 1979). Although all are important, transaction-cost economics attaches special significance to this last (Williamson, 1975, 1979; Klein, Crawford, and Alchian, 1978; Grossman and Hart, 1986).

Asset specificity has reference to the degree to which an asset can be redeployed to alternative uses and by alternative users without sacrifice of productive value. Asset-specificity distinctions of six kinds have been made: (1) site specificity, as where successive stations are located in a cheek-by-jowl relation to each other so as to economize on inventory and transportation expenses; (2) physical asset specificity, such as specialized dies that are required to produce a component; (3) human-asset specificity that arises in learning by doing; (4) brand name capital; (5) dedicated assets, which are discrete investments in general purpose plant that are made at the behest of a particular customer; and (6) temporal specificity, · which is akin to technological nonseparability and can be thought of as a type of site specificity in which timely responsiveness by on-site human assets is vital (Masten, Meehan, and Snyder, 1991). Asset specificity, especially in its first five forms, creates bilateral dependency and poses added contracting hazards. It has played a central role in the conceptual and empirical work in transaction-cost economics.

The analysis here focuses entirely on transaction costs: neither the revenue consequences nor the production-cost savings that result from asset specialization are included. Although that simplifies the analysis, note that asset specificity increases the transaction costs of all forms of governance. Such added specificity is warranted only if these added governance costs are more than offset by production-cost savings and/or increased revenues. A full analysis will necessarily make allowance for effects of all three kinds (Riordan and Williamson, 1985). Only a truncated analysis appears here.

Reduced-Form Analysis

The governance-cost expressions set out herein are akin to reduced forms, in that governance costs are expressed as a function of asset specificity and a set of exogenous variables. The structural equations from which these reduced forms are derived are not set out. The key features that are responsible for cost differences among governance structures are nonetheless evident in the matrix version of the model set out below.[2]

Although asset specificity can take a variety of forms, the common consequence is this: a condition of bilateral dependency builds up as asset specificity deepens. The ideal transaction in law and economics—whereby the identities of buyers and sellers is irrelevant—obtains when asset specificity is zero. Identity matters as investments in transaction-specific assets increase, since such specialized assets lose productive value when redeployed to best alternative uses and by best alternative users.

Assume, for simplicity, that asset specificity differences are entirely due to physical or site specificity features. I begin with the situation in which classical market contracting works well: autonomous actors adapt effectively to exogenous disturbances. Internal organization is at a disadvantage for transactions of this kind, since hierarchy incurs added bureaucratic costs to which no added benefits can be ascribed. That, however, changes as bilateral dependency sets in. Disturbances for which coordinated responses are required become more numerous and consequential as investments in asset specificity deepen. The high-powered incentives of markets here impede adaptability, since each party to an autonomous exchange that has gotten out of alignment and for which mutual consent is needed to effect an adjustment will want to appropriate as much as possible (ideally, all but epsilon) of the adaptive gains to be realized.

---

[2]Developing the deeper structure that supports the reduced forms—by explicating contractual incompleteness and its consequences in a more microanalytic way and by developing the bureaucratic cost consequence of internal organization more explicitly—is an ambitious but important undertaking.

When bilaterally dependent parties are unable to respond quickly and easily, because of disagreements and self-interested bargaining, maladaptation costs are incurred. Although the transfer of such transactions from market to hierarchy creates added bureaucratic costs, those costs may be more than offset by the bilateral adaptive gains that result.

Let $M = M(k;\theta)$ and $H = H(k;\theta)$ be reduced-form expressions that denote market and hierarchy governance costs as a function of asset specificity (k) and a vector of shift parameters (θ). Assuming that each mode is constrained to choose the same level of asset specificity, the following comparative-cost relations obtain: $M(0) < H(0)$ and $M' > H' > 0$.[3] The first of these two inequalities reflects the fact that the bureaucratic costs of internal organization exceed those of the market because the latter is superior in adaptation (A) respects—which is the only kind that matters if asset specificity is negligible. The intercept for market governance is thus lower than is the intercept for hierarchy. The second inequality reflects the marginal disability of markets as compared with hierarchies in adaptation (C) respects as asset specificity, hence bilateral dependency, becomes more consequential.

As described above, the hybrid mode is located between market and hierarchy with respect to incentives, adaptability, and bureaucratic costs. As compared with the market, the hybrid sacrifices incentives in favor of superior coordination among the parts. As compared with the hierarchy, the hybrid sacrifices cooperativeness in favor of greater incentive intensity. The distribution of branded product from retail outlets by market, hierarchy, and hybrid, where franchising is an example of this last, illustrates the argument.

Forward integration out of manufacturing into distribution would be implied by hierarchy. That would sacrifice incentive intensity but would (better) assure that the parts do not operate at cross-purposes with one another. The market solution would be to sell the good or service outright. Incentive intensity is thereby harnessed, but suboptimization (free riding on promotional efforts, dissipation of the brand name, etc.) may also result. Franchising awards greater autonomy than hierarchy but places franchisees under added rules and surveillance as compared with markets. Cost control and local adaptations are stronger under franchising than hierarchy, and suboptimization is reduced under franchising as compared with the market. The added autonomy (as compared with hierarchy)

---

[3]A more general optimizing treatment in which the level of asset specificity varies with organization form is set out in Riordan and Williamson (1985). Also see Masten (1982).

and the added restraints (as compared with the market) under which franchisees operate nevertheless come at a cost. If, for example, quality assurance is realized by constraining the franchisee to use materials supplied by the franchisor, and if exceptions to that practice are not permitted because of the potential for abuse that would result, then local opportunities to make "apparently" cost-effective procurements will be prohibited. Similarly, the added local autonomy enjoyed by franchisees may get in the way of some global adjustments.

Transactions for which the requisite adaptations to disturbances are neither predominantly autonomous nor bilateral, but require a mixture of each, are candidates to be organized under the hybrid mode. Over some intermediate range of k, the mixed adaptation (A/C) that hybrids afford could well be superior to the A-favoring or C-favoring adaptations supported by markets and hierarchies, respectively.

Letting $X = X(k;\theta)$ denote the governance costs of the hybrid mode as a function of asset specificity, the argument is that $M(0) < X(0) < H(0)$ and that $M' > X' > H' > 0$.[4] The relations shown in Fig. 1 then obtain. Efficient supply implies operating on the envelope, whence, if k^* is the optimal value of k, the rule for efficient supply is as follows: I, use markets for $k^* < \bar{k}_1$; II, use hybrids for $\bar{k}_1 < k^* < \bar{k}_2$; and III, use hierarchy for $k^* > \bar{k}_2$.

In a very heuristic way, moreover, one can think of moving along one of these generic curves as moving toward more intrusive controls. Thus, consider two forms of franchising, one of which involves less control than the other. If $X^1(k)$ and $X^2(k)$ refer to franchising with little and much control, respectively, then $X^2(k)$ will be located to the right of $X^1(k)$ in Fig. 2. Or consider the M-form (multidivisional) and U-form (unitary or functionally organized) corporation. Because the former provides more market-like divisionalization than does the latter, the M-form is given by $H^1(k)$ and is located closer to $\bar{k}_2$ in Fig. 2.

A Matrix Representation

Suppose that disturbances are distinguished in terms of the type of response—autonomous or bilateral—that is needed to effect an adaptation. Suppose further that the type of adaptation depends on

---

[4]This assumes that $X(0)$ is less than $H(0)$ to a nontrivial degree, since otherwise the hybrid mode could be dominated throughout by the least-cost choice of either market or hierarchy, which may occur for certain classes of transactions, as discussed below.

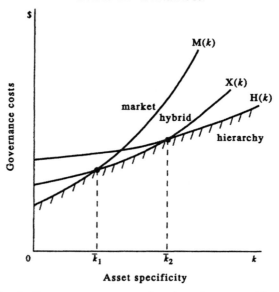

FIG. 1. Governance costs as a function of asset specificity.

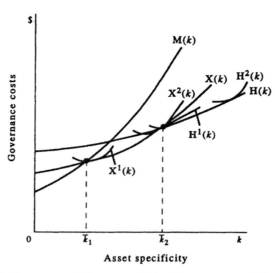

FIG. 2. Governance differences within discrete structural forms.

the degree of asset specificity. Let asset specificity be denoted by k_j and suppose that it can take on any of three values: $k_1 = 0$ (generic investment), $k_2 < 0$ (semi-specific investment), or $k_3 \gg 0$ (highly specific investment). Assume that adjustments to disturbances can be any of four kinds: I, strictly autonomous; II, mainly autonomous; III, mainly coordinated; or IV, strictly coordinated. Let p_{ij} be the probability than an adaptation of type $i = $ I, II, ... , IV will be required if asset-specificity condition k_j ($j = 1, 2, 3$) obtains and let the matrix $[p_{ij}]$ be given by

		k_1	k_2	k_3
	I	1.00	.25	.10
	II	.00	.25	.10
$[p_{ij}]$:	III	.00	.25	.40
	IV	.00	.25	.40

Note that, the k_1 column excepted, positive probability is associated with every element in the matrix. What added asset specificity does is shift the distribution of required responses in favor of greater cooperativeness.

Assume that each adaptation, if costlessly and successfully implemented, would yield identical expected cost savings. For the reasons given above, however, the efficacy with which different modes adapt to disturbances of different kinds varies. Let e_{im} be the efficacy with which mode m ($m = $ M, X, H) is able to implement adaptations of type i ($i = $ I, II, ... , IV) and assume that the matrix e_{im} is given by

		M	X	H
	I	1.0	0.9	0.7
	II	0.7	0.9	0.4
$[e_{im}]$:	III	0.2	0.5	0.5
	IV	−0.2	0.0	0.5

where 1.0 is the ideal degree of adaptiveness and 0.0 is equivalent (in terms of efficacy) to no adaptation.

The efficacy assumptions embedded in this last matrix warrant remark: (1) Only the entry e_{IM} has a value of 1.0. This condition—market adaptations to a disturbance for which strictly autonomous adaptation is appropriate—corresponds to the ideal transaction in law and economics (classical market contracting); (2) The efficacy of the market falls off as bilateral dependency builds up, becoming negative (worse than no adaptation at all) for the strictly cooperative case (IV). This last reflects the conflictual nature of market exchange for transactions of the bilaterally dependent kind; (3) The hybrid mode is almost as good as the market for strictly autonomous adaptations, is better than the market in all other adaptation categories, and is as good or better than hierarchy in all categories save that for which strict coordination is indicated; (4) Hierarchy is burdened by bureaucracy and never scores high in efficacy for any category of adaptation.[5] What matters, however, is comparative efficacy. The hierarchy comes into its own (comparatively) where adaptations of a strictly cooperative kind are needed; and (5) The efficacy of hierarchy is lowest for disturbances requiring a mainly autonomous adaptation. As compared with strictly autonomous disturbances, where bureaucratic costs are held in check by an objective market standard, ready recourse to the market is compromised by the need for some coordination. Because, however, the gains from coordination are not great, efforts to coordinate are problematic. If efforts to adapt autonomously are protested (my costs are greater because you moved without consulting me) while failures to adapt quickly are costly, the hierarchy is caught between the proverbial rock and a hard place.

Let C_{jm} be the expected maladaptation cost of using mode m to effect adaptations if asset specificity is of type k_j. Since inefficacy is given by $1 - e_{im}$, the expected maladaptation costs are $C_{jm} = \Sigma_i\, p_{ij} (1 - e_{im})$. That matrix is given by

		M	X	H
	k_1	.000	.100	.300
$[C_{jm}]$:	k_2	.575	.425	.475
	k_3	.830	.620	.490

The lowest values in each row are realized by matching market, hybrid, and hierarchy with asset specificity conditions k_1, k_2, and k_3, respectively. These costs are consonant with the reduced-form relations shown in Fig. 1. Thus if $\beta \geq 0$ is the irreducible setup costs of economic participation, then the bureaucratic cost intercepts associated with zero asset specificity (k_1) for market, hybrid, and hierarchy will be given by β plus .000, .100, and .300, respectively. Also, the relation between the implied slopes associated with each mode in the matrix (expressed as a function of asset specificity) is that $M' > X' > H'$, which corresponds exactly to the relations shown in Fig. 1.

[5]Hierarchy is able to deal with type I (strictly autonomous) disturbances reasonably well by instructing the operating parts to respond to local disturbances on their own motion and by using the market as an alternate source of supply and/or standard.

Comparative Statics

Transaction-cost economics maintains that (1) transaction-cost economizing is the "main case," which is not to be confused with the only case (Williamson, 1985, pp. 22–23; 1989, pp. 137–138), and (2) transaction costs vary with governance structures in the manner described above. Assuming that the institutional environment is unchanging, transactions should be clustered under governance structures as indicated. Variance will be observed, but the main case should be as described.

The purpose of this section is to consider how equilibrium distributions of transactions will change in response to disturbances in the institutional environment. That is a comparative static exercise. Both parts of the new institutional economics—the institutional environment and the institutions of governance—are implicated. The crucial distinctions are these (Davis and North, 1971, pp. 6–7):

> The *institutional environment* is the set of fundamental political, social and legal ground rules that establishes the basis for production, exchange and distribution. Rules governing elections, property rights, and the right of contract are examples. . . .
>
> An *institutional arrangement* is an arrangement between economic units that governs the ways in which these units can cooperate and/or compete. It . . . [can] provide a structure within which its members can cooperate . . . or [it can] provide a mechanism that can effect a change in laws or property rights.

The way that I propose to join these two is to treat the institutional environment as a set of parameters, changes in which elicit shifts in the comparative costs of governance. An advantage of a three-way setup—market, hybrid, and hierarchy (as compared with just market and hierarchy)—is that much larger parameter changes are required to induce a shift from market to hierarchy (or the reverse) than are required to induce a shift from market to hybrid or from hybrid to hierarchy. Indeed, as developed below, much of the comparative static action turns on differential shifts in the intercept and/or slope of the hybrid mode. The critical predictive action is that which is located in the neighborhood of $\bar{k}_1$ (M to X) and $\bar{k}_2$ (X to H) in Fig. 1. Parameter changes of four kinds are examined: property rights, contract law, reputation effects, and uncertainty.

Among the limitations of the discrete structural approach is that parameter changes need to be introduced in a special way. Rather than investigate the effects of increases (or decreases) in a parameter (a wage rate, a tax, a shift in demand), as is customary with the usual maximizing setup, the comparative governance cost setup needs to characterize parameter changes as improvements (or not). It is furthermore limited by the need for these improvements to be concentrated disproportionately on one generic mode of governance. Those limitations notwithstanding, it is informative to examine the comparative static effects.

Property Rights

What has come to be known as the economics of property rights holds that economic performance is largely determined by the way in which property rights are defined. Ownership of assets is especially pertinent to the definition of property rights, where this "consists of three elements: (a) the right to use the asset [and delimitations that apply thereto] . . ., (b) the right to appropriate returns from the asset . . ., and (c) the right to change the asset's form and/or substance" (Furubotn and Pejovich, 1974, p. 4).

Most discussions of property rights focus on definitional issues. As is generally conceded, property rights can be costly to define and enforce and hence arise only when the expected benefits exceed the expected costs (Demsetz, 1967). That is not my concern here. Rather, I focus on the degree to which property rights, once assigned, have good security features. Security hazards of two types are pertinent: expropriation by the government and expropriation by commerce (rivals, suppliers, customers).

Governmental Expropriation. Issues of "credible commitments" (Williamson, 1983) and "security of expectations" (Michelman, 1967) are pertinent to expropriation by the government. If property rights could be efficiently assigned once and for all, so that assignments, once made, would not subsequently be undone—especially strategically undone—governmental expropriation concerns would not arise. Firms and individuals would confidently invest in productive assets without concern that they would thereafter be deprived of their just deserts.

If, however, property rights are subject to occasional reassignment, and if compensation is not paid on each occasion (possibly because it is prohibitively costly), then strategic considerations enter the investment calculus. Wealth will be reallocated (disguised, deflected, consumed) rather than invested in potentially expropriable assets if expropriation is perceived to be a serious hazard. More generally, individuals or groups who either experience or observe expropriation and can reasonably anticipate that they will be similarly disadvantaged in the future have incentives to adapt.

Michelman (1967) focused on cost-effective compensation. He

argued that if compensation is costly and if the "demoralization costs" experienced by disadvantaged individuals and interested observers are slight, then compensation is not needed. If, however, demoralization costs can be expected to be great and losses can be easily ascertained, compensation is warranted. Michelman proposed a series of criteria by which to judge how this calculus works out. Suppose that the government is advised of these concerns and "promises" to respect the proposed criteria. Will such promises be believed? This brings us to the problem of credible commitments.

Promises are easy to make, but credible promises are another thing. Kornai's (1986, pp. 1705–1706) observation that craftsmen and small shopkeepers fear expropriation in Hungary despite "repeated official declarations that their activity is regarded as a permanent feature of Hungarian socialism" is pertinent. That "many of them are myopic profit maximizers, not much interested in building up lasting goodwill ... or by investing in long-lived fixed assets" (1986, p. 1706) is partly explained by the fact that "These individuals or their parents lived through the era of confiscations in the forties" (Kornai, 1986, p. 1705).

But there is more to it than that. Not only is there a history of expropriation, but, as of 1986, the structure of the government had not changed in such a way as to assuredly forestall subsequent expropriations. Official declarations will be more credible only with long experience or if accompanied by a credible (not easily reversible) reorganization of politics. As one Polish entrepreneur recently remarked, "I don't want expensive machines. If the situation changes, I'll get stuck with them" (Newman, 1989, p. A10). Note, in this connection, that the objectivity of law is placed in jeopardy if the law and its enforcement are under the control of a one-party state (Berman, 1983, p. 37). Credibility will be enhanced if a monarch who has made the law "may not make it arbitrarily, and until he has remade it—lawfully—he is bound by it" (Berman, 1983, p. 9). Self-denying ordinances and, even more, inertia that has been crafted into the political process have commitment benefits (North and Weingast, 1989).

That this has not fully registered on Eastern Europe and the Soviet Union is suggested by the following remarks of Mikhail Gorbachev (advising U.S. firms to invest quickly in the Soviet Union rather than wait): "Those [companies] who are with us now have good prospects of participating in our great country ... [whereas those who wait] will remain observers for years to come—*we will see to it*" (*International Herald Tribune*, 1990, p. 5). That the leadership of the Soviet Union "will see to it" that early and late movers will be rewarded and punished, respectively, reflects conventional carrot-and-stick incentive reasoning. What it misses is that ready access to administrative discretion is the source of contractual hazard. The paradox is that fewer degrees of freedom (rules) can have advantages over more (discretion) because added credible commitments can obtain in this way. Effective economic reform thus requires that reneging options be foreclosed if investor confidence is to be realized.

Lack of credible commitment on the part of the government poses hazards for durable, immobile investments of all kinds—specialized and unspecialized alike—in the private sector. If durability and immobility are uncorrelated with asset specificity, then the transaction costs of all forms of private-sector governance increase together as expropriation hazards increase. In that event, the values of $\bar{k}_1$ and $\bar{k}_2$ might then change little or not at all. What can be said with assurance is that the government sector will have to bear a larger durable investment burden in a regime in which expropriation risks are perceived to be great. Also, private-sector durable investments will favor assets that can be smuggled or are otherwise mobile—such as general-purpose human assets (skilled machinists, physicians) that can be used productively if emigration is permitted to other countries.

Leakage. Not only may property rights be devalued by governments, but the value of specialized knowledge and information may be appropriated and/or dissipated by suppliers, buyers, and rivals. The issues here have recently been addressed by Teece (1986) in conjunction with "weak regimes of appropriability" and are related to earlier discussions by Arrow (1962) regarding property rights in information. If investments in knowledge cannot lawfully be protected or if nominal protection (e.g., a patent) is ineffective, then (1) the ex ante incentives to make such investments are impaired and (2) the ex post incentives to embed such investments in protective governance structures are increased. As Teece (1986) discussed, vertical or lateral integration into related stages of production where the hazards of leakage are greatest is sometimes undertaken for precisely these protective purposes. Trade secret protection is an example.

Interpreted in terms of the comparative governance cost apparatus employed here, weaker appropriability (increased risk of leakage) increases the cost of hybrid contracting as compared with hierarchy. The market and hybrid curves in Fig. 1 are both shifted up by increased leakage, so that $\bar{k}_1$ remains approximately unchanged and the main effects are concentrated at $\bar{k}_2$. The value of $\bar{k}_2$ thus shifts to the left as leakage hazards increase, so that the distribution of transactions favors greater reliance on hierarchy.

Contract Law

Improvements or not in a contract law regime can be judged by how the relevant governance-cost curve shifts. An improvement in excuse doctrine, for example, would shift the cost of hybrid governance down. The idea here is that excuse doctrine can be either too lax or too strict. If too strict, then parties will be reluctant to make specialized investments in support of one another because of the added risk of truly punitive outcomes should unanticipated events materialize and the opposite party insist that the letter of the contract be observed. If too lax, then incentives to think through contracts, choose technologies judiciously, share risks efficiently, and avert adversity will be impaired.

Whether a change in excuse doctrine is an improvement or not depends on the initial conditions and on how these trade-offs play out. Assuming that an improvement is introduced, the effect will be to lower the cost of hybrid contracting—especially at higher values of asset specificity, where a defection from the spirit of the contract is more consequential. The effect of such improvements would be to increase the use of hybrid contracting, especially as compared with hierarchy.

Hadfield (1990, pp. 981–982) has recently examined franchise law and has interpreted the prevailing tendency by the courts to fill in the gaps of an incomplete contract "by according the franchisor unfettered discretion, much as it would enjoy if it [the franchisor] were a vertically integrated corporation" as a mistaken application of forbearance reasoning from hierarchy (where the logic holds) to neoclassical contracting (where the logic fails). Such a failure of franchise law would increase the cost of franchising in relation to forward integration into distribution (Hadfield, 1990, p. 954). This would imply a shift in the value of $\bar{k}_2$ in Fig. 1 to the left.

A change in forbearance doctrine would be reflected in the governance cost of hierarchy. Thus, mistaken forbearance doctrine— for example, a willingness by the courts to litigate intrafirm technical disputes—would have the effect of shifting the costs of hierarchical governance up. This would disadvantage hierarchy in relation to hybrid modes of contracting ($\bar{k}_2$ would shift to the right).

Reputation Effects

One way of interpreting a network is as a nonhierarchical contracting relation in which reputation effects are quickly and accurately communicated. Parties to a transaction to which reputation effects apply can consult not only their own experience but can benefit from the experience of others. To be sure, the efficacy of reputation effects is easily overstated (Williamson, 1991b), but comparative efficacy is all that concerns us here and changes in comparative efficacy can often be established.

Thus, assume that it is possible to identify a community of traders in which reputation effects work better (or worse). Improved reputation effects attenuate incentives to behave opportunistically in interfirm trade—since the immediate gains from opportunism in a regime where reputation counts must be traded off against future costs. The hazards of opportunism in interfirm trading are greatest for hybrid transactions—especially those in the neighborhood of $\bar{k}_2$. Since an improvement in interfirm reputation effects will reduce the cost of hybrid contracting, the value of $\bar{k}_2$ will shift to the right. Hybrid contracting will therefore increase, in relation to hierarchy, in regimes where interfirm reputation effects are more highly perfected, ceteris paribus. Reputation effects are pertinent within firms as well. If internal reputation effects improve, then managerial opportunism will be reduced and the costs of hierarchical governance will fall.

Ethnic communities that display solidarity often enjoy advantages of a hybrid contracting kind. Reputations spread quickly within such communities and added sanctions are available to the membership (Light, 1972). Such ethnic communities will predictably displace nonethnic communities for activities for which interfirm reputation effects are important. Nonethnic communities, to be viable, will resort to market or hierarchy (in a lower or higher k niche, respectively).

Uncertainty

Greater uncertainty could take either of two forms. One is that the probability distribution of disturbances remains unchanged but that more numerous disturbances occur. A second is that disturbances become more consequential (due, for example, to an increase in the variance).

One way of interpreting changes of either kind is through the efficacy matrix, above. I conjecture that the effects of more frequent disturbances are especially pertinent for those disturbances for which mainly coordinated or strictly coordinated responses are required. Although the efficacy of all forms of governance may deteriorate in the face of more frequent disturbances, the hybrid mode is arguably the most susceptible. That is because hybrid adaptations cannot be made unilaterally (as with market governance) or by fiat (as with hierarchy) but require mutual consent. Consent, however, takes time. If a hybrid mode is negotiating an adjustment to one disturbance only to be hit by another, failures of adaptation predictably obtain (Ashby, 1960). An increase in market and hierarchy and a decrease in hybrid will thus be associated with an (above threshold) increase in the frequency of disturbances. As shown in Fig. 3, the hybrid mode could well become nonviable when the frequency of disturbances reaches high levels.[6]

If an increase in the variance of the disturbances uniformly increases the benefits to be associated with each successful adaptation, then the effect of increasing the consequentiality of disturbances can again be assessed through the effects on efficacy. Since outliers induce greater defection on the spirit of the agreement for hybrid modes, the efficacy of the hybrid is adversely affected by added variance. Unless similarly disabilities can be ascribed to market or hierarchy, the hybrid is disfavored by greater variance, ceteris paribus.

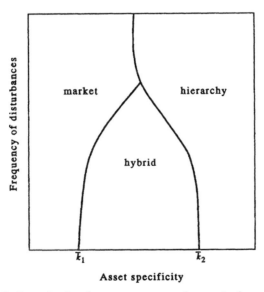

FIG. 3. Organization form responses to changes in frequency.

[6]The range of asset specificity is from zero (purely generic) to complete (purely firm-specific). The range of frequency is from "low" (a positive lower bound in a nearly unchanging environment) to "very high."

Discussion

The foregoing is concerned with the organization of transactions for mature goods and services and introduces parameter shifts one at a time. Added complications arise when innovation is introduced and when a series of parameter shifts occur together.

Innovation

Some of the added problems posed by innovation take the form of weak property rights. These are discussed above in conjunction with leakage. A second class of problems that confront innovation is that of timeliness. Nonstandard forms of organization, such as parallel R&D (Nelson, 1961) and joint ventures, are sometimes employed because these facilitate timely entry.

Timing can be crucial if a party expects to be a "player" when events are fast-moving or if learning-by-doing is essential. Although transaction-cost economics can relate to some of the pertinent issues, such as those posed by tacit knowledge (Polanyi, 1962) and the limits of imitation (Williamson, 1975, pp. 31–32, 203–207), added apparatus is needed to deal with the full set of issues that arise when responsiveness in real time, rather than equilibrium contracting, is the central concern. Awaiting such developments, the apparatus developed here should not be applied uncritically. For example, joint ventures are sometimes described as hybrids. If, however, joint ventures are temporary forms of organization that support quick responsiveness, and if that is their primary purpose, then both successful and unsuccessful joint ventures will commonly be terminated when contracts expire. Successful joint ventures will be terminated because success will often mean that each of the parties, who chose not to merge but, instead, decided to combine their respective strengths in a selective and timely way, will have learned enough to go it alone. Unsuccessful joint ventures will be terminated because the opportunity to participate will have passed them by. Joint ventures that are designed to give a respite should be distinguished from the types of hybrid modes analyzed here, which are of an equilibrium kind.

The need to distinguish continuing from temporary supply does not, however, mean that transaction-cost economizing principles do not apply to each. To the contrary, although the particulars differ, I would urge that the same general transaction-cost economizing framework has application (Williamson, 1985). The quasi-firms described by Eccles (1981), for example, can be interpreted as the efficient solution to a particular type of recurrent contracting problem. But the details do matter.

Simultaneous Parameter Shifts

The comparative static analysis set out above treats each generic form of organization as a syndrome of attributes and introduces parameter shifts one at a time. Suppose, instead, that a series of shifts were to occur together. Could these be processed as a sequence of independent changes? If such changes were in fact independent, that is precisely what I would propose. If, however, a related set of changes is made simultaneously, it will not do to treat these independently. If strong interaction effects exist, these must be treated as a cluster.

Relying extensively on the recent work of Aoki (1988, 1990), I have elsewhere interpreted the Japanese corporation as follows: (1) three key factors—employment, subcontracting, and banking—are fundamentally responsible for the success of the Japanese firm; (2) the efficacy of each of these rests on distinctive institutional supports; and (3) the three factors bear a complementary relation to each other (Williamson, 1991a).

The search for key factors and their institutional supports is wholly consistent with the spirit of this paper. Because employment, subcontracting, and banking changes are linked, however, the American corporation cannot expect to replicate the Japanese corporation by making changes in only one of these practices and not in the others. That is not to say that American firms cannot learn by observing subcontracting practices in Japanese firms. Exact replication of individual practices will be suboptimal, however, if linkages are important.

Similar considerations apply to economic reforms in China and Eastern Europe. If, for example, the efficacy of privatization turns crucially on the manner in which banking is organized and on the security of property rights, then piecemeal proposals that ignore the support institutions are fraught with hazard. The study of viable clusters of organization is a combined law, economics, and organizations undertaking. Although the apparatus in this paper is pertinent, applications to economic reform need to make express provision for contextual differences between alternative forms of capitalism (Hamilton and Biggart, 1988).

Conclusion

This paper advances the transaction-cost economics research agenda in the following five respects: (1) the economic problem of society is described as that of adaptation, of which autonomous and coordinated kinds are distinguished; (2) each generic form of governance is shown to rest on a distinctive form of contract law, of which the contract law of forbearance, which applies to internal organization and supports fiat, is especially noteworthy; (3) the hybrid form of organization is not a loose amalgam of market and hierarchy but possesses its own disciplined rationale; (4) more generally, the logic of each generic form of governance—market, hybrid, and hierarchy—is revealed by the dimensionalization and explication of governance herein developed; and (5) the obviously related but hitherto disjunct stages of institutional economics—the institutional environment and the institutions of governance—are joined by interpreting the institutional environment as a locus of shift parameters, changes in which parameters include shifts in the comparative costs of governance. A large number of refutable implications are derived from the equilibrium and comparative static analyses of governance that result. The growing empirical literature, moreover, is broadly corroborative (for summaries, see Williamson, 1985, ch. 5; Joskow, 1988; Shelanski, 1990).

Further developments of conceptual, theoretical, and empirical kinds are needed. Taken together with related developments in information economics, agency theory, and population ecology, there is reason to be optimistic that a "new science of organization" will take shape during the decade of the 1990s (Williamson, 1990). Whether that materializes or not, organization theory is being renewed in law, economics, and organizational respects. These are exciting times for interdisciplinary social theory.

References

Alchian, Armen, and Harold Demsetz (1972) Production, information costs, and economic organization. American Economic Review, 62 777–795.

Aoki, Masahiko (1988) *Information, Incentives, and Bargaining in the Japanese Economy*. New York: Cambridge University Press.

Aoki, Masahiko (1990) Toward an economic model of the Japanese firm. *Journal of Economic Literature*, 28 1–27.

Arrow, Kenneth J. (1962) Economic welfare and the allocation of resources of invention. In National Bureau of Economic Research (ed.), *The Rate and Direction of Inventive Activity: Economic and Social Factors*: 609–625. Princeton, NJ: Princeton University Press.

Arrow, Kenneth J. (1969) The organization of economic activity: Issues pertinent to the choice of market versus nonmarket allocation. In *The Analysis and Evaluation of Public Expenditure, Vol 1: The PPB System*: 59–73. U.S. Joint Economic Committee, 91st Congress, 1st Session. Washington, DC: U.S. Government Printing Office.

Ashby, W. Ross (1960) *Design for a Brain*. New York: Wiley.

Barnard, Chester (1938) *The Functions of the Executive*. Cambridge, MA: Harvard University Press.

Bergson, Abram (1948) Socialist economics. In Howard Ellis (ed.), *Survey of Contemporary Economics*: 430–458. Philadelphia: Blakiston.

Berman, Harold (1983) *Law and Revolution.* Cambridge, MA: Harvard University Press.

Buxbaum, Richard M. (1985) Modification and adaptation of contracts: American legal developments. *Studies in Transnational Economic Law,* 3 31–54.

Chandler, Alfred D., Jr. (1962) *Strategy and Structure.* Cambridge, MA: MIT Press.

Chandler, Alfred D., Jr. (1977) *The Visible Hand: The Managerial Revolution in American Business.* Cambridge, MA: Harvard University Press.

Clausewitz, Karl von (1980) *Vom Kriege,* 19th ed. (Originally published in 1832.) Bonn: Dremmler.

Coase, R. H. (1952) The nature of the firm. In George J. Stigler and Kenneth E. Boulding (eds.), *Readings in Price Theory:* 331–351. Homewood, IL: Irwin.

Commons, John R. (1924) Law and economics. *Yale Law Journal,* 34 371–382.

Commons, John R. (1934) *Institutional Economics.* Madison, WI: University of Wisconsin Press.

Cox, Archibald (1958) The legal nature of collective bargaining agreements. *Michigan Law Review,* 57 1–36.

Davis, Lance E., and Douglas C. North (1971) *Institutional Change and American Economic Growth,* Cambridge: Cambridge University Press.

Demsetz, Harold (1967) Toward a theory of property rights. *American Economic Review,* 57 347–359.

Eccles, Robert (1981) The quasifirm in the construction industry. *Journal of Economic Behavior and Organization,* 2 335–357.

Fama, Eugene F. (1980) Agency problems and the theory of the firm. *Journal of Political Economy,* 88 288–307.

Farnsworth, Edward Allan (1968) Disputes over omissions in contracts. *Columbia Law Review,* 68 860–891.

Fuller, Lon L. (1963) Collective bargaining and the arbitrator. *Wisconsin Law Review,* January: 3–46.

Furubotn, Eirik, and Svetozar Pejovich (1974) *The Economics of Property Rights.* Cambridge, MA: Ballinger.

Gilson, Ronald (1986) *The Law and Finance of Corporate Acquisitions.* Mineola, NY: Foundation Press.

Goldberg, Victor (1976) Regulation and administered contracts. *Bell Journal of Economics,* 7 426–452.

Grossman, Sanford J., and Oliver D. Hart (1986) The costs and benefits of ownership: A theory of vertical and lateral integration. *Journal of Political Economy,* 94 691–719.

Hadfield, Gillian (1990) Problematic relations: Franchising and the law of incomplete contracts. *Stanford Law Review,* 42 927–992.

Hamilton, Gary, and Nicole Biggart (1988) Market, culture, and authority. *American Journal of Sociology* (Supplement), 94: S52–S94.

Hayek, Friedrich (1945) The use of knowledge in society. *American Economic Review,* 35 519–530.

Holmstrom, Bengt (1989) Agency costs and innovation. *Journal of Economic Behavior and Organization,* 12 305–327.

Holmstrom, Bengt, and Paul Milgrom (1991) Multi-task principal-agent analysis. *Journal of Law Economics, and Organization* (in press).

International Herald Tribune (1990) Soviet economic development, June 5: 5.

Jensen, Michael, and William Meckling (1976) Theory of the firm: Managerial behavior, agency costs, and capital structure. *Journal of Financial Economics,* 3 305–360.

Joskow, Paul (1988) Asset specificity and the structure of vertical relationships. *Journal of Law, Economics and Organization,* 4 95–117.

Klein, Benjamin (1980) Transaction cost determinants of "unfair" contractual arrangements. *American Economic Review,* 70 356–362.

Klein, Benjamin, R. A. Crawford, and A. A. Alchian (1978) Vertical integration, appropriable rents, and the competitive contracting process. *Journal of Law and Economics,* 21 297–326.

Knight, Frank H. (1941) Review of Melville J. Herskovits, Economic Anthropology. *Journal of Political Economy,* 49 247–258.

Koopmans, Tjalling (1977) Concepts of optimality and their uses. *American Economic Review,* 67 261–274.

Kornai, Janos (1986) The Hungarian reform process. *Journal of Economic Literature,* 24 1687–1737.

Lange, Oskar (1938) On the theory of economic socialism. In Benjamin Lippincot (ed.), *On the Economic Theory of Socialism*: 55–143. Minneapolis: University of Minnesota Press.

Light, Ivan (1972) *Ethnic Enterprise in America: Business and Welfare among Chinese, Japanese, and Blacks,* Berkeley, CA: University of California Press.

Llewellyn, Karl N. (1931) What price contract? An essay in perspective. *Yale Law Journal,* 40 704–751.

Macneil, Ian R. (1974) The many futures of contracts. *Southern California Law Review,* 47 691–816.

Macneil, Ian R. (1978) Contracts: Adjustments of long-term economic relations under classical, neoclassical, and relational contract law. *Northwestern University Law Review,* 72 854–906.

Malmgren, Harold (1961) Information, expectations and the theory of the firm. *Quarterly Journal of Economics,* 75 399–421.

Manne, Henry (1967) Our two corporation systems: Law and economics. *University of Virginia Law Review,* 53 259–285.

Masten, Scott (1982) Transaction costs, institutional choice, and the theory of the firm. Unpublished Ph.D. dissertation, University of Pennsylvania.

Masten, Scott (1988) A legal basis for the firm. *Journal of Law, Economics, and Organization,* 4 181–198.

Masten, Scott, James Meehan, and Edward Snyder (1991) The costs of organization. *Journal of Law, Economics, and Organization,* 7 (in press).

Michelman, Frank (1967) Property, utility and fairness: The ethical foundations of "just compensation" law. *Harvard Law Review,* 80 1165–1257.

Milgrom, Paul, Douglass North, and Barry Weingast (1990) The role of institutions in the revival of trade. *Economics and Politics,* 2 1–23.

Milgrom, Paul, and John Roberts (1990) The economics of modern manufacturing: Technology, strategy, and organization. *American Economic Review,* 80 511–528.

Montias, Michael (1976) *The Structure of Economic Systems,* New Haven, CT: Yale University Press.

Nelson, Richard R. (1961) Uncertainty, learning, and the economics of parallel R&D. *Review of Economics and Statistics,* 43 351–364.

Newman, Barry (1989) Poland's farmers put the screws to leaders by holding back crops. *Wall Street Journal,* October 25: A1 and A10.

North, Douglass (1986) The new institutional economics. *Journal of Theoretical and Institutional Economics,* 142 230–237.

North, Douglass, and Barry Weingast (1989) Constitutions and commitment: The evolution of institutions governing public choice in 17th century England. *Journal of Economic History,* 49 803–832.

Polanyi, Michael (1962) *Personal Knowledge: Towards a Post-Critical Philosophy.* New York: Harper & Row.

Riordan, Michael, and Oliver Williamson (1985) Asset specificity and economic organization. *International Journal of Industrial Organization,* 3 365–378.

Scott, W. Richard (1987) *Organizations,* 2nd ed. Englewood Cliffs, NJ: Prentice-Hall.

Shelanski, Howard (1990) A survey of empirical research in transaction cost economics. Unpublished manuscript, University of California, Berkeley.

Simon, Herbert (1951) A formal theory of the employment relation. *Econometrica,* 19 293–305.

Simon, Herbert (1978) Rationality as process and as product of thought. *American Economic Review,* 68 1–16.

Teece, David J. (1986) Profiting from technological innovation. *Research Policy,* 15 (December) 285–305.

Topkis, Donald (1978) Maximizing a submodular function on a lattice. *Operations Research,* 26 305–321.

Ward, B. N. (1967) *The Socialist Economy: A Study of Organizational Alternatives.* New York: Random House.

Williamson, Oliver E. (1975) *Markets and Hierarchies,* New York: Free Press.

Williamson, Oliver E. (1976) Franchise bidding for natural monopoly—In general and with respect to CATV. *Bell Journal of Economics,* 7 73–104.

Williamson, Oliver E. (1979) Transaction-cost economics: The governance of contractual relations. *Journal of Law and Economics,* 22 233–261.

Williamson, Oliver E. (1983) Credible commitments: Using hostages to support exchange. *American Economic Review,* 73 519–540.

Williamson, Oliver E. (1985) *The Economic Institutions of Capitalism.* New York: Free Press.

Williamson, Oliver E. (1988) The logic of economic organization. *Journal of Law, Economics and Organization,* 4 65–93.

Williamson, Oliver E. (1989) Transaction cost economics. In Richard Schmalensee and Robert Willing (eds.) *Handbook of Industrial Organization,* 1 136–182. New York: North-Holland.

Williamson, Oliver E. (1990) Chester Barnard and the incipient science of organization. In Oliver E. Williamson (ed.), *Organization Theory* 172–207. New York: Oxford University Press.

Williamson, Oliver, E. (1991a) Strategizing, economizing, and economic organization. *Strategic Management Journal* (in press).

Williamson, Oliver, E. (1991b) Economic institutions: Spontaneous and intentional governance. *Journal of Law, Economics, and Organization* (in press).

Coase, Hayek, and Hierarchy

HEIN SCHREUDER[1]

Introduction

Economists have traditionally been fascinated by the problem of coordination of economic activities in society. Since Adam Smith postulated the operation of an "invisible hand" guiding self-interest seeking individuals to collectively efficient outcomes, much of the economists' attention was directed toward the coordination through markets. For a long time market coordination was mainly contrasted with coordination through "planning" in centrally directed economies. Of course, economists recognized that an increasing portion of the required economic coordination took place not "across markets" but "within organizations". However, it was not until Coase (1937) posited the fundamental question why ". . . in view of the fact that it is usually argued that coordination will be done by the price mechanism,. . . is organization necessary?", that the systematic comparison of markets and organizations commenced.

Coase is recognized by Williamson (1975) as one of the antecedents of his Markets and Hierarchies (M&H) approach. So is Hayek (1945) with his seminal article on "The use of knowledge in society". Williamson provided a major impetus to the rapid development of organizational economics (Barney and Ouchi, 1986) in the seventies after several decades of slow progress, if not stagnation. The M&H approach, which later became better known as "Transaction Cost Economics" (Williamson, 1985), constitutes one of the branches of organizational economics. Others include agency theory, property rights analysis, and information economics.

[1]DSM Polymers, Sittard, and Faculty of Economics and Business Administration of the University of Limburg, Maastricht, The Netherlands. Author's note: This paper was written while the author was a Fellow of the Netherlands Institute for Advanced Study in the Humanities and Social Sciences (NIAS). It benefitted from discussions at the NIAS workshop on Current Issues in Organization Studies and from comments received from colleagues at the Faculty of Economics and Business Administration of the University of Limburg, Maastricht, The Netherlands.

Generically these approaches belong to the contracting perspective on economic allocation and coordination.

In this article I focus on the M&H approach to argue that the nature of organizations, and their distinctive features *vis-à-vis* markets, are not adequately captured in the notion of hierarchy. Hierarchy and authority are the basis of only one of the communication and coordination mechanisms available to organizations. Taking the alternative mechanisms into account leads to a richer view on organizational coordination. Moreover, it forces us to rethink the conceptual distinctions between (ideal typical) markets and organizations. A proposal for a conceptual reformulation is developed. The proposal is shown to alleviate some problems with the current concepts, as identified by other authors.

First, however, the history of the idea of hierarchy/authority as the opposite coordination mechanism of markets is examined with reference to Coase and Hayek. The seminal work of these influential authors has not only inspired subsequent developments, but has also constrained them in certain respects. In order to see this we have to return to our intellectual roots.

Coase and Hayek

Coase's answer to his own fundamental question (why we observe so many firms in spite of the allocative efficiency of the price mechanism) ran along the following lines. He first of all established that the main difference between market coordination and coordination within firms is that the price mechanism is superseded within firms. It is replaced by the authority of an entrepreneur. The reason why this may be more efficient is sought by Coase in the existence of costs of market coordination. These costs pertain to the actual operation of markets (e.g., finding out the relevant prices) but more importantly to the difficulty of drawing up contracts for particular transactions. Transactions which cannot be well specified in advance, due to uncertainty and the necessity of longer term relationships, are not amenable to the market type of short-term contracting. An example is the long-term labor contract, which leaves the actual services to be rendered unspecified.

A sample of quotations from Coase (1937) may communicate this gist of the argument in his own words. Moreover, they will suffice to illustrate the main focus of the present analysis: Coase's assumption that market coordination is replaced by *authority* which is embodied in an entrepreneur who *directs* the allocation of resources within the firm. Consider the following passages:

> Outside the firm, price movements direct production, which is coordinated through a series of exchange transactions on the market. Within a firm, these market transactions are eliminated and in place of the complicated market structure with exchange transactions is substituted the entrepreneur-coordinator, who directs production.. . .
>
> It can, I think, be assumed that the distinguishing mark of the firm is the supersession of the price mechanism.. . .
>
> The main reason why it is profitable to establish a firm would seem to be that there is a cost of using the price mechanism.. . .
>
> We may sum up this section of the argument by saying that the operation of a market costs something and by forming an organization and allowing some authority (an "entrepreneur") to direct the resources, certain marketing costs are saved.. . . A firm, therefore, consists of the system of relationships which comes into existence when the direction of resources is dependent upon an entrepreneur.

As we shall see in a following section, this concept of entrepreneurial direction is one of the coordination mechanisms recognized in current organization theory. It is particularly prevalent in organizations of the "simple structure" type (Mintzberg, 1979). Start-up firms as well as small- and medium-sized firms with a strong entrepreneurial influence are often of this type. It is thus appropriate to state that market coordination is often superseded by this type of coordination. And in the thirties a larger part of the firm sector would have consisted of such firms. However, then as well as now this type of coordination is not sufficient to explain the coordination of economic activity within *organizations*. We return to this point in the next section.

Hayek's paper on "The use of knowledge in society" (1945) was concerned with the problem of the construction of a rational economic order. This problem was formulated as follows: ". . . how to secure the best use of resources known to any members of the society, for ends whose relative importance only these individuals know. Or, to put it briefly, it is a problem of the utilization of knowledge not given to anyone in its totality." Hayek proceeds to compare the price system with "planning" as mechanisms for communicating throughout society the knowledge which people need to engage in economic activities. Planning can be done by individuals, but Hayek prefers to restrict the term here to "central planning—direction of the whole economic system according to one unified plan". He emphasizes that certain types of knowledge can not be communicated without loss of information. Particularly, "local knowledge" (knowledge of particular circumstances of time and place) cannot be summarized in aggregated statistics without losing its usefulness for specific decisions. To make specific decisions, however, general information is necessary as well. Hayek shows how prices act as "sufficient statistics" to summarize this general information on the value of scarce resources. The combination of this general (price) information with local knowledge leads to the best decisions on the use of these resources.

Again, some quotations may illustrate the flavor of the argument in Hayek's own words:

> This is not a dispute whether planning is to be done or not. It is a dispute as to whether planning is to be done centrally, by one authority for the whole economic system, or is to be divided among many individuals.. . .
>
> If we can agree that the economic problem of society is mainly one of rapid adaptation to changes in the particular circumstances of time and place, it would seem to follow that the ultimate decisions must be left to the people who are familiar with these circumstances, who know directly of the relevant changes and of the resources immediately available to meet them. We cannot expect that this problem will be solved by first communicating all this knowledge to a central board which, after integrating *all* knowledge, issues its orders. We must solve it by some form of decentralization.. . .
>
> Fundamentally, in a system where the knowledge of the relevant facts is dispersed among many people, prices can act to coordinate the separate actions of different people in the same way as subjective values help the individual to coordinate the parts of his plan.

We see here that the price system is contrasted with *central* planning by one *authority* for an *entire* economic system.[2] Only through this line of reasoning can the price system be equated with decentralization. Organizational coordination can, of course, be effected in a relatively centralized or decentralized way. The price system is an important, but not the only way to decentralize decision-making in society. Centralization versus decentralization is an issue, but it is not the main distinction between market and organizational coordination. As Meckling and Jensen (1986, p. 11) have observed: "Pushed to its logical extreme, Hayek's focus on knowledge of particular circumstances implies more or less complete atomization of the economy." Hayek's analysis fails to explain why we observe so much organizational coordination in societies where reliance on the price system is a ready alternative.

The reason for returning to Coase and Hayek in the context of the present argument will be clear. Both contrast market coordination through the price mechanism with some type of coordination through *authority*. In Coase's analysis this authority is embodied in an entrepreneur directing resources within the firm. In Hayek's

---

[2]The reason is that Hayek wanted to contribute to the "capitalism versus socialism" debate. As we shall observe in the next section, his basic distinction was carried over into the "market versus hierarchy/organization" literature.

argument the authority rests with a central planning board for the entire economic system, issuing orders on the allocation of resources. In both cases coordination is achieved by directions or orders given in the setting of a hierarchical relation. By framing the analysis in these terms, important alternative coordination mechanisms are overlooked. This will be shown later. First, Williamson's use of these ideas—including his extension and modification of them—will be discussed by focusing on the M&H approach. This enables us to see (a) how Coase's and Hayek's view of coordination still exert a powerful influence on current approaches in organizational economics, but (b) also how a certain unease with this view has begun to emerge.

Markets and Hierarchies

In his book *Markets and Hierarchies* Williamson (1975) laid the foundation of what later was renamed Transaction Cost Economics (Williamson, 1985). In the 1975 book Williamson used the labels "Markets and Hierarchies approach" and "Organizational Failures Framework" interchangeably. Since the former term became used more widely (Williamson and Ouchi, 1981), and depicts the central issue of the current argument more vividly, I shall continue to use it here. In the M&H approach, markets and firms are seen as alternative instruments for completing a related set of transactions. Whether transactions will be executed across markets or within a firm depends on the relative efficiency of each instrument, given the transactional characteristics. These characteristics include human factors of the decision makers involved as well as environmental characteristics. A basic proposition of the M&H approach is that the same transactional characteristics apply to both market and firm coordination of transactions. Markets and firms (hierarchies) are, however, differentially equipped to deal with these characteristics. Hence, their relative efficiency in dealing with *particular* transactions will differ. The M&H approach attempts to explain which kinds of transactions will be coordinated across markets and within firms respectively.

Williamson's (1975, p. 9) introductory statement of this approach includes the following succinct passage:

> The markets and hierarchies approach attempts to identify a set of *environmental factors* which together with a related set of *human factors* explain the circumstances under which complex contingent claims contracts will be costly to write, execute, and enforce. Faced with such difficulties, and considering the risks that simple (or incomplete) contingent claims contracts pose, the firm may decide to bypass the market and resort to hierarchical modes of organization.

Transactions that may otherwise be handled in the market are thus performed internally, governed by administrative processes.

The legacy of Coase clearly shines through this quotation: contracting difficulties lead to hierarchical coordination superseding market coordination. Williamson's very important contribution, however, was to specify the human and environmental factors involved. The human factors were bounded rationality and opportunism. The environmental factors uncertainty and small numbers exchange. Derived transactional characteristics were information impactedness and, later, asset specificity (Williamson, 1981). By specifying these characteristics major steps were taken toward the explanation of the trade-off between market and firm coordination.[3]

There is, however, also evidence of a certain unease—already in the original exposition of the M&H approach—with the dichotomy of markets versus hierarchies. One signal of this is in the terminology used. The term "hierarchy" is often replaced by "firm", particularly when it is clear that the argument does not apply to *all* hierarchies (including, for example, the church or governmental bureaus). More significantly, it is also often substituted by *"internal organization"*. In chapter 2 of the 1975 book the approach is outlined. The four sections which deal with the comparative advantages of "hierarchies" are all captioned "Internal organization". Thus, it comes as no surprise that in the summary we read the following (emphases added):

To recapitulate, the advantages of *internal organization* in relation to markets are:

1. In circumstances where complex, contingent claims contracts are infeasible and sequential spot markets are hazardous, *internal organization* facilitates adaptive, sequential decision making, thereby to economize on bounded rationality.

2. Faced with present or prospective small-numbers exchange relations, *internal organization* serves to attenuate opportunism.

3. Convergent expectations are promoted, which reduces uncertainty.

4. Conditions of information impactedness are more easily overcome and when they appear, are less likely to give rise to strategic behavior.

5. A more satisfying trading atmosphere sometimes obtains.

---

[3]It is, in addition, recognized by Williamson (1975, pp. 37–39) that exchange will take place in a context with a certain *atmosphere*. This concept remains remarkably underdeveloped, however, an issue to which I return later. See also Spangenberg (1989) for a discussion of this issue and for an elaboration of the concept.

It *is* a surprise, however, that the immediately following sentences, which conclude the summary, read as follows (emphases added again):

> The shift of a transaction or related set of transactions from market to *hierarchy* is not all gain, however. Flexibility may be sacrificed in the process and other bureaucratic disabilities may arise as well. The failures of *internal organization*, in relation to markets, are examined in chapter 7 (Williamson, 1975, pp. 39–40).

The surprise, at least my surprise, comes from the observation that the five factors listed above are certainly related to internal organization, but their relation to hierarchy is often tenuous, to say the least.

Apart from these terminological signals, there are other, more substantive indications of the inappropriateness of the view that hierarchical coordination replaces market coordination. Two of the clearest examples are Williamson's own discussions of "peer groups" and "atmosphere".

Williamson's (1975, p. 41) discussion of the *peer group* evolves from the assumption ". . . for expositional purposes, that autonomous contracting is ubiquitous . . ." and the related question ". . . Why might such contracting be supplanted by non-market organization, and what internal forms of organization will first appear?" His answer is that market coordination will at first coexist with peer group coordination, dependent upon individual preferences for market versus non-market relationships. Peer groups are defined in the following quote:

> In order to avoid imputing benefits to hierarchy that can be had, in some degree, by simple nonhierarchical associations of workers, it will be useful to begin with an examination of worker peer groups. These groups involve collective and usually cooperative activity, provide for some type of other-than-marginal productivity and income-sharing arrangement, but do not entail subordination (Williamson, 1975, pp. 41–42).

Such groups will have certain advantages over the market (pp. 42–45), but experience very real limitations as well (pp. 45–49). As a consequence, Williamson (p. 45) conjectures that ". . . neither mode will fully displace the other, but both modes will coexist and each will selectively appeal to that part of the population to whose involvement tastes it most nearly corresponds, *ceteris paribus*". Peer groups may be attractive to individuals who prefer ". . . a transformation of 'involvement' relations, from a calculative to a more nearly quasimoral mode. . ." (p. 44). Because of its limitations, associative coordination will soon give way to "simple hierarchy" (p. 49).

We see in this line of reasoning that markets are *not* replaced by hierarchies but by associative groups in Williamson's own exposition. Here Williamson departs from Coase's view. For Coase, authority was the coordinative mechanism replacing the price system. For Williamson, it is apparently something else (to be named "mutual adjustment" in the next section). Something *not* captured in the notion of hierarchy which is to be reserved to "... a continuing superior-subordinate relationship ..." (p. 45). Hence, the dichotomy of markets versus hierarchies breaks down in this exposé.

The concept of *atmosphere* is hardly elaborated in Williamson (1975) or in his later works, although it was originally presented as a central concept in the M&H approach (see also Spangenberg, 1989). Reference is made to issues such as "... supplying a *satisfying exchange relation* is ... part of the economic problem, broadly construed" (p. 38) and to the values of some groups which may imply that "... efficiency and a sense of well-being (that includes, but transcends, equity) are intrinsically (nonseparably) joined" (p. 39). Hence, "attitudinal spillovers" are important for some transactional settings, and Williamson chooses to focus especially on differences in "metering intensity" (p. 39). Given this choice, it is again surprising to find a conclusion of the book stated as follows (p. 258):

> *Atmosphere.* As compared with market modes of exchange, hierarchy provides, for some purposes at least, a less calculative exchange atmosphere. *A footnote adds*: Note, however, that the peer group may be preferred to hierarchy in this respect—at least in small organizations.

One reason for the surprise is related to the argument above. *If* it is conceded that the peer group has the superior atmosphere characteristics, it is not possible to argue that hierarchies will replace markets because of this characteristic. The major reason for the surprise, however, is that we normally do not associate "satisfying exchange relations" or a "sense of well-being" with the hierarchical nature of organizations. Neither is it evident that it is the hierarchical nature of organizations which leads to decreased "metering intensity". When these arguments are (justifiably) invoked, the analysis could lead to other modes of organizational coordination which are overlooked by the emphasis on hierarchy. This will be attempted in the next section.

To summarize the argument so far, it is useful to start with the observation that complex organizations indeed usually have a hierarchical structure. This is not the issue here. The issue is whether it is the hierarchical nature of organizations which explains why they may serve as alternative instruments for completing a related set of transactions. For Coase and for Hayek this was the case, since they emphasized the *authority* embedded in the hierarchical structure as the alternative coordination mechanism. Williamson acknowledged both authors as precursors to his M&H approach. He retained the concept of hierarchy as the alternative "governance structure" for transactions. It was shown, however, that he appeared not to be very comfortable with the dichotomy thus introduced. At the terminological level, he continually switches between the use of hierarchy, firm, and internal organization. More substantively, he moved away from the emphasis on authority (see also Williamson, 1975, pp. 101–102). He imputes a number of advantages to hierarchies/firms/internal organization which are hardly associated with the hierarchical nature of organizations. Moreover, his analysis becomes internally inconsistent when non-hierarchical peer groups are also acknowledged as alternatives to market coordination. And, finally, it was shown that it is no coincidence that the central concept of atmosphere remained underdeveloped in the M&H approach. This concept, too, sits uneasily with any emphasis on hierarchy.

Williamson (1985, p. 402) recognized that "Transaction cost economics stands to benefit from the infusion of greater organizational content. More generally, economics should both speak and listen to organization theory." It is in the spirit of this observation that a richer picture of organizational coordination is painted in the following section.

Organizational Coordination

Mintzberg (1979) has provided a synthesis and typology of organizational structures and coordination, which will be adopted to illustrate an organizational theory perspective. The starting-point of his analysis is familiar to economists, but his reference to various organizational coordinating mechanisms may not be:

> Every organized human activity . . . gives rise to two fundamental and opposing requirements: the *division of labor* into various tasks to be performed and the *coordination* of these tasks to accomplish the activity. *The structure of an organization can be defined simply as the sum total of ways in which it divides its labor into distinct tasks and then achieves coordination among them* . . . Coordination . . . (involves) . . . various means. These can be referred to as *coordinating mechanisms*, although it should be noted that they are as much concerned with control and communication as with

coordination.[4]. . . *These . . . (coordinating mechanisms) . . . should be considered the most basic elements of structure, the glue that holds organizations together. From these all else follows . . .*" (Mintzberg, 1979, pp. 2–3).

It is important to note at this stage that organizations are thus perceived as having various coordinating mechanisms at their disposal. Their structures reflect the *sum total* of ways in which coordination is achieved.

What are these coordinating mechanisms? They are introduced in Mintzberg (1989, p. 101) as follows:

1. *Mutual adjustment,* which achieves coordination by the simple process of informal communication (as between two operating employees).

2. *Direct supervision,* in which coordination is achieved by having one person issue orders or instructions to several others whose work interrelates (as when a boss tells others what is to be done, one step at a time).

3. *Standardization of work processes,* which achieves coordination by specifying the work processes of people carrying out interrelated tasks (those standards usually being developed in the technostructure to be carried out in the operating core, as in the case of the work instructions that come out of time-and-motion studies).

4. *Standardization of outputs,* which achieves coordination by specifying the results of different work (again usually developed in the technostructure, as in a financial plan that specifies subunit performance targets or specifications that outline the dimensions of a product to be produced).

5. *Standardization of skills* (as well as *knowledge*), in which different work is coordinated by virtue of the related training the workers have received (as in medical specialists—say a surgeon and an anesthetist in an operating room—responding almost automatically to each other's standardized procedures).

6. *Standardization of norms,* in which it is the norms infusing the work that are controlled, usually for the entire organization, so that everyone functions according to the same set of beliefs (as in a religious order).

Comparing this approach with the economic perspective outlined before, it is clear that the latter has tended to focus on one particular type of organizational coordination: "direct supervision" in Mintzberg's terms. Only in this case is coordination achieved by the authority of one person to issue orders or instructions. Only when direct supervision is effected, is coordination actually associated with ". . . a continuing superior-subordinate relation-

[4]In a footnote Mintzberg quotes Litterer (1965, P. 233): "Recent developments in the area of control, or cybernetics, have shown (control and coordination) to be the same in principle." This may be true from a cybernetic point of view, but seems a conflation of terms from a broader perspective. As Schreuder et al. (1989, p. 5) have argued, control should be conceptualized as instrumental in achieving coordination in organizations. While coordination refers to the tuning of different tasks or activities, control denotes the ways and means in which coordination is monitored and preserved.

ship" (Williamson, 1975, p. 45). When direct supervision is the *key* coordinating mechanism in an organization, the associated type of structure is called the "Simple Structure" (Mintzberg, 1979) or the "Entrepreneurial Organization" (Mintzberg, 1989). When the coordination demands increase, this structure breaks down rapidly, essentially for the reasons already indicated by Hayek (1945). This does not imply, however, that organizational coordination is replaced by market coordination. It is usually replaced by some other form of organization. Mintzberg (1979, ch. 22; 1989, ch. 14) may be consulted for an overview of propositions pertaining to changes in organizational forms.

Even if it is accepted that organizational coordination is a richer phenomenon than it is usually conceptualized in organizational economics, it may still be argued that ultimately all other co-ordination mechanisms depend on the existence of hierarchy within organizations. After all, isn't it necessary that the top decision makers in the organization approve, say, the standardization of work processes? The answer is: Yes, sometimes it is. But organizations are not only "rational systems", deliberately designed and purposefully controlled. They are also to some extent "natural systems" (Scott, 1981), evolving without (and sometimes opposite to) intentional design. Mutual adjustment, for instance, may develop without any hierarchical authority being involved, as Williamson noted for the peer group (which, incidentally, also exists *within* organizations). And organizations are also "open systems" (Scott, 1981), in contin-uous interaction with their environments. The environment may directly determine organizational coordination and control. Ex-amples include legislative requirements on organizational structure, resource dependence (Pfeffer and Salancik, 1978), or the external change in skills training of professionals or of norms which infuse the organization and regulate behavior.

So, there are organizational reasons not to posit hierarchy as the ultimate source of organizational coordination. But there are further reasons. Consider the market relationship between an automobile manufacturer and its subcontractors. The latter are required to produce exactly to order, as specified by the former. The automobile manufacturer often has stipulated the right to inspect the subcon-tractors' facilities, to monitor and supervise their parts production, and to order any changes in production methods that are quality-related (within a certain acceptable range, of course). When we focus on the mechanisms involved in coordinating the work of these firms, it is clear that authority (or hierarchy) plays a significant role (cf. Simon, 1957; Williamson, 1975, p. 71). Part of the property rights of the subcontractor have been assigned to the automobile manufacturer. For that part, a hierarchical relationship may be said to exist between the firms. Market coordination and hierarchical coordination are, hence, not necessarily mutually exclusive, but may be complementary as well. A simple market-hierarchy dichotomy would obscure this fact (as indeed Williamson's recent work also acknowledges; see Williamson 1993).

More generally, coordination through the price mechanism and coordination through the six organizational mechanisms identified above often coexist. Within firms, transfer prices may regulate the internal flow of goods (see Eccles and White, 1988). An internal capital market may operate with rates of return (co-)determining which strategic projects will obtain internal funding. And internal labor markets may exist, upon which departments or divisions compete for the best human resources, also by bidding up their potential salaries.[5] *Market coordination may thus penetrate hierarchies.*

But organizational mechanisms may operate in combination with markets as well. Across markets, norms may be standardized, as businessmen discover when dealing with other cultures. A dramatic example is the Islamic prohibition to charge interest. If some foreign practices seem strange to us, we should realize that our norms, too, are "standardized" to allow us to engage in economic transactions with roughly the same expectations of what is fair and what is not.[6] Mutual adjustment may also play a role in market settings, as in the case of "tacit collusion" within oligopolies. Standardization of work processes may have been legislated, leading to regulated markets. Or such standardization may have simply evolved, as Grinyer and Spender (1979) show for certain "industry recipes". And, finally, outputs may have been standardized, as in the case of computer operating systems or international product standards. In all these examples organizational mechanisms operate in conjunction with

[5]Interestingly, from an economist's perspective internal labor markets are characterized by the existence of formalization (see Doeringer and Piore, 1971). However, given that we are dealing with markets which are internal for organizations, and that organizations are generally characterized by some degree of formalization, for an organization theorist the distinguishing characteristic of internal markets is that competition is allowed, partly by price.
[6]One illustration of this is provided by Stewart Macaulay (1963, p. 61) in the following quote: "One purchasing agent expressed a common business attitude when he said, 'if something comes up, you get the other men on the telephone and deal with the problem. You don't read legalistic contract clauses at each other if you ever want to do business again. One doesn't run to lawyers if he wants to stay in business because one must behave *decently*" (emphasis added).

market coordination. In some cases these organizational mechanisms are associated with an ultimate source of hierarchy, in others they are not. Hierarchy cannot be regarded as a necessary condition for organizational coordination. What is more, these few examples show that *a combination of market and organizational coordination is probably the rule rather than the exception.*

If it is accepted:

(1) that is not the hierarchical nature of organizations which explains why they are alternative coordination devices,

(2) that organizations have various coordination mechanisms at their disposal, and

(3) that, empirically, market and organizational coordination will be combined more often than not,

we are forced to reconsider the dichotomy between markets and hierarchies/organizations (or, alternatively, between prices and authority as the two mutually exclusive coordination mechanisms).

In the remainder of the paper two alternative routes for such a reconsideration will be outlined. The first leaves an ideal typical "market versus *organization*" distinction intact. It aims for a conceptual reformulation of organizational coordination, which enables us to preserve such a distinction. The other route dispenses with the "market versus organization" dichotomy. It inquires directly into the comparative advantages of the alternative coordination mechanisms and attempts to explain the "bundles" of mechanisms we commonly observe.

Markets and Organizations

If we want to retain a "markets versus organizations" distinction, we need to reformulate our conceptual apparatus.

How can we conceptually demarcate markets from organizations? Again, a return to the roots of organizational economics may provide the beginning of an answer. For both Coase and Hayek market coordination was characterized by the operation of the price system as coordination mechanism. This characterization is retained in the following proposal. It was shown, however, that their seminal contributions started the field off on too narrow a path by contrasting the price system solely with authority (or hierarchy). The full range of organizational mechanisms should be taken into account.

Hayek's (1945) problem formulation remains intact, however:

> The various ways in which the knowledge on which people base their plans is communicated to them is the crucial problem for any theory explaining

the economic process. And the problem of what is the best way of utilizing knowledge initially dispersed among all the people is at least one of the main problems of economic policy—or of designing an efficient economic system.

In Hayek's view this is the central problem, since it is necessary to convey ". . . to the individuals such additional knowledge as they need in order to enable them to fit their plans in with those of others".

It will be clear that from an organizational point of view all the coordination mechanisms contribute to achieving this very purpose. Knowledge may be communicated in informal contacts (mutual adjustment) or by issuing orders (direct supervision). Manuals contain information how to fit your plans with those of others (standardization of work processes). So do product and performance specifications (standardization of output) and professional training (standardization of skills). And, finally, norms strongly regulate behavior and lead to convergent expectations (standardization of norms). Mintzberg's (1979, pp. 2–3) remark that ". . . coordinating mechanisms . . . are as much concerned with . . . communication as with coordination" is apposite here. His organizational view and Hayek's economic perspective are perfectly congruent in this respect.

This observation provides the basis for *the proposal to demarcate markets from organizations by means of the coordination mechanisms used to communicate the necessary knowledge to the actors involved in economic transactions.*

Market coordination remains characterized by use of the price system. Organizational coordination can then be complementarily defined as non-price communication, which includes the six coordination mechanisms identified above.

It will be clear that markets and organizations are thus defined as mutually exclusive at the conceptual level. When prices signal the information actors need to engage in transactions, market coordination obtains. When non-price communication is involved, organizational coordination is said to exist. An ideal typical market is characterized by the *exclusive use* of the price system as communication and coordination device. The model of perfect competition is a case in point. An ideal typical organization would *not* rely on prices for its internal coordination. Williamson's peer group may serve as an example.

In the real world, we would expect to find more mixed cases than ideal types, as has been argued above. While the *concepts* of market and organizational coordination are mutually exclusive, *empirically* they may be combined. The proposal for a conceptual demarcation of market and organizational coordination is premised on the belief that these mechanisms involve differences in kind. This belief is by no means shared by all organizational economists. Barney and Ouchi (1986, pp. 432–435), for instance, argue that adoption of the transaction cost perspective forces us to abandon concepts like organizational boundaries, environments and structures (see also Barzel, 1989, ch. 4). In the next section an alternative route will be sketched which disposes of any sharp conceptual distinctions between markets and organizations. In the final section, the two routes will be compared.

Organized Markets and Organizational Markets

Two objections to the foregoing proposal may be used as an introduction to the alternative route. The first objection is of an empirical nature: it is very hard to find examples of "pure" market coordination. The model of perfect competition was mentioned as a case in point. However, as Samuelson (1980, p. 39) has observed: "... A cynic might say of perfect competition what Bernard Shaw said of Christianity: The only trouble with it is that it has never been tried." Markets are almost always organized in the sense that some organizational mechanism is usually operative in combination with the price mechanism. Of course, it is no objection against an ideal type that it is hard to find "pure" empirical examples of that type. However, it is much less difficult to find examples of "pure" organizational coordination under the definition presented above. Small voluntary associations, religious orders, and small firms would all seem to qualify. This leads to the suspicion that markets and organizations are treated differently under the preceding proposal.

The second objection is of an analytical nature. Market coordination is equated with exclusive use of the price system. Organizational coordination, however, is identified as the use of any one of *six* mechanisms or *a mix of these*. We can thus see that two levels of analysis are involved. One level of analysis involves the coordination mechanisms used. The other level of analysis pertains to the ideal types of coordination identified (i.e., market or organizational). In the case of market coordination these two levels of analysis are conflated: coordination by the price system is identical to market coordination. In this case, one of these levels is redundant. For organizational coordination, however, the two levels of analysis remain necessary. Any (combination) of the six mechanisms may be involved. Identifying a particular transaction as organizationally coordinated, still leaves open the more microanalytic question how this was actually achieved. Probably, this analytically different treatment of market and organizational coordination explains the empirical observation above to a large extent.

These objections point toward the need to base the analysis on the most microanalytic concepts involved, i.e., the coordination mechanisms. Instead of the dichotomy between markets and organizations, the potential coordination mechanisms governing the execution of economic transactions form the basic units of analysis. In effect, this second route is much more in line with the gist of the fundamental transactions cost argument. The amendments made are:

1. Instead of two coordination mechanisms (price and authority/ hierarchy), seven basic mechanisms are identified; and
2. Combinations of these mechanisms are recognized as analytically possible and empirically abundant.

Thus, we would expect many transactions to be governed by *bundles* of coordination mechanisms. The actual (bundle of) coordination mechanism(s) used for particular transactions can be predicted on the basis of the usual assumption of economizing on production and transaction costs.

In the spirit of Hayek's problem diagnosis, however, the elusive concept of transactions costs may need further scrutiny. The reason is that the *communication costs* involved in any transaction are perhaps underspecified. Recall that Hayek identified the basic problem as communicating the necessary knowledge to the actors involved in economic transactions. This implies that the basic property of any coordination mechanism is its ability to communicate knowledge of a particular kind. At the present stage of development, our understanding of the association between particular types of knowledge and particular types of coordination mechanisms seems fragmentary. What is more, if alternative mechanisms are available to communicate a particular type of knowledge, a procedure has to be followed to identify which mechanism allows for the most *efficient communication.*[7]

The analytical procedure to determine the communication costs would be to first establish the knowledge required by the actors involved in the transaction. Then, the knowledge which has to be communicated for coordination purposes should be determined.

---

[7]As usual, efficiency would have a static and a dynamic aspect. Static efficiency is discussed further in the following example in the text. Dynamic efficiency would refer to the ease of adaptation allowed by a particular coordination mechanism. Fragmentary understanding of the latter issue is evident in organization theory (e.g., Mintzberg, 1979) and transaction cost economics (e.g., Williamson, 1990).

Finally, the mechanisms through which this knowledge can be communicated most efficiently, need to be ascertained. The latter requirement implies that an important part of the broadened research program in transaction cost economics should involve the investigation of the communication costs associated with alternative coordination mechanisms (cf. Demsetz, 1988; Meckling and Jensen, 1986).[8]

To illustrate, consider the case of the automobile manufacturer and its subcontractor, discussed earlier. Assume that this relationship started out as a pure market relation, in which the subcontractor produced a fully specified part for the automobile manufacturer. However, as the product life cycles of cars shorten, production technology speeds up, new materials emerge, quality becomes more important, etc., it becomes very costly to renegotiate the terms of the contract every time a product respecification is called for. For the reasons outlined by Williamson (1975; 1985) a hierarchical relationship may come into being. Note, however, that this hierarchical relationship does not fully replace the market relationship. The automobile manufacturer may have limited rights to monitor and supervise particular aspects of the subcontractor's production program, for instance with respect to on-site quality control. Prices will still be used as communication devices to summarize the value dimension of the actions taken. Furthermore, it may well be that the contracts cannot be fully specified for the quality dimension. Supervision may be too costly to implement on a real-time basis, and may only be feasible by means of sampling. In such a case, the automobile manufacturer may attempt to create a shared (quality) culture with its subcontractor. The shared culture may fill the gaps in the contracts and the supervision. As Camerer and Vepsalainen (1988, p. 115) observed: "Corporate culture solves the problem by specifying broad, tacitly understood rules—'the way we do things around here'—for appropriate action under unspecified contingencies." Note that in this illustrative case, we have a *bundle* of market, hierarchy and culture (standardization of norms) coordination.

Of course, this is only an illustration of the second route indicated above. Much work will be required to specify the transaction costs (including the communication costs) associated with the use of the various coordination mechanisms. The purpose of this article was

[8]Work of this nature has also been carried out in information economics (Arrow, 1984), in the "architecture of economic systems" program of Sah and Stiglitz (1986, 1988; see also Schreuder and Van Witteloostuyn, 1990) and on an *ad hoc* basis (e.g., Camerer and Vepsalainen, 1988).

to outline two proposals to deal with the untenable dichotomy between markets/the price system and hierarchies/authority. In the next and final section these will be summarized and discussed.

Summary and Discussion

In his introductory essay to the reader on *The Economic Nature of the Firm*, Putterman (1986) lists seven distinctions between markets and firms. The first reads (p. 6):

> Agents interact as "free" individuals and as equals in markets but under organizational directives and in accordance with their station in a hierarchy in firms.

Later the following "disavowal" is added:

> The contrast between agent autonomy and equality in markets, on the one hand, and subordination and hierarchy in firms, on the other, runs the risk of obscuring actual agent discretion and the ambiguities of interagent relations within firms leading to a view of the firm as a strictly regimented hierarchy that . . . is an oversimplification for many purposes. (p. 15).

This paper has addressed the conflict inherent in these two statements. It has argued that firms, and complex organizations generally, indeed usually have a hierarchical element, but that it is certainly an oversimplification to equate organizational *coordination* with hierarchy or authority. The reason is not only "actual agent discretion and the ambiguities of interagent relations within firms". Far more important is the fact that a focus on hierarchy obscures a large part of the actual coordination mechanisms that may operate in organizations. Once this is recognized, it may also be seen that all forms of organizational coordination may operate in conjunction with market coordination by the price mechanism.

These insights lead to the need to reconsider the familiar distinction between markets/the price system and hierarchies/authority. This has been attempted along two routes. The first route was premised on the belief that it is useful to retain an ideal typical distinction between markets and organizations. This has been achieved by contrasting organizational coordination anew with market coordination. The latter is generally equated with communication and coordination through the price system. Organizational coordination can then be complementarily defined as non-price communication, which includes the six coordination mechanisms identified by Mintzberg (1989). This reformulation directs the attention toward the *knowledge* necessary for actors to engage in economic transactions. Whereas market and organizational *coord-*

ination are thus conceived of as mutually exclusive at the conceptual level, they may be combined empirically.

This first route was shown to present some difficulties in view of the differential treatment of markets and organizations. Analytically, organizational coordination requires two levels of analysis, while these levels are conflated in the case of market coordination. Therefore, a second route was suggested which focuses on the most microanalytic level of analysis: the various potential coordination mechanisms. Instead of the two mechanisms, which are traditionally identified, seven were recognized. What is more, combinations of these mechanisms are recognized as analytically possible and empirically abundant. Thus, it has been argued that many transactions will be executed under the regime of a *bundle* of coordination mechanisms. Each bundle will be specifically geared to the transactional properties involved. The familiar assumption of cost minimization may be retained as the explanatory device, if the concept of cost includes communication costs as an element of production and transaction cost.

The second route seems preferable from an analytical point of view. It disposes of the conceptual dichotomy between markets and organizations, but it retains the focus on the most microanalytic level of analysis: the coordination mechanisms employed. Furthermore, there is a way to bring a (reformulated) distinction between markets and organizations back into our analytical vocabulary, if this is deemed useful.[9] In line with the typological approach outlined in the section on organizational coordination, markets can be identified as the governance structures associated with the *dominant use* of the price mechanism. Organizations then remain the governance structures associated with the dominant use of any of the other mechanisms. Of course, this introduces the difficulty of establishing an operational definition of "dominant use". Since organizational theorists of the typological inclination have not yet provided such an operational definition either,[10] a challenging task would then remain for economists and organizational researchers alike.

This paper was written in the spirit of Williamson's (1985, p. 402) recommendation that "... economics should both speak and listen to organization theory".[11] It was shown that at the

---

[9]Since institutions are slow to change, it is not to be expected that the edifices of economics and organization theory will give up their core concepts easily.

[10]See Schreuder et al. (1988) for a discussion of this issue.

[11]Similarly, Holmstrom and Tirole (1989, p. 126) conclude their review of the theory of the firm by noting three outstanding problems, one of which is "... to integrate observations from neighboring fields such as sociology and psychology—in a consistent (not *ad hoc*) way into the theoretical apparatus".

level of these basic concepts an integration of organizational and economic perspectives was possible. Of course, this represents only a first step in the elaboration of a truly integrated organizational economics.

References

Barney, J. B. and W. G. Ouchi (1986) *Organizational Economics*. San Francisco: Jossey-Bass.

Barzel, Y. (1989) *Economic Analysis of Property Rights*. Cambridge University Press.

Camerer, C. and A. Vepsalainen (1988) The economic efficiency of corporate culture. *Strategic Management Journal*, 115–126.

Coase, R. H. (1986 (1937)) The nature of the firm. *Economica*.

Demsetz, H. (1988) The theory of the firm revisited. In *Ownership, Control, and the Firm*, edited by H. Demsetz. Basil Blackwell.

Doeringer, P. and M. Piore (1971) *Internal Labor Markets and Manpower Analysis*. Boston: D. C. Heath and Co.

Eccles, R. G. and H. C. White. (1988) Price and authority in inter-profit center transactions. *American Journal of Sociology*, 94, S17–S51.

Grinyer, P. E. and J. Spender (1979) Recipes, crises, and adaptation in mature businesses. *International Studies of Management and Organization*, 9, 113–133.

Hayek, F. (1945) The issue of knowledge in society. *The American Economic Review*.

Holmstrom, B. R. and J. Tirole (1989) The theory of the firm. In *Handbook of Industrial Organization*, Vol. 1, edited by R. Schmalensee and R. D. Willig. North-Holland.

Lindenberg, S. (1990) A new push in the theory of organization. In *The New Institutional Economics. Different Approaches to the Economics of Institutions*, p. 76–84 edited by E. Furubotn and R. Richter. Special Issue of the *Journal of Institutional and Theoretical Economics*, Vol. 146 (1).

Litterer, J. A. (1965) *The Analysis of Organizations*. John Wiley.

Meckling, W. H. and M. C. Jensen (1986). Knowledge, control and organizational structure: Parts I and II. Working paper.

Mintzberg, H. (1979) *The Structure of Organizations*. Englewood Cliffs: Prentice Hall.

Mintzberg, H. (1989) *Mintzberg on Management*. New York: The Free Press.

Pfeffer, J. and G. R. Salancik (1989) *The External Control of Organizations*. New York: The Free Press.

Putterman, L. (1986) The economic nature of the firm: overview. In *The Economic Nature of the Firm*, edited by L. Putterman. Cambridge University Press.

Sah, R. K. and J. E. Stiglitz (1986) The architecture of economic systems. *American Economic Review*, 716–727.

Sah, R. K. (1988) Committees, hierarchies and polyarchies. *Economic Journal*, 98, 451–470.

Schreuder, H., J. Spangenberg, P. Kunst and S. Romme (1988) *The Structure of Organizations: An Empirical Assessment of Mintzberg's Typology*. European Institute for Advanced Studies in Management.

Schreuder, H. and A. van Witteloostuijn (1990) *Dispersed Knowledge and Economic Organization*. Research memorandum. Maastricht: University of Limburg.

Scott, W. R. (1981) *Organizations: Rational, Natural and Open Systems*, 2nd edition. Englewood Cliffs: Prentice Hall.

Simon, H. A. (1957) *Models of Man*. New York: John Wiley.

Spangenberg, J. F. A. (1989) *Economies of Atmosphere*. Assen/Maastricht: Van Gorcum.

Williamson, O. E. (1975) *Markets and Hierarchies*. New York: The Free Press.

Williamson, O. E. (1985) *The Economic Institutions of Capitalism*. New York: The Free Press.

Williamson, O. E. (1993) Comparative economic organization: the analysis of discrete structural alternatives. In *Interdisciplinary Perspectives on Organization Studies* edited by S. Lindenberg and H. Schreuder. Oxford: Pergamon.

Notes on the Use of Power and Efficiency Constructs in the Economics and Sociology of Organizations

ANNA GRANDORI[1]

Introduction

An important barrier to an effective dialogue between economists and sociologists of organizations—a dialogue which has been initiated from both sides (Huppes, 1976; Williamson, 1987b)—is the widely used distinction between "power" and "efficiency" variables as *explanans* of organizational arrangements. For example, in his conclusions to the debate at the EGOS Conference on the "Markets and Hierarchies Persepctive", Turk (1983, p. 189) reported that "there had been a direct opposition between economic and sociological arguments in many instances(. . .). Economists (and some organization theorists) tended to contend that organizations are all about efficiency; sociologists (and other organization theorists) retorted that organizations are all about power." Analogous positions have been adopted in the recent past on both sides of the controversy. Pfeffer (1982) characterizes economic and sociological perspectives on organizations as respectively arguing from an "efficiency" or a "power" point of view; and has suggested that the dispute be resolved by means of empirical tests. On the other side, Williamson and Ouchi (1981) and Teece (1981a) represent the challenge in analogous terms by arguing that a power motive explanation of observable organizational forms fails to give an account of the selective rather than universal expansion of organizational boundaries.[2]

---

[1]Bocconi University, Milan.

[2]This controversy has been stimulated by the development of models of organizations developed by new institutional economics (Williamson, 1975 and 1985). They emphasize the superior long-run survival chances of least cost organizational forms. This seems ironic considering that the "old" institutional

Before resorting to empiricial tests in order to discriminate between "efficiency" and "power" explanations of organization forms, and indeed in order to be able to conduct such tests, further clarification of the two constructs is warranted. In fact, not only are both concepts admittedly very complex and somewhat ill-defined (Turk, 1983) but any dialogue or comparison between different scientific theories poses problems of commensurability of concepts and variables (Feyerabend, 1975) which require careful translation before communication becomes possible.

The Efficiency Variable

In organizational economics, the efficiency variable notoriously occupies a very central position. More "efficient" organization forms are those under which the sum of production and transaction costs is lower; and they are said not only to outperform other forms but also to replace them "in nature" in the long run. For example, the multidivisional organizational form is hypothesized to be more efficient than the functional form in large enterprises because of the decrease in communication and decision costs brought about by decentralization, and because of a reduction in the costs of sub-goal pursuit produced by internal control and incentive mechanisms based on profitability (Teece, 1981b). Analogously, at the level of inter-firm organization, more internalized solutions are supposed to be more efficient when the partners of exchange are not easily replaceable and context uncertainty creates occasions for opportunistic behaviors and provokes costly renegotiations of exchange conditions (Williamson, 1981 and 1985).

The currently most active research programs in organizational economics, namely transaction cost and agency cost economics, have focused on the costs deriving from conflict resolution in goods/services exchanges (i.e., opportunism and negotiation costs)

---

economists, the great tradition of Veblen, Myrdal, Galbraith and Schumpeter, criticized and sought to reform neoclassical economics precisely by including, as an important antecedent of economic behavior, its embeddedness in social and power relations and by constructing dynamic and evolutionary rather than static models (Kapp, 1976). Yet, from this point of view, organizational economics is more similar to neoclassical than to institutional economics (Bauer and Cohen, 1983; Rullani, 1986), given its emphasis on strict cost reduction considerations and on equilibrium solutions. However, a distinctive achievement of the "new" institutional economics has been that of challenging pred-existing organizational theories, many of which have sociological bases, on the grounds of organization design about which economics (the "old" institutional economics included) was traditionally silent.

in addition to the traditional information search, communication and decision-making costs. However, these expanded economic approaches still use a particular or limited notion of efficiency. In the first place, organizational economics is concerned with problems of shirking and motivation, waste and control, opportunism and communication, in short with what Leibenstein (1976) called "*x*-efficiency" problems as opposed to allocative efficiency problems. Leibenstein had complained that economics was concerned only with allocative efficiency and not with *x*-efficiency. But in recent organizational economics, the situation is reversed. Attention to allocative efficiency is lacking. Specifically, economic approaches to organization do not consider the possibility that different parties in a transaction have conflicting interests concerning the organizational forms by which exchanges are to be regulated and that therefore a problem of efficient allocation of organizational resources to the different actors may arise.

In the second place, organizational economics has often been criticized for using a static rather than dynamic notion of efficiency (Mariotti, 1989; Bauer and Cohen, 1983). In the third place, it can be noticed that an "absolute" notion of an efficient organizational solution as the least-cost arrangement may run into problems for bounded rationality reasons (Winter, 1975; Grandori, 1989a). In sum, the way in which the efficiency variable is used in these models of organization is far from being comprehensive or unproblematic. In the remainder of this section we specify three additional or "reformed" concepts of organizational efficiency, which complements the static cost efficiency criterion employed by current organizational economics.

Pareto Efficiency

The more general case in organization design, as far as preference structures are concerned, is that in which the different parties hold different transaction cost functions (or more generally different utility functions) with respect to alternative organizational arrangements. These differences cannot be dismissed as epiphenomena due to volatile tastes but can often be reconstructed as rational preferences due to higher transaction costs borne by the structurally weaker party. For example, in interfirm networks, those firms contributing abilities and resources that are relatively more substitutable, often (although not always) prefer more integrated agreements than their more monopolistic counterparts. Examples are: sub-contractors in the Italian fashion industry prefer more long term and obligational contracts than the fashion houses which externalize production; in complex engineering projects, construction firms prefer sub-contracting to joint ventures, the opposite of what engineering firms do; firms who confer labor in a project often prefer a more internalized form of association than the capital conferers would like to subscribe to. In these asymmetric conditions the traditional notion of a single most efficient solution for the whole system becomes insufficient (if arbitrary interpersonal comparisons of utilities are not introduced), and the problem of devising "efficient" organizational arrangements should be tackled as a game problem, usually a cooperative game (Grandori, 1991).

For example, it is true that in a franchising agreement it is in the common interest of the associating firms that a central agent monitors franchisees' behaviors in order to guarantee their compliance to the chain's quality standards and to prevent free-riding (Williamson, 1985; Rubin, 1978). However, other dimensions of a franchising organizational arrangement are relevant, on which interests diverge: the amount of royalties paid, a division of expenses for chain specific assets that protects the franchisee from quasi-rent expropriation, an amount of know-how transfers and of contract obligations for the franchisee that defend the franchisor from the risk of opportunistic participation and early exit of the franchisee (Grandori, 1989b; Ioannilli, 1989).

As a whole, the problem of designing an efficient organizational solution is not simply one of choosing the least-cost arrangement (for everybody), but is one of finding the undominated solutions of a game, some of which will be more favorable to one party and some others to the counterpart.

Dynamic Efficiency

A notion of dynamic efficiency can widen the static efficiency analysis of standard organizational economics, thereby responding to the possible objection that designing organizational structures and mechanisms to best fit actual transactional and productive requirements may entail future costs. Specifically, costs of malsuitability may emerge where the requirements are variable over time; and the elimination of organizational slack aimed at enhancing present efficiency can impoverish innovation capability.

Analytical responses to the need to reform the concept of efficiency in these directions might be the following. First, we can hypothesize that the production and transaction costs attached to a given exchange randomly vary over time. For example, suppose that the demand for a good or service is subject to frequent variations in volume and qualitative specifications. As described by Mariotti and

Cainarca (1987) for the textile/clothing industry, a dynamic efficient criterion may suggest the externalization of production in spite of the specificities and interdependencies that link the production to the design phase. In this sense dynamic efficiency includes a "flexibility" notion. To take into account these dynamic factors we can consider a series of future probability distributions of production and transaction costs contingent on different transactional conditions. Analytically, we can compare the present expected values of the sums of all these costs (C=production + transaction costs) under each arrangement, given by an expression of this type:

$$\bar{C} = \Sigma_i c_i a_i = \int_0^\infty c_i f_i(c) dc \cdot a_i$$

where C is the present expected value of total costs under any given organization form, i is the accounting period, f is the probability density function of costs in each period and a is an actualization rate.

Second, if we consider that organizational slack is a major source of a firm's innovation capacity (Cyert and March, 1963), we can assign positive preferences to slack, at least up to a certain level, and at least to a certain type of slack. For example, for purposes of innovation, it may be more interesting to maintain a reserve of unallocated attention (work time) rather than to distribute extra emoluments. In any case, "dynamically efficient" firms in this sense should be expected to have wider organizational boundaries than statically efficient firms. This conclusion is by no means counterintuitive on the basis of the consideration that a firm has to maintain extra staff in order to provide them with extra time. Analytically, the proposition that optimal organizational boundaries are wider where positive preferences are assigned to slack has been demonstrated by Williamson (1970), although the purpose of his analysis was to demonstrate the effects of managerial objectives of control over resources (i.e., "power" objectives) and not the effects of innovation objectives (i.e., dynamic efficiency objectives).

Bounded Efficiency

Efficient organizational forms are often thought of as optimal forms, but this is neither necessary nor adequate. Bounded rationality is likely to limit choice at the meta-level of organization design as well as at the level of the transactions they regulate.

It would be a logically impossible task to generate all the possible relevant structural alternatives. An evolutionary theory according to which "better" or "superior" arrangements replace less efficient forms is all that an efficiency model of organizations may be able to produce. This approach has been very explicit in some economic models of organizational behavior (Nelson and Winter, 1982) but, if we take bounded rationality seriously, it seems the only reasonable version for a model of comparative assessment of organization efficiency.

Even a relative or evolutionary way of conceiving organizational efficiency, however, may be too extreme if it is expected that superior forms will replace more costly arrangements by means of an inescapable natural law. The natural selection argument, dear as it is to positivistic economists, has been convincingly criticized in general (Winter, 1975) and it has been raised in particular against organizational economics (Grandori, 1987 and 1989a; Robins, 1987). If we accept these criticisms, we must conclude that efficiency models of organizations are not "positive" models, nor even "normative" models—in the strict sense in which these terms are used in economics (Keynes, 1917; Simon, 1977). In fact, they do not provide universally valid laws of "what happens" nor of "what should happen" (because often firms do not minimize costs and nevertheless survive, even in the "long run"). Rather, they belong to the third type of economic models defined by John Neville Keynes (1917): "practical" or "instrumental" models which state that *if* a result of superior economic performance is "desired", then the XY organizational arrangement should be adopted in a given context.

Some research implications of this view of efficiency theories of organizations should be mentioned. In the first place, an instrumental theory of efficient organization cannot be falsified by the mere observation that often firms do not reduce costs as they might and pursue other objectives (as sometime it is maintained). A correct way to test instrumental theories of efficiency would be to demonstrate that firm performance does not correlate with organizational characteristics as predicted. In the second place, a notion of "intended" or relative, rather than "absolute" efficiency need not lead to a strictly "satisficing" mode of deciding on organization structures. It is true that the choice of a partner for a business agreement is conditioned by the existing networks of personal ties, as Granovetter (1985 and 1989) has shown, and that the choice of an architecture of agreement is bounded by all the heuristics and biases which intervene in any complex judgment (Kahneman, Tversky and Slovic, 1982). However, one can always try to improve the rationality of decision and negotiation processes even in the absence of an optimum, by supporting the breadth of information search, accuracy of judgment, correctness of inference and learning, etc. (Bell, Raiffa and Tversky, 1988; Grandori, 1984). For example there is a high failure rate of joint ventures and of inter-firm agreements for innovation in general. It does not seem that these failures are mainly due to the inadequacy of the organizational form of joint venture with respect to the nature of transactions. Such agreements usually regard the launch of new complex activities, requiring transfers of specific know-how. Therefore, a highly formalized equity agreement, with the hostage-exchange mechanism of capital conferments on both sides, seems appropriate. Other hypotheses for the explanation of this phenomenon, alternative to that of cost inefficiency of the adopted organization form, are provided by the additional efficiency criteria outlined here. In particular, there is the possibility that an excessively heuristic and biased search for acceptable partners leads to poor choices. In fact, the design of organizational forms for innovation is subject to a much higher degree of uncertainty than the comparison of alternative arrangements for conducting known activities. Therefore, we should expect that organization forms regulating innovative transactions are particularly vulnerable to inefficiencies of cognitive origin. For instance, given the nature of the task, we should find that firms often get trapped by commitments toward current transactional partners where better alternatives could be found; by forecasting the partner's future performance in the relationship by over-weighting case-specific information and neglecting hard information about industry or mother country economic trends; by anchoring the judgment about each partner's appropriate share of resources in the agreement on internal parameters (such as the firms' operating conditions, costs, usual mark ups, etc.) rather than on external, less available information on what product/price/conditions combinations can be sustained by demand in the long term.

The point about the paramount role of heurstics on innovative organization design that I would like to make here, is that no "optimally efficient" solution can be suggested in these problems; by contrast, the design process can and should be supported so that a wider and more accurate information domain is considered and "more efficient" solutions are discovered.

The Power Variable

It has been admitted that power is an even more complex concept than efficiency (Turk, 1983). A number of definitions and traditions of analysis, both with a sociological and an economic origin, exist. Let us focus here on the structural notions of power, which are more relevant for organization design than the process views of power. Even within these limits, we can distinguish a variety of concepts of power, each of them having a particular relation to the various concepts of efficiency outlined above. We maintain that at least three significantly different constructs of structural power are used in current theories of organization for explaining observed arrangements. They are: (a) power as pursuit of particularistic objectives by organizational sub-systems; (b) power as pursuit of control of critical uncertainties and interdependences; (c) power as pursuit of dominance over other actors.

Particularistic Rationality

Power-seeking behavior in organizations has been often operationalized as sub-goal or parochial interest pursuit by internal actors (Pfeffer and Salancik, 1978; Williamson, 1964). Let us separate this definition, for analytic purposes, from any hypotheses about the content of these particular goals. Following this convention, the hypothesis of sub-goal pursuit is equivalent to the assertion that a firm is not a monolithic actor but a coalition of actors with possibly different objectives. This assumption, in turn, does not imply by itself "power" issues, but only a different, (in this case) more micro level of analysis.

A variety of objectives can be of interest for individuals and groups, such as achievement, technical perfection, social relations, innovation and professional development. Most of them differ from an overall organizational efficiency criterion, but also differ from power objectives in the sense of the pursuit of control or dominance.

The issue of conflict between general system efficiency and sub-system objectives therefore, is not in general a power-versus-efficiency question. Rather, it is an issue of level of analysis. Leibensten (1979) has put it neatly denouncing that a branch of economics is entirely missing: that of micro-micro-economics. In a sense, the Schumpeterian principle of methodological individualism has been betrayed by the habit of economics of treating firms as individual decision makers and of applying the efficiency notion only at this level. By contrast, as Barnard (1938) has taught a long time ago in the organizational field, any methodologically accurate analysis of an organizational system efficiency should begin with the individuals' efficiency, in the sense of a balance between incentives and contributions.

The problem of conflict between systems at different levels arise not only at the intra-firm level but also at the inter-firm level. One case in point may be Williamson's (1975) analysis of dominant firms. He provides an explanation of the emergence of dominant firms in terms of efficiency, i.e., in terms of transaction cost advantages of this institutional form over the alternative of a group of "conspiring oligopolists". Nevertheless, he does not conclude, as one would expect on the basis of this explanation alone, that dominant firms are welcome because of their transaction cost reduction properties. On the contrary, Williamson recommends resolute legal action for the dissolution of these firms, by appealing to a superordinate criterion: the prevention of consumer losses. Again, we do not need to introduce a power concept to say that a cost efficiency criterion at the firm level conflicts with more general allocative efficiency principles. Rather we probably need the Pareto-efficiency criterion, illustrated in the second section, as we try to solve a problem of organization design with multiple-efficiency functions.

All the above notwithstanding, we should admit that some notion of power creeps into any multiple actors organization design problem, as we face the question of selecting one solution among a variety of Pareto-efficient organization forms. The fathers of game theory (Von Neumann and Morgenstern, 1944) left this choice open to the influence of "psychological factors", in that it was not possible to determine it on the basis efficiency criteria alone. More recent game theory has offered a number of techniques for solving this problem by employing *fairness* criteria: for example, the maximum sum or the maximum product of parties' utilities, the maximum of the payoffs of the most disadvantaged party, the equal proportion sharing rule, and others. For our purposes, it is relevant to notice that the choice of any particular fair selection scheme (as well as the choice of not adopting a scheme and leaving the outcome to be determined by free play), calls for a judgment on the relative weights of parties' preferences, i.e., on parties "power". Consider the following example.

A number of engineering firms have some relevant part in constructing a complex plant, but no one firm alone can win the contract for this job and each particular combination of firms can construct a plant with different characteristics and pay-off. Suppose that bidding firms can form coalitions of $k \leq n$ members, and that a larger coalition can obtain a larger job. The process of coalition formation entails a negotiation of how to divide activities and gains within a coalition. Raiffa (1982) has illustrated two different ways of solving this type of game. A first strategy involves offering to any other firm such a share that no other player can offer it more without reducing his own pay-off. The equilibrium shares in this play reflect the coalition power of each actor: i.e. the share of player X depends on the increases in any sub-coalition's total pay-off caused by the participation of X in the coalition. A second strategy is to cooperate with at least $n-1$ other firms in order to form the largest possible joint venture and then to divide the gains in function of the average marginal contribution conferred by each player to all possible sub-coalitions that could be formed by other players. Within this solution, shares still reflect a party's relative strength but weaker parties receive a larger share than in the previous scheme, because it is assumed that their contributions are in any case necessary to increase the size of the pie as much as possible.

The choice of a procedure for agreeing on one organizational solution among a number of Pareto-efficient ones seems to be a largely arbitrary one. Given that different procedures produce different allocations of resources to the players, an implicit judgment on the relative weights to be assigned to parties' preferences seems unavoidable.

Control of Critical Uncertainty and Interdependence

Part of the conflict about the power issue between economic and sociological views of organization stems from a misunderstanding of the different roles that this variable plays in the two types of models. It is not right to say that economic models "neglect" power, as is often heard. Rather, an actor's power usually enters economic models only under two forms.

1. Power can be a given, a feature of the context in which exchanges take place. For example, two partners in an exchange may come to be "locked into" the transaction for learning by doing motives. Then they can exert influence, they "have power" over one another. *If* this is the situation, organizational economics argues, *then* their interaction should be regulated in certain ways (i.e. *ceteris paribus*, through highly integrated forms) in order to be efficient.

2. Power can be a dependent variable, i.e., a distribution of resources deriving from efficiency criteria. If a subset of organizational activities is critical for organizational success, R&D for example, then the R&D unit should be more powerful (have more resources, count more in organizational decision making, etc.).

Economic models traditionally do not admit the inclusion of power as an independent variable, in the sense of a possible objective to be pursued in the shaping of organizations.

In sociological contributions these three different uses of the power variable—as a context datum, as a dependent variable and as an independent variable—are usually intertwined. This is the case, for example, of the influential and original analysis of organizations as arenas and outcomes of social actors' power games elaborated by Crozier and Friedberg (1977).

Their theory explains organizational arrangements as results of games among social actors endowed by resources that are used as power bases in the game (e.g., time, exclusive competences, first mover advantages, decision making capacity). The exclusive control over "sources of uncertainty" for other actors and the organizational system in general is considered to be an actor's most important base of structural power, and, in turn, the fundamental objective the actor pursues in organizational action in general and in organizational form negotiation in particular. Control of uncertainty stems from an actor being in a "gate-keeper" position with respect to any important and variable input of organizational operations. It can be exclusive technical competences (expert power), on contacts with important clients, suppliers or environment segments in general (*rélé* power), or rights over the life and death of the firm (property power).

I submit that as far as an actor's power is considered as a given or as something which stems from an actor's "control of critical uncertainties and interdependencies", no rivalry with efficiency variables is in order. For example, information processing, efficiency-based models of organization design such as those belonging to the "structural contingency theory" tradition (Lawrence and Lorsch, 1967; Thompson, 1967) assert that, in highly performing firms, power in the form of resources and decision making opportunities is distributed according to competence and to the locus where relevant information is available. Departments which face more critical and uncertain sub-environments should have more power.

Even in the case of power as an independent variable, however, no genuine rivalry with organizational efficiency pursuit arises when power pursuit is conceived of as an effort to "reduce critical uncertainties and interdependences" relative to current transactions. Let us compare what predictions are yielded by such a hypothesis with those generated by a "reduction of information and transaction costs". As I have argued more extensively elsewhere (Grandori, 1987), they yield analogous predictions. That is, they both predict that the organizational boundaries of firms or sub-units will expand selectively in order to internalize or quasi-integrate the sources of critical uncertainties and interdependencies. In fact, information and transaction costs arise precisely from uncertainty and "specificity" (interdependence) in the relations between activities. "Transaction and information cost reduction" and "uncertainty reduction and control" seem therefore to be substantially equivalent hypotheses, divided to a large extent by differences in languages.

To assume that the current web of transactions is given and to design a form of regulation which reduces the costs of managing the uncertainties and interdependences associated to them, however, is not the sole way to achieve superior performances. The share of resources and the hierarchical intensity an actor can achieve in an organizational agreement depend on his own relative replaceability with respect to that of other actors. It would be naïve to think that an actor, knowing this fact, does not attempt to change asymmetries in small number conditions towards a more favorable state of things for its own party.

This more strategic power games, aimed at changing transactional parameters, are not contemplated in current organizational economics models, whereas they are central in contemporary non functionalist sociology of organizations (Crozier and Friedberg, 1977; Pfeffer and Salancik, 1978). There is a long way, however, from here to saying that this implies rivalry between perspectives. At present, the difference seems to be between domains of analysis, a matter of division of labor. In perspective, one may ask what intrinsic obstacles prevent the consideration of the "design of the rules of the game" in an economic perspective. After all this aspect could provide a common interest between the sociology and economics of organizations.

Dominance Pursuit

To what extent is the pursuit of wealth by an actor, possibly also through the manipulation of "power" conditions, legitimate; and when does it hurt other, more legitimate or general interests thereby becoming illegitimate? This is a clearer way, I submit, to pose the question of conflict between power and efficiency if there is any conflict at all. Transaction cost reduction, as pursued by oligopolist firms in order to give rise to a dominant integrated firm, can be judged as illegitimate (or inefficient by a more general point of view) because of the dead-weight losses it implies. Unionization, and the right to strike in defense of workers' party interests that goes with it, is and ought to be much more strictly regulated in public interest services than elsewhere. Managers are expected to pursue the sub-goals of their departments; but they are said to engage in political behavior if they pretend to share a greater pie than the market can support for their firm.

All these examples of behaviors of resource appropriation are normally considered illegitimate in liberal societies. Let us refer to this type of conduct as dominance pursuit, in order to distinguish it from the other notions of power seeking analyzed above. Naturally, there is in this distinction an element of arbitrariness, or a dependence upon social customs, in that it is necessary to weight preferences in order to discriminate between legitimate and illegitimate self-interest seeking behaviors. Yet, this choice seems to be unavoidable, although there are ways of structuring it rationally.[3]

Models of dominance pursuit, relevant for the explanation of organization forms, exist. Their meaning and their relationship with the organizational efficiency variables obviously differ according to whether these models are descriptive or prescriptive. Empirical *descriptive* research can demonstrate and does demonstrate that managers, firms, unions and other economic actors sometimes decide on organizational and institutional arrangements for dominance reasons (Francis, 1983). This proposition need not conflict with the proposition, empirically grounded as well, that some organizational forms are more efficient than others in given circumstances. These two empirical propositions would conflict only if we were willing to subscribe to the Hegelian claim of orthodox economics that "all that's real is rational", thanks to the *deus ex machina* of natural selection. On the contrary, descriptive research on the conditions enabling dominance pursuit is complementary to descriptive research on the conditions facilitating the adoption of efficient organization forms.

As to *prescriptive* models, we should distinguish between negative and positive prespective models of dominance pursuit. Prescriptive models of dominance pursuit in organizational design are predominantly *negative*, i.e., they "proscribe" rather than prescribe organization forms shaped by dominance motives. The most important example of this type of theorizing is probably represented by marxist approaches to the understanding of organizations. For example, radical economists have offered interpretations of the spreading of bureaucratic forms of organization within firms (with high formalization and completely centralized authority) as an outcome of successful dominance strategies effected by capitalists and enterpreneurs (Marglin, 1971; Edwards, 1979). Specifically, it is maintained that the hierarchical centralized shape of organization

---

[3]As far as organization design is concerned, Williamson (1987a) has proposed to solve this problem through an analytic trade-off between transaction cost reduction benefits and dead-weight losses for consumers. I would prefer a game or negotiation approach to the problem (Grandori, 1991) given that the bearers of costs and those of benefits are different actors.

in capitalist firms entails high structural costs, while it does not allow to achieve higher productive results with respect to more democratic forms of intra-firm organization. Then, it is argued, centralized hierarchy is conserved because the privileged party under this form of governance, i.e., the "capitalists", resists to change, by using hierarchy itself as a *divide et impera* mechanism. These contributions have been received by more orthodox economists as "conspiring views of history" (Stiglitz, 1975) or naive power models (Williamson, 1980). However, in spite of their political flavor, at least some core theses by radical economists are actually efficiency arguments: hierarchical forms are opposed because alternative organizational arrangements, such as peer groups, are supposed to be more efficient. The survival of hierarchies represents a deviation with respect to their efficiency hypothesis and *therefore* it is explained in terms of dominance and proscribed. This procedure is the same as would be adopted by any organizational economist prescribing efficient organization forms (see Williamson and Ouchi, 1981, for an explicit pronouncement in this sense). The conflict here is not between different theories of organizations but between observational propositions: is hierarchy or peer group a more efficient form of internal organization, and under what circumstances? To be sure, this complex measurement question cannot be answered by an armchair verdict, such as that contained in the otherwise thought-provoking essay by Williamson (1980), without raising controversy.[4]

A question then arises about whether the dominance versus efficiency dilemma is perhaps lacking firm foundation. Once descriptive models of organizing for dominance are admitted as possibly

---

[4]Radical economists seem to have largely preserved, on this point, Marx's approach. As it is more widely understood in European, as compared to American, social science literature, Marx (1848) was basically arguing from a long term efficiency viewpoint. He theorized that hierarchy and central planning would be more efficient than market "anarchy", and that power should go to those social actors who have, at any given time, 'objective interests' in the most efficient organizational arrangements of institutions and economic systems (e.g., to the bourgeoisie rather than to landlords in the industrial revolution phase, and to the working class rather than to capitalists in the era of the collective use of the means of production). Resistance to these efficiency-based "historical laws" was seen as an arbitrary power exercise (this principle was, for example, applied also "against" workers as they resisted technological advance). As assessed today, the "universalistic" theories of Marx can be said to be wrong, not because they argued from a power rather than efficiency perspective, but because they mispredicted which organizational solutions would have been more efficient in industrialized countries in the long run, in a wide range of circumstances.

TABLE 1 *The Power-efficiency Debate: a Possible Inter-theoretical Translation*

"Efficiency" perspectives variables		"Power" perspectives variables
Fundamentally equivalent	1a. Reduction of information/ transaction costs.	1b. Reduction/control of critical uncertainties and interdependences.
	2a. Pareto efficency/ superiority of organization forms.	2b. Organizations as results of games among actors with different objectives.
	3a. Intended efficiency/ bounded rationality in organization design	3b. Social construction of institutions.
Genuinely rival	4a. Selective dominance acceptance or rejection for efficiency reasons (prescriptive).	4b. Universalistic dominance pursuit or refusal (prescriptive).
Possibly complementary	5a. Any version of efficiency pursuit or equivalent variable (descriptive).	5b. Dominance pursuit or refusal (descriptive).
Tentatively common	6. Organizational fairness. 7. Strategic change of transaction parameters	

complementary to descriptive models of efficiency-driven organization; and once Marxist perspective is reinterpreted as an efficiency approach, not much is left out. Nevertheless, some discourses about power as dominance have been made which are genuinely different from all those considered up to now. These are those contributions which advise the pursuit of power and even dominance in organizational strategy simply because it is beneficial to the winning actor; and, symmetrically, those which advise against dominance and any power asymmetry because it is costly for the dominated party.

The first posture, a "positive" prescriptive view of dominance, can be found in various areas of managerial literature: firms are often instructed as to how to achieve dominance over competitors, clients and suppliers, and managers are advised on how to acquire power in organizations. These recipes, however, rarely meet the standards of scientific propositions.[5]

The second posture, a negative view of power differences and dominance relations *as such*, has been recently defended by Perrow (1981). Dear as it is to ideological discourse on organizations, such a value judgement is however difficult to accept in scientific theorizing about organizations.

Conclusions

One specific purpose of the analysis of the constructs of efficiency and power carried out in this paper is to contribute to the opening of communication channels between organizational economics and the sociology of organizations. Indeed, the opposition between "efficiency" and "power" perspectives, which often divides scholars of the two disciplines, seems to be far too general to be useful and scientifically meaningful. Table 1 summarizes a variety of sub-variables to which the concepts of "power" and "efficiency" can be reduced, and the type of relationship by which they are linked. As argued throughout the paper, there is only a restricted zone of genuine rivalry between these variables. A quite consistent number of sub-variables result to be nearly equivalent, if a translation effort is undertaken. The more interesting zone, as far as future research is concerned, may be a ground of possibly common interest and hopefully common language, which I see as inhabited by at least two concepts: that of fairness of organization forms, and that of the strategic modification on transaction parameters.

References

Barnard, Chester (1938) *The Functions of the Executive*. Cambridge, Mass.: Harvard University Press.

Bauer, Michael and Elie Cohen (1983) The invisibility of power in economics: beyond markets and hierarchies. In *Power, Efficiency and Institutions*, edited by A. Francis, J. Turk and P. Willman, London: Heinemann.

Bell, David E., Hovard Raiffa and Amos Tversky (1988) *Decision Making, Descriptive, Normative and Prescriptive Interactions*. Cambridge, Mass.: Cambridge University Press.

Crozier, Michael and Erhard Friedberg (1977) *L'acteur et le système*. Paris: Ed. du Seuil.

[5]If adopted by everyone, this kind of advice would often be self-defeating. A criticism of business policy models in this respects is contained in Rugiadini (1985).

Cyert Richard M. and James J. March (1963) *A Behavioral Theory of the Firm.* Englewood Cliffs: Prentice-Hall.

Edwards, R. C. (1979). *Contested Terrain.* New York: Basic Books.

Feyerabend, Paul (1975) *Against Method.* New York: Verso.

Francis, Arthur (1983) Markets and hierarchies: efficiency or domination? In *Power, Efficiency and Institutions,* edited by A. Francis, J. Turk and P. Willman, London: Heinemann.

Grandori, Anna (1984) A prescriptive contingency view of organizational decision making. *Administrative Science Quarterly,* **29,** 192–209.

Grandori, Anna (1987) *Perspectives on Organization Theory.* Cambridge: Ballinger.

Grandori, Anna (1989a) The transaction cost approach: problems and prospects. *Economia Aziendale,* **viii,** 393–409.

Grandori, Anna (1989b) Efficienza ed equità delle reti interorganizzative: una prospettiva negoziale. *Economia e Politica Industriale,* **64,** 349–362.

Grandori, Anna (1991) Negotiating efficient organization forms. *Journal of Economic Behavior and Organization,* **16,** 319–340.

Grandovetter, Mark (1985) Economic action and social structure: the problem of embeddedness. *American Journal of Sociology,* **91,** 481–510.

Granovetter, Mark (1989) Nuova e vecchia sociologia economica: evoluzione storica e prospettive di ricerca. *Economia e Politica Industriale,* **61,** 135–163.

Huppes, Tjerk (ed) (1976) *Economics and Sociology: Towards an Integration.* Leiden: Martinus Nijhoff.

Ioannilli, Andrea (1989) Analisi negoziale delle reti interorganizzative: gli accordi di franchising. *Tesi di laurea.* Università Bocconi.

Kahneman, Daniel, Amos Tversky and Paul Slovic (eds.) (1982) *Judgment Under Uncertainty: Heuristics and Biases.* Cambridge, Mass.: Harvard University Press.

Kapp, William K. (1976) In defence of institutionalism In *Economics and Sociology: Towards an Integration,* edited by T. Huppes. Leiden: M. Nijhoff.

Keynes, John Neville. (1917) *The Scope and Method of Political Economy,* 4th ed. New York: Macmillan.

Lawrence, Paul and Jay Lorsch (1967) *Organization and Environment.* Boston: Harvard Business School.

Leibenstein, Harvey (1976) *Beyond Economic Man.* Cambridge, Mass.: Harvard University Press.

Leibenstein, Harvey (1979) A branch of economics is missing: micro-micro theory. *Journal of Economic Literature,* **17,** 477–502.

Marglin, S. A. (1974) What do bosses do? The origins and functions of hierarchy in capitalist production. *Review of Radical Political Economics,* **6,** 33–60.

Mariotti, Sergio (1989) Efficienza dinamica e sistemi di imprese. *Economia e Politica Industriale,* **64,** 91–124.

Mariotti, Sergio and Gian Carlo Cainarca. (1986) The evolution of transaction governance in the textile-clothing industry. *Journal of Economic Behavior and Organization,* **7,** 351–374.

Marx, Karl (1867) *Das Kapital. Kritik der politischen Oekonomie. (Capital.* New York: International Publishing Company. 1967).

Nelson, Richard and Sidney Winter (1982) An Evolutionary Theory of Economic Change. Cambridge: Harvard University Press.

Perrow, Charles (1981) Markets, hierarchies and hegemony. In *Perspectives on Organization Design and Behavior,* edited by A. M. Van de Ven and W. F. Joyce. New York: Wiley.

Pfeffer, Jeffrey (1982) *Organizations and Organization Theory,* London: Pitman.

Pfeffer, Jeffrey and Gerald Salancik (1978) *The External Control of Organizations: A Resource Dependence Perspective.* New York: Harper and Row.

Raiffa, Howard (1982) *The Art and Science of Negotiation.* Cambridge: Harvard University Press.

Robins, James (1987) Organizational economics: notes on the use of transaction cost theory in the study of organizations. *Administrative Science Quarterly,* 32, 68–86.

Rubin, Paul H. (1978) The theory of the firm and the structure of the franchise contract. *Journal of Law and Economics,* 21, 223–233.

Rugiadini, Andrea (1985) L'efficienza delle scelte manageriali fra organizzazione e mercato. In *Organizzazione e mercato,* edited by R. C. D. Nacamulli and A. Rugiadini. Bologna: Il Mulino.

Rullani Enzo (1986) Economia delle transazioni e informazioni. Saggio sulla nuova teoria economia dell'organizzazione. *Annali di storia dell'impresa,* no. 2, 9–117.

Simon, Herbert (1977) *Models of Discovery and Other Topics in the Method of Science.* Dordrecht, Boston: Reidel.

Stiglitz, Joseph E. (1975) Incentives, risk and information: Notes towards a theory of hierarchy. *Bell Journal of Economics,* 6, 552–579.

Teece, David (1981a) The multinational enterprise: market failure and market power considerations. *Sloan Management Review,* 22, 3–17.

Teece, David (1981b) Internal organization and economic performance: an empirical analysis of the profitability of principal firms. *The Journal of Industrial Economics,* xxx, 1–27.

Thompson, James D. (1967) *Organization in Action.* New York: McGraw Hill.

Turk, Jeremy (1983) Conclusions: power, efficiency and institutions: some implications of the debate for economics. In *Power, Efficiency and Institutions,* edited by A. Francis, J. Turk and P. Willman, London: Heinemann.

Von Neumann, John and Oskar Morgestern (1944) *Theory of Games and Economic Behavior.* Princeton: Princeton University Press.

Williamson, Oliver E. (1964) *The Economics of Discretionary Behavior.* Englewood Cliffs: Prentice Hall.

Williamson, Oliver E. (1970) *Corporate Control and Business Behavior.* Englewood Cliffs: Prentice Hall.

Williamson, Oliver E. (1975) *Markets and Hierarchies.* New York: Free Press.

Williamson, Oliver E. (1980) The organization of work. *Journal of Economic Behavior and Organization,* 1, 5–38.

Williamson, Oliver E. (1981) The economics of organization: the transaction cost approach. *American Journal of Sociology,* 87, 548–577.

Williamson, Oliver E. (1985) *The Economic Institutions of Capitalism.* New York: Free Press.

Williamson, Oliver E. (1987a) *Antitrust Economics.* Oxford: Blackwell.

Williamson, Oliver E. (1987b) Economics and sociology: promoting a dialog. Paper presented at the 8th EGOS Colloquium, Antwerp.

Williamson, Oliver E. and William G. Ouchi (1981) The markets and hierarchies programme of research: origins, implications and prospects. In *Perspectives on Organization Design and Behavior,* edited by A. H. Van de Ven and W. F. Joyce. New York: Wiley.

Winter, Sydney (1975) Optimization and evolution in the theory of the firm. In *Adaptive Economic Models,* edited by R. H. Davis and T. Groves. San Diego: Academic Press.

Properties of Rational Organizations

JAMES S. COLEMAN[1]

In this paper I want to examine properties of formal organizations that make them function more or less efficiently. To do this, I want to begin by distinguishing the organization that I will examine from other social organization. I will make a distinction between what I will call constructed social organization and what I will call spontaneous social organization. Hayek (1972) distinguishes "made order" from "spontaneous order", a distinction corresponding to the one I will make here. Constructed organization or made order is organization designed for a purpose. The construction is necessary in order to accomplish the purpose: Specific positions or roles are defined, their obligations to, and expectations from, other positions in the organization are specified independently of the occupants of the positions. This implies that constructed social organization consists of a structure of positions, and that the relations that make up the structure are between positions, not persons.

All this contrasts with spontaneous social organization, in which obligations and expectations are between persons directly, and the structure emerges only in a cumulative fashion, as these relations concatenate. Spontaneous social organization consists entirely or primarily of two-person relations which continue so long as both parties find the relation profitable, ending when one of them finds the relation no longer beneficial. In order for the relation to continue, both persons must have positive account balances for that relation, getting more out of it than they put into it. A system composed of these relations exhibits a particular form of viability, *reciprocal viability*, as I will call it, depending on the two positive account balances for each relation. The incentives to continue in the relation are intrinsic as the incentives to each are created by what the other brings to the relation. I have elsewhere called these relations "simple" social relations, in contrast to the "complex" social relations of which constructed organization

[1]Department of Sociology, The University of Chicago.

consists (Coleman, 1990). In the latter, a third party is an implicit member of each relation, having established the obligations and expectations. Because of the implicit third party—the organization itself as actor—it need not be the case that each person has a positive account balance, in each relation. To continue as a participant in the organization, each person need have only an overall positive account balance. This I call *independent viability*, in contrast to the reciprocal viability of spontaneous social organization.

Independent viability is equivalent to Chester Barnard's (1938) characterization of the firm as requiring a balance of inducements and contributions. Inducements from the firm must be greater for the employee (an overall positive account balance for the employee), and the contributions from the employee must be of greater value to the firm than what is must give up to keep him (a positive account balance for the firm in its relation with that employee).

It is in fact possible—though dangerous—for the firm to have accounts for some employees that are negative (the cost of the inducements is greater than the value of the contributions), so long as other employees' contributions are sufficient to make up for the loss. This is a still weaker level of viability and may be called *global viability*. That is, the organization may be profitable even if some employees are not worth their cost to the firm. The danger of global viability lies in the fact that loss of some highly productive employees can destroy the viability of the organization, leaving it only with those whose contribution to the organization's account balance is less than their cost.

This orientation to formal organization, that it involves a set of account balances for each of the employees of the organization, and one or more for the organization itself, is a very different orientation than has been traditional in sociology. It regards each actor as purposive, rationally determining whether to continue an activity that has been begun, or to stop. The classical conception of rational organization among sociologists is one handed down from Max Weber, who fit all forms of authority into three classes: traditional, charismatic, and rational. His conception of rational authority was that of bureaucracy. He specified, in fact, ten properties of this type of "rational organization". These are as follows:

1. Office holders are subject to authority only with respect to their impersonal official obligations.
2. They are organized in a clearly defined hierarchy of offices.
3. Each office has a clearly defined sphere of competence.
4. The office is filled by a free contractual relation.
5. Candidates are selected on the basis of technical qualification.

6. Officials are remunerated by fixed salary, in money.
7. The office is treated as the sole, or at least the primary occupation of the incumbent.
8. The occupation constitutes a career, punctuated by promotions.
9. The official does not appropriate or own the position.
10. The official is subject to strict and systematic discipline and control in the conduct of his office.

Note that these so-called "properties of rational organization" are nearly all properties of the *structure* of the organization. The structure consists of offices or positions, not of persons. The authority relations are defined as between offices, the obligations are defined as obligations of the offices. The persons are merely transient occupants of offices, with entrance to the office established by qualifications associated with the office.

My contention in this paper is that Max Weber made a serious mistake in equating rational authority with bureaucracy, as defined in these ten properties, a mistake that arose from not taking the idea of rationality seriously. Rationality implies an efficient means to a goal; by specifying the structural properties. Weber was implicitly making a set of ten propositions: that each of these properties of an organization would independently contribute to its efficiency. It was a standard error of Weber's that he bundled a large number of properties together to create an "ideal type", not recognizing that by specifying this bundle he was doing more than giving a definition. He was stating propositions about causal interconnections between their properties. The unfortunate consequence of this error in the case of rational organization is that, for many sociologists, it hid the fact that it is an open question whether an efficient organization takes on the form of Weber's "rational organization" a question which might be decided differently in different cases. Some examples of properties of organization that lead to efficiency through very different structures will help erase this conception.

Diamond Markets and Merchant Bankers

Two arenas of activity that involve high degrees of functional rationality are merchant banking firms and firms engaged in wholesale diamond markets. In both of these arenas, a structure seen by Weber as antithetical to rational authority is pervasive: family members are employed extensively in the firms, and the higher officials in the firm are often sons, brothers, or nephews of the head of the firm.[2] In addition, diamond markets are ordinarily

[2]See Wechsberg (1966) for a discussion in the case of merchant bankers.

made up of firms whose principal officials have extensive relations with one another outside the market. The diamond market of 47th Street in New York, for example, consists of Orthodox Jews who attend the same synagogues in Brooklyn, who have extensive ties of community and kin. Relations extending beyond the market are also characteristic, to a lesser extent, of persons at higher levels of merchant banking firms.

Thus in both of these arenas of activity, functional rationality in the organization appears to be realized by structures ordinarily seen as quite the opposite of rational authority structures. Why is this? The answer appears to be quite simple: The officials of these firms regularly deal with commodities of great value, and the opportunity to abscond with or siphon assets of the firm is very high. If a firm's activities are to be facilitated, these employees must have the freedom which carries with it the possibilities of profiting at the firm's expense. One device for ensuring against defection in such situations is bonding, in which the firm pays a fee to have its employees bonded. Another, however, which appears to be more efficient for these firms (since this is the device they use) is to employ persons whose attachments to other members of the firm are so extensive that breaking the trust that has been placed would have repercussions in all areas of the offender's life. Thus trustworthiness, which greatly increases the firm's efficiency, is insured by extensive use of nepotism.

It is, of course, not always true that the benefits gained by trustworthiness outweigh the costs due to the reduced ability that will on average occur when persons are employed and promoted on the basis of communal or kinship relations rather than ability. The computer industry, as exemplified by the firms of Silicon Valley in California, is one in which a large part of a firm's assets are carried around in the heads of some of the employees. The assets consist of information, whether of software design or hardware design. Thus the setting is, like the merchant banker or diamond merchants, one in which trust of employees, and accompanying trustworthiness, greatly facilitates a firm's activities. These firms do not ordinarily employ or promote through nepotism, however. The reasons may be several: the absence of kin structures and close, stable communities among the populations involved in these firms, the greater relative importance of talent. Yet these firms do not merely employ the usual criteria of the bureaucratic form. They attempt to bind the top employees to the firm through various patterns of shared ownership: stocks, stock options, and other devices. Other firms (Intel is perhaps the best example) employ a variety of non-bureaucratic devices to create strong communal bonds among employees. The devices used by these firms are not sufficient to prevent some loss of intellectual capital (primarily through employees leaving and taking with them company secrets). The principal point, however, is that in such a setting, firms use non-bureaucratic devices, whether it is nepotism or stock options, to increase their efficiency.

None of this is to say that the devices used by firms in these industries—merchant banking, wholesale diamond merchants, and computers—are optimal for the setting in which these firms find themselves. Yet the widespread existence of non-bureaucratic structures in these industries suggests the strong likelihood that at least some of these forms come closer to realizing functional rationality—that is, the goal of the organization—than would the structurally rational, bureaucratic forms that they supplant.

Quality Control Circles in Japanese Industry

In many firms in Japanese export industries (such as the automobile industry), much of the supervision that is carried out through a hierarchical structure in Western firms is carried out through the use of "quality control circles" (see Koshiro, 1983). A quality control circle consists of a small group of workers working on the same section of an assembly line or on a related group of machines who collectively exercise authority over one another and make local decisions about work organization. These groups are formally organized and given authority by the firm, and the firm may induce inter-group comparisons by posting group performance charts in the plant. These formal actions in turn encourage the growth of informal norms which develop and through which the collective authority over group members is exercised.

The quality circles represent the organizational use of social processes of informal social control discovered by Roethlisberger and Dickson (1939) in the classic Western Electric studies. Subsequent to the Roethlisberger and Dickson finding that informal social norms among groups of workers could act either to increase or to decrease production, industrial sociologists have used these processes to improve the performance of the firm. For example, group incentives in wages and group target rates (which is a nonlinear form of group incentives; see Peterson, 1989) depend for the effectiveness on the group processes they stimulate. Similarly, quality circles depend for their effectiveness on informal group processes. They constitute an example of formal organization designed to foster informal social processes that aid in realizing the organizational goal.

Lessons from the Examples

The central element of the diamond market and merchant banker is that the firm makes use of social organization *outside* the firm in which its members are embedded. The organization provides insurance against defection, through the embeddedness of its employees, and of persons in firms with which it does business, in social organizations that encompass the rest of their lives, and is of extreme importance to them. This is not the only way firms use social organization outside the firm to increase their efficiency. Much of the hiring of new employees, especially at lower levels in the organization, occurs through friendship or kinship ties with current employees. A firm can use the performance of the already-employed worker as a predictor of the future performance of that worker's friend, and thus reduce the possibility of hiring bad workers. A relatively new organizational use of extended social organizations in a few American firms is the use of family relationships to bind the employee to his firm through day care centers, nursery schools, and even schools in the working place where one or both parents work. Altogether, the general statement that can be made is that it may very well be rational for a firm to make use of already existing social relations outside the firm. Those relations may increase its efficiency through the sanctioning power they contain (as in the diamond market case), or through the information they provide (as in the case of hiring friends and relations of good workers), or through their capacity to reduce turnover (as in the case of child-care centers in the work place). But the use of such relations destroys the picture of the rational organization as a simple machine, in which the skills of persons are combined with other inputs to produce an output—as if those persons had no interests, or had completely abandoned their interests, in the exchange of labor for money.

The central element of the Japanese quality circles is a different one, again involving social organization. By a reallocation of rights in the formal organization (taking authority from superiors and reallocating it to work groups, collectively), the firm creates the conditions in which spontaneous organization an grow, and can increase the viability of the firm. Numerous research results have shown the impact of spontaneous social organization that grows up within a constructed organization on the efficiency of an organization. The Japanese quality circles, and their American imitations (called Quality of Work Life, or QWL, program), as well as group incentive plans, attempt to generate such organization, including informal norms and sanctions, and including support networks, to increase the firm's efficiency. This was, indeed, the explicit aim of the human relations in industry movement which developed in American industrial sociology of the 1930s, 40s, and 50s, centered at the University of Michigan.

One can see these developments—use of social organization outside the firm and encouraging spontaneous organization within the firm, as recent stages in a long-term movement away from the conception of rationally constructed organization as a machine consisting of parts, one of which was the labor inputs of persons. The earlier stages may be seen as follows:

1. The systematic use of knowledge about the *psychological* and *physiological* properties of individuals. This began with Frederick W. Taylor in the 1880s, became known as "Taylorism" with its efficiency experts and time and motion study engineers, and in what has come to be called human factors psychology.

2. The second stage was the systematic use of knowledge that persons are *purposive* not *passive*, and never abandon their individual interests. It can be seen especially in the use of incentive systems, ranging from piece work to bonuses to stock options. The important intellectual development represented by this stage is the recognition that, unlike Weber's conception of the worker or the official as robot-like, persons continue to have personal interests as employees, and those interests can work either to increase the firm's efficiency or to decrease it. Much of the field of industrial psychology is directed toward implementation of this recognition.

3. The third stage, described earlier, is the systematic use of the *social relations* in which a person is or may come to be embedded, to increase the organization's efficiency.

The incorporation of these three properties of persons—physiological and psychological, personal interests, and social relations— into the design of constructed organizations can make the organization both more efficient and more apparently idiosyncratic. The resulting view of an organization's structure is a view not of a structure with specific properties, but of a structure tailored to the specific kinds of persons who will, or can be, employed in it, and the specific kinds of external social organization in which they are embedded. Optimal organizational design will not attempt to insulate the organization from the harm that can result from the interests and social relations of persons as, for example, the prohibition against employment of family members, or nepotism, is intended to do, but will instead attempt to *use* the interests and social relations of persons to increase organizational efficiency.

Beyond Efficiency

Until now, I have used the term "efficiency" without a clear statement of what I mean by it. The concept of efficiency of an economic system is defined only within a particular distribution of resources, or as I will call it, a particular constitutional allocation of rights and resources. If in a given system, with a given constitutional allocation, all externalities are internalized and transaction costs are reduced to zero, the system has achieved efficiency. But if rights are allocated differently, to persons with different interests, then the "efficient" outcomes of the system may differ, even in the absence of transaction costs.[3]

This creates a dilemma for public policy which establishes rules for the constitutions of constructed organizations, as the following two examples of rights allocations indicate.

Codetermination in Germany

In Germany in 1976, a comprehensive *Mitbestimmung* or codetermination law was enacted to give new rights to workers. This law makes extensive changes at two levels. At the board of directors level, it fixes the size—at twenty for large firms—and specifies that half will be representatives of stockholders and half representatives of employees.

At the level of the workplace, it requires creation of workers' councils, with procedures for election of representatives and with specific powers, such as those concerning grievances of workers. The powers of the workers' councils include some which have previously been prerogatives of management, exercised through supervision. The workers' councils, as well as the newly-constituted board of directors, greatly increase workers' power in the organization.

Germany's codetermination law (which has counterparts in Scandinavia) is an example of a general movement toward "industrial democracy" in Western societies, particularly in Western Europe. The law, and the movement behind it, reflects a modified conception of the corporation, away from a single-purpose organization.

Ownership Rights to Innovations

In capitalist corporations, the standard employment agreement for persons engaged in activities which might result in patents includes the assignment of patent rights to the corporation. The agreement also places restrictions on the employee's rights to employment or consultation by competing firms for a period following employment. The employment agreement for such employees of state-owned

---

[3]This fact, incidentally, invalidates the usual statement of the Coase theorem that the allocation of rights does not, in the absence of transaction cost, affect systemic outcome.

enterprises is similar, containing a provision that patent rights will be assigned to government. In effect, this agreement vests ownership rights to innovations made by an employee in the corporation or the government.

The terms of faculty appointments at most universities in the United States are entirely different. Ownership rights to ideas and innovations that originate in universities are vested in the person rather than the university, except where a contract with a government, corporation, or other source of research funds specifies otherwise. This has led to an extensive development of what may be termed "professorial spinoffs", in which one or a group of faculty members who have developed a set of ideas as part of their university research form a corporation to carry the ideas to commercial realization. This has occurred not only in the physical sciences (where it is especially evident in electronics), but also extensively in the biological sciences (where firms for genetic engineering have been formed by groups of faculty members, sometimes in a joint venture with existing corporations) and even in the social sciences (especially data bases in law and economics, and statistical software).

In some corporations, the principle that ownership rights to ideas and innovations lie with the corporation has begun to erode. One corporation where this change came early was the 3M Company in Minneapolis. Donald Schon (1970) described the development:

> They got Scotch tape out and it seemed to work and they sold a lot of it. Then along came research with magnetic tape. They said, "We know how to make tape. We'll make magnetic tape . . ." They had an invention along with this: the invention was that the man who developed the idea would go off and take a piece of the business and become in effect a semi-autonomous firm based around the product which he had developed. The company then kept P & L—profit and loss—control over that division, but in no other way attempted to manage that man.

In the 3M Company, there is an implicit acceptance of the principle that ownership rights to ideas and innovations are shared by the corporation and the person or group where the idea originated. However, it is the personal computer software and hardware industry in which the problems of ownership rights to ideas, and the potential variations in structure, are greatest. Here, ideas are especially easily transportable. In this industry, spin-offs of the sort that Schon described in the case of 3M have been one response to the flow of ideas between firms. Another has been to give partial ownership of the firm to an employee with an especially important idea.

Another evolutionary change is evident in high technology and biological industries, especially in the genetic engineering industry.

A kind of joint activity is created, in which university faculty members, working on their own time, make use of a company's laboratories and facilities under a contractual arrangement in which the ownership of ideas is regarded as being shared by the person and the corporation. The extensive growth of high technology industrial parks and industrial research parks in the vicinity of universities is in part evidence of the professorial spinoffs and in part evidence of the symbiotic relation between faculty members and corporations under a variety of property-rights arrangements.

These two examples of changes in rights allocations illustrate how certain changes lead to distributional questions that go beyond the question of efficiency. Consider the codetermination case. Before enactment of the law, the governing board of the automobile firm Adam Opel, a subsidiary of the multinational General Motors, had made a decision to build a plant in Spain to manufacture a new small car, the Corsa. The location of this plant in Spain was a decision based on lower wages in Spain, and greater expected profits for the firm than if the new plant had been located in Germany. But my conjecture is that if the decision had been made *after* the board had come to consist not merely of shareholder's representatives, but also of workers' representatives, the plant would have been located in Germany. Assume I am right. That outcome might have been more efficient for the firm under the *new* constitutional allocation of rights, and the Spanish location more efficient under the *old* allocation. If the result of a German location would have been lower profits (and thus smaller dividends and lower share prices for stockholders) and more jobs for German workers, this could be an outcome that was optimal under the new allocation of rights and suboptimal under the pre-1976 allocation of rights.

A different issue is raised by the rights to innovations case. Suppose, as I conjectured, the transportability of ideas to a new firm with low capital investment increases the innovativeness of an industry because persons may, in spite of the existing rights allocation which gives ownership rights to the firm, abscond with the ideas and set up a new firm. If this is so, then in those industries in which ideas are not so easily transportable, a new law requiring ownership rights to inventions to be vested jointly in the firm and the inventor(s) (with private contracts for assigning rights being unenforceable), would increase the innovativeness, and thus very likely, the profitability of the industry. But it could do so at the expense of the profitability of existing firms, with new firms' earnings made in part at the expense of those of existing firms.

Here it might be in the interests of a nation state, for example, to increase the innovativeness of an industry, to increase competitiveness of firms in international markets, or to create higher productivity in the industry for general economic benefits. But the policies that would do so, changing the constitutional allocation of property rights within the firm, might well be harmful to this firm as originally constituted, or to the firm minus its newly endowed innovators, who could leave the firm with their new property rights.

What do we mean by properties of a rational organization?

These last examples, involving reallocation of constitutional rights within the firm, raise more fundamental questions about properties of a rational organization than I have raised earlier. They expose the fact that in all the earlier parts of the paper, I assumed that the constructed organization was constructed for a particular purpose (for example, to realize a certain set of interests, such as to maximize the benefits of a firm's residual claimants, the shareholders) and that the allocation of rights in the organization's institutions reflected this. When that assumption is abandoned then the goal of the constructed organizations are no longer well defined. Even less can be said about the properties of a rational, or efficient, constructed organization than we said in the earlier section, i.e., that the psychological properties of the persons involved in it, and their interests and social relations, must shape its properties. The properties of a rational organization now become contingent as well on its constitutional allocation of rights, and what they imply for the goals (i.e., efficient outcomes) of the organization.

This might seem to be a generally negative conclusion, advocating a stance of hopelessness with respect to the initial task. It is, however, otherwise. What is necessary before beginning the positive task of specifying what the properties of a rational constructed organization would be in certain circumstances, is first to get rid of old simplistic ideas that have led to premature closure. That is what I have tried to do here.

References

Barnard, C. (1938) *The Functions of the Executive.* Cambridge, MA: Harvard University Press.

Coleman, J. S. (1990) *Foundations of Social Theory.* Cambridge, MA: Harvard University Press.

Hayek, F. A. (1973) *Law, Legislation, and Liberty*, Vol. 1. London: Routledge & Kegan Paul.

Koshiro, D. (1983) The quality of working life in Japanese factories. In *Contemporary Industrial Relations in Japan*, edited by T. Shirai. Madison: University of Wisconsin Press.

Peterson, T. (1989) Group based reward systems. Paper presented at the Annual
    Meeting of the Public Choice Society, in Florida, (March).
Roethlisberger, F. and W. Dickson (1939) *Management and the Worker*,
    Cambridge, MA: Harvard University Press.
Schon, D. (1970) The future of American industry. *The Listener*, 2 July, Vol. 84,
    pp. 8–12.
Wechsberg, J. (1966) *The Merchant Bankers*. Boston: Little, Brown.

PART II

Decision-making, Leadership and Innovation

Dimensions and Types of Strategic Decision-Making: an Empirical Check of a Typology[1]

JEROEN POOL and PAUL L. KOOPMAN[2]

Introduction

Strategic decision-making has drawn the attention of the organizational sciences for quite some time. Barnard (1938) worked on it even before World War II, and later it was mainly Simon (1947, 1957) and March (with Simon, 1958) who published many books and articles. In the past 20 years contributions have been made to the study of strategic decision-making by many disciplines and from many points of view (e.g., Allison, 1971; Cohen et al., 1972; Mintzberg et al., 1976), while recently a number of important books have been published (e.g. Heller et al., 1988; Hickson et al., 1986; Quinn et al., 1988; Schwenk, 1988).

The first major step was made when normative theories were abandoned in favor of descriptively more accurate theories (Simon, 1947, 1957; March and Simon, 1958). The second leap forward was made towards classification of different models of decision-making, and towards clarification of the context in which they occur (Mintzberg et al., 1976; Hickson et al., 1986). What is missing still is a third step enlarging insight in how decision-making processes are controlled and how demands stemming from the context and the content of the decisions are fine-tuned.

In this chapter we present a typology of decision-making processes

[1]This research project was financed (partly) by the Foundation of Social-Cultural Sciences of the Netherlands Organization of Scientific Research (NWO). The authors wish to thank Prof. Dr. P. J. D. Drenth and Prof. Dr. C. J. Lammers for their supervision of the IDE-2 project, and Gerry Hermsen-Pooley, Drs. Jan de Groot, Marjolein van Offenbeek and Aleid Otto for their contribution in the fieldwork.
[2]Dr. J. Pool is working as a senior researcher in the National Hospital Institute in the Netherlands, and was research fellow in the Department of Work and Organizational Psychology of the Vrije Universiteit Amsterdam during the research project. Dr. P. L. Koopman holds a professorship in this department.

and some preliminary results of a research project which was performed in the context of a broader study of decision-making and participation in the 80s (known by the abbreviation IDE-2). We compare the typology to an analysis of twenty-five empirically obtained cases of strategic decision-making. As strategic decisions we regard important decisions on the structuring and restructuring of the organization and on innovation and automation.

Theory

Depending on various context factors, the topic of decision-making and the policy of management, organizational decision-making processes can assume very different shapes (Koopman and Pool, 1990). The classification proposed here attempts to include as much empirical research as possible, and models based upon it.

To exemplify, Hickson et al. (1986) distinguished sporadic, fluid and limited processes. Schwenk (1988), following Allison, differentiated the rational choice perspective, the organizational perspective and the political perspective. Thompson and Tuden (1959) distinguished decisions through computation, majority judgement, compromise and inspiration. Axelsson and Rosenberg (1979) and McMillan (1980) used similar typologies. Fahey (1981) reduced reality to two contrasting types of decision-making: rational analytical versus behavioral-political. McCall and Kaplan (1985) spoke of quick versus convoluted action. Our classification most clearly corresponds to that of Shrivastava and Grant (1985). These authors distinguished the managerial autocracy model, the systematic bureaucratic model, the political expediency model and the adaptive planning model. Another more or less related classification is that of Quinn and Cameron (1983), who described the rational goal model, the internal process model, the human relations model and the open systems model.

A typology of four basic models of decision-making can reasonably accommodate most literature in this field (see Fig. 1). We distinguish: the neo-rational model, the bureaucratic model, the arena model and the open-end model. The models are not only configurations of dimensions; there is often also a clear relationship between the various models and the context in which they take place. We have summarized the expected constellations in Table 1.

The *neo-rational model* is characterized by not very complex decision-making processes that are guided and controlled from one point: the top management. There is a high concentration of power in the organization. According to Fredrickson (1986a) and Shrivastava and Grant (1985), this type of decision-making process

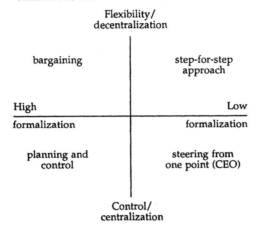

FIG. 1. Four models of decision making (Koopman and Pool, 1990).

may primarily be expected in the organizational type that Mintzberg (1979, 1983) termed a "simple structure" or "autocracy". In terms of organizational culture, Harrison's (1972) "power culture" would be most conducive to this type of decision-making process. The model is rational in the sense that decision-making aims to maximize the goals of top management. Like a spider in its web or like Zeus in Greek mythology (Handy, 1985), the top manager leaves his personal mark on decision-making, and in so doing, strives to maximize his goals. Intuition and quick decisions are more typical of this model than extensive analysis and study of alternatives. (Shrivastava and Grant, 1985). We speak of the neo-rational model because it takes account of some fundamental characteristics relating to human cognitions and emotions. Because of this, the behavior of decision-makers is characterized by "bounded rationality" and "satisficing" (as opposed to maximal) goal achievement (Simon, 1976). A dynamic and/or threatening environment can lead decision-making processes to follow the neo-rational model (McCall and Kaplan, 1985; Pettigrew, 1986; Mintzberg, 1983): it demands quick reaction.

Characteristic of the *bureaucratic model* is that decision-making is "constricted" by rules and regulations. They may be rules of the organization itself, such as job descriptions, tasks and competencies, meeting rules, etc., but also rules that are laid down outside the organization, as by legislation or by directives from the head office. The decision-making comes to be formalized by all manner of rules and methods of planning and control. Different actors or groups are expected to make their contribution at various stages, even if it merely means initialling a document. Various alternatives are explored and officially documented. The selection of the best solution is conducted by way of existing procedures (Shrivastava and Grant, 1985). In contrast to the neo-rational model, the bureaucratic model usually involves fairly complex decision-making processes. Its counterpart in Mintzberg's structural typology is the "machine bureaucracy" or the "closed system". In Harrison's culture typology this model resembles the "role culture". As in these counterparts, the environment is characterized by stability and predictability. When time pressure or external threats increase, decision-making increasingly leans toward the neo-rational model (temporary centralization, Mintzberg, 1983). If innovation requirements are central, then characteristics of the open-end model (still to be discussed) gain the upper hand.

Decision-making in the *arena model* is dominated by negotiations between various interested parties, which form coalitions around certain subinterests. These groups defend a point of

TABLE 1. *The Four Decision-Making Models and Their Hypothetical Relationships with Various Context Factors*

	Neo-rational model	Bureaucratic model	Arena model	Open-end model
Context factors:				
Environment:				
—complexity	low	low	high	high
—dynamics	high	low	low	high
—hostility	high	low	high	low/high
Organization:				
—power distribution	low	low	high	high
—type of org. (Mintzberg)	autocracy	machine bureaucracy	professional bureaucracy	adhocracy
—type of culture (Harrison)	power culture	role culture	person culture	task culture
Characteristics of decision-maker	proactive, intuitive	reactive, analytic	autonomous, intrapreneur	innovative, willing to take risks
Type of subject:				
—complexity	low	high	low/high	high
—dynamics	high/low	low	high	high

view or alternative as the only correct and legitimate view of reality (Shrivastava and Grant, 1985). Power in the organization is relatively evenly distributed; power differences are small. There is no central machinery that can easily impose its will. Although there is a certain degree of coordination (primarily through professional training, Mintzberg, 1983), the organization must constantly contend with the problem of acquiring sufficient consensus and acceptance for decisions. Mutual contention and lack of cooperation threaten the quality of the decision-making. This type of decision-making, with controversial topics, is primarily found in organizations that are composed of relatively independent units, such as universities, hospitals or other "conglomerate firms". The decision-making sometimes takes place at two levels: at the first level a small group of insiders arrives at the critical choices which are subsequently legitimized for the constituency by the official bodies and by means of arguments which are accepted by these bodies. The natural counterpart in Mintzberg's structural typology is the professional bureaucracy; in the culture typology of Harrison we should think of the "person culture".

Decision-making in the *open-end model* is characterized by a limited view of the goals or of the means by which to achieve them (Thompson and Tuden, 1959). Chance circumstances and unpredictable events cross the path of this approach. Again and again, people must adapt to new demands and possibilities. Furthermore, political opposition or emotional resistance are often hard to predict. This forces decision-makers to take a step-by-step approach (Quinn, 1980). Another characteristic of the model is that, depending on the problem in question, expertise of various types and locations must be gathered on a temporary basis (project management). The message here is: organize flexibly. Gradually, by way of iterations and recycling, the end product comes into view (Boehm, 1986). Complex innovative decisions (e.g., automation) often take place in this way. Mintzberg's adhocracy forms the organizational structure conducive to this type of decision-making. The environment is complex and dynamic. Such an organization generally has a "task culture" (Harrison, 1972).

In addition to the two dimensions in Figure 1 this analysis of the literature shows that other dimensions are of importance as well. Most specifically, the use of information and the measure of confrontation seem to be significant dimensions on which decision-making processes can vary. Table 2 presents a schedule reflecting the most likely configuration of dimension scores for each of the four decision-making types discussed above. Thus, decision-making can show much or little centralization, but also much or little formalization, for centralization and formalization do not always go together (Robbins, 1987). Sometimes information plays an important role in the preparation of decisions, sometimes power processes determine the contents of the decision and information primarily serves the purpose of legitimating after the fact (O'Reilly, 1983; Langley, 1990).

TABLE 2. *Four Models of Decision-Making and Their Relationships with the Process Dimensions*

	Neo-rational model	Bureaucratic model	Arena model	Open-end model
Characteristics of decision-making process:				
Centralization	high	moderate/ high	low	low
Formalization	low	high	moderate/ high	low
Information	high/ low	high	low	high/ low
Confrontation	low	low	high	high

The amount of *centralization* is one of the most important parameters of decision-making. Much research has been done of the manner in which decentralization and participation take place in decision-making and of the question in how far participation is effective. (e.g. Bacharach and Lawler, 1980; IDE, 1981; Pfeffer, 1981; Heller et al., 1988).

A second important dimension is the extent to which the decision-making is *formalized* (Fredrickson, 1986a; Hickson et al., 1986). Decisions can take place according to an established procedure set down in advance, or they can proceed more flexibly, according to informal considerations of what is required or desirable (Stein, 1981).

Third, the way in which the substance of a decision comes about is important. On the basis of what *information* is a decision made? What alternatives are developed or sought, and from where do they come? Have important possibilities or consequences been overlooked? These questions involve the extent to which the requirements set by the traditional rationality perspective of decision-making are met (Miller, 1987; Nutt, 1984; O'Reilly, 1983).

The fourth and final dimension is the extent to which there is *confrontation* and conflict in the decision-making process. This last dimension comes from models of decision-making as a political process, in which parties try to achieve their own interests on the basis of their power positions (Allison, 1971; Hickson et al., 1971; Pettigrew, 1973).

Theoretically, classification based on the four dimensions would yield sixteen different models. In our view, such diversity is not wise, nor can it be defended empirically. In addition, the four dimensions are not completely independent. A high score on one dimension frequently implies a low score on another. Within the neo-rational model, highly centralized processes are often also fairly informal and show little conflict. Sometimes, however, the dimensions are more independent. One and the same centralized process can be allowed to operate intuitively, or management can adopt a broad, comprehensive information strategy. What we then see are actually two subforms of the neo-rational model (Koopman and Pool, 1990).

Expanding on earlier research on the control of organizational change processes, which led to a list of ten management dilemmas (choice opportunities with both advantages and disadvantages, see Koopman, Kamerbeek, Pool and Van Vuuren (1986)), the four dimension of decision-making are seen as control possibilities in the management of strategic decision-making. Mintzberg et al. (1976) speak of "meta decision-making". Analyzing decision-making processes using these four dimensions opens up the possibility to focus on control processes in strategic decision-making.

Method

Companies and cases: the study took place in the same organizations that had taken part in the replication studies IDE-2 and ZIDE-2 (Pool et al., 1988). This implies that the group of companies and hospitals was fixed, and contained a maximum of sixteen organizations. Twelve agreed to participate, and twenty-five case studies were ultimately completed (see Table 3).

Case selection: as the first step, an inventory was made of important decisions that had taken place in the last few years in the organizations involved. In consultation with management, it was then decided what cases would be studied. Primarily, we selected cases on two areas, reorganizations and technological innovations. If cases on these areas were not available, other topics were studied instead.

Respondents: immediately after the case selection, it was discussed what informants would be interviewed. First a "key respondent" was decided upon per case; in an initial interview, this person informed us of the decision-making process in general lines. In this meeting it was also decided who would serve as further informants. It was attempted to achieve as good a coverage as possible of all viewpoints and aspects of the decision-making process. A minimum of three respondents per case was agreed upon, including one member of management or the board of directors and one representative of the works council. It was also agreed that, depending on the needs of the study, more people could be interviewed for each case. This possibility was frequently utilized, so that the number of respondents per case in these companies varied between three and nine. Overall, a total of 123 managers and employee representatives were interviewed, several of them twice.

Data: the primary source on which the analysis was performed was the interview material. The interviews served to obtain a chronological survey of the course of the decision-making process, and to sound out the opinions of the respondents on a number of relevant aspects (mainly the process indicators and the subject aspects). The interviewees also completed a questionnaire in which their opinion was asked about the influence distribution during the various phases, as well as a brief evaluation of the process.

In addition, relevant documentation was collected (minutes of management, work council and other meetings, memos, reports, etc.) on each case, so far as it was (or was made) available. This written information was used to support, supplement and check the oral information (Schwenk, 1985).

Processing: processing mainly qualitative information is difficult and not without risks. Two of the inherent dangers are subjective influencing by the researcher and selective representation of the information. We tried to minimize these risks by producing well-documented case reports, which were subsequently fed back to the respondents. The revised case reports were then analyzed by the researchers, following a "case survey" approach (Yin, 1984). A check on six cases showed equal scores on 90% of the aspects of the cases, when two independent researchers analyzed the case material (Pool, 1990).

Some Preliminary Results

The twenty-five cases studied were analyzed in terms of the degree of centralization, formalization, use of information and confrontation. Each dimension was scored on a number of aspects and a total score per dimension was calculated. The total score was then split into three categories of approximately equal size: high, medium and low. Table 3 shows the profiles per case, based upon the four process dimensions.

We subsequently investigated whether there was a relationship between the four control dimensions distinguished, or whether certain patterns could be discovered in the relationships between the dimensions. We wanted to find out whether the cases could

TABLE 3. *Standardized Total Scores Process Dimensions per case*
(scale is partitioned in three values: L (low)—H (high))

Sectors and cases		Centrali- zation	Formali- zation*	Informa- tion	Confron- tation
			Process dimensions		
Insurance branche:					
F1	Take over supplier	H	L	H	L
F2	Automation	L	M	H	M
F3	Sales campaign	H	L	H	L
G1	Working hours arrangement 1987	M	L	L	H
G2	Change name of company	M	M	M	M
G3	New consultation procedures	M	L	M	M
G4	Automation life-insurance dept.	L	M	L	H
G5	New location headquarters	M	M	H	H
H1	Reorganization 1987	H	H	M	M
H2	Automation fire-insurance dept.	L	M	L	M
Metal industry:					
J1	Reorganization 1987	M	H	M	H
K1	Reorganization 1987	M	H	L	M
N1	Automation attendance registration	M	H	H	M
N2	Clode down factory	H	H	M	L
U1	New consultation-procedures	H	L	M	L
U2	Automation/standard, product line	H	H	L	L
W1	Reorganization 1983	H	—	L	L
Hospitals:					
ZA1	Reorganization 1987	L	L	M	L
ZA2	Closure of ward	H	M	L	H
ZB1	Reorganization 1987	L	H	M	H
ZB2	Buy CT-scan	L	L	H	L
ZC1	New management-team	M	—	L	H
ZC2	Buy CT-scan	M	L	M	M
ZE1	Reorganization 1988	L	M	H	H
ZE2	Buy CT-scan	L	M	H	L

*Two cases are assigned missing values on this dimension because of insufficient data on some aspects.

be classified into groups or clusters on the basis of such patterns. We will come back to this directly.

To answer the first question, we calculated the correlations between the standardized total scores on the four dimensions (see Table 4). This brought to light a few clear relationships between the dimensions. The highest correlation ($r = .57$, $p < .05$) was found between the dimensions of formalization and confrontation. It indicates that more formalized decision-making strategies typically show more conflicting interests and more forms of conflict management. The question of causality (for example, whether the presence of conflict brings about stronger formalization) cannot be answered on the basis of these data.[3]

TABLE 4. *Pearson Correlations Between Process Dimensions (standardized total scores)*

	1	2	3	4
1. Centralization	—			
2. Formalization	-.37*	—		
3. Information	-.17	.08	—	
4. Confrontation	-.37*	.57**	-.06	—

*$p < .1$ **$p < .05$

There also appeared to be a significant correlation between the degree of centralization and formalization. On theoretical grounds it can be argued that there is less need to formalize matters when fewer people are involved in the decision-making (high degree of centralization). This is understandable, and the correlation we found is in line with findings from organizational theory (i.e., Child, 1972; Pugh, Hickson, Hinings and Turner, 1968). This finding does however raise the question of whether the two dimensions used in Fig. 1 are independent.

Centralization also correlates negatively with confrontation. The involvement of several parties may lead to more opinions and more interests in the "decision set" (Hickson et al., 1986, pp. 58–59), and thus to more potential conflict and more conflict management. By the same line of reasoning, centralization of the decision-making leads to fewer opportunities for conflict. If the decision-making primarily takes place within the "inner circle", where there is broad agreement on the policy lines to be followed, the chance that conflicts arise is limited. Finally, the information dimension was separate from the other three dimensions. Centralization of the

[3]It may be that there is a correlation of both formalization and confrontation with the size, or scope, of a decision. The relationship between these two dimensions would then be spurious, because of the invisible influence of a confounding variable (Drenth, 1984, ch. 1.2, p. 21). Unfortunately, the scope of this paper does not allow us to go more deeply into this question of causality.

decision-making is thus not associated with less use of information, nor formalization with more. Also, no negative relationship with confrontation (which would be expected in either information-oriented or conflict-dominated decision-making) could be found.

Secondly, a cluster analysis was performed on the basis of the profiles. It was intended to investigate whether certain groups could be distinguished on the basis of the profiles. This analysis (hierarchical cluster analysis according to the method of Ward) yielded clustering into four groups of cases. These groups are shown in Fig. 2 along with the profiles corresponding to each of the clusters. Analysis of variance showed significant differences between the four clusters on all four dimensions, which may be seen as a confirmation of the cluster classification. The complete results of these analyses are included as an Appendix.

The clustering in Fig. 2 is simple to interpret. Comparison of the profiles of the four groups with the classification in Fig. 1, which was based upon the literature and previous research, shows a clear correspondence.

The first cluster, with three cases (F1, F3 and U1), is the smallest in size, and its profile bears a clear resemblance to the *neo-rational model*. The cases in this group show strong centralization linked to low values on formalization and confrontation. In this type of process the decision remains in the hands of those in power, which means there is little necessity to formalize matters and the chance of confrontation and conflict is limited. There is some variation in the use of information, which was anticipated in the predicted pattern of the neo-rational model.

The second cluster is also relatively small, containing four cases (H1, N1, U2 and W1). In the pattern of the scores on the four dimensions, this group shows the most correspondence to the *bureaucratic model*. Especially decisive here are the high values on centralization and formalization, linked to a medium to low use of information with little confrontation.

The cases in the third cluster, which contains eight cases (G1, G4, H2, J1, K1, ZA2, ZB1 and ZC1) show a profile strongly reminiscent of the *arena model*. This type of process is characterized by a high degree of confrontation linked to a low use of information. In addition, this type of process shows low to medium centralization and high to medium formalization. However, these dimensions exhibit more variance.

The fourth and final cluster is the largest in size. It includes ten cases (F2, G2, G3, G5, N1, ZA1, ZB2, ZC2, ZE1 and ZE2) which can be typified as *open-ended processes*. This cluster is essentially characterized by a high use of information linked to a

Cluster 1 (N=3): neo-rational processes

	L	M	H
Centralization			3
Formalization	3		
Information		1	2
Confrontation	3		

Cluster 2 (N=4): bureaucratic processes

	L	M	H
Centralization			4
Formalization			4
Information	2	2	
Confrontation	3	1	

Cluster 3 (N=8): political processes

	L	M	H
Centralization	3	4	1
Formalization	1	3	3
Information	6	2	
Confrontation		2	6

Cluster 4 (N=10): open-end processes

	L	M	H
Centralization	5	5	
Formalization	4	5	1
Information		4	6
Confrontation	3	5	2

FIG. 2. Profiles of four clusters of decision-making processes (standardized total scores, divided in three categories high, medium and low).

low degree of centralization. The degree of formalization, although generally low, shows a fairly wide spread. With a few exceptions, the level of confrontation generally lies in the middle. In view of the variance on the latter dimensions, this cluster could be subdivided into two groups: a group with lower values on formalization and confrontation (cases G2, G3, ZA1, ZB2, ZC2 and ZE2), and a second group with higher values on these two dimensions (cases F2, G5, N1 and ZE1). The low values on formalization and confrontation put the first subgroup closer to the neo-rational model, while the second subgroup—with higher values on formalization and confrontation—tends more towards the arena model.

Summary of Results

The correspondence of these clusters—both in the number of models and in the pattern of dimensions that fits each model—with the classification of models based on the literature reinforces our confidence in the typology. Although our data relate to the control of decision-making processes, the resulting typology bears great resemblance to that from other research. Decision-making processes can be classified into one of the four process types on the basis of the degree of centralization and formalization they show, the amount of information they utilize and the degree of confrontation and conflict management. From the point of view of the emphasis on factors in the control of decision-making processes, we may speak of a classification into four types of strategy.

In this section we have discussed the methods of control used in the decision-making processes studied. It proved to be possible to distinguish decision-making processes on the degree of centralization and formalization, on the amount of information utilized and on the amount of conflict management and balancing of preferences.

Based on the pattern that emerged when the four dimensions were combined, the twenty-five decision-making processes studied could be satisfactorily subdivided into four groups. These four groups may be seen as distinct strategies in the approach to decision-making processes. The dominant patterns in the scores on the dimensions show a clear correspondence with the profiles as they were theorized to exist on the basis of previous research. Beyond describing the options for control of decision-making, some key questions remain unanswered: what are the outcomes, or: is there a relationship between the various forms of control and the outcome of decision-making? A further question is the influence of the decision-making situation. Is it of decisive influence on the use of a certain form of control? Or do characteristics of the organization and of the topic under consideration primarily influence the relationship between control and effectiveness? These questions are discussed in the final report of the research project (Pool, 1990).

Future Research

As stated at the beginning of this paper, research of decision-making in organizations does not yet have a long tradition. Much work must still be done in a number of areas to increase our insight into these basic and central organizational processes. Below is a summary of important fields for future research.

1. Most studies of decision-making start their analysis at a

moment when a problem has been pointed out, and it has been decided that, no matter what, something must change. Several authors (Kanter, 1983; McCall and Kaplan, 1985) have shown that important steps or events may have preceded this, which can have a substantial influence on decision-making. Lyles (1987) and Lyles and Thomas (1988) have done preliminary work on the topic of problem recognition and formulation. Further elaboration in the direction of political aspects in the earlier phases [expanding on the non-decision topic of Bacharach and Baratz (1963)] and the cognitive, personal and political processes of the emergence of decisions (e.g., Narayanan and Fahey, 1982) seems promising.

2. A second field of research is to obtain more insight into the way in which important changes, often referred to as paradigm shifts, occur in organizations. A crisis, perhaps accompanied by changes in key officials, seems to be one important factor (Donaldson and Lorsch, 1983; Miller and Friesen, 1982; Pettigrew, 1986). Further research of the existence of organizational mind sets, belief systems, dominant logics (Bouwen, De Visch and Steyart, 1992) and other synonyms for what is held to be shared reality in an organization, and especially of the ways in which and circumstances under which they change (Pettigrew, 1985), is recommended.[4]

3. In our view, further research of the relationship of personality, personal characteristics and skills to decision-making seems necessary. Although preliminary work has been done in this field (see section 2), better knowledge of these relationships is of crucial importance to a good policy in the selection, training and career support of managers, and to the design of good management training. We must guard against a revival of the "great men" concept.

4. More research should be performed on the relationship between organizational characteristics and decision-making. The basic assumption should be that there is no such thing as unidirectional causality, but reciprocal influence and interaction. The organization influences the way in which decisions are made, but these decisions can—directly or indirectly—influence organizational characteristics. Manipulation of the structural context (Bower, 1970) can even be adopted as a conscious strategy, to facilitate later decisions. Finally, it may be stated that many interpersonal contacts are often intended as strategic, and that networking (Hosking, 1988) is used as an intentional tactic for future decision-making. With this in mind, more study of the interaction between the organization and decision-making seems particularly fruitful.

[4]See also Bouwen (1993).

5. Much research of decision-making in organizations is descriptive in nature, and at best quasi-experimental. There is a dichotomy between field research, which sticks close to reality and often works with case studies, and the more experimental laboratory research to improve decision-making methods (e.g., dialectical inquiry and devil's advocacy (Cosier, 1978; Schweiger, Sandberg and Ragan, 1986)). By converging these two schools, perhaps in the form of experimental field research, real life data could be obtained. Managers could be trained in decision-making techniques and then the effects could be evaluated based on an analysis of decisions made before and after training.

6. Although we have not devoted any attention in this paper to Decision Support Systems (DSS) and Management Information Systems (MIS) (Davis and Olsen, 1984; Koopman et al., 1988), it seems to us of eminent importance to study the effects of the emergence of such systems on the course and the effectiveness of organizational decision-making. In an area where bounded rationality is one of the best known explanatory concepts, making the bounds smaller may have great consequences. The rapid increase in the information processing capacity of organizations does not leave decision-making unaffected. Although initial results of DSS have not been earth-shaking (Monger, 1987)—and part of the explanation is that better information does not alter the political side of decision-making but may even emphasize it—it is important to increase our insight into its operation. In addition, the availability of a multitude of data files and the possibility to transport and manipulate them (telematics) appears to have a great influence on organizations and their decision-making and should also be studied carefully.

7. Finally, as a possible further development we mention the necessity to arrive at a more methodical research approach. The previously mentioned case study method, one which has proved to be very fruitful, should be further developed to make the comparison of studies possible. Another step on the road to comparative methods of decision-making research is the scenario method developed by Fredrickson (1986b). The advantage of this method, in comparison to case study, lies in the larger scale. It would even be possible—and extremely interesting—to set up international comparative research in this way.

References

Allison, G. T. (1971) *Essence of Decision: Explaining the Cuban Missile Crisis.* Boston: Little Brown.

Axelsson, R. and Rosenberg, L. (1979) Decision-making and organizational turbulence. *Acta Sociologica*, 22, 45–62.

Bachrach, P. and Baratz, M. S. (1963) Decisions and non-decisions: An analytical framework. *American Political Science Review*, 57, 641–651.

Bacharach, S. B. and Lawler, E. J. (1980) *Power and Politics in Organizations.* San Francisco: Jossey Bass.

Boehm, B. W. (1986) A spiral model of software development and enhancement. *ACM Sigsoft Software Engineering Notes*, 11, 22–42.

Bouwen, R. (1993) Organizational innovation as a social construction: managing meaning in multiple realities. In *Interdisciplinary Perspectives on Organization Studies* S. Lindenberg and H. Schreuder (eds.) Oxford: Pergamon Press.

Bouwen, R., De Visch, J. and Steyart (1992) Innovation projects in organizations: Complementing the dominant logic by organizational learning. In *Organizational Change and Innovations: Psychological Perspectives and Practices*, ch. 6, edited by D. M. Hosking and N. Anderson. London: Routledge.

Bower, J. L. (1970) *Managing the Resource Allocation Process: A Study of Corporate Planning and Investment.* Boston: Harvard University School.

Child, J. (1972) Organization structure and strategies of control: A replication of the Aston study. *Administrative Science Quarterly*, 17, 163–177.

Cohen, M. D., March, J. G. and Olsen, J. P. (1972) A garbage can model of organizational choice. *Administrative Science Quarterly*, 17, 1–25.

Cosier, R. A. (1978) The effects of three potential aids for making strategic decisions on prediction accuracy. *Organizational Behavior and Human Performance*, 22, 295–306.

Davis, G. B. and Olson, M. H. (1984) *Management Information Systems.* New York: McGraw-Hill.

Donaldson, G. and Lorsch, J. W. (1983) *Decision Making at the Top: The Shaping of Strategic Direction.* New York: Basic Books.

Drenth, P. J. D. (1984) Research in work and organizational psychology: Principles and methods. In *Handbook of Work and Organizational Psychology*, Vol. 1, Ch. 1.2, edited by P. J. D. Drenth, H. Thierry, P. J. Williems, and C. J. de Wolff. New York: Wiley.

Fredrickson, J. W. (1986a) The strategic decision process and organizational structure. *Academy of Management Review*, 11, 280–297.

Fredrickson, J. W. (1986b) An exploratory approach to measuring perceptions of strategic decision process constructs. *Strategic Management Journal*, 7, 473–483.

Handy, C. B. (1985) *Understanding Organizations.* New York: Penguin.

Harrison, R. (1972) Understanding your organizations character. *Harvard Business Review*, 50, 119–128.

Heller, F. A., Drenth, P. J. D., Koopman, P. L. and Rus, V. (1988) *Decisions in Organizations: A Three Country Comparative Study.* London: Sage.

Hickson, D. J., Hinings, C. R., Lee, A. C., Schneck, R. E and Pennings, J. M. (1971) A strategic contingency theory of intra-organizational power. *Administrative Science Quarterly*, 16, 216–229.

Hickson, D. J., Butler, R. J., Cray, D., Mallory, G. R. and Wilson, D. C. (1986) *Top Decisions: Strategic decision-making in Organizations.* Oxford: Basil Blackwell.

Hosking, D. M. (1988) Organization, leadership and skilful process. *Journal of Management Studies*, 25, 147–166.

IDE-International Research Group (1981) *Industrial Democracy in Europe*. Oxford: Clarendon Press.

Kanter, R. M. (1983) *The Change Masters: Innovation for Productivity in the American Corporation*. New York: Simon and Schuster.

Koopman, P. L., Broekhuysen, J. W. and Wierdsma, A. F. M. (1988) Complexe besluitvorming in organisaties (Complex decision making in organizations). In *Nieuw Handboek Arbeids-en Organisatiepsychologie*, Ch. 4.11 edited by P. J. D. Drenth, Hk, Thierry and Ch. de Wolff. Deventer: Van Loghum Slaterus.

Koopman, P. L. and Pool, J. (1990) Decision making in organizations. In *International Review of Industrial Psychology*, pp. 101–148 edited by C. L. Cooper and I. T. Robinson. New York: Wiley.

Langley, A. (1990) Patterns in the use of formal analysis in strategic decisions. *Organization Studies*, 11, 17–45.

Lyles, M. A. (1987) Defining strategic problems: Subjective criteria of executives. *Organization Studies*, 8, 263–280.

Lyles, M. A. and Thomas, H. (1988) Strategic problem formulation: Biases and assumptions in alternative decision-making models. *Journal of Management Studies*, 25, 131–145.

March, J. G. and Simon, H. A. (1958) *Organizations*. New York: Wiley.

McCall, M. W. and Kaplan, R. E. (1985) *Whatever it Takes: Decision-makers at Work*. Englewood Cliffs, NJ: Prentice-Hall.

McMillan, C. J. (1980) Qualitative models of organizational decision-making. *Journal of General Management*, 5, 22–39.

Miller, D. (1987) Strategy making and structure: analysis and implications for performance. *Academy of Management Journal*, 30, 7–32.

Miller, D. and Friesen, P. (1983) Strategy making and the environment. *Strategic Management Journal*, 4, 221–235.

Mintzberg, H. (1979) *The Structuring of Organizations: A Synthesis of the Research*. Englewood Cliffs, NJ: Prentice-Hall.

Mintzberg, H. (1983) *Power In and Around Organizations*. Englewood Cliffs, NJ: Prentice Hall.

Mintzberg, H., Raisinghani, D. and Théorêt, A. (1976) The structure of "unstructured" decision processes. *Administrative Science Quarterly*, 21, 246–275.

Monger, R. F. (1987) *Managerial Decision Making with Technology*. New York: Pergamon Press.

Narayanan, V. and Fahey, L. (1982) The micro-politics of strategy formulation. *Academy of Management Review*, 7, 25–34.

Nutt, P. C. (1984) Types of organizational decision processes. *Administrative Science Quarterly*, 29, 414–450.

O'Reilly, C. A. (1983) The use of information in organizational decision-making: A model and some propositions. In *Research in Organizational Behaviour*, pp 103–139, edited by L. L. Cummings and B. M. Shaw, Greenwich, CN: JAI-Press.

Pettigrew, A. M. (1973) *The Politics of Organizational Decision Making*. London: Tavistock.

Pettigrew, A. M. (1985) *The Awakening Giant: Continuity and Change in ICI*. Oxford: Basil Blackwell.

Pettigrew, A. M. (1986) Some limits of executive power in creating strategic change. In *The Functioning of Executive Power*, edited by S. Shrivastva. London: Jossey Bass.

Pfeffer, J. (1981) *Power in Organizations*. Boston: Pitman.

Pool, J., Drenth, P. J. D., Koopman, P. L. and Lammers, C. J. (1988) De volwassenwording van de medezeggenschap: Invloedsverhoudingen in de jaren '80 (The maturation of codetermination: Influence relations in the eighties). *Gedrag en Organisatie*, 1, 37–58.

Pool, J., Koopman, P. L. and Kamerbeek, E. (1986) Veranderingsprocessen bij de rijksoverheid: Cases en keuzemomenten (Change processes in government: Cases and choices). *M & O, Tijdschrift voor Organisatiekunde en Sociaal Beleid*, 40, 516–531.

Pool, J. (1990) *Sturing van strategische besluitvorming: Mogelijkheden en grenzen* (Control of strategic decision making: Possibilities and limits). Amsterdam: VU-Uitgeverij.

Pugh, D. S., Hickson, D. J., Hinings, C. R. and Turner, C. (1968) Dimensions of organization structure. *Administrative Science Quarterly*, 13, 65–105.

Quinn, J. B. (1980) *Strategies for Change: Logical Incrementalism*. Homewood: Irwin.

Quinn, J. B., Mintzberg, H., and James, R. M. (Eds.) (1988) *The Strategy Process: Concepts, Contexts and Cases*. London: Prentice-Hall.

Quinn, R. E. and Cameron, K. (1983) Organizational life cycles and shifting criteria of effectiveness: Some preliminary evidence. *Management Science*, 29, 33–51.

Robbins, S. P. (1987) *Organization Theory: Structure, Design and Applications*. Englewood Cliffs, NJ: Prentice-Hall.

Schweiger, D., Sandberg, W. and Ragan, J. (1986) Group approaches for improving strategic decision-making: A comparative analysis of dialectical inquiry, devil's advocacy and consensus. *Academy of Management Journal*, 29, 51–71.

Schwenk, C. R. (1984) Cognitive simplification processes in strategic decision-making. *Strategic Management Journal*, 5, 111–128.

Schwenk, C. R. (1988) *The Essence of Strategic Decision Making*. Massachusetts: D. C. Heath and Co.

Shrivastava, P. and Grant, J. H. (1985) Empirically derived models of strategic decision-making processes. *Strategic Management Journal*, 6, 97–113.

Simon, H. A. (1947) *Administrative Behavior*. New York: Free Press.

Simon, H. A. (1957) *Models of Man*. New York: Wiley.

Simon, H. A. (1976) *Administrative Behavior*, 3rd ed. New York: Free Press.

Thompson, J. D. and Tuden, A. (1959) Strategies, structures and processes of organizational design. In *Comparative Studies in Administration*, edited by J. D. Thompson, P. B. Hammond, R. W. Hawkes, B. H. Junker and A. Tuden. Pittsburgh: Pittsburgh University Press.

Yin, R. K. (1984) *Case Study Research: Design and Methods*. Beverly Hills: Sage Publications.

Appendix I

Appendix 1: Cluster-analysis process dimensions

Profiles dimensions

Ce	Fo	In	Co		Distances:
					0.000 .... 5.000
M	–	L	H	zc1	0.000
M	L	L	H	g1	0.856
H	M	L	H	za2	1.695
M	H	M	H	j1	0.500
L	H	M	H	zb1	1.152
L	M	L	H	g4	0.500
L	M	L	M	h2	0.882
M	H	L	M	k1	3.838
M	M	M	M	g2	0.667
M	L	M	M	g3	0.000
M	L	M	M	zc2	1.724
L	L	M	L	za1	0.500
L	L	H	L	zb2	0.638
L	M	H	L	ze2	2.029
L	M	H	H	ze1	0.500
L	M	H	M	f2	0.638
M	M	H	H	g5	0.856
M	H	H	M	n1	4.684
H	H	M	M	h1	0.500
H	H	M	L	n2	1.050
H	H	L	L	u2	0.000
H	–	L	L	w1	2.851
H	L	M	L	u1	0.667
H	L	H	L	f3	0.000
H	L	H	L	f1	

APPENDIX 1. Cluster-analysis process dimensions.

The Role of Dialogue in Organizational Change Programs

Introduction

There is today a fairly broad agreement on what a "good enterprise" should look like. Depending on which side is talking, we hear aspects like high productivity, to be able to produce at competitive costs, an ability to be innovative, quality-minded and flexible, etc. On the other side we hear high and secure wages, safe jobs, interesting and developing tasks, good work environment, promotion opportunities, etc. Expressions containing these aspects can be found in official statements of managers and unionists and they are credos in conferences and public speeches.

These characteristics are of course not new, they have been around for a long time. But today, the conditions for their realization have changed. We can illustrate this with four areas where considerable changes have taken place and are expected to take place in the future. Great changes have occurred in the product market where we can observe a shift from mass products to customized quality products. In the field of technology, we see the explosion of a micro-electronics which can be applied in all manufacturing and administrative processes. Developments in the last few years have also resulted in more user-friendly computer equipment. Labor markets have also changed considerably, even if there are great national differences regarding unemployment level, barriers of entrance to the labor market and other features. In virtually all industrialized countries, the level of education has risen, and expectations regarding work environment, tasks, learning and promotion opportunities, etc., have changed. At least young workers no longer accept work conditions which their parents were willing to tolerate. In many countries, attempts to democratize and to achieve influence for employees over matters of production have been codified in laws and agreements.

[1]Swedish Centre for Working Life, Stockholm.

113

The development in all four areas have called for rethinking the issue of work organization. There is now a fairly strong consensus that the traditional work organization with its rigid hierarchy of positions, with emphasis on external coordination and control, narrow skills, and where man is seen as an extension of a machine, no longer fits the demands of efficiency or individual expectations. There is much less agreement on new work organization and there is even less agreement on who the relevant actors in a change process should be and how they should interact with each other. Specifically, what should the role of science be in all that? Against the expressed hope of proponents of "scientific management" to come up with "the best" strategy, the insight is gaining that there is no single "best way" to reach the vision of the "good enterprise".

In this confused situation, the Swedish approach has been to have solutions emerge from a sustained dialogue among all actors, culminating in the so-called Program on Leadership, Organization and Participation, or LOM Program. The Program started 1985 with an annual budget of about 1.7 million US dollars. In all sixty-six firms and institutions were—and most of them still are—formally engaged in LOM projects, many others were inspired and are loosely coupled to the formal program structure.

Because this program is so thoroughly oriented towards dialogue rather than control and because this orientation is so much against the received views of scientific management, it is important to ask first whether there is a theoretical basis for this approach, and second what other programs the Swedes have tried before they adopted the LOM Program. While both questions say little about the actual functioning of the LOM Program, they say something about the degree to which the dialogue principles are simply "a Swedish thing" or, alternatively, to what degree they connect to a wider theoretical analysis of industrial relations and are based on a wealth of experience with less dialogue-oriented approaches. In the discussions of the Swedish model in the literature, there has been little attention paid to both aspects. Partially this is due to the fact that the theoretical basis has not been sufficiently explicated by the Swedes themselves and that there has been little explicit reference to the collective learning experience from other programs in Scandinavia.

The purpose of this paper is to explicate the theoretical basis of the LOM Program and to look at the efforts prior to the LOM Program with the question: in what way did these prior programs contribute toward the development of the dialogue principles?

A Point of Department and Elements of a Theoretical Frame

"An organization is a consciously coordinated social entity, with a relatively identifiable boundary, that functions on a relatively continuous basis to achieve a common goal or a set of goals" (Robbins, 1987, p. 3). This definition is the kind of standard formulation found in textbooks and is perhaps useful at this level. A closer look at how organizations can be conceptualized soon give a different and varied picture. Organizations can be viewed as rational entities in pursuit of goals, or information-processing units, or open systems, etc. Organizations can also be viewed as coalitions of powerful constituencies, as political systems, or instruments of domination. From the latter viewpoint, organizations are means for structuring, steering and control of labor. This view express perhaps an extreme but nevertheless common opinion and defines the core of the so-called control paradigm. It goes back to Karl Marx and his analysis of the labor process. In capitalism, the process of production must combine the labor process with the creation of surplus value. It is human labor power which is capable of creating the surplus value which becomes the legal property of the employer. To translate legal ownership into real possession, the employer must therefore erect structures of control over the conditions under which the speed, skill and dexterity of the worker operate (Marx, 1976).

As Braverman (1974) has pointed out, "Scientific Management", as developed by Taylor, can be seen as the direct expression of this need to control. But other authors showed that there is a variety of other control methods and responses of workers. Friedman (1977), Edwards (1979) and Burawoy (1979) developed alternative theories of control and their joint feature is the rejection of the orthodoxy of Marx and Braverman concerning the necessity for capital to control the labor force directly. Instead they stress the need of the capitalist to take into consideration workers' resistance and involvement through more complex means of control and integration. This gave rise to what may be called the control debate. In this debate, the new and important element is that Burawoy and others opened the field for analysis of consent and positive participation in "self-control" by workers.[2]

A related development can be found in the strategic use of value commitment, a discussion that has been revived in Sweden by the publication of by organizational consultants like *In Search of Excellence* (Peters and Waterman 1982) and *Theory "Z"* (Ouchi, 1981). In Sweden they were followed up very quickly by Swedish

[2]See also Cressy and MacInnes (1980) and Coriot (1980).

publications in the same field. *Riv pyramiderna!* (Carlzon, 1985) is perhaps the most well-known title. One main topic was the so-called soft components in an organization. Values, norms, feelings and rituals are seen as much more important than the so-called hard components of the organization-like structures. Another important feature in the literature was the concentration on leadership and the emphasis on the leader as a person. The leader is no longer an administrator but a creator of values who is expected to be "elevating, mobilizing, inspiring, exalting, uplifting, exhorting, evangelizing" (Peters and Waterman 1982, p. 83). In many cases these books are an expression of the need for steering and control of an organization, and in certain cases it is very clear that they are "social techniques" for steering.

One important problem of the extensions so far has been the inability to analyze these control structures in combined forms.[3] Control structures are both coordination (through technical or organizational measures) and subjective consensus and these issues should therefore be treated together. In the discussion, these two parts are recognized but treated as separate spheres. Against this still dominating "dual" approach, the LOM Program claims that an organization's activity and efficiency is bound to the daily reproduction through their member's actions and we can only understand and change organizations if we take into consideration the whole person both as labor power and as an individual subject. The reference is to German critical theory, French post-structuralists and democratic theory (Gustavsen, 1985, Kalleberg, 1984). Yet, there is no explicit theoretical discussion. I believe that the most relevant theoretical development for this issue is Habermas's theory of communicative action. For this reason, I will discuss his contribution first.

Habermas Theory of Communicative Action

Habermas departs at an early stage in his theoretical development from two concepts which Hegel and Marx discussed at length and which had become central in the so-called Critical Theory of the Frankfurter School. Habermas breaks down Marx's concept of "sensuous human activity" into two components which are

---

[3]This difficulty is common to all attempts in this field, also for the Weberian approach of Hill (1981).

analytically distinguishable, even though they are interdependent in social practice: labor or purposive-rational action and social interaction or communicative action. This is developed most clearly in *Technology and Science as "Ideology"* (Habermas, 1968). By "labor" (work) he understands either instrumental or rational action. Instrumental action is governed by technical rules based on empirical knowledge. Rational action is governed by strategies based on analytical knowledge By "interaction" he understands communicative action or symbolic action which is governed by binding consensual norms which define reciprocal expectations about the behavior of acting subjects. These social norms are enforced through sanctions and their meaning is objectified in ordinary language communications. Both concepts are the core of different rationality systems and follow rationalization processes in society. "Work" is purposive-rational action which uses and controls objects. Its problem is uncertainty and it demands knowledge about "objective" causal relations. "Rationalization" in this case means an expansion of this form of action.

"Interaction" is communicative action intended to reach understanding between subjects. Its problem is disagreement which can be solved by dialogue or discourse. Dialogue allows a intersubjective consensus over meanings. Dialogue concerns ends and norms, and the term "rationalization" here means an expansion of communicative possibilities for understanding.

These two forms of action with their different rationalities are related to two different spheres of action, systems of purposive-rational action or "system" and systems of communicative understanding or *Lebenswelt*. The concept of *Lebenswelt* has its origin in Edmund Husserl's phenomenology and its refers to the area in everyday life which has always been there and which is taken for granted without question (Schütz and Luckmann 1975, pp 27ff). This *Lebenswelt* is not static. Conventional world views, theoretical interpretation of the world and practical, normative lines of actions are gradually liberated from mythical or metaphysical-religious content (Habermas 1981b, pp. 119f). Instead there will be more consequential forms of communicative consensus. Conventional world views, value systems, forms of action and institutions will be more open to augmentative criticism. In the words of Habermas (1981a, p. 455), a normatively prescribed consensus (*Einverständnis*) is being replaced by augmentative understanding (*Verständnis*).

The normative content will no longer be institutionalized in society, instead the formal structure of communication, which is the medium for understanding, will be formalized and institutionalized. But because there will be an increasing need for communicative

Bernd Hofmaier

understanding, the medium will undergo a differentiation of means of communication. Viewed in a historical perspective we can see the emergence of a process-oriented legal system, democratic forms of political systems of volition and institutionalized public sphere (see Habermas, 1962).

Even if *Lebenswelt* is basic, it cannot be understood without referring to the emergence and rationalization of functional sub-systems. When traditions are being dissolved, there is demand for change-over from normative social integration to functional system-integration (see Habermas, 1973, p. 13; 1981b, pp. 226f). Here Habermas seeks to integrate in this theory both the action-theoretical and the system-theoretical perspective In regarding the system-theoretical perspective, Habermas's theoretical reasoning is based on Parsons's theory of generalized media which he used in his famous four-function paradigm the so-called AGIL schema (Parsons et al., 1953). The communicative coordination of action is on the whole or partly replaced by structures and mechanism for purposive-rational action. Society is divided into different subsystems such as the economic system, the state, science, etc. These subsystems have developed as a result of the greater complexity of society and they are goal-rational structures. System integration is reached not by discourse, but through objectified, formalized steering media like money or power. These are independent of persons and quasimechanical. Money is the integrative medium for the market, and power the integrative medium for political and administrative institutions. Both media can be viewed as a kind of language which can be used for interaction without friction. The typical situation in which money functions as a medium of control or steering is that in which persons exchange goods for money or through money. Habermas is describing this situation as one where participants "pursue economic interests" and in doing so they seek to optimize the relations of expense and return "according to the generalized value of utility" (Habermas, 1981b, p. 395). The difference with interactions regulated by communicative understanding is that the latter offers the possibility of a "rationally motivated consensus", i.e., an agreement based on the convincing force of reason, while in the situation regulated by money, the exchange is motivated towards the "satisfaction of needs, not recognitions of claims of validity" (Habermas, 1981b, p. 398). Power functions in a parallel way. According to Habermas, power-mediated interaction implies in the standard situation that orders are being followed. The generalized value is effectiveness and efficiency of goal—attainment. As in the case of money, the possessor of power can use different sanctions to force other people into obedience, and both money and power are used strategically.⁴ They replace linguistic "communication" which also means they are replacing linguistic understanding and consensus. They are therefore contributing to the "uncoupling" of the subsystems from the *Lebenswelt*.

Does this mean that dialogue in working life is not possible? Habermas believes it is possible. But for this end, we have to combine ideal reciprocity with human praxis. He (and recently Ulrich) formulated this combination as the double *a priori* of the communication community (Habermas, 1973, p. 329; Ulrich, 1987, p. 286). The first one is an argumentation *a priori* which resembles the ideal communication community. The second one is an *a priori* of the real argumentation situation. In the junction of these two, which forms a kind of vague open space, we can strive to make the ideal real.

Habermas claims that if one is serious about establishing an exchange of arguments, e.g., establishing a dialogue in an effort to reach understanding, then one is also serious about this argumentation being meaningful. In other words, we are making a counterfactual presumption on an ideal speech situation. In this speech situation every factual consensus will be seen as a rational consensus. The core of the argumentation *a priori* is that people are augmentation subjects with whom reasonable understanding is possible in principle. The point is reciprocity. One whose intention it is to argue in a reasonable manner claims also that other people should respect his arguments when he acknowledges them as equal subjects. In the ideal communication situation this includes all human beings. Because one cannot rely on some objective principles for success in a discourse, criteria for the ideal communication structure need to be designed and operationalized.⁵ But even these criteria must be formed in a discourse process and cannot be deduced

---

⁴Parsons had originally suggested two more media of exchange: influence and value commitment. However, according to Habermas, these do not qualifying as steering media in the system sphere. Influence can be like power with strategic-instrumental orientation but it is different from power execution in the sense that influence is based on the use of language in an attempt to establish consensus. Here the same claims for validity, thruth and sincerity are raised, which means that peoples can accept or reject claims. Value commitment is linked to moral appeals and therefore also to language and consensus.

⁵Karl-Otto Apel takes this, form a slightly different approach, as a starting point for a communicative ethic: "sie verpflichtet alle, die durch den Sozialisations-prozess 'kommunikative Kompetenz' erworben haben, in jeder Angelegenheit, welche die Interessen (die virtuellen Ansprüche) Anderer berührt, eine Übereinkunft zwecks solidarischer Willensbildung anzustreben" (Apel, 1976, p. 426).

from some superior principle. This implies that an operationalization of dialogue criteria should be embedded in human praxis.

In the next section, we turn to the LOM Program. The criteria and organizational principles for this program came indeed out of a combination of such two *a priori*. First of all, there was a considerable learning experience from organizational praxis, as described in the next section.

Learning from Earlier Change Programs

Several Scandinavian programs heavily influenced the LOM Program, mainly through their shortcomings. The important programs in Scandinavia were the Norwegian Industrial Democracy Program and the following Swedish programs.

The Norwegian Industrial Democracy Program

The Norwegian Industrial Democracy Program started in 1962 with two phases of research, one concentrated on the experiences gained in formal systems of participation through representative arrangements (see Thorsrud and Emery, 1969). The second phase dealt with field experiments and sociotechnical changes.

The initiator of the program saw two fallacies in the most common models of organizational change. First, organizational experiments carried out under real industrial conditions are basically different from physical experiments. Secondly, if the experiments are to become part of a democratic process, they cannot be set up by specialists in a traditional way. Results cannot be "handed out to others who need to be democratized".

Therefore a then new strategy was developed, which can be described in nine different parts:

1. A joint national committee helped to define problem area and advised research and development plans.
2. The choice of experimental sites was made by the joint committee according to criteria suggested by researchers (type of technology, size, location, potential diffusion).
3. A search phase preceded each experiment (goals, problems, criteria to measure progress).
4. A local action committee was set up where managers, local union representatives, workers, staff, and researchers were represented.
5. Sociotechnical analyses were carried out in collaboration with the members of the action committee.
6. A program of change should be put into effect by the personnel of the departments involved in collaboration with the specialists and the action committee (redesign of jobs, systems of pay, systems of communication and control, etc.).

7. Stepwise evaluation of change should have to be agreed on and carried out according to predetermined criteria (joint union–management evaluation was essential).
8. Continued learning and organizational change were basic objectives of the experiments.
9. Diffusion of results was assumed to take place as a consequence of the evaluation and policy-making process. The national committee had major responsibility for this process of diffusion.

Four larger so-called field experiments were conducted at Christiania Spigerverk, a wire drawing industry, Husfors paper and pulp industry, the NOBÖ experiment in metal products industry, and the experiments at Norsk Hydro fertilizer. It is not necessary to go into detail here about the circumstances and development of these experiments. The first reports were published in 1969 (Thorsrud and Emergy, 1969).[6]

A highly structured plan was adopted, mainly to avoid misuse of experiments as new management tools or consultant techniques. But centrally controlled diffusion did not work. Instead, real diffusion took place in all sorts of unexpected ways. Another weakness was the researchers' role, which was too active and difficult to change later. Researchers were acting as motor in the change processes. Neither unions or management felt confident at an early stage of the project to give a free hand to all sorts of activities emerging from local developments. Those who were not directly involved were too inclined to consider the projects as pure, scientific experiments, and the results as something which could be copied. Concepts which were used by the researchers (as semi-autonomous groups) initially either remained specialist "tools", or they were considered obligatory even in cases where they did not apply to local requirements.

Another problem was the problem of encapsulation. Experiments in enterprises quickly became isolated and the expected learning effect never occurred. Critics are also pointing to a glamor effect for the first experiment groups, but the following groups had many difficulties. Several experiments stagnated because they did not lead to the necessary diffusion beyond the initial group or department involved.

A final weakness of the strategy was that it took too long to trigger the expected changes in the system of bargaining necessary to support continued organizational changes. There is also another important aspect to which we will return later. This concerns the role of the unions which needs to be redefined. Unions will need

---

[6]For a more detailed description see Gustavsen and Hunnius (1981).

to reconsider their functioning not only as political institutions but also as work organizations. For instance, if unions are bureaucratic and centrally controlled, they will not be effective in supporting diffusion of such forms of democratization as indicated.

Three Swedish programs

The Norwegian ID Program was one of the "learning arenas" for the initiators of the LOM Program. Other learning opportunities were provided by Swedish programs which the parties on the labor market started. The first one was a similar program, the so-called URAF Program. It was centrally organized and jointly controlled by a small committee consisting of representatives of management and unions. But only one element of the Norwegian sociotechnical approach was incorporated in the URAF Program, it was the concept of the semi-autonomous group. In general the goal of the URAF Program was to demonstrate the viability of new forms of work organization by means of enterprise experiments. It included about ten projects, all but one of which were located in industry. One was located in an insurance company. The program was finished formally in 1973. The emphasis on semi-autonomous groups turned out later to be an impediment for people working with change projects.

Another program was launched in the public sector. It was the so-called Delegation Program, which consisted of committees or delegations appointed by the government. The aim was the initiation of workplace democratization within state-owned enterprises, departments and authorities. The program started in 1968 and ended formally in 1975. Both programs ended in disputes between all parties involved, unions, employers and researchers.

There was a third program which had a certain impact on both development in industry and the ideological debate in the early seventies. This was the so-called New Factory Program which was conceived by the Swedish Employers Confederation (SAF) and guided by its technical department. The employers foresaw clearly the importance of production engineering as the key to enhancing Sweden's competitive position on the international market. Therefore they launched a series of about 500 local experiments, or rather development projects, which were guided by production engineering principles such as work flow, product shops, and others. There were some joint lines of concepts such as the basic principle of "coordinated independence in small systems", but usually they where very loosely coupled. A few "star cases" achieved international reputations, such as, for instance, the Volvo assembly plant in Kalmar. The main target of experiments in this program were not democratization but higher productivity and better working conditions, but even this was seen as part of a productivity strategy. Unlike the other programs, the New Factory Program was dominated by management and performed without the formal participation of unions; even researchers were not accepted in the experiments.

Two of these programs, the URAF Program and the Delegation Program, started as a joint effort of the parties on the labor market. Even if there was little enthusiasm from the employers side, the unions were very serious about changes in a more democratic direction, at least in the beginning. Unlike the New Factory Program, researchers were also engaged in both establishing and evaluating these programs. In a more detached perspective, these researchers obtained a more conspicuous role than both they and the parties involved expected to play. Most critical were representatives of the employers who objected to the "scientific" manner in which the experiments in the URAF and Delegation Programs were carried out. Extensive data collection and diagnosis followed by carefully monitored changes and evaluation were typical for these projects. In SAF's view, this was inconsistent with the normal change procedures in enterprises and therefore seen as slowing down the pace of the change process. The employers also felt that the ideas behind the URAF approach (e.g., group work) were too general and not sufficiently adapted to local circumstances. There also was criticism of the group concept used because it would be a threat to the first line supervisors, who are crucial for the employers if new forms of work organizations are to survive.

Even on the union side, similar objections could be heard, even if there were differences. The unions felt disappointed with the pace of change and there were serious attacks against researchers, especially from the white collar union (TCO). But there were also objections from the blue-collar union confederation (LO) which felt that the focus of the experiments was limited to issues on the shop floor and that management was against any expansion of its scope. Even in the Delegation Program there were some critical voices, although for obvious reasons the management was not as critical as in the private sector.

The URAF and the Delegation Programs faded away and the unions decided to take a step in a more legislative direction. For that, the prior change programs had created a favorable context. Within a few years, major portions of existing legislation were revised and a wide range of new labor legislation was adopted. A so-called Labor Law Committee was established, whose work culminated in the proposal for the Co-determination Act (MBL) and the Public Employment Act (LOA), both introduced in 1977.

The MBL has become the legal framework for industrial democracy in Sweden. The MBL prescribes that management should be a joint effort by capital and labor. Both sides should have equal rights to information. It stipulates that management has to consult unions before any decision on major changes in the company is taken (from reorganization to the introduction of new technology. Although management is not obliged to reach agreement, it has to allow time for unions to investigate the matter and negotiate at either local or central level before implementation.[7]

There where even several other laws of importance for organizational change projects which came into effect at this time. One was an "Act on Security of Employment" of 1977, the other was "The Work Environment Act" of 1978 which replaced an earlier workers' protection law and increased the rights of trade unions to help improve the working environment. The statutory rules of the Act have been supplemented by work environment agreements, which can also be seen as a kind of codetermination agreement. While these laws protected the worker and increased his say, further negotiations placed these legal instruments squarely into a market context. After considerable conflict and delay, the "Agreement on Efficiency and Participation" (the Development Agreement or UVA with Swedish abbreviations) was signed between the Employers Federation (SAF), the Swedish Trade Union Confederation (LO), and the Federation of the Salaried Employees Union (PTK) in 1982. The agreement starts out from the general premise of mutual understanding of the need for efficiency, profitability, and competitiveness in enterprise, this being a requirement for employment opportunities, job security and development at work. The UVA includes clauses concerning the goals and direction of joint development, forms of codetermination, the role of local agreements in small firms, information to members of the local union during working hours, employee consultants and the access of researchers to enterprises. It is a framework law and contains very little on how various issues should be treated.

This legal framework is now the base for change efforts of both technical and organizational issues, also in change projects not organized through the LOM Program. But there are several problems in using these. One has to do with two different principles which

---

[7]MBL gives the unions priority rights in interpreting agreements in some cases. By law, two local union-based directors (and two deputies) have the right to belong to the board of most private companies which employ at least twenty-five people.

are underlying at least two of the laws/agreements. MBL is aimed to promote employees' influence through providing information and traditional negotiations. The idea with this law was that it should be followed by agreements on the branch and local level and end in local forms for codetermination. This was only partly the case. The "Development Agreement" can be seen as a step in the direction of a joint understanding about development. The problem is to combine the two principles of negotiations and development.

The LOM Program

Although the legal development created a favorable context for dialogue, the experience of the prior programs clearly showed that it was wrong to depend on the idea that in a favorable context solutions based on dialogue would spread more or less by themselves. Experiments were always isolated and dependent on individual researchers or dependent on so-called souls of fire (Phillips, 1989). Even if there was support in one organization and the local union supported the experiments, there was no structure for support in a more general sense. Central unions sometimes were consistently positive and enthusiastic, central employer associations did not consistently trust local initiatives. Researchers or consultants who needed expert help in certain fields had no network of fellow researchers to rely on. And when they left and other researchers from the outside came into an organization, the whole process of adaptation and trial and error process started again. Learning from these negative experiences, the core of the LOM Program was developed to provide a much more stable dialogue interaction. Of course, the dialogue should be embedded in the political and cultural reality of working life, but there had to be a concrete context for this "democratic dialogue," as Gustavsen, one of the major driving forces behind the programs development, pointed out (Gustavsen, 1987). First of all, we need criteria for dialogue that clearly connect to the practical conditions of working life and to the democratic system. Second, arenas for the dialogue should be provided in such a way that power consideration entered as little as possible. Third, the basic unit of change efforts should not be an isolated enterprise but a network of enterprises. Fourth, there should be an infrastructure for the routine communication among the various parties. Let me briefly go into each of these points.

Criteria

The following criteria are used in the LOM Program. They emanated from theoretical discussions, practical conditions in working life and demands in a change process (Gustavsen, 1987, 1988).

1. The dialogue is a process of exchange: points and arguments moving between the participants.
2. All concerned must have the possibility of participating.
3. Possibility for participation is, however, not enough: everybody should also be active in the discourse.
4. At the outset, all participants are equal.
5. Work experience is the foundation for participation.
   This criterion is a modification with respect to Habermas, and the reason is to "strengthen the role of work in democratic dialogue" (Gustavsen, 1985).
6. At least some of the experiences which the participant has when entering the dialogue must be considered legitimate.
7. It must be possible for everybody to develop an adequate understanding of the issue at stake.
8. All arguments which pertain to the issues under discussion are legitimate. No argument should be rejected on the grounds that it emerges from an illegitimate source.
9. The points, arguments, etc., which are to enter the dialogue must be made by a participating actor. Nobody can participate "on paper".
10. Each participant must accept that other participants can have better arguments.
11. The participants should be able to tolerate an increasing degree of difference of opinion.
12. The dialogue must continuously produce agreements which can provide platforms for practical actions.

This last point establishes a connection to praxis and to the democratic system. It does not contradict no. 11, because "the major strength of a democratic system compared with all others is that it has the benefit of drawing upon a broad range of opinions and ideas which inform practice" (Gustavsen, 1988, p. 13). Criterion no. 12 is important because it is directly connected to practical change. Without a moment of action the whole dialogue would be more of a play than a serious attempt to be the driving force in change projects.

Arenas

Normally, power—or authority—is executed through the organizational line with some organs where employees are represented. Influence is usually executed in minor informal groups like projects groups, groups where managers and experts and others are temporarily working together, or through informal ties. Communicative understanding or a real dialogue can usually only be found in certain strata of the organization, as among groups where members share the same background assumptions, experiences and culture and with little status or formal subordination (see Lysgaard's theory about the "workers collectivity", Lysgaard, 1967; see also Hofmaier, 1980). In the LOM projects, the idea is to establish arenas where this kind of dialogue can be executed. When such a dialogue is more permanently established, existing locales or "meeting places" can be used even if they sometimes have to be transformed into a more adequate forum. In the starting phase of LOM projects, an example of such arenas are search or start conferences, which can be seen as an operationalization of the principles for dialogue. At the same time they function as learning situations for participants in the projects.[8]

A "start conference" has several steps. The LOM Program is usually concerned with inviting a selection of personnel and managers from four companies of a branch to join such a series of conferences. The first is the starting point for a change program; the following conferences are seen as meetings where experiences can be discussed and where the individual enterprises can learn from each other. As such they are also the main component in the network structure of the LOM Program.

The conference is usually designed for small groups with group discussion and with plenary sessions playing an important part. They are temporary or casual arrangements, and therefore usually arranged in meeting places outside the enterprises. The duration is usually between one and two days. The groups normally consist of a vertical slice of the organization with line management at different levels, workers and representatives of staff and unions. Four topics are discussed over the period. The first session is concerned with the vision of the future of the firm or of the workplace for the next five years. This session is normally comprised of homogenous groups which means that people with the same characteristics (men or women, management, workers, etc.) are discussing this topic. The group discussions, arguments and opinions which have been discussed in the different groups are then presented in plenum. The second topic is about problems which are likely to be encountered in trying to realize the vision. Here discussions are made in groups consisting of vertical slices of an organization. If there are several organizations, the groups can also be formed diagonally, by mixing functions from different organizations. Through this arrangement one can avoid situations where the traditional subordination in organizations will hinder an open and frank discussion. The results are also presented in plenum. The third topic is about the ideas and suggestions of how to overcome these problems. Even here the

[8]Conferences of this type were first created at the end of the sixties at the Tavistock Institute in London and have since been developed by researchers and consultants in change projects in Norway, Canada, Australia and other countries (see Gustavsen and Engelstad, 1985; Emergy, 1982; Wright and Morley, 1989).

groups are mixed as in the earlier session, but in different groups, and the results are again presented in plenum. The fourth session is about the concrete work of participants back in their organizations. They should define a plan on how to proceed and how to implement some of the ideas they met at the conference, or how they will work with their own ideas. The groups in this session are composed of people from the same organization. After all, they are expected to work jointly when back in their organizations.

The real work to establish a change project takes place after the conference in the enterprise, where the agenda set by the initial conference is further refined and anchored in the organization. The likelihood that this will happen is much enhanced through the fact that whole networks of enterprises are involved in one change project.

Networks

As the idea of so-called "star cases" had proven to be inadequate, the strategy conceived by the LOM Program (especially Gustavsen, 1985) was that the basic unit for change efforts should not be a single enterprise but a cluster of four or more enterprises. Usually they would be located in a certain geographical area and cut across industrial boundaries.

Today, a total of forty-six LOM projects are in progress in the private sector. The range is from manufacturing (12 projects), hotel and restaurants (10), retail (8), process industries (4), paper and pulp (4), banks and insurance (4), graphical industries (3), to timber industries (1). Some of them are located close to each other in one region (as hotel and restaurants, graphical industries, etc.), others are spread over the country, like the paper and pulp industry projects. Besides these, there are also twenty projects in the public sector, mostly in regional authorities, police and municipalities (4 each), hospitals (3), day care (2), postal services (2) and colleges (1).

The above-mentioned conference methodology is broadly applied as a linking mechanism throughout the program. Start conferences with clusters of four enterprises are arranged, followed by conferences where experiences can be diffused. But also conferences with local and regional participants or participants from other branches are arranged. A cluster of four as a starting point was chosen in a pragmatic way, but there is an effort to go beyond this form of cluster and regional networks to create broader systems of links and relationships. An example is the development of a social-ecological approach for creating change in organizations which is seen by some researchers as the basic model for further industrial and democratic development (Van Beinum, 1990).

Infrastructure

Part of the LOM strategy was to create an infrastructure for support. This was also the reason for choosing different clusters of four enterprises. At the practical level the so-called branch committees which were established together with the Development Agreement (UVA) were the basis for the discussions with the companies. They consist of representatives of the parties in the labor market in a specific sector who usually have a good knowledge of circumstances in the particular branch. They usually also take part in the first start conferences and have the ability to spread ideas and results to other organizations.

In regional clusters, organizations other than enterprises are usually part of this network. Here we can find institutions like health institutions for enterprises, but also the regional branches of unions and interest organizations. When there is a regional university, its departments are normally part of this structure.

All the research work in the LOM Program today is organized in a network which consists of forty-eight researchers representing different disciplines, universities, regions and different background experiences. Many of them are part of an interdisciplinary group which often has a local university as its base. Several academic fields are represented in the groups, with an equal share for economists, psychologists, sociologists, technical engineers and others. The LOM Program also organizes joint seminars, conferences and other activities as a doctoral course for nearly sixty researchers from all over the country. This program will continue even in the years after the formal LOM Program has ended.

Conclusion

There are many problems and open questions left concerning the LOM Program. But it is instructive to see where the direction of development is going: into more rather than less dialogue, including the basic understanding that the entire economy is operating in a market economy. And although this development has been going on for quite some time in Sweden, I have attempted to show that this direction is by no means just a traditional Swedish way of doing things. It is based on theoretical insight and a great wealth of learning from experience.

130   *Bernd Hofmaier*

References

Apel, K. O. (1976) *Transformation der Philosophie*, Band 2. Frankfurt/Main: Suhrkamp.

Braverman, H. (1974) *Labor and Monopoly Capital. The Degradation of Work in the Twentieth Century.* New York: Monthly Review Press.

Burawoy, M. (1979) *Manufacturing Consent: Changes in the Labor Process Under Monopoly Capitalism.* Chicago: University of Chicago Press.

Carlzon, J. (1985) *Riv pyramiderna!* Stockholm: Bonniers.

Coriot, B. (1980) The restructuring of the assembly line: a new economy of time and control. *Capital and Class*, 11, 34–43.

Cressey, P. and MacInnes, J. (1980) Industrial democracy and the control of labor. *Capital and Class*, 11, 5–33.

Edwards, R. (1979) *Contested Terrain: The Transformation of the Workplace in the Twentieth Century*, London: Heineman.

Emery, M. (1982) *Searching: for New Directions, in New Ways, for New Times.* Canberra: CCE, Australian National University.

Emery, M. (ed.) (1989) *Participative Design for Participative Democracy.* Canberra: CCE, Australian National University.

Friedman, A. (1977) *Industry and Labour: Class Struggle at Work and Monopoly Capitalism.* London: Macmillan Press.

Gustavsen, B. (1985) Workplace reform and democratic dialogue. *Economic and Industrial Democracy*, 16(5), 461–479.

Gustavsen, B. (1987) Reformer på arbetsplatser och demokratisk dialog. In *Arbetets rationaliteter*, edited by Odhnoff, Von Otter. Stockholm: Swedish Centre for Working Life.

Gustavsen, B. (1988) *Creating Broad Changes in Working Life—The LOM Programme.* Toronto: Ontario Quality of Working Life Centre.

Gustavsen, B. and Hunnius, G. (1981) *New Patterns of Work Reform: the Case of Norway.* Oslo: Universitetsforlaget.

Gustavsen, B. and Engelstad, P. (1985) The design of conferences and the evolving role of democratic dialogue in changing work life. *Human Relations*, 39(2), 101–116.

Habermas, J. (1962) *Strukturwandel der Öffentlichkeit.* Neuwied: Luchterhand.

Habermas, J. (1968) *Technik und Wissenschaft als 'Ideologie'.* Frankfurt/Main: Suhrkamp.

Habermas, J. (1973) *Erkenntnis and Interesse.* Frankfurt/Main: Suhrkamp.

Habermas, J. (1981a) *Theorie des kommunikativen Handelns. Band 1 Handlungsrationalität und gesellschaftliche Rationalisierung.* Frankfurt/Main: Suhrkamp.

Habermas, J. (1981b) *Theorie des kommunikativen Handelns. Band 2 Zur Kritik der funktionalistischen Vernuft.* Frankfurt/Main: Suhrkamp.

Hill, S. (1981) *Competition and Control at Work.* London: Heineman.

Hofmaier, B. (1980) *Permanent tillfällighet.* Göteborg: University of Gothenburg, Department of Sociology.

Kalleberg, R. (1984) Demokratisering av foretak. In *Demokrati og demokratisering*, pp. 265–404, edited by Hagtved, Lafferty. Oslo: Universitetsforlaget.

Lysgaard, S. (1967). *Arbeiderkollektivet.* Oslo: Universitetsforlaget.

Marx, K. (1976). *Capital*, Vol. 1. Harmondsworth: Penguin.

Ouchi, W. G. (1981) *Theory "Z": How American Business Can Meet the Japanese Challenge.* Reading, MA: Addison-Wesley.

Parsons, T., Bales, R. F. and Shils, E. A. (1953) Working paper in the Theory of Action. Glencoe, IL: Free Press.

Peters, T. and Waterman, R. Jr. (1982) *In Search of Excellence*. New York: Harper and Row.

Phillips, Å. (1989) *Eldsjälar*. Stockholm: Stockholm School of Economics.

Robbins, S. P. (1987) *Organization Theory. Structure, Design and Applications*. Englewood Cliffs, NJ: Prentice-Hall.

Schütz, A. and Luckmann, T. (1975) *Strukturen der Lebenswelt*. Neuwied: Luchterhand.

Thorsrud, E. and Emery, F. (1969) *Democracy at Work*. Leiden: Nijhoff.

Ulrich, P. (1987) *Transformation der ökonomischen Vernuft. Fortschrittsperspektiven der modernen Industriegesellschaft*. Bern: Haupt.

Van Beinum, H. (1990) Observations on the development of a new organizational paradigm. Unpublished paper. Stockholm: Swedish Centre for Working Life.

Wright, S. and Morley, D. (eds.) (1989) *Learning Works: Searching for Organizational Futures*. Toronto: York University, Faculty of Environmental Studies.

Organizational Innovation as a Social Construction: Managing Meaning in Multiple Realities

Introduction

Organizational innovation requires the understanding of, and the dealing with, multiple realities: the perceptions of the existing reality and the emerging new reality of the different parties involved. A new idea has to be introduced and implemented through balancing diversity and conflict, on the one hand, and common directedness and joint action, on the other. Dealing with discontinuous change is an important challenge for most organizations, and expectations of a quick-fix solution are very much alive. Among organization theorists, there is also disagreement about the appropriateness of a soft versus a hard approach to "turnarounds" (Poole, Gioia and Gray, 1990; Dunphy, 1988). Multiplicity of perspectives on social events is considered to be the very nature of organizational innovations. Organizational innovation is defined here as the organizational behavior process components that underlie product market, technological process and management innovations. This will be illustrated by a case study on a management innovation: the introduction of the "team concept" in a production facility.

This article uses *a social constructionist approach* to understand organizational behavior and, in particular, innovations in organizations (Gergen, 1978). The constructionist paradigm assumes that an organization is not a given social reality that only has to be discovered by means of appropriate instruments and methodologies. An organization is conceived as being continuously in-the-making (Weick, 1979). It is the result of an ongoing negotiation process among the parties involved, all using their own perspectives to frame organizational events. Organizational innovation can be very well understood as being an organization-in-the-making. The

[1]University of Leuven Center for Organization and Personnel Psychology.

133

organizational negotiation aims to achieve a new domain of minimum "shared meaning" necessary to allow for effective common action. The existing dominant social reality and the emerging innovative social reality continuously strive to influence the definition of what the future common reality is going to be. By not using the noun "organization" but the verb "organizing", K. Weick emphasizes the dynamic nature of the interaction process. This approach has been used by several authors in the study of organizational behavior (Pondy, Frost, Morgan and Dandridge, 1983). But empirical research is still scarce (Brown and Hosking, 1986) because appropriate methodologies need to be developed for the different applications.

A four-step approach will be used to illustrate analysis and behavior in the unfolding innovation effort. This approach is intended to provide an in-depth insight into what organizational innovation really means to those involved. It must also make it possible to have a more appropriate view of the ongoing dynamics, so that management or consulting efforts can better deal with the issues at stake.

The first question is about the *composition of the cognitive maps* developed by the different parties. Each party has his or her own image of the situation. The second question concerns *the configuration of the cognitive maps*. How do the cognitive and causal maps relate to each other and what dynamics characterize these relationships? Third, a step for *dereifying the organization* is required, a shift from "this is the organization", being a "real thing", towards "this is my picture of the social events at hand". Dereification is necessary to allow change to be considered seriously. Finally, *coping strategies* to deal with the diversity will emerge from the configuration of dominant logics and new emerging logics in the organization. The critical question here is to what extent management can steer action strategies while still allowing for effective and lasting innovative outcomes.

The necessary conditions that inhibit organizational innovation have been described in previous studies on innovation: lack of adequate internal and external communication processes, lack of interdisciplinary teamwork, bureaucratization, a culture of "standard operating procedures", inappropriate reward systems and inappropriate attitudes of managerial personnel. The process approach does not intend to extend this list of factors determining the innovation, but rather to describe and articulate the characteristics of the process itself. The development towards shared meaning, the action strategies to deal with diversity, and the resulting learning effects will be the object of this study. We will study not so much the "variables" that can be identified and related to each other, but the evolution of the process itself. We know from previous studies that the quality of the communication among the parties is crucial (Rothwell,1977). In using a "process" approach, we take the quality of the dialogue among the parties as a critical issue. This quality will be understood as emerging from the configuration and dynamics of different meanings among the parties involved in the process.

A Social Constructionist Paradigm

How can we think and theorize about organizations when an essential element is the multiplicity of perspectives taken by those involved? Berger and Luckman (1967) formulated the constructivist paradigm in sociology, and Gergen (1978) provided the most explicit phrasing of a social psychological problem in constructionist terms. Weick (1979) elaborated this paradigm for the social construction process in an organization. Making meaning always starts from some enactment or behavior or exchange that is produced and retrospectively understood. A certain selection process "brackets" a view of the social events and is retained in the memory. The more retention guides the process, the more past experiences shape the selection process and the more the enactment is framed in previously known terms. Enactment is stimulated or recreated by ecological change or change in the environment. By being in a certain situation or behaving in a specific way, one enacts or implements certain aspects of the situation. Being at the top or at the bottom of an organization gives a completely different enactment followed by specific selection and retention processes.

Weick supposes a "natural world" underlying the ecological change. For Gergen and many other social constructionists, there is no "given outside reality". There is only the construction of meanings by the participants as a source for the social negotiation process to agree upon shared meanings and minimal common action (Donnellon, Gray and Bougon, 1986). Morgan (1986) is another source of inspiration, since he emphasizes the imaging of the organizational participant and observer and the "reading" of the cognitive maps. The second step in our approach here is an illustration of that process.

The behavioral meaning cycle of Weick also underlies our four-step approach to meaning management. The cognitive maps can be studied by describing the retention content. Cognitive maps are the result of a selection process leading to a configuration of meaning among the parties. Action strategies emerge from cognitive maps and lead back to the creation of new selection and retention. Dereification is made possible by introducing ecological change.

The author of this article played both the roles of researcher and consultant in this case study. In a social constructionist perspective, one can only participate in a social system by being another party with a specific perspective and interest: insight into the configuration of the multiple realities and facilitating the process of management's effort towards shared meaning. The role of researcher/consultant can be described as a "process" role, collecting cognitive map data, feeding it back, and facilitating the emerging dialogue, mainly from a learning perspective. It is not a traditional observer role in the anthropological tradition. It is a participant observer role with the participation being of a facilitating kind.

Case Study: Introduction of the Team-unit Concept in Extruco

Extruco is a Belgian subsidiary of an American multinational company that produces food packaging with special characteristics and in different forms. It employs about 600 people, 350 of whom are blue-collar workers in a continuous shift system. There are two production departments: one producing flat products and the other hollow products. They are supported by service departments: finance and administration, human resources, safety and environment, material management, technical services, quality control, and customer services. Each department is led by a manager assisted by specialists and technical and administrative employees. The general manager of this plant is also responsible for other European activities in Germany and the Netherlands. Each manager also reports to world headquarters in the USA for the long-term policy in his functional domain.

The firm leads the market and has only a few smaller competitors. The extrusion technology is protected by patents. The Belgian plant intends to position itself within the larger company as a very modern and advanced production facility. Therefore, the strategy was to cut delivery times, to demonstrate high flexibility towards the market, and to produce high quality, but certainly not to engage in price competition. An important element of this strategy was optimization of the production process. The general manager mainly stressed cost reduction, but the other "stake holders" emphasized quality, safety, a favorable social climate, involvement of employees and favorable organizational and general working conditions, such as a rewarding and flexible shift system.

This case study will concentrate on the diversity of meanings

among the different parties, how these differences are experienced
and handled by those involved, and especially by the managerial
staff. Within this general strategy of optimization of the production
process, the introduction of the "team-unit" concept in the production department will be the focus of this analysis.

The production manager of Department A came in contact with
this concept in the USA. He visited several sites where this approach
was being used and became a strong protagonist of it to improve the
internal functioning of the production departments. Briefly defined,
the "team-unit" concept is the creation of multifunctional semi-
autonomous work groups, each producing a specific, identifiable
product. Planning and quality control functions are integrated in
the group task, and people from the staff and service departments
are assigned to specific groups and spend a considerable amount of
time (6%) on structured work consultation.

In 1986 a "quality improvement process" was initiated with
several training sessions and a system to detect and correct errors.
A "zero defect day" officially launched the quality improvement
process. A survey of the personnel later on indicated that the
employees saw little opportunity for responsibility, that they considered the work as not challenging, and that they experienced very little
involvement in general. The introduction of the team-unit concept
(TC further on) was intended to respond to this problem. Production
Manager A and staff people developed a plan for the composition,
tasks, organization and introduction schedule of these self-managing
team units. The purpose was to increase the number of technically
trained people and to reduce the number of supervisory personnel
and operators. In the TC, production teams are formed under the
guidance of a "team leader" around an indentifiable product. The
team members perform interchangeable tasks at work stations for a
particular product. These tasks included running the machinery to
make the product, switching to other products, transport of goods,
routine maintenance, executing quality checks, evaluating results,
and making agreements about improvements during the 25-minute
overlap between the work shifts. The "support" or "service"
groups had a heterogeneous composition of technicians, planners,
laboratory workers, quality specialists, and material handlers. The
production teams worked in a new five-shift system.

The new teams started on March 1, 1988. A few months after the
introduction, four of the nine team leaders were considered not to
be functioning adequately in their new role. The number of team
leaders was reduced to five. The overlapping consultation added
significant cost to the product, and results were not emerging.
The operators in the TC group were envied by the workers in

other departments, as they had a good time schedule and a special shift bonus.

At the end of 1988, an interim evaluation by the personnel department indicated that the high expectations were not being met. Interviews with key persons revealed very diverse experiences of the change effort. According to management, it was too slow and too costly. The team leaders did not live up to their task and did not feel they were supported sufficiently by the management. The time for consultation was experienced as not being used efficiently, and the service departments did not know how to deal with the new groups, the so-called "teams".

From meetings with the general manager, interviews with middle management, and a two-day management team meeting, a very large diversity of meanings emerged, which were attributed to the changes occurring in the organization. This was the context for a more extensive inquiry among middle and lower management. These data were fed back to several groups of supervisory personnel during two-day seminars to answer the question with them: where are we coming from, what do we see ourselves doing now, and where do we go from here? Further on, in this paper, we will describe the range of meanings throughout the production department during the fall of 1989 and how this diversity was handled.

At the end of 1989, role clarifications were being made on all levels. An internal "change manager" was appointed for coaching the team leaders and for following up on the total change process. A system and measurement group was installed. Special attention was given to clear and congruent communication between the top and the operators and between the production and service groups. A concept was developed to frame and shape measurement, follow-up and improvement activities in all groups. A new all-organization meeting was planned to anchor the new steps. The concept of "craftsmanship for everyone in every job" was a new way of connecting the effort of the employees with the quality and flexibility strategy of management.

Unfolding the Cognitive Maps of the Stakeholders

In this situation of organizational innovation, the existence of multiple realities could clearly be observed among the important stakeholders involved in the change process. At the end of 1988, eight months after the first introduction of the TC, an extended "steering committee" of representatives of staff and managers from all levels and departments was asked to assess the progress of the project. The General Manager and the Human Resource Manager did not participate in the meeting. This probably enhanced the very open and non-evaluational expression of ideas. In answer to the question, "What have we been doing up to now?", a broad variety of ideas was expressed. Very different names were used to characterize the change process they all were involved in:

> *Quality Manager*: "This is in the first place a quality improvement program to respond to the demands of the clients."
> *Personnel Officer*: "TC is an irreversible step in the creation of involvement of the operators."
> *Technical Manager*: "This is in fact a cultural change program. Therefore, resistance to change is understandable."
> *A Supervisor*: "Too much energy has been invested in selling the program to the operators."
> *Administration Manager*: "We have been naive and too socially oriented. The operators benefit from the new shiftwork system, but they don't increase their personal initiative and involvement."
> *A Team Leader*: "Most operators are not interested in having more responsibility and prefer to be passive."
> *Production Manager B*: "There is a double message 'stop' and 'go' at the same time in the organization."
> *Materials Manager*: "In fact top management is after a quick-fix solution."
> *Quality Manager*: "We have to increase our knowledge of the process, do more measuring, and stick to those facts".
> *Technical Manager*: "It has never been clear in this organization where we are going."
> *Quality Manager*: "There are at least three different change processes going on."
> *Administration Manager:* "The main problem is that management tried to buy into the operators; it was a demand from the top. Also the other departments want a five-shift system but not the disadvantages of it."
> *A Supervisor*: "The core is a skill problem. Up-grading the people to team leaders will not succeed. We reached the limit of their competence."
> *Technical Manager*: "The service groups don't see their role in relation to the production teams. The information does not come through."
>
> Reacting to the question "What is the highest priority action now to make any progress?", the response was nearly unanimous: "It is important to reduce all change efforts to the lowest common denominator. We are going different directions now and neutralize each other's efforts." But this common definition of the desired future is immediately followed by very divergent action proposals: "We finally have to implement the Crosby system we have been teaching", said the Quality Manager. "We don't have adequate measurements" was the position of the Materials Manager. "There is an overemphasis of the team-unit concept as if it were the solution for everything", said a Production Manager, who was still working in the former shift system. "We lose sight of the costs", warned the Financial Manager.

After a report to the General Manager, an appointment was made between the consultant and the management team to work on three levels to deal with the equivocality of the situation. A change manager would be appointed to organize the coaching of team leaders and production teams, a two-day seminar would be conducted with the whole group of middle and lower management, and the management team would start this process with a two-day off-site meeting. The purpose was to pick up the thread of the development and to agree on attainable steps towards the goal for the future. After the first management team meeting, the general conclusion was: "The question is not whether we have to change and in what general direction, but *how* we should change and at what pace.'

A Kaleidoscope of Meanings: Cognitive Maps

The first step in the "management of meaning" process is the exploration and the reading of the cognitive maps of all the significant parties involved. As this case very clearly illustrates, at this moment in the life of the organization, there was a lot of diversity of meaning. The organization-in-the-making can be observed at a moment of internal activity. The organizational innovation disrupted the existing configuration of shared and opposed meanings and all existing diversity was expressed.

One way to represent the diversity of the described situation is to construct cognitive maps for the parties involved. In several disciplines, there is a growing interest in knowledge structures. Walsh (1989) gives a list of about fifty terms used to describe a specific knowledge structure in an organization. "Cognitive map" is one of those concepts to describe the constellation of meanings for a person or a group. The sense-making paradigm refers to meaning as a way to frame similarities and differences (Weick and Bougon, 1986). In previous research, four frames have proven useful in this task: content frames, relational frames, procedural-structural frames, and political frames. Figure 1 gives a schematic representation of the kaleidoscope of frames of meaning.

Each party will use a set of frames to attribute meaning to social events. The change situation in Extruco was constructed in very different ways by the parties involved using different frames. The *content* frame allows the actor to define a situation as a technical or economic problem. The *relational* frame refers to how each party perceives the relation or change in relation to the others involved. The *procedural* frame concerns the extent to which the approach to the task at hand is structured and what kind of structures or rules are used. The *interest* frame mainly indicates how the party using this frame perceives the distribution of the rewards resulting from the situation or the change.

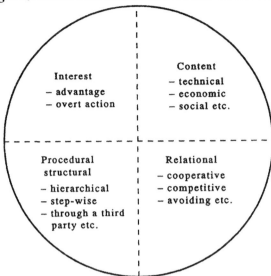

FIG. 1. Kaleidoscope of frames of meaning.

The metaphor of the kaleidoscope is introduced here to characterize the specificities of the process of sense making. This process is idiosyncratic, dynamic, self-evident, and perspectivistic for a particular party. For children before the days of the computer, a kaleidoscope was a source of excitement and astonishment. Pieces of colored glass in a tube with mirrors were randomly ordered to form very symmetrical and obvious configurations. Each movement or turn of the kaleidoscope gave a new and an equally obvious but totally different configuration. The parts and the combination rules are the same, but the result is new for each viewer. Donald Schön (1979) talks about a generative metaphor, which also creates an image about how to handle the situation given a particular image. "Turning the kaleidoscope" allows other perspectives and recognizes the unique and dynamic character of each perspective.

In this case study, it is not difficult to identify the main actors: the general management, the operators, the team leaders, and middle management.[2] Their respective cognitive maps were also not difficult to detect:

The *general manager* conceived the change program mainly as an improvement of the efficiency of the production process. Profit was

[2]The service departments also had a somewhat distinctive cognitive map, but they did not belong to the important parties.

how much "sales" exceeded "costs" $(P = S - C)$. The production department could lower the costs. This was an expression of his content and interest frame. The relation frame was more subtle: he felt it necessary to emphasize this again and again, and the operators were expected to live up to his expectations. The procedural aspects were not very explicit, but he did expect plantwide application of TC.

The cognitive map of *the operators* was very different. They saw their interest primarily in the change program because it gave them an improved shift and bonus system. The content of the project was considered to be just another management technique to get things done. Most of the operators filled the relational frame with the traditional hierarchical view of leadership, although some did have positive expectations about work consultation in the production teams.

The cognitive map of the *team leaders* was very conflictual. They saw the TC as a top-down initiative. A change in their role was at the core of the TC project. From an authoritarian foreman, they had to become an "educator" or a "guide". All of them experienced this as a problem. The relational frame was very crucial for them. The work consultation sessions required new social skills, and the limited training they received was perceived as inadequate. Their big concern was: "How can we discipline people?" because discipline was considered to be the most important lever for getting things done. The reduction of the number of team leaders caused serious damage to relations with higher management. Regarding the content frame, they considered change to be one element of the many new management techniques related to quality and flexibility. The structural aspects were also evaluated negatively: the change came too fast, and the teams were much too large. Their interest frame concerned the additional work they got and also the special attention from management and other groups.

Another cognitive map prevailed among *middle management*, and it was shared by the *quality department and human resource department*. Those directly related to Department A, where the TC was first introduced, felt very strongly involved. Staff people of Department F, where TC was going to be introduced later on, wanted the advantages of the new approach but certainly tried to avoid the problems encountered in Department A. TC was considered to be a new management method and a challenge for organizational improvement. They complained about not having enough resources and asked for more training and guidance during the change process. Their relational frame was "being put under pressure to succeed and to show their competencies". Procedurewise, they had a lot of concern about the pressure for a quick introduction by top management. They felt it in their personal interest to succeed and as a challenge to their professional competency.

Thus, as can be seen, each party had a specific frame as first priority and added to this a specific constellation of background frames. But what did this indicate? Weick and especially Bougon (1986) extended the thinking about cognitive maps on this point to include cognition about causal chains.

Building Causal Maps

Building causal chains involves looking into the dynamic structure of a cognitive map and deriving pictures about supposed causal links. Behavioral charting, as we can call this approach, helps to obtain insight into the dynamics at stake during change efforts. Figure 2 depicts a causal map for the cognitive structure of the general manager and some staff people. The observation of not reaching the expected outcome is diagnosed in a very different way and is embedded in a different causal chain. The steering mechanism can be called the governing logic within a party. This dominant logic is a combination of the cognitive style of the actor, the type of structure one is relying on, and a set of values supporting this logic (Prahalad and Bettis, 1986). Extruco was mainly steered by an economic logic. The introduction and the implementation of TC asked for an organizational logic. These logics, the dominant logic of the organization and the innovation

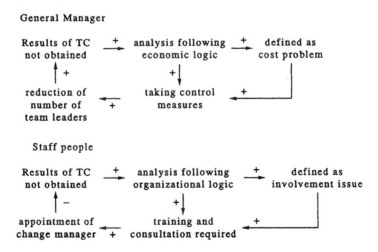

FIG. 2. Causal maps of general management and staff members.

logic of the TC system conflict with each other. The organizational task is precisely to work on this tension, which can be handled in various ways. What is important is to diagnose the different paths followed and to watch the results, carefully. The capacity to innovate for this organization depended largely on the way the tension between the dominant and the innovation logic was handled. The social construction process of the organization can be made visible using cognitive and causal maps, and the main threats and opportunities can be identified. For this purpose, it is useful to look at the relationship between cognitive and causal maps, i.e., at configurations of meaning (Bouwen et al., 1988).

The Configuration of the Cognitive Maps

The relation, framed and experienced among the parties, and consequentially also the power relationship influences the course of the negotiation process (Smircich and Morgan, 1982). Following Weick (1979), one can characterize the relationships among the cognitive maps as "loose" or "tight coupling".[3] A tight coupling, which is not allowing for diversity, can lead towards stagnation (Van Dijk, 1989). Polarization can create this condition. Complete overlap of cognitive maps can also be an indication of stagnation, making it very difficult to be in contact with the changing environment. The retention process is then completely dominating the selection and enactment process.

In Extruco, only the service department took some distance from the sense making process. All the other parties were involved in some way. General management polarized the sense-making process by harsh decisions and there was a danger for the elimination of other meanings by the management's emphasis on the cost related aspects. In turn, team leaders and operators have a polarized view *vis-à-vis* the management. These configurations can be called the organizational "reality".

Dereification from "Organization" to "Organizing"

In the beginning of this paper, we already referred to Weick's emphasis on "organizing" as opposed to "organization". It is a difference in view that is very important to a change process. An important step in such a process is the "dereification" of a

---

[3]Weick uses the concept of coupling to describe clusters within a collective structure, whereas here the concept is used to describe relationships between cognitive and causal maps.

more or less stagnated situation. Dereification here means that the parties switch their perception of the organization from a realistic to a cognitive perspective: they change their position from "this organization is functioning this way" to "our perspective or our image of the social events is like this". This dereification is facilitated by a variation in the context, which leads to new images of the social reality (Van Dijk, 1989). In our present case, context variation was achieved by inviting in outsiders, by meetings of the steering committee, and by the organization of the two-day workshop. Another important stimulus for dereification was the experience of a gap between the original concept of the TC project and the experience of the operators, the team leaders and supervisors after a few months. Especially among the staff, there was a "gap experience" or a growing awareness that the intended consequences were not emerging. A superficially shared meaning was broken, or, more correctly, was revealed after a short time. Managing the *diversity* of meaning is thus an important task for the leadership in organizational innovation processes.

Action Strategies to cope with Diversity of Meaning

Developing a new common script can be considered as a step to relate new ideas to continuity in an organization (Bouwen and Fry, 1989) and to develop a shared directness among the parties, allowing for minimal joint action in the future (Bouwen and De Visch, 1989). The concept "script" is used in the literature on symbolic management to indicate collective cognitive maps among the members of an organization (Wilkins, 1989). In cognitive psychology, too, this concept is used to name the cognitive program of the operator of a task (Abelson, 1976).

In this case study "common script" signifies the "shared cognitive maps" of the parties involved that allow for some common action. The team concept can be a shared model of operations to achieve very different goals, but a "common sense" on the means is necessary to support further existence of common action. A variety of strategies is possible. In previous research on innovation projects four models of action strategies are distinguished: the power model, the sales model, the expert model and the learning or confrontation model (Bouwen and De Visch, 1989).

How was this common script achieved in Extruco? During the preparation phase, the Production Manager who initiated the concept was experienced as a "product champion". He, personally was well informed and was closely related to all the parties involved and spent much time talking and share opinions with them. When he was transferred, the process of creating a common script was suddenly interrupted. The intensity of consultation among the parties decreased sharply and a large diversity of perspectives came on the fore. By starting the process review, stimulated by the quality and human resources people, management subsequently opened up the steering of the project for questioning and context variation.

During the process of reduction of equivocality around the team concept a whole range of action strategies was used to attain a "common script". For a long time, the General Management considered the project as its own responsibility and tried to impose the meaning of the team concept by pushing cost awareness. This was done in the first revision meeting to stop the discussion; the definition by other parties was qualified as not valid. The result originally was compliance and lack of further interaction. This can be seen as a power model strategy. The leader is attributed the authority to impose an idea based on the interest of the organization. In a crisis situation and when time is short, this can be a legitimate coping strategy.

Some people in middle management say that "management has sold the team concept to the operators, with the operators not fully realizing the consequences". There was, indeed, a lot of persuasion going on, and the advantages of the new shiftwork system were stressed to remove resistance. Other illustrations of this sales strategy could be cited. The quality and safety program was communicated to the shop floor using persuasion. If the other party is indifferent or no favorable outcome for the other party can be achieved, then a sales model can be an appropriate coping strategy.

The quality Department acted following an expert model. Developing procedures, executing measurement, developing data gathering techniques, etc., are illustrations of an expert model. When insight and understanding are a necessary and satisfactory condition, then a straight step-by-step expert model is advisable.

During the organization revision, with an external consultant and researcher joining in, one can observe a shift more and more to a learning or confrontation model. "Double interacts", in Weick's terms, could be created or "double loop learning", as Argyris (1978) has it, was achieved more and more. Through unstructured interviews with key people, an overview of their cognitive maps was fed back to management. Valid information could be collected and shared. A procedure for role clarification was started from the top. A "change manager" was appointed to follow up on the agreements made and to act as a day-to-day coach for the team leaders. A concrete behavioral description of this change manager, who had a technical and a human resource background, revealed that he worked with a process consultation approach. When interdependence among parties has to be promoted, the learning model is a necessary condition for real involvement of the parties.

Conclusion: Managing Meaning as Social Construction

Organizational innovation is characterized by a high level of diversity and tension among parties involved. The social constructivism paradigm provides a way of thinking and acting in a world of multiple realities. The context of an organizational innovation is especially prone to create a multiplicity of realities. Tension between parties is a natural consequence of this. One can picture the cognitive maps and the causal maps of the parties involved. Among the parties, the cognitive maps form a specific configuration, which describes relations and dynamics among parties. In an innovation situation it is important to clarify and understand the tension between the perspective underlying the dominant logic versus the logic of innovation. The nature of the action strategies enacted by the parties and resulting from the configuration of logics will define the quality of the ongoing dialogue. One can distinguish one-sided (power, sales, expert) strategies from two-sided (learning model) strategies and observe the consequences. A hypothesis based on this kind of analysis is that "real" organizational learning will only emerge following a two-sided confrontational approach. When sales strategies or power strategies dominate the dialogue, one can expect only very limited learning to take place. Involvement will only be the outcome of a two-sided process. These statements can be tested in further research.

The kind of knowledge we can obtain from this type of analysis can be called "process knowledge" in context. It is in-depth understanding of the quality of the dialogue process that is being produced. To get to know how social reality can be deconstructed and reconstructed and how the emergence of a "common script" takes place in a specific context will be the benefits of this kind of approach.

References

Abelson, R. P. (1976) Script processing in attitude formation and decision making. In *Cognitive and Social Behavior*, edited by J. S. Carroll and J. W. Payne. New York: Erlbaum.

Argyris, C. and Schön, D. A. (1978) *Organizational Learning: A Theory of Action Perspective*. Reading, MA: Addison-Wesley.

Berger, P. and Luckmann, T. (1967) *The Social Construction of Reality*. New York: Anchor Books.

Brown, M. H. and Hosking, D. M. (1986) Distributed leadership and skilled performance as successful organization in social movements. *Human Relations*, 39(1), 65–79.

Bouwen, R. and De Visch, J. (1989) *Innovation projects in organizations: complementing the dominant logic by organizational learning*. Paper presented at the 4th European Congress of Work and Organizational Psychology, April 10–12, Cambridge, U.K.

Bouwen, R. et al. (1988) *Het Management van Innovatieprocessen: het evenwicht vinden tussen gelijkgerichtheid en nieuwe ideeën bij de verschillende betrokken partijen*. Onderzoeksrapport: K.U. Leuven.

Bouwen, R. and Fry, R. (1988) An agenda for managing organizational innovation and development in the 1990s. In *Corporate Revival*, edited by M. Lambrecht. Leuven: University Press.

Donnellon, A., Gricar, B. G. and Bougon, M. G. (1984) *Communication, Meaning and Action*. Paper presented at the National Academy Meetings, Boston, August.

Dunphy, D. C. and Stace, D. A. (1988) Transformational and coercive strategies for planned organizational change: beyond the O.D. model. *Organization Studies*, 9(3), 317–334.

Gergen, K. J. (1978) Toward generative theory. *Journal of Personality and Social Psychology* 36(11), 1344–1360.

Glaser, B. and Strauss, A. (1967) *The Discovery of Grounded Theory*. Chicago: Aldine.

Gray, B., Bougon, K. and Donnellon, A. (1985) Organizations as constructions and destructions of meaning. *Journal of Management*, 11(2), 77–92.

Morgan, G. (1986) *Images of Organization*, London: Jossey-Bass.

Pondy, L. R., Frost, P. J., Morgan, G. and Dandridge, T. C. (eds.) (1983) *Organizational Symbolism*. London, England: JAI Press.

Poole, P. P., Gioia, D. A. and Gray, B. (1990) Influence modes, scheme change and organizational transformation. *The Journal of Applied Behavioral Science*, 11.

Prahalad, C. K. and Bettis, R. A. (1986) The dominant logic: a new linkage between diversity and performance. *Strategic Management Journal*, 7, 485–507.

Schön, D. (1979) Generative metaphor: a perspective on problem-setting in social policy. In *Metaphor and Thought*, edited by A. Ortony. Cambridge: University Press.

Smircich, L. (1983) Organizations as shared meanings. In *Organizations Symbolism*, edited by L. R. Pondy et al. Greenwich: JAI Press.

Smircich, L. and Morgan, G. (1982) Leadership: the management of meaning. *The Journal of Applied Behavioral Science*, 3, 257–273.

Van Dijk, N. M. H. (1989) *Een methodische strategie van organisatie-verandering*. Delft: Eburon.

Walsh, J. P. (1989) Knowledge structures and the management of organizations: a research review and agenda. Paper presented at the Academy of Management Meeting, Washington, August.

Weick, K. E. (1979) *The Social Psychology of Organizing*. Reading, MA: Addison-Wesley.

Weick, K. E. and Bougon, M. G. (1986) Organizations as cognitive maps: charting ways to success and failure. In *The Thinking Organization*, edited by H. P. Sims and D. A. Gioia. London: Jossey-Bass.
Wilkins, A. (1989) *Corporate Character*. London: Jossey-Bass.

PART III

Organizations and Environments

From Organizations to Concrete Systems of Action[1]

ERHARD FRIEDBERG[2]

In a recent introduction to a selection of his articles (March, 1988), March has said that the history of choice theory is the story of simple notions becoming more and more complex. The same can be said about organization theory. If one excepts the bulk of contingency theory studies with their emphasis on "formal organization" and their positivistic and technico-economical biases, the recent history of organization theory can be read as the story of the deconstruction of the classical model of organization and its replacement by a more complex and fragmented view of organized action. Not least thanks to the contribution of organizational economics, organizations are not viewed any more as tightly integrated, coherent and clearly delineated structures of functions held together by unambiguous overall goals and one dominant rationality actually guiding the behavior of its participants. Consensus is growing that the phenomenon is not orderly and tidy, and the potentially anarchic nature of all organizations (not just universities) is now widely recognized.

Today, organizations are seen as nexuses of contracts, as game structures, as political arenas or more generally as *contexts of action* in which a multiplicity of divergent if not contradictory strategies meet and adjust through processes of power and negotiation. The *local order* which prevails is not given. It is the product of these processes of negotiation, and as such always *precarious and problematic,* for it is threatened by a threefold "deficit" (in regard to the illusions of the classical model of organization):

[1]This paper has greatly benefitted from the comments of the participants in the International Symposium on Interdisciplinary Perspectives on Organization Studies at NIAS in Wassenaar in May 1990. I should like to thank the organizers of this symposium for inviting me and thus giving me the opportunity to meet and discuss with so many stimulating people. Neither the organizers nor any of the participants can of course be held responsible for the persistent errors and misinterpretations contained in this paper.
[2]Paris Centre de Sociologie des Organisations.

—a *"deficit"* of *rationality* which stems from the bounded rationality of all human behavior and all human action, and its inbuilt opportunism and adjustment to local conditions.

—a *"deficit"* of *legitimacy* which results from the bounded legitimacy and validity of overall goals and values which are always relativized by the development of "factional" interests, rationalizations and values: the normative integration of participants, even under the conditions of the traditional "paternalistic" or the modern "cultural" management, is always incomplete.

—a *"deficit"* of *interdependence* which is the result of the pervasiveness of loose coupling in all organized systems and of the continuous attempt of participants to protect and widen their autonomy by activating decoupling mechanisms and reducing their dependence on contributions from other participants.

In other words, organizations as objects of research lose much of what used to be considered their peculiarities. Their borders become unclear and fuzzy. Their internal ordering and functioning is subject to the same limitations of rationality and to the same ambiguity which characterize decision-making in general. Hierarchical control is relativized, conflict is accepted as normal, decoupling is seen as a general phenomenon.

For all these reasons the distinction between formal organization and less explicit forms and structures of collective action has become blurred—it is not a difference of kind any more, only a difference of degree. Organizations are just the most artificial form of what Crozier and I (Crozier and Friedberg, 1977) have called *"concrete action systems"*. These are a general class of structures of collective action producing a local and contingent order whose characteristics and "rules of the game" are the result of, and at the same time also a constraint on, the strategic interaction and power processes among the participants.[3]

Every context or field of collective action can be conceptualized as a concrete action system which as such is prestructured, that is organized and regulated (Reynaud, 1989), by game mechanisms by means of which the "objective" interdependencies between participants and the resulting exchange processes are mediated and regulated. The difference, therefore, does not lie so much in the existence or non-existence of such mechanisms, but in the extent to which these mechanisms are acknowledged by the participants, codified and formalized. And it becomes evident that formal organizations constitute a particular class of action systems with certain special characteristics, such as explicit structuration, the existence of (more or less) clearly defined goals, articulation of the games around these goals, conscious awareness of these by

---

[3]Some of the implications of this conceptualization will be elaborated further on in this paper.

the participants and partial responsibility by some participants for certain of the regulations.[4]

However vague these characteristics may seem (and it is difficult to define and describe them more precisely if one is not to fall into the trap of unduly emphasizing the only measurable dimension, which is formalization of structure), they provide the possibility to order the various empirical cases on a continuum which ranges from the unconscious exchange processes and corresponding games of the system of action which produces, say, a fashion of clothing, to the conscious regulation of a perfectly rationalized organization where the distance between formal organization and actual games would be minimal.

As organizational analysis shows, few organizations achieve this extreme degree of rationalization, and action systems never do. On the other hand, it seems obvious that more and more sectors of society have moved towards the medium range of this continuum, as organized complexity has increased in modern societies. Inter-organizational network analysis and the neo-corporatist literature on public policymaking, to take only these areas, are full of examples of such "concrete action systems". These analyses can be understood as attempts to focus on the action systems underlying macro-economic management and to theorize on the emergence and existence of certain "rules of the game" by means of which each participant is enabled (or constrained) to depart from purely adaptive "market" behavior and to cooperate despite conflicting interests and objectives. The pluralist approach to public policy-making has produced an impressive amount of evidence in this field. Indeed, showing the influence of some pressure groups on the content of public policy amounts to nothing less than showing the existence of enduring exchange and bargaining processes between public agencies and their "private" counterparts, bargaining processes which are regulated by more or less implicit "rules of the game".[5]

---

[4]The organization has thus become at least partially a legally autonomous territory, or—to use Williamson's terms—internal transactions are characterized by the juridical regime of forbearance: most disputes that arise within a formalized organization are exempted from court-ordered enforcement (Williamson, 1990). With the important and weighty exception of labor and employment disputes (which interestingly enough are hardly mentioned by Williamson), courts will refuse to be drawn into the litigation of internal conflicts.

[5]For an attempt to analyze the game structures underlying the industrial policymaking in France, see Friedberg (1974). For a general theoretical formulation of these processes, and its application on the case of the Austrian macro-economic management, see Wagner and Marin in Marin (1990).

The result of this all is a growing embeddedness of organizations in organized contexts or organizational matrices (Emery and Trist, 1965) and a diminishing contrast between the two. This *banalization of organizations* as objects of research brings about a new emphasis on the study of *processes of organizing*, i.e., on the nature and characteristics of these "constructs of collective action" by means of which fields of collective action are structured, "organized" and regulated, as well as on the conditions and dynamics of their emergence, development and maintenance.

This shift in research focus carries with it some important implications and raises a great number of substantive and/or methodological issues. To examine them all would by far exceed the limits of this paper. I shall therefore concentrate on only a few which seem to me the most significant.

The conflation of Exchange and Power Theory[6]

The concept of a concrete system of action is the result of the transposition, to the field of human systems in general, of a mode of reasoning which was initially developed for the analysis of organizations (Crozier, 1963; Friedberg, 1972). In this mode of reasoning, both are conceptualized and understood as a socially constructed, i.e., artificial and therefore always contingent order. This order solves the basic problem of collective, i.e., organized, human action by structuring and regulating the mutual dependencies it produces in such a way as to make possible the necessary cooperation in spite of conflicting interests and goals.

This transposition is thus no simple extrapolation of descriptive laws on organizations to the level of more complex human systems. Nor does the notion of a "concrete action system" say anything about the characteristics and properties of such systems. To say that the conduct of any cooperative effort presupposes the existence of such a human, i.e., political construct implies a simple hypothesis: if it is possible to empirically observe patterns of relations and dependencies between actors, then there must also exist some game structures which coordinate and integrate the conflicting strategies of the various participants, as well as an encompassing concrete system

---

[6]Many of the following considerations are very much in agreement with Grandori (1993) when she compares the implications of the efficiency and power constructs used in the economics and the sociology of organization. I would only contend that transaction and information cost minimization is of a much more restricted applicability than the concept of uncertainty reduction.

of action which articulates and regulates the relations between the game structures it contains.[7]

As such it is only a *heuristic hypothesis* concerning the necessary existence of a human construct without which collective action is not feasible. This hypothesis has no substantive implications concerning the properties and characteristics of these constructs, which are necessarily specific and contingent and can only be inductively reconstructed from the observation of the actual behavior and patterns of relationships of the various participants. But it does imply and call for a conflation of power and exchange theories and confers a central place to the analysis of power processes as the fundamental coordinating mechanisms, i.e., as the basis of organization.

In order to better understand the issue at hand, a short discussion of the basic dynamics of power relations is necessary. In any field of action, power can be defined as the unbalanced exchange of possibilities of behavior between a set of interdependent institutional and/or social actors. Such a definition, which builds on, and enlarges, the now classic perspective on power developed first by Dahl (1957), Emerson (1962) and Crozier (1963), has three major implications.

First, it stresses the relational nature of power. Power cannot be possessed, it can only be exercised. It is not a commodity which could be carried around in one's pocket and which could be saved like money. Just like trust or love, it is inseparable from the relation by means of which it is exercised. It does not exist outside of this relation; indeed it is nothing but this relation.

Second, this definition emphasizes the link between power and interdependence, that is between power and cooperation, power and exchange. Power relations are not entered for their own sake, but in order to get the cooperation of others in view of managing and solving a more or less commonly perceived problem. Power and cooperation are not contradictory but rather the consequence one of the other.

Third, such a definition stresses the bilateral and most frequently multilateral nature of power relations. Power is not something that is imposed by those who "possess" it upon those who do not

---

[7]A concrete action system can thus be defined as a contingent social construct which uses relatively stable game mechanisms to coordinate the behaviour of its members and which maintains its structure, that is the stability of its games and their articulation, by means of certain specific mechanisms of regulation, which in turn are the content and the outcome of still other games. See Crozier and Friedberg (1977) for a more detailed discussion of the issues raised by this concept.

"possess" it. It can and has to be defined as the capacity of structuring *ongoing and enduring*[8] exchange processes in one's favor, by imposing terms of trade favoring one's own interests. And it therefore always has a component of reciprocity. It is an exchange relation which is structured in such a way that, while all participants get something out of it, some are able to get more than the others.[9]

The power of any one partner in an exchange process, i.e., his capacity to structure it in his own favor, in turn is based on two main sources.

The first source of power is the *relevance* of each actor's possibilities of behavior for the desired outcomes of the others, i.e., the fact that through his behavior he can control uncertainties threatening, and thus relevant for the desired outcomes of the other participants. The better he is able to control relevant uncertainties of his partners, the more they will be willing to offer in exchange to his goodwill.

The second source of power is the *freedom of action or leeway* which each participant in the exchange process has in his transactions with the others and which determines the predictability of his behavior for the others. The more A's behavior is unpredictable for B, C and D, and the more A has simultaneously succeeded in confining B, C and D to predictable behaviors, the more A is able to structure the relationship to his advantage. It is as if there were an equivalence between an actor's predictability and his bargaining capacity.

---

[8]An important dimension is here of course the time perspective. We are not talking about spot transactions but of enduring exchange processes which allow for compensations between possibly very unbalanced spot transactions: short-term losses can be traded for long-term benefits, and each transaction is also seen by the transactors in the light of longer term trade-offs. But the point seems to me to be that any such spot transaction is part of an ongoing exchange process and can hardly be considered independently from it.

[9]This analysis of power and exchange is situated in an action perspective, i.e., a perspective interested only in the mechanisms whereby power can be mobilized and translated into concrete results. It therefore has no use for a refined typology distinguishing between domination, power and influence. It would by far exceed the limits of this note to discuss the merits and drawbacks of such typologies which often induce reifications of *a priori* categories. Be that as it may, the point made here is to stress the fact that whatever their characteristics, domination, power and influence are mobilized in much the same way and by means of much the same mechanisms and they amount to much the same results in the field. Domination which cannot be translated into a concrete power relation just will not change the results in the field which can be observed.

Suppose we have an actor A whose behavior is crucially relevant for the desired outcomes of B and C, whereas B's and C's behavior is of little relevance to A. Suppose further that A is quite free not to behave in the desired way, whereas B and C are quite predictable, having nowhere else to turn for the behavior necessary to enhance and bring about their desired outcome. A is then in a very comfortable bargaining position, being at any moment able to threaten B and C with behavior undesirable to them, while the others have hardly any choice but to deal with him which makes them very predictable.[10]

This being so, all the parties to a power relation therefore always follow two simultaneous strategies in their transactions with their "partners": an offensive one aimed at increasing the predictability of the others by reducing their leeway, and a defensive one aimed at diminishing their own predictability by systematically protecting and whenever possible widening their own freedom of behavior.

This explains why the *replaceability* of each participant always becomes one of the crucial stakes in every power relation, one which will be as important as the "instrumental" reason for which it was sought in the first place. In other words, the behavior of each of the counterparts in the relationship cannot solely be understood from the standpoint of its "*instrumental*" (or if you prefer *economic*) rationality as an attempt to obtain from the others the behavior instrumental and necessary for enhancing one's own desired outcomes. It must also be understood and analyzed from the standpoint of its *political* rationality, as an attempt to structure the ongoing exchange process in such a way as to increase the replaceability of one's partners by opening up for oneself substitute solutions and/or partners, and to simultaneously restrain one's partners' margins of freedom and choice by making one's own replacement more difficult.[11]

This perspective provides a key for the understanding of the reasons why the logic at work which structures the strategies of the actors behind the diversity of empirical configurations and

[10]It should be quite clear that we are talking here about potential unpredictability. Each party can refrain from using his unpredictability if he thinks it in his interest. Power and exchange thus always include blackmail as an ultimate weapon which lingers in the background, even if it rarely used. The power of A over B and C always also has to do with the capacity of A to blackmail them into doing something by threatening to withhold a behavior on which B and C have come to depend in the pursuit of their desired outcomes.
[11]Or, to use Williamson's terms (Williamson, 1975 and 1985), by increasing the specificity of the assets controlled by him in regard to his counterparts.

consequently conditions the games they are involved in, is a *logic of monopoly.*

Striving for the monopolistic control of certain social functions (or relevant outcomes for the other participants) in a relatively unstructured or only very loosely organized field of action, becomes a rational strategy for all the actors involved, as it promises them a favorable bargaining position.

This does not mean that there are no situations where—for reasons to be specified in each case—it would be in the interest of each participant to play a game of differentiation rather than monopoly.[12] Nor do I want to imply that it is impossible for any one actor to pressure the others without being in a monopolistic position, or that all exchange processes always and necessarily end in bilateral monopoly.

What is being said is simply that there are two ways of playing the exchange game, which have to be distinguished even if one tends to spill over into the other, blurring the borderline between them. On the one hand, there is *economic exchange*: in a purely instrumental perspective, players exchange resources on a tit-for-tat basis, without drawing into their bargaining the conditions and "rules" which structure it. On the other hand, there is *political exchange*: here players still exchange resources as before, but they do so while simultaneously trying to manipulate the conditions and "rules" of the exchange.

The basic problem raised by this distinction lies in the fact that "economic" exchange (market) is essentially unstable. Unless structural and/or normative constraints prevent players from doing so, they will always tend to include the conditions and "rules" of the exchange in their bargaining ("organization" will complement "market"). The slope leading from "pure" to "political" exchange is steep and slippery. A context of action which is neither fluid nor transparent and where the construction of asset specificity (to use Williamson's terms again) is therefore a tempting alternative for each participant. The underlying dynamic of political exchange leads, if not controlled and counterbalanced, to situations of bilateral monopoly. On this account, market and organization, market and hierarchy cannot be opposed, as Williamson (1990) seems inclined to do. Even without any formalization, participants in any enduring exchange process look for means for reducing the autonomy of the

---

[12]Although one could argue that differentiation or—to say it in marketing terms—market segmentation is another way of avoiding or at least reducing competition, that is playing the monopolistic game in a more sophisticated way.

other participants, that is their capacity to interrupt and quit the exchange process. Organization or hierarchy will merely try and make such strategies more difficult, as well as lower the incentive for them, as it will guarantee the permanence of these processes. But so will markets. Indeed, one could argue that markets, in order to be working, have to be more efficient than hierarchy in checking the monopolistic tendencies of (political) exchange. They are therefore more sophisticated and complex systems of action as their existence presupposes the social construction and maintenance of all sorts of constraints and of highly elaborate modes of regulation. Markets are not the first and quasi-natural stage in an evolutionary process towards more complex and "organized" forms of cooperation and coordination. In a way, they come *after* organization or hierarchy.

The Autonomy of Organization as a Political Construct and the Problem of the Measurement or Evaluation of Performance

Let us take the argument further. Power relations in this perspective are not only conflictual. By their very inception, they also entail a collusive dimension, as each participant, in order to enhance his own bargaining capacity, will try and reduce the possibility of choice for his counterparts, thus contributing willingly or unwillingly, knowingly or unknowingly to the stability of the relation. This all the more so as this stability also guarantees him the benefits he gets out of the relation.

This is where the game mechanism comes into the picture. The "rules of the game" guarantee this stability by defining the minimal requirements each participant has to meet if he wants to stay in the game and to continue his transactions with the others. The more or less explicit and conscious modes of structuration and organization of the field of action which they provide are irreducible to the original purposes and instrumental rationality of the transaction process that brought them into being. They only make sure that each participant, while cooperating, still maintains his possibility to negotiate and to act, and that no cheating will radically endanger the exchange process itself.

The extent of this autonomization of the transaction and bargaining processes around implicitly accepted "rules of the game" will in turn depend on contextual variables, which more or less narrowly limit the development of this dynamic. Put differently, the more a given context insures the stability of the transaction processes, the greater will be their autonomization. This depends in part on structural factors themselves, such as technical, economical, juridical and other barriers to entry into the field which determine the extent to which any one actor can more or less easily replace his traditional partners by new ones. Such "competition", however, will only have real impact if at the same time there exists a measurement technique which is accepted by all the parties involved and which allows their respective "performance" in responding to the needs of their counterparts to be evaluated.[13]

Suppose, on the one hand, a field of action where all participants are placed in a situation of perfect competition and where a measuring technique known and accepted by everybody makes it possible to evaluate the performance of everyone. Then the various actors' power strategies are rigorously subject to rational evaluation, and the autonomy of the "game" in regard to the instrumental rationality of the transaction processes will be minimal. This is the well-known (and purely theoretical) economic marketplace with perfect competition, which in this perspective reveals itself to be a social construct, and not natural given, since it can only be maintained by a series of socially constructed, i.e., "artificial", constraints which prevent the establishment of monopolistic control of relevant resources by any of the participants.

Suppose, on the other hand, a field of action where the objectives, "needs" or requirements of the different partners are ambiguous, diffuse and hard to articulate, where at the same time no partner is really able to measure the degree of actual satisfaction of his requirements by his partners and where therefore no information about the respective performance of the various participants is available. We are then faced with a situation where the theoretical possibility of changing partners loses much of its attractiveness for all participants involved and will usually occur only in exceptional circumstances. The autonomy of organization as a political construct will then be maximal, that is we are in the (again purely theoretical) case of a transaction process regulated only through power equilibria, influence peddling and political logrolling.

Empirical action fields will always be in between these two extremes of the continuum. Access to resources (information, support, legitimacy, influence, etc.) will always be partially structured and restricted and dependence of the various participants never

---

[13]A third dimension could be added which tends to stabilize cooperative arrangements. This dimension is the capacity of participants to externalize the cost of their cooperative arrangements onto third parties or onto actors not directly participating in the exchange processes. For instance, cooperation between firms and public agencies for pollution control will be the easier the less difficult it is to shift the cost of pollution control to the consumers.

equal. Measurement of the "performance" of the various participants will never be complete, and—more important still—will never
be free from manipulation. The replaceability of participants in
an action field will thus always be imperfect and made more
difficult by the ongoing exchange processes whose underlying game
mechanisms tend to close the field of participants and to lead to
a stabilization and strengthening of existing modes of negotiation
and cooperation. Purely adaptive "market" behavior seems in this
perspective to be exceptional. Most interaction carries with it an
embryo of organization.[14]

Thresholds of Organization and the Problem of Learning the Management of Interdependence

A third issue raised by the focus on organizing and the processes
of organization relates to how it comes about, to the conditions of
emergence and development.

Empirical analysis will in fact show a wide spectrum of situations:
systems where regulation is unconscious, others where it is conscious; systems whose participants are aware of common results,
systems where these common results have been transformed into
goals, and systems where some participants have been (tacitly
or overtly) entrusted with responsibility for internal government.
It seems possible to tentatively outline a genetical sequence for
increasingly more explicitly organized concrete action systems leading to increasingly more conscious modes of regulation and formalized forms of integration of the participants' strategies.

A first threshold in such a sequence would be the passage of tacit
collusion to conscious and overt cooperation. A great number of
situations come to mind where *de facto* collusion between actors
not only remains completely tacit, but is moreover thoroughly
covered up by hostile rhetoric, with none of the participants able
to accept the risk of letting the tacit arrangements come out into
the open, if they are to remain in control of their respective
constituencies. As a typical example one could think of the early

---

[14]It is because most of the action fields are unbalanced and produce dependencies
that even in a non-formalized exchange process, the account balance of each
participant is not necessarily positive, as Coleman claims (Coleman, 1990). It
can also be that an actor has no better possibility (at least in the short run) for
getting the contributions he needs—he is dependent and has to abide. Codification
in a formal structure of the rights and duties of the different participants does
not fundamentally change this fact. "Spontaneous" as well as "constructed"
organization are both artificial products of "rules of the game" which themselves
are underpinned by power relations.

stages in the development of systems of industrial relations, of the
very complex situation which characterized the relationship between
the government and the Catholic Church in communist Poland, or
of the often very strained and ideological relations between public
authorities and private enterprise (especially small and medium
size firms) in a liberal economic order.[15] In order for the various
participants to accept open cooperation, they will have to develop
some sort of awareness of the positive results of cooperation or the
negative results of non-cooperation (the latter being more likely to
become apparent than the former), and with this awareness some
sort of measurement of these results.

The introduction and acceptance of explicit measurement of
the results of cooperation and the transformation of these results
into commonly accepted and internalized goals could therefore
be considered a second threshold in the evolution towards more
consciously managed action fields. Cooperation here is not just
valued for itself, but for the results it helps to obtain and these
results more or less explicitly become the measure of the relevance
of the possibilities of action to be exchanged in the power relations
between participants. A great number of systems of industrial
relations could today be situated in this stage, especially in those
societies with a high degree of neo-corporatist guidance. One could
also find examples of this in policy fields where implementation of
public policy *de facto* if not *de jure* involves the active cooperation
of private bodies whose relations to the public agencies responsible
for these policies are permanent, structured and subject to more and
more explicit evaluation.

A third and final threshold would be passed when participants
agree to explicitly allocate some responsibility for regulation and
guidance within the system, which may amount to the emergence of
some formal procedures and hierarchies. An example which comes
to mind here, is the evolution in German and even more so Japanese
industry from competition to (more or less formalized and officially
accepted) forms of cartelization to organizational integration into
huge sectoral or intersectoral trusts.[16]

---

[15]For a seminal analysis of such an apparently hostile, but actually collusive
relationship in the area of French local politics, see Worms (1966), Gremion
(1976) and of course the basic study of Pizzorno (1968).
[16]It is probably this last sequence which is best accounted for by transaction cost
economics. Indeed it would probably be the only one to which transaction cost
economics could be applied. The transaction cost consciousness it presupposes it
inconceivable without the existence of a set of highly elaborate constraints and
modes of regulations, and the concomitant existence of entrepreneurs, to cite just
two preconditions.

It should be stressed that this admittedly very sketchy outline of a genetical sequence of more and more formalized action systems, i.e. of more and more consciously constructed and formalized modes of regulation of the processes of political exchange through which collective action is produced, is not a continuum. It highlights a series of thresholds, the passage of which is not the product of a "natural" evolution and will not come about automatically. Tacit collusion does not "naturally" lead into more consciously agreed upon modes of cooperation and regulation. Indeed, as many analysts have shown (Schelling, 1960; Morel, 1981), it is a very inefficient mode of regulation which is based upon very complicated, counterproductive and paralyzing arrangements and negotiation patterns in which misunderstandings are frequent and can easily lead to the interruption of the interaction and exchange process. If and when it gives way to a new mode of cooperation and regulation in an action field, this transformation will be equivalent to profound social change and to the acquisition of new and higher collective capacities by all the participants.

We know very little of the relevant processes of social innovation and collective learning at work. Even if market organizations (and their managers) are transaction cost conscious and construct their firms also (if not exclusively) on grounds of transaction cost minimization, the emergence, the development and the maintenance of organizational constructs in any field of action (even in the economy) is not just a question of economic calculus. In order for anybody to be able to calculate the costs and benefits of hierarchy (organization), cost awareness and instruments of measurement and of calculus have to be developed, as well as the conditions for trust and confidence and with it a capacity to cooperate. And this is not just a technical or if you will an intellectual problem. It is a social problem, and it supposes collective learning, i.e., the acquisition of new cognitive and relational capacities by all the actors involved.

Historical studies as well as more basic studies on the conditions and the dynamics of processes of collective learning in organizations and in less formalized contexts of action would be especially interesting in this perspective and will have to complement the economic and sociological understanding of the advantages (or positive functions) of organization (hierarchy). We all have various explanations of why organizations emerge, but we do not have that many good descriptions of how they emerged and developed. What we need are studies of the emergence and creation of concerted forms of economic management; of the diffusion of new techniques of management and organization; of the progressive institutionalization of systems of collective bargaining; or of the impact over time of the evaluation of the results of public intervention in a policy field on the structuration of the relations between the state agencies responsible for that intervention and their respective "clienteles", to mention but a few examples.

The Dangers of Overemphasizing Formalization and Hierarchical Control: The Problem of Methodology and Research Design

The last issue I would like to raise follows from the preceding considerations and has both substantive as well as methodological implications.

The emphasis on organizing rather than organization means priority to the study of processes of organizing. The central problem in this perspective is the problem of collective action. How does it come about, what are the concrete mechanisms that have been invented to coordinate the actors' behavior and to regulate their strategic interaction, and how are they kept in operation? It is the question of the creation, development and maintenance of social rules (coordinating mechanisms) without which the conflicting interests and behaviors of the participants could not be integrated and no enduring cooperative effort would be feasible.

In this perspective, formalization and hierarchical control lose much of the privileged position they have been enjoying in organization theory for so long. Their existence cannot be considered sufficient proof of effective integration of behavior, and their premature measurement is not of much use.

Empirical analysis of action fields indeed shows that the real influence of hierarchical structures is often very small, and that formalization of structure is not synonymous with effective organization. The universities would be a good case in point. They have been characterized as organized anarchies, as the prototype of loosely coupled systems. And yet it is difficult to imagine more formalized, not to say more bureaucratized, settings. To some extent one could say that there is a negative correlation between the amount of procedures and rules and the amount of organization, i.e., integration of behavior, they achieve. The organizations described by Coleman (1993) provide other cases on the opposite side of the spectrum. He describes organizations whose capacity to effectively integrate the behavior of their members in the pursuit of the organization's goals relies heavily on informal mechanisms and modes of regulation which have their roots far beyond the official borders of these organizations.

The same point can of course be made in regard to the embeddedness of the processes of organization and to the necessity of empirically reconstructing the relevant field of action which may or may not coincide with the formal institutions and boundaries which can be observed. Here again, universities can be a case in point. In a recent study on the functioning of French and German universities (Friedberg and Musselin, 1989), we found that under very similar constraints, German universities could be said to have higher decision-making capacities and a higher organizational density than French universities. If universities in both countries resembled organized anarchies, German universities seemed less anarchical than their French counterparts. Probably not the only reason for this difference, but certainly one of the main reasons, seemed to us to be rooted in the capacity of German universities to negotiate with candidates for a professorship the conditions for their recruitment. The implicit contractual relationship thus created between a German university and its professors endows professors with entrepreneurial capacities in exchange for their greater commitment. The organizational capacities of German universities are thus enhanced. Note that in order to explain a difference observed in the internal functioning of the universities, we had to go beyond their formal borders and take into account the embeddedness of universities in larger systems of action (in this case the organization of the career systems of French and German university teachers and their different articulations in the universities).

I do not want to overstress this particular point and case. Many other examples come to mind which all point in the same direction. They highlight one major research difficulty which has important methodological implications. We have no way of knowing in advance the real significance of hierarchical and/or formalized structures. But we do know by experience that even where they exist, they are only the tip of the iceberg of all the informal power processes and coordinating mechanisms whereby behavior is integrated and a minimum of order and/or efficiency is maintained. Only the clinical and inductive reconstruction of the limits as well as the actual configurations of the processes and mechanisms active in a given action field and for a given problem will enable us to appreciate the significance of whatever formalized and hierarchical elements or dimensions can be found in that field.

Before measuring these elements, much more must be known about the configuration of actual mechanisms of coordination, about the way they work, about how they are empirically bundled and how they are linked or not to formalization and formalized hierarchy.[17] For the time being, organizational analysis should therefore opt for the gradual discovery and construction of grounded theory, both substantive and formal (Glaser and Strauss, 1968), not for measurement. What Etzioni (1988) so aptly formulated for economics applies perfectly well to organization theory: above all we need more induction. Not hypthetico-deductive reasoning, even if it aims at decreasing abstraction (Lindenberg, 1990), but the progressive founding of a theory of social regulation (Reynaud, 1989) through a hypothetico-inductive approach and research design (Friedberg, 1990).

References

Baldwin, D. A. (1978) Power and social exchange. *The American Political Science Review*, 70, 1229–1242.

Coleman, J. S. (1990) *Foundations of Social Theory*. Cambridge, Mass.: Harvard University Press.

Coleman, J. S. (1993) Properties of rational organization. In: S. Lindenberg and H. Schreuder (eds.), *Interdisciplinary Perspectives on Organization Studies*. Oxford: Pergamon.

Crozier, M. (1963) *The Bureaucratic Phenomenon*. Chicago: Chicago University Press.

Crozier, M. and Friedberg, E. (1977) *L'Acteur et le Système*. Paris, Ed. du Seuil. English translation: *Actors and Systems*. Chicago. Chicago University Press, 1980.

Dahl, R. A. (1957) The concept of power. *Behavioral Sciences*, 2, 201–215.

Emerson, R. M. (1962) Power-dependence relations. *American Sociological Review*, 27, 31–41.

Emergy, F. E. and Trist, E. L. (1965) The causal texture of organisational environments. *Human Relations*, 18, 21–33.

Etzioni, A. (1988) *The Moral Dimension*. New York: The Free Press.

Friedberg, E. (1972) *L'Analyse Sociologique des Organisations*. Paris, POUR. 2nd edition, Paris, L'Harmattan, 1987.

Friedberg, E (1974) Administration et entreprises. In *Où va l'Administration Française*, edited by M. Crozier, E. Friedberg et al. Paris: Ed. d'Organisation.

Friedberg, E. (1990) La méthode de l'analyse stratégique. Paper presented at the International Colloquium on Le raisonnement de l'analyse stratégique: sa génèse, ses applications et ses problèmes actuels, Cerisy La Salle, June 1990.

Friedberg, E. and Musselin, Ch. (1989) *En Quête d'Universités*. Paris: L'Harmattan.

Glaser, B. G. and Strauss, A. (1968) *The Discovery of Grounded Theory*, London; Weidenfeld and Nicolson.

---

[17]In this respect, I completely agree with Schreuders' (1993) second alternative which dispenses with the "market versus organization" distinction altogether and calls for the analysis (*which can only be empirical and inductive*) of the "bundles of coordination mechanisms" through which economic (and I would add: all other) transactions are regulated and made possible.

Grandori, A. (1993) Notes on the use of power and efficiency constructs in the economics and the sociology of organizations. In: S. Lindenberg and H. Schreuder (eds.), *Interdisciplinary Perspectives on Organization Studies*. Oxford: Pergamon.

Gremion, P. (1976) *Le pouvoir périphérique*. Paris: Ed. du Seuil.

Lindenberg, S. (1990) A new push in the theory of organization. *Journal of Institutional and Theoretical Economics*, 146, 76–84.

March, J. G. (1988) *Decisions and Organizations*. London: Basil Blackwell.

Marin, B. (ed.) (1990) *Generalized Political Exchange* 2 vols. Frankfurt/New York: Campus/Westview.

Morel, C. (1981) *La Grève froide*. Paris: Ed. d'Organisation.

Pizzorno, A. (1968) Political exchange and collective identity in industrial conflict. In *The Resurgence of Class Conflict in Western Europe since 1968*, Vol. 2, edited by C. Crouch and A. Pizzorno. New York: Holms & Meier.

Reynaud, J. D. (1989) *Les règles du jeu*. Paris: A Colin.

Schelling, T. C. (1960) *The Strategy of Conflict*. Cambridge: Harvard University Press.

Schreuder, H. (1993) Coase, Hayek and hierarchy. In S. Lindenberg and H. Schreuder (eds.), *Interdisciplinary Perspectives on Organization Studies*. Oxford: Pergamon.

Williamson, O. E. (1975) *Markets and Hierarchies*. New York: Free Press.

Williamson, O. E. (1985) *The Economic Institutions of Capialism*. New York: The Free Press.

Williamson, O. E. (1990) A comparison of alternative approaches to economic organization. *Journal of Institutional and Theoretical Economics*, 146(1).

Worms, J. P. (1966) Le prefet et ses notables. *Sociologie du Travail*, no. 3.

Organizational Ecology Approaches
to Institutions

WILLIAM P. BARNETT[1] and GLENN R. CARROLL[2]

Institutions matter—about that there seems little disagreement among organization theorists. Yet when it comes to more specific questions about how and why institutions affect organizations, it is sometimes difficult to find even two analysts who apparently agree. Organization theory today abounds with a diversity of arguments, methodologies and even definitions about institutions (see Scott, 1988).

Many of the popular ideas about institutions come from work falling within either the "neo-institutional" perspective in sociology (Meyer and Rowan, 1977; DiMaggio and Powell, 1983) or the "new" institutional school of economics (Williamson, 1975, 1985). However, some fresh approaches to studying the effects of institutions come from recent research in organizational ecology (Hannan and Freeman, 1989). These developments may surprise those who see ecological research as involving mainly the study of unrestrained competitive processes. Yet, as we review in this chapter, ecological researchers study institutions because they have powerful effects on the shape and form of competitive systems of organizations.

Our purpose here is to review some of the ways that institutional forces affect the ecology of organizations. Ecological studies of organizations typically take a long historical view and examine environmentally driven patterns of organizational founding and mortality. The challenges of an institutionally informed approach to organizational ecology include, first, identification of the important institutional changes occurring within an organizational population's arena over vast sweeps of time and, second, finding ways to

---

[1]Stanford University.
[2]University of California at Berkeley. This chapter was written while Carroll was a Fellow at the Netherlands Institute for Advanced Study, Wassenaar, the Netherlands.

incorporate representations of these changes into ecological models of competition.

Although it is not widely recognized, researchers currently use two different general approaches to incorporate institutional theory into organizational ecology. One of these is implicit in the model of density-dependent evolution advanced by Hannan (1986). As we explain in greater detail below, this approach involves taking institutions as informally constructed norms. The other approach involves looking more directly at readily identifiable social institutions. It takes institutions as formally constructed laws and rules. Both approaches focus primarily on the consequences of institutions for organizational populations, but each reveals a distinct type of effect on competition.

Formal and Informal Institutions

It may seem odd to distinguish explicitly between formally and informally constructed institutions, especially since traditional conceptions do not. In fact, some of the most influential early social theorists argued just the opposite: that formal institutional rules and informally institutionalized norms comprise a single process. For example, Commons (1924) argued that the institutional framework for economic transactions—the formal rules that dictate what actors must, can, cannot, and may do—evolves over time through an informal process of social acceptance. Similarly, Durkheim (1893, 1933) claimed that social order based on conformity ("mechanical solidarity") results when formal sanctions enforce the "collective conscience." In the same way, Parsons (1956) proposed that formal rules are required to ensure conformity to informally institutionalized norms.

Despite this tradition, we think it makes sense to study separately the formal and informal aspects of institutionalization. Our reasoning derives from Berger and Luckmann (1966), who observe that informal, normative institutionalization implicitly predefines certain actions as "unthinkable." Formal sanctions, by contrast, necessarily target only behavior that is "thinkable." (After all, if an action is unthinkable, so is its formal prohibition.) Thus, formally constructed rules and informally constructed norms operate distinctly, with the former occurring sometimes only when the latter have broken down.

What difference does this conceptual distinction make? In the next sections, we review how each type of institutional process has been studied from an ecological perspective. First we review the model of density dependence (Hannan, 1986) and explain how it views institutions as norms. Then we review research that conceives institutions as laws and formal rules. To conclude, we then discuss how the two approaches may be combined, and how mainstream institutional theories would do well to integrate these findings into their literatures.

Institutions as Informally Constructed Norms

The primary use of institutions as norms by organizational ecologists is found in Hannan's (1986) model of density dependence in organizational evolution. The underlying theoretical rationale for this model derives from assumptions about general sociological processes of legitimation and competition. Density (the number of organizations) drives both processes, although in different ways. Density increases legitimacy at a decreasing rate but increases competition at an increasing rate. Legitimation increases founding rates and depresses mortality rates, intensified competition lowers founding rates and heightens mortality rates. When coupled, these arguments imply that the legitimation process dominates in a region of low density while the competition process dominates at high density. According to the model, organizational density and vital rates have specific nonmonotonic relationships such that: (1) founding rates rise and then decline as a function of density and (2) mortality rates drop and then increase with rises in density. Empirical testing focuses on these readily testable predictions (see Hannan and Freeman, 1989).

In developing the density model, Hannan draws his concept-ualization of legitimacy from the institutional theory of Meyer and Rowan (1977). According to this theory, an organizational form is legitimated or institutionalized to the extent that it is "taken for granted" by relevant actors and publics. By this view legitimation involves the emergence and acceptance of norms about the organizational form and the activities it encompasses. That is, norms develop informally about the proper ways to organize for particular activities and the institutional environment sanctions organizations on the basis of these norms whether it makes sense to do so technically or not. As a result of the existence of form-specific norms there is a limited range of appropriate ways to organize for, say, schooling or restaurants. (Imagine, for instance, the technically plausible but virtually unthinkable restaurant form serving quality French fast food.) At a more general level, Meyer and Rowan (1977, p. 343) argue that in modern society the institutional norms about formal organizations are "rationalized and impersonalized prescriptions that identify various social purposes as technical ones and specify in rulelike way the appropriate means to pursue these technical purposes rationally."

The appeal of the density model is that it specifies a single general process as driving the early evolution of all organizational populations: legitimation through the development of norms about the organizational form used by the population. While the content of these norms may vary considerably by organizational form, the expected qualitative effects of their emergence and acceptance do not. Moreover, the effects of these norms are not seen as negating competitive pressures, as they often are in institutional theory, but as governing evolution when competition is low or negligible. Legitimation and competition are thus complementary processes.

An important theoretical feature of the model is the endogenous nature of its institutional mechanism. Norms about the organizational form are not imposed from the outside by actors or agencies but are instead constructed informally as a result of the growth and diffusion of the population. As the population initially expands in numbers, its organizational form gets defined, codified and promulgated. After a certain density is reached, norms have developed about the organizational form. This means that the form is taken for granted and further increases in the population have no additional effects of this kind.

One highly commendable strength of the density model is its straightforward reliance on observable characteristics of organizational populations. The model can be estimated with data on the timings of vital events and counts of density. Such ease of estimation allows the model to be applied over extremely long periods of time and to be compared across very different types of organizational populations. Comparability of this scope is virtually unprecedented in organizational studies and promises to open up important new theoretical questions (Hannan and Carroll, 1992).

Empirical support for the model is robust, at least in studies of long-lived organizational populations with untruncated observation windows. These include studies of American national labor unions from 1836 to 1985 (Hannan and Freeman, 1989); Argentinean newspapers from 1800 to 1900 (Carroll and Hannan, 1989); Irish newspapers from 1800 to 1975 (Carroll and Hannan, 1989); San Francisco newspapers from 1845 to 1975 (Carroll and Hannan, 1989); American breweries from 1633 to 1988 (Carroll and Swaminathan, 1991); German breweries from 1880 to 1988 (Wiedenmayer and Ziegler, 1990); U.S. trade associations from 1900 to 1983 (Aldrich et al., 1990). Although the theory is not supported by studies of truncated data (Delacroix, Swaminathan and Solt, 1989), few theories of organization have been independently replicated across so many comprehensive samples.

Institutions as Formally Constructed Rules and Laws

The second popular way of incorporating institutional theory into organizational ecology involves taking institutions as formal rules and laws. Researchers using this approach typically begin with the glib general notion that rules and laws affect the development of organizational populations and vice versa. Once an organizational population is chosen for study, the research task then consists of identifying the relevant rules and laws that have emerged during the course of the population's history and of exploring their effects on organizational evolution.

An example of this approach can be found in our analysis of the early American telephone industry (Barnett and Carroll, 1993). We examined the effects of formally constructed rules and laws—which we called institutional constraints—on competition between organizational forms in the industry from 1902 to 1942. The early twentieth century was a period of great competition in the telephone industry; literally thousands of telephone companies populated the American landscape. Moreover, telephone companies of the time faced a variety of institutional constraints, ranging from those imposed by municipalities and other local authorities, to those arising from state governments and commissions, to those emanating from the federal government. By examining each set of constraints separately, we found that the effects of these various rules and laws differed markedly. For instance, telephone interconnection laws enacted by the states increased mutualism among the organizational forms of the telephone industry while the famous Kingsbury Commitment between Bell and the federal government calmed the war between Bell and the large independents but started another one between the large and small independents.

One major difference between this approach and that of the density model reviewed above is that here institutions are assumed to be exogenous. Obviously, this assumption is not entirely justified; some institutional change is at least partly endogenous to the organizational population. For instance, in the analysis of the telephone industry Bell undoubtedly had some influence with state and federal authorities about the construction of new laws and regulations. However, from a research point of view, assuming laws and rules to be exogenous allows the effects of institutions on organizational populations to be modelled with statistical tools. Moreover, if the actual effects of formal rules and laws differ from their intended effects, little is lost in such analysis and much may be gained (in particular, inappropriate retrospective rationality in interpretation is avoided, a problem of some institutional research). In addition, there are significant research design advantages to this strategy; formally constructed institutions such as laws and rules are readily identifiable across social contexts and historical time; the political processes behind their development are less so.

One serious drawback of this approach is that much analysis is potentially idiosyncratic. Laws and formal rules are designed by authorities to deal with specific problems arising in particular historical contexts (e.g., prohibition of alcohol sale and consumption). It is no mystery that they often have strong effects on organizations; if they did not presumably they would be changed until they did. Demonstrating such effects, however, in many instances means simply restating the obvious (who is surprised that the Prohibition caused high mortality among brewers?). Worse yet, historically specific analysis of this kind does little to inform about the effects of institutions on other organizational populations. To be useful, institutional theory needs to be general. The major challenge of the approach viewing institutions as formal rules and laws is to recast the effects of such historical phenomena into more general theoretical statements.

Organizational theory of this kind is currently rare and almost always underdeveloped. Theories of regulation may provide some help (i.e., public interest theory, capture theory and pre-capture theory). But they typically focus more on the causes and intended effects of laws and rules than on their actual consequences. These theories also do not make explicit predictions about the issues of primary concern to organization theorists. So at best they require translation to be useful.

The most common tact used to develop general organizational theory within this approach to institutions involves not looking directly at rules and laws but at the organization of authorities behind them. In examining mortality rates among voluntary social service organizations in Toronto, for instance, Singh et al. (1987) identified several agencies that they argued provided external legitimacy including the Community Directory and Revenue Canada. Their analysis demonstrates that organizations which conform to the rules of these legitimating bodies experience greater survival chances.

A different line of general theory of this kind examines the level of fragmentation in the authority structure of superordinate units (Scott and Meyer, 1983). When authority is centralized, policies are easily coordinated and imposed on subordinate organizations. By contrast, a fragmented authority structure is likely to suffer from ambiguity, dissension and conflict. A general lack of coordinated direction prevails. Monitoring and enforcement are also difficult activities under these circumstances. For these reasons, institutional theorists predict that fragmented authority structures lead to more diversity in organizational forms and to greater differentiation among individual organizations. Empirical support has been found in analyses of school districts in the U.S. (Meyer, Scott and Strang, 1987) and agricultural cooperatives in Hungary (Carroll, Goodstein and Gyenes, 1988).

Using this and related theory as the takeoff point, our analysis of the early telephone industry made some minor headway in developing a framework for ecological analysis of institutions as rules and laws. At a general level, we distinguished between the form of institutional constraints and their content. As the theory about fragmentation in authority suggests, one important aspect of form concerns the socially constructed boundaries of governmental bodies, which vary in both structure and number. Accordingly, our analysis shows that the more political units there are within a state, the greater the number of telephone companies.

In terms of content, institutional constraints differ on innumerable dimensions. But we believe that one especially important distinction concerns how comprehensively the requirements of legal constraints affect an interdependent organizational community. Laws and rules can be either universalistic or particularistic in content with respect to the organizations in the community. That is, they apply either to all organizations in the community (universalistic) or to only some segment of the community (particularistic).

We argue generally that particularistic regulation of dominant organizations is likely to produce unexpected consequences. An unconstrained dominant organization threatens the survival of others in the organizational community. Those subordinate organizations which survive often do so only by devoting considerable resources to defending their niche. Such action typically includes collaborating defensively with other similarly threatened organizations. For example, as conglomerate banks have become more aggressive under deregulation, small banks have begun to form regional consortia in order to compete against this common threat (Gart, 1985). When the dominant organization is legally constrained, the common threat diminishes. This usually means the end of defensive collaboration and subordinate organizations may devote their resources to competition among themselves. In this way, regulation meant to reduce competition by dominant organizations leads to unintended increased competition among those not regulated, a process we call "competitive release." In the telephone industry, the particularistic Kingsbury Commitment set off such competition among large and small independent companies by the restraints it imposed on Bell.

Two recent empirical studies of other organizational settings yield findings consistent with those of the telephone study and with the theoretical predictions. In one of these studies, Edelman (1990) examines the effects of American federal civil rights mandates about employment on organizational structures and processes. These mandates were universal in nature, intended to force all employing organizations to implement procedures that would diminish discrimination on the basis of race, color, religion, sex or national origin. Edelman demonstrates that despite initial ambiguity about how to accomplish such ends, the effects of these laws were consistent with intentions in that they involved the adoption of the organizational structures which eventually got defined and accepted as the appropriate means. That organizations themselves helped define these appropriate means and adopted them at varying rates only illustrates some of the possible processes underlying the outcomes predicted by our theory.

The second study is by Sutton (1990) and looks at child welfare reform in turn-of-the-century America. During this period, delinquent and dependent children were housed in either private agencies (often run by churches) or public institutions. Although they had similar purposes, the two organizational forms were competitive in the sense that growth in, say, the private form diminished the potential size of the public form. Most regulation of child reform activities at the time was enacted by the states. Sutton describes how political factors internal to a state affected its ability to create a strong regulatory board with comprehensive powers over both organizational forms. States with weak boards implied particularistic regulation since they typically had authority over only the public homes. As Sutton shows with systematic empirical analysis, those states with such weak boards and particularistic regulation experienced diminished growth of public homes and rapid growth of private agencies for children. That regulations designed to protect deviant children lead to an expansion of unregulated homes has to be seen (at least from the regulator's perspective) as an unintended outcome.

Conclusion

Much current institutionally oriented work on organizations ignores or downplays the role of competition. The highly influential theory of Meyer and Rowan (1977), for instance, divides the world of organizations into two sectors, a competitive one where technical efficiency is rewarded and an institutionalized one where conformity to rules and norms determines sanctions. DiMaggio and Powell (1983) reinforce this division by distinguishing between various types of isomorphism in organizations and environments generated by forces other than competition. Most institutional research follows in these directions by investigating organizations operating in contexts other than competitive markets (for example, schools).

By contrast, organizational ecology has always claimed to be a theory about the entire world of organizations and competition has until recently always played the central role within it. Incorporating institutional ideas into organizational ecology represents a refinement of this approach rather than a fundamental rethinking of the theory. Accordingly, it should not be surprising that various researchers have developed different strategies to integrate institutional theory into organizational ecology. Among these, the approach using institutions as informally constructed norms seems inherently different than the approach using institutions as formally constructed rules and laws, and each approach reveals distinct and powerful ways that institutions affect organizational selection processes.

By way of contrast, it is interesting to note that researchers within the more visible so-called institutional schools usually pursue a single approach, focusing on either the informal or formal aspects of institutions. This is especially true in economics, where Commons' interest in the social legitimation of formal institutional rules has been entirely neglected by those following in his tradition. Most notably, Coase (1937) paid no regard to normative processes, instead confining his view to coordination through either markets or formal institutions. More recent work remains within Coase's narrow focus. In fact, Arrow (1974) explicitly assumes away the effects of "shared collective rationality." As Granovetter (1985) observes, such assumptions prevent researchers from seeing how normative processes, such as trust and social cohesion, affect organizational behavior.

Seen in this light, the recent developments in organizational ecology are somewhat novel. One possibility for future research would be to examine the combined effects of both types of institutional processes. For example, formal sanctions sometimes prohibit behavior that is normatively acceptable. An illustration of this occurred earlier in this century in the United States, when the production and sale of alcoholic beverages was banned despite the fact that in many areas the consumption of alcohol was a well-established tradition. Did formal sanctions affect organizations differently under those normative conditions? In general, are normatively institutionalized organizational forms more robust, making for a more rapid recovery from such temporary formal sanctions? Questions of this kind suggest intriguing new research directions, but require that researchers distinguish between the formal and informal aspects of institutions.

References

Aldrich, Howard, Udo Staber, Catherine Zimmer and John Beggs (1990) Minimalism and organizational mortality: patterns of disbanding among U.S. trade associations, 1900–1983. In J. Singh (ed.), *Organizational Evolution: New Directions*, pp. 21–52. Newbury Park: Sage.

Arrow, Kenneth J. (1974) *The Limits of Organization*. New York: W. W. Norton and Co.

Barnett, William P. and Glenn R. Carroll (1993) How institutional constraints affected the organization of early American telephony. *Journal of Law, Economics and Organization*, forthcoming.

Berger, Peter L. and Thomas Luckmann (1966) *The Social Construction of Reality*. New York: Doubleday.

Carroll, Glenn R. and Michael T. Hannan (1989) Density dependence in the evolution of newspaper populations. *American Sociological Review*, 54 524–541.

Carroll, Glenn R. and Anand Swaminathan (1991) Density dependent organizational evolution in the American brewing industry from 1633 to 1988. *Acta Sociologica*, 34 155–175.

Carroll, Glenn R., Jerry Goodstein and Antal Gyenes (1988) Organizations and the state: effects of the institutional environment on agricultural cooperatives in Hungary. *Administrative Science Quarterly*, 33 233–256.

Coase, R. H. (1937) The nature of the firm. *Economica*, 4 386–405.

Commons, John R. (1924) *The Legal Foundations of Capitalism*, Madison: University of Wisconsin Press.

Delacroix, Jacques, Anand Swaminathan and Michael E. Solt (1989) Density dependence versus population dynamics. *American Sociological Review*, 54 245–262.

DiMaggio, Paul J. and Walter W. Powell (1983) The iron cage revisited: institutional isomorphism and collective rationality in organizational fields. *American Sociological Review*, 48 147–160.

Durkheim, Emile (1893) *The Division of Labor in Society*. Translated 1933 by George Simpson. Glencoe, IL: Free Press.

Edelman, Lauren B. (1990) Legal environments and organizational governance: the expansion of due process in the American workplace. *American Journal of Sociology*, 95 1401–1440.

Gart, Alan (1985) *Banks, Thrifts and Insurance Companies*. Lexington, MA: Heath.

Granovetter, Mark (1985) Economic action and social structure: the problem of embeddedness. *American Journal of Sociology*, 91 481–510.

Hannan, Michael T. (1986) Competitive and institutional processes in organizational ecology. *Technical Report 86–13*, Department of Sociology, Cornell University.

Hannan, Michael T. and Glenn R. Carroll (1992) *Dynamics of Organizational Populations.* New York: Oxford University Press.
Hannan, Michael T. and John Freeman (1989) *Organizational Ecology.* Cambridge, MA: Harvard University Press.
Meyer, John W. and Brian Rowan (1977) Institutionalized organizations: formal structure as myth and ceremony. *American Journal of Sociology,* 83 340–363.
Meyer, John W., W. Richard Scott and David Strang (1988) Centralization, fragmentation and school district complexity. *Administrative Science Quarterly,* 32 186–201.
Parsons, Talcott (1956) Suggestions for a sociological approach to the theory of organizations—1. *Administrative Science Quarterly,* 1 63–85.
Scott, W. Richard (1988) The adolescence of institutional theory. *Administrative Science Quarterly,* 32 493–511.
Scott, W. Richard and John W. Meyer (1983) The organization of societal sectors. In John W. Meyer and W. Richard Scott (eds.), *Organizational Environments: Ritual and Rationality,* pp. 129–153 Beverly Hills: Sage.
Singh, Jitendra V., David J. Tucker and Robert J. House (1986) Organizational legitimacy and the liability of newness. *Administrative Science Quarterly,* 31 171–193.
Sutton, John R. (1990) Bureaucrats and entrepreneurs: Institutional responses to deviant children in the U.S., 1890–1920. *American Journal of Sociology,* 95 1367–1400.
Tirole, Jean (1988) *The Theory of Industrial Organization.* Cambridge, MA: MIT Press.
Wiedenmayer, Gabriele and Rolf Ziegler (1990) Interdependence in the West German brewing industry: an ecological approach. Unpublished manuscript, University of Munich.
Williamson, Oliver E. (1975) *Markets and Hierarchies: Analysis and Antitrust Implications.* New York: Free Press.
Williamson, Oliver, E. (1985) *The Economic Institutions of Capitalism: Firms, Markets, Relational Contracting.* New York: Free Press.

Organization Studies and the Ideology of Technological Determinism

JAN BERTING[1]

Technology and Organizations

Theoretical thinking in the social sciences pertaining to the technological factor is not only rather weakly developed, but also strongly influenced by ideas of a technological determinism. This is also true of organization studies in which organizational forms and labor relations are often seen to be the result of the exigencies of technological development. Within organization, similar ideas often prevail and investments are primarily related to science and technology, not to labor. Or, if attention is paid to labor, it is often as part of a smoothly-working industrial machine which is part human, part non-human, but equally mechanical in both aspects.

Technological determinism is also related to a dominant, rationalistic machine image of organizations that plays a pivotal role in the process of the design of new technologies.[2] The evidence against technological determinism in one form or another (and there is considerable evidence by now) is slow to change thinking about organizations. Why? As I will try to show, there are mainly two reasons, each one forming a stumbling block for a fresh approach to the role of technology, including the analysis of the social shaping of technology. First, technological determinism is deeply rooted in Western civilization and second, technology is often meant to cover virtually every aspect of human rational action, so that technological determinism lumps disparate aspects together and thus fails to stimulate analysis of many important separate social processes connected with technological development. In this contribution I discuss both aspects and will advocate the necessity to "de-construct" technological determinism.

[1]Department of Sociology, Erasmus University, Rotterdam.
[2]Council for Science and Society, 1981, p. 21.

Technological Determinism and Organizations

Many writers regard technology as the "prime mover" that has an important, standardizing impact on organizations. Technological development plays a pivotal role according to the adherents of the industrial convergence thesis, because each nation seeks to utilize the best modern technology. As Kerr remarks about industrial development: "There is only one best technology in any given situation and at any moment of time, and it requires production of the same materials to make it and training of the same skills to create and to operate it" (Kerr, 1983, p. 78). Other theorists, such as Saint-Simon, Marx, Veblen, Ogburn and Lenski defended the same thesis.[3] This thesis implies a close relationship between a specific technology and a specific type of organization in such a way that the technology determines strongly the organization: only the most efficient and effective combination of "the best technology" and "the best organization" will survive in an international, open market. In this perspective, the organization has to adapt to the exigencies of technological development and is thus "culture free."

Woodward discovered during her research in the United Kingdom that production organizations could be categorized into three types according to their dominant technology: (1) the small-batch, or unit-production, system (e.g., ship-building, aircraft factories); (2) large-batch, or mass-production organization (e.g., automobile production); (3) continuous production or process-industry (e.g., chemical plants or oil refineries). Her findings show that the nature of the dominant technology determines strongly the structure of the organizations; the number of levels in the management hierarchy, the span of control of first-line supervisors, and the ratio of the managers and supervisors to other personnel. Moreover, the effectiveness of the organizations is related in her study to the ways in which the firms' management had succeeded in structuring the organization according to the exigencies of the technical systems (Woodward, 1958). Other authors also found specific relationships between dominant production technologies, organizational structure and workers' attitudes and workers' conscience (see Blauner, 1966), while authors like Thompson (1967) and Perrow (1971) attempted to go beyond Woodward by developing a typology of technologies that encompasses all organizations.

Notwithstanding those long-standing, sweeping generalizations, more recent empirical research has shown that the industrial convergence thesis is not tenable (when formulated in this crude

[3]See Veblen (1922), Ogbum (1964) and Lenski (1966).

way) and that the results on the Woodward kind of typologies are mixed at best (see Hall, 1987, pp. 107f.). International comparative and cross-cultural research has demonstrated that the same type of technology can go together with important differences between the organizations in which it is applied and without producing indications that those differences are related to varying degrees of efficacy and efficiency. New technologies, such as CNC machines, may be accompanied by quite different types of organizations (see Berting and van de Braak, 1989, pp. 296ff). International comparative studies show us that specific consequences of the introduction of new technologies are primarily not contingent upon the nature of technology itself, but on the organizational conceptions of the interest groups that decide on the type of introduction and the nature of the application of technologies. Moreover, this research demonstrates that the same technologies may have different social consequences in different countries, depending on both the nature of institutional arrangements existing between relevant interest groups and on the educational system.[4] Another recent example is the comparative study by D'Iribarne (1989). He showed that organizations with the same formal, "universalistic" structure and technological processes (aluminium melting works in France, the USA and the Netherlands, belonging to the same French multinational organization) differed widely with respect to such variables as the nature of interactions between superiors and workers, discipline, the workers' definitions of their relationship to their tasks and ways of handling interactions between co-workers. D'Iribarne demonstrates in his study that these differences are interrelated with differences in the cultural environment of these three organizations. Despite these research results, technological determinism of some kind or another is still widely accepted and in the next section I try to show why.

The Classical Approach to Technology

Organizational analysis in the light of technological determinism has profound roots in Western history, being related to both the coming of modern science in the sixteenth century and the advent of industrial society. As I have elaborated upon this theme elsewhere (see Berting, 1990), I will restrict myself to a few brief observations. Moreover, Van der Pot (1985) has amply

---

[4]Important studies in this area are Maurice, Sellier and Silvestre (1982) Gallie (1978), Lutz (1976), Kern and Schumann, (1985), Dore (1973), Smith, (1983), and the theoretical analyses of Winner, (1977) and Hirschhorn, (1984).

demonstrated the important role of the Jewish and Christian religions in the creation of the necessary conditions for the rise of Western technology. The analysis of Dijksterhuis shows us, in his *The Mechanization of the Image of the World* (*De mechanisering van het wereldbeeld*, 1980) the long line of development of the natural sciences, leading to the coming of *modern* natural sciences in the period between 1543, when Copernicus published his *De Revolutionibus Orbium Coelestium,* and 1687 when Newton's *Philosophiae Naturalis Principia Mathematica* is published. This period represents an enormous progress of human knowledge and of opportunities, and changes deeply the dominant view of life. It did set the course of the natural sciences for the centuries to come, based on a mechanistic image of material processes, not to be conceived of as a complex machine designed by the Creator, but as processes which can be understood by applying the concepts of mechanics: the physics and mathematics of energy and forces. Only the West witnessed the development of such a conception of science based on rationality (especially mathematics) and systematic observation (especially controlled experiments).[5]

Here we are, in fact, referring to the Enlightenment and its tremendous impact on the industrial development of Western Europe. Moreover, it generated in Western thinking the sharp opposition between modernity—related to scientific truth as the major element in a new image of societal development ("progress")—and tradition, the resistance of the existing social institutions to the forces of progress.

As Herrera put it succinctly: "For Enlightenment, all things in nature are disposed in harmonious order, regulated by a few simple laws, in such a way that everything contributes to the equilibrium of the Universe. The same rational order is the basis of the human world and manifests itself through the instincts and tendencies of men. The main obstacle to this linear unending human progress is, for the Enlightenment, ignorance and the education of all strata of society in the light of reason and science will finally lead to a perfect and happy society. Indeed, the rational analysis of the physical and social world will gradually unveil most ideas of the established traditional order as errors, to be replaced by scientific truth. Moreover, in connection with these ideas, a new type of society evolved and conscious attempts were made to change

[5]Weber (1961, pp. 232f.) observed that "a rational science and in connection with it a rational technology remained unknown to those (non-occidental, JB) civilizations." According to him, only the Occident possessed science in the present-day sense of the word.

political and social orders into the direction of a 'rational society'. It was, as Eisenstadt phrased it, the birth of "the civilization of modernity' which is, among other things, characterized by growing structural differentiation and specialization, the establishment of universalistic organizational frameworks and the articulation of relatively open, nontraditional systems of stratification and mobility in which criteria of achievement are dominant" (see Herrera, 1990).

The Enlightenment model of industrial development implies that industrialism will have a far-reaching and overwhelmingly positive impact on society. This model of development, for the first time formulated by Saint-Simon, has become known in modern economics and sociology as the "industrial convergence thesis" (other references being, as we explained earlier, "technological functionalism" and "technological imperialism") and is, as we already remarked, still a powerful image of development.

In this model, two main forces determine the development of society:

1. The march of rationality, resulting from the inquiring human mind that follows the rules of the positivist—logico-empirical—science while analyzing the physical and social world in the pursuit of truth. Moreover, this also leads to the development of new technologies, being—partly at least—applications of the growth of knowledge.
2. The open international large-scale markets which urge industry to adopt quickly the best available technology in the production processes. Failing to do so by an enterprise or branch of industry would result in a quick deterioration of their international competitive position.

The general idea is that of all the available technologies only one can be the most efficient and effective one. Relative benefits will flow to that company or branch of industry that succeeds in developing new technologies or in acquiring the most efficient and effective technologies in an early stage. This is, in fact, technological Darwinism: the survival of the fittest technology by the fittest organization.

It is, however, not only the adoption of the best technology that counts but also the successful combination of (new) technologies with the best type of organization of the production process and of the organization of the company or system of companies. In connection with a certain type of technology, the argument runs, there is also only one type of the most efficient and effective way of organization.

Furthermore, it follows from what we have said, that a specific combination of technology and organization determines the nature of the tasks in the division of labor. This, in its turn, determines the job requirements with which the workers are being confronted, requirements related to the contents of the available jobs, working relations, working conditions, organization's hierarchy and opportunities for advancement in the organization. This logic of industrialism implies that social life can only *adapt* to the deterministic line that has been described above.

In this line of argument, the origin of scientific discoveries and technological innovations does not need to be explained by other factors than the inquisitive mind, following the rules of positivist science. Society has just to wait and see what comes out of these processes of discovery and to adapt to their results. There are no other possibilities to control this "march of rationality" than the control by the scientists and technologists themselves, who do not control the direction of the scientific development but who have to see to it that their fellow-scientists abide to the tenets of logico-empirical science. The development of science and of new technologies based on these scientific developments, is as such not susceptible to human needs. In fact, the logic of the model implies that societal development is a process of reduction of human subjectivity by *rational calculation* (see Eisenstadt, 1978). Control over men and things is secured by substituting technological rationality for human interpretation when organizing any activity. "Subjectivity" is being subordinated to "objectivity". An important consequence of this development is that "Technology tends to shape the user and not simply in ways suggested by cultural materialism; specifically, technology shapes the user as it alters society's paradigms"[6] (e.g., by replacing social relationships by technically determined links).

These uses of technology in this model of development stand in a sharp contrast to the utilization of technical instruments in the pre-industrial period. While all societies developed technologies to cope with the problems of their existence, it is only in the West that a model of development is applied for the first time in which human beings are systematically brought under the yoke of technology and in which most energy is invested in the improvement of technologies and technological systems, not in the improvement of craftsmanship in which technologies are being used in accordance with the standards of craftsmanship of those who apply technologies and who compensate, by their skill, for the deficiency of the tools they used when accomplishing these productive tasks.

Ellul described very aptly this difference between pre-industrial and industrial technology: "Technical progress today is no longer conditioned by anything other than its own calculus of efficiency.

[6]Murphy and Pardeck (1986, p. xv).

The search is no longer personal, experimental, workmanlike; it is abstract, mathematical, and industrial. . . . The individual participates only to the degree that he is subordinated to the search for efficiency, to the degree that he resists all the currents today considered secondary, such as aesthetics, ethics, fantasy. Insofar the individual represents this abstract tendency, he is permitted to participate in technical creation. . . ." (Ellul, 1965, p. 74).

At this point it is important to note that the Enlightenment model of industrialism is based on a cluster of values—the "technological culture" or the "culture of rationality"—that comprises universalism, instrumental rationality (*Zweck-rationalität* in the Weberian sense), calculability of processes and outcomes, control, efficiency, effectiveness or efficacy, contract relationships, materialism, economic growth as the primary source of welfare, individualism and individual remuneration (primarily material remunerations).

Conceptions of Technology

Yet another support of technological determinism comes from an encompassing concept of technology. Consider the following meaning of technology (see also Berting, 1990):

1. Technology as sets of physical objects, designed and constructed by man. In a (post-) industrial society this term refers especially to "artificial" things, and more particularly to modern machines: artificial things that (a) require engineering knowledge for their design and production, and (b) perform large amounts of operations themselves (see Joerges, 1988). In this context the term may be used to refer to inventions and processes with extensive potentialities for application, such as laser technology, chip technology and DNA recombinant technology, and the applications of such technologies within existing or new machines and production processes.

2. Technology as a term which refers to human activities in connection with the utilization of artifacts. Moreover, technology implies the knowledge to use these technical things. "Technological" things are meaningless without the "know-how" to use them, repair them, design them and make them. As such this know-how can, partly at least, . . . be systematised and taught, as in the various disciplines of engineering (see MacKenzie and Wajcman, 1985).

3. Finally, "technology" may refer to a body of knowledge that is necessary to generate new rules for the design, construction and application of technical potentialities in relation with different types of problems (such as, e.g., the control of environmental pollution). Here the term technology refers to the *theory* of the application (logia), not just to "artificial things", the ways in which they are used in practice and the transmission of this practical knowledge ("technics"; German: *Die Technik;* French: *la technique*) as is being emphasized in the first and second meaning of the concept "technology".

Understandably, those writers who start from an encompassing definition of technology, comprising the three meanings of technology as described in the preceding paragraph, or even from a still wider concept of technology, "as a mean of transforming raw materials (human, symbolic, or material) into desirable goods and services" (Perrow[7]) end up with a closer connection between "technology and organization" than those researchers who refer to technology as "artifacts and the human activities in connection with their utilization" (the first two levels of our definition).

Ironically, the ideology of technological determinism may also have received some extra support from recent technological developments that blur the distinction between science and technology even more and therefore support a broad definition of technology. This is shown in Bell's analysis of the post-industrial society when he says that "What has become decisive for the organization of decisions and the direction of change is the centrality of *theoretical* knowledge—the primacy of theory over empiricism and the codification of knowledge into abstract systems of symbols that, as in any axiomatic system, can be used to illuminate many different and varied areas of experience" (Bell, 1976, p. 20). Bell points at the importance of the rise of new intellectual technologies, enabling the management of organized complexity—the complexity of large organizations and systems, the complexity of theory with a large number of variables—and the identification and implementation of strategies for rational choice in games against nature and games between persons. Bell argues that ". . . by the end of the century [a new intellectual technology] may be as salient in human affairs as machine technology has been for the past century and a half" (Bell, 1976, p. 28).

It follows from what has been put forward that in the third meaning of technology not only the distinction between "science" and "technology" becomes blurred, but also that this meaning is strongly associated with a new, emerging mode of production in which these intellectual technologies play a pivotal role. As such the third meaning of technology goes together with specific types of artifacts (hardware) and a specific way the hardware of production has been laid out in a factory or other place of work. This implies "the division of labor and work organization which is built into, or required for efficient operation by the productive technique", as Hill (1981, p. 86) remarks. Habermas, approaching

---

[7]C. Perrow (1971, p. 75). He continues: "In this view of technology, machines and equipment are merely tools; they are not the technology itself. Indded, the personnel man uses a technology that has little to do with tools" (pp. 75–76).

Bell's encompassing delineation of technology, states that technology means "scientifically rationalized control of objectified processes. It refers to the system in which research and technology are coupled with feedback from the economy and the administration" (Habermas, 1971, p. 57).

Conclusion

The idea of technological determinism is deeply rooted in our Western civilization. Yet, by leaning on an encompassing definition of technology as rational control, the idea of technological determinism tends to blur the distinction between theoretically distinct aspects, especially those of structural constraints and individual decisions.

Therefore, technological determinism has to be dismissed both on the macro-level as a "theory" explaining societal forms and change[8] and on the level meso-level as a theory of organizational form and organizational change. Hall, referring to Argyris, summarizes this problem as follows: "Because organizations change, albeit slowly, there must be a reason for change. If technology is the sole source of structures, then technology must change before structure. If the technology is imported into the organization from outside, then *someone or some set of individuals within the organization must decide* to import the technological change. If the change is from within, *again decisions have to be made.* In addition, the technological approach *does not include considerations of the role of individuals,* separately or collectively, as they respond to or try to lead organizations" (Hall, 1987, pp. 108f., *italics supplied*). Indeed, and we may add that "technology" itself is not something unpredictable that imposes itself on an organization, but that it is developed and designed by people under specific cultural and social circumstances. This social shaping of technology has to be an important element in the debate (see, for instance, MacKenzie and Wajcman, 1985). Moreover, also the introduction of new technologies and their application leave room for different alternatives, as has been demonstrated by the results of many cross-cultural or international comparative studies. Often this room for alternatives is not really used because many decision-makers either (tacitly) accept the tenets of technological determinism as valid, or only implement, as managerial elites, the opportunities for choice to enhance *their* level of control within the organization while using "technological determinism" as an ideology. This social shaping of

[8]See also Berting (1988) and Boudon (1984, p. 191).

both technologies and organizations by powerful groups within organizations tend to produce, to a certain extent, convergences with respect to the division of labor, organizational hierarchies and the ways of introduction of new technologies within organizations.

There is thus a systematic neglect of the following aspects pertaining to the relationship between technology and organization:

1. The societal and cultural conditions of technological development and of technological applications. In which ways are technological developments themselves determined by sociopolitical factors which impinge on the selection of technological trajectories? (e.g., in which ways are national interests and pride related to, e.g., space programs, the Concorde and TGV projects?).

2. The research process with respect to the development of new technologies. Which cultural or social factors play a role in the development and designing of technology? Which are the main opportunities for choice and in which ways are they (not) used in the technical laboratories?[9] It may be that some technological constraints management is confronted with, when implementing technological changes within their organization, could be less constraining or even absent when in a preceding stage and in other organizations certain opportunities for choice had been used in the development/designing of new technologies.

3. The nature and types of introduction of new technologies within organizations. In which ways are new technologies selected, by whom, how are they introduced, on which assumptions and with which consequences? In which ways does an organization "learn" when it is confronted with the fact that its earlier objectives are not realized?

4. The opportunities that are provided by the different options in the process of implementation of new technologies with respect to human dignity, human rights and collective or solidarity rights.

5. The consequence of the contemporary *systemic* character of technological developments and the increasing interconnection of technological and (societal) or organizational systems.

Since the ubiquitous ideology of technological determinism glosses over the distinction between constraints and decisions, it may also have worked against the integration of various kinds of analysis, especially of the structuralist and the methodological individualist approaches. Actively abandoning the ideology of technological determinism may thus not only help to put important research questions on the agenda but it may also help to develop the tools to answer them.

[9]See Latour (1987) and Latour and Woolgar, (1979).

References

Bell, D. (1976) *The Coming of Post-Industrial Society. A Venture in Social Forecasting.* New York: Basic Books, Inc.

Berting, J. (1988) The goals of development in developed countries. In *Goals of Development,* edited by E. Agazzi et al. Paris: Unesco.

Berting, J. (1990) Models of development, science and technology, and human rights. In C.G. Weeramantry (1993).

Berting, J. and H. van de Braak (1989) Technological changes in two Dutch factories: control, flexibility and learning. In *New Technologies and Work. Capitalist and Socialist Perspectives,* pp. 296ff. edited by A. Francis and P. Grootings. London and New York: Routledge.

Blauner, R. (1964) *Alienation and Freedom. The Factory Worker and His Industry.* Chicago and London: The University of Chicago Press.

Boudon, R. (1984) *La place du désordre. Critique des théories du changement social.* Paris: Presses Universitaires de France.

Council for Science and Society (1981) *New Technology. Society, Employment and Skill.* London: Blackrose Press, London.

Dijksterhuis, E. J. (1980) (1950) *De mechanisering van het wereldbeeld.* Amsterdam: Meulenhoff.

D'Iribarne, P. (1989) *La logique de l'honneur. Gestion des entreprises et traditions nationales.* Paris: Éditions du Seuil.

Eisenstadt, S. N. (1978) *Revolution and Transformation of Societies. A Comparative Study of Civilizations.* New York: The Free Press/London: Collier Macmillan.

Ellul, J. (1965) *The Technological Society.* New York: Alfred A. Knopf.

Gallie, D. (1978) *In Search of a New Working Class: Automation and Social Integration within the Capitalist Enterprise.* London: Cambridge University Press.

Habermas, J. (1971) Technical progress and the social-life world. In *Toward a Rational Society. Student Protest, Science and Politics,* p. 57, edited by J. Habermas (translated by G. J. J. Shapiro). London: Heinemann.

Hall, R. (1987) *Organizations. Structures, Processes and Outcomes,* 4th edition. Englewood Cliffs, New Jersey: Prentice-Hall, Inc.

Herrera, A. O. (1991) Science, technology and human rights: a prospective view. In C. G. Weeramantry (1991).

Hill, S. (1981) *Competition and Control at Work. The New Industrial Sociology.* London: Heinemann Educational Book.

Hirschhorn, L. (1984) *Beyond Mechanization. Work and Technology in a Postindustrial Age.* Cambridge, Mass., London: MIT Press.

Joerges, B. (1988) Technology in everyday life: conceptual choices. *Journal for the Theory of Social Behaviour,* 18 2.

Kern H. and M. Schumann (1985) *Das Ende der Arbeitsteilung? Rationalisierung in der industriellen Produktion.* München: Verlag C. H. Beck.

Kerr, C. (1983) *The Future of Industrial Societies. Convergence or Continuing Diversity?* Cambridge: Harvard University Press.

Latour, B. (1987) *Science in Action.* Open University Press.

Latour B. and S. Woolgar (1979) *Laboratory Life. The Social Construction of Scientific Facts.* Beverly Hills, London: Sage Library of Social Research.

Lenski, G. (1966) *Power and Privilege.* New York: McGraw-Hill Book Company.

Lutz, B. (1976) Bildungssystem und Beschäftigungsstrukturen in Deutschland und Frankreich. Zum Einfluss des Bildungssystems auf die Gestaltung betrieblicher

Arbeitskräftestrukturen. In *Betrieb, Arbeitsmarkt, Qualifakation*, edited by I. S. F. München. Frankfurt am Main.

MacKenzie D. and J. Wajcman (1985) Introductory essay. In *The Social Shaping of Technology. How the Refrigerator Got Its Hum*, pp. 3–4, edited by D. MacKenzie and J. Wajcman. Milton Keynes, Philadelphia: Open University Press.

Maurice, M., F. Sellier and J. J. Silvestre (1982) *Politique d'éducation et organisation industrielle en France et Allemagne*. Paris: Presses Universitaires de France.

Murphy J. W. and J. T. Pardeck (1986) Introduction. In *Technology and Human Productivity. Challenges for the Future*, p. xv, edited by J. W. Murphy and J. Pardeck. New York: Quorum Books.

Ogburn, W. F. (1964) *On Culture and Social Change*. Chicago, London: University of Chicago Press.

Perrow, C. (1971) *Organizational Analysis. A Sociological View*. London: Tavistock.

Smith, R. J. (1983) *Japanese Society. Tradition, Self and the Social Order*. London: Cambridge University Press.

Thompson, J. D. (1967) *Organizations in Action*. New York: McGraw-Hill.

Touraine, A. (1966) *La conscience ouvrière*. Paris: Aux Editions du Seuil.

Van der Pot, J. H. J. (1985) *Die Bewertung des technischen Fortschritts. Eine systematische Uebersicht der Theorien*. Assen-Maastricht: Van Gorcum.

Veblen, T. (1922) *The Theory of the Leisure Class*. New York: Viking Press.

Weber, M. (1961) *General Economic History*. Collier Books.

Weeramantry, C. G. (ed.) (1993) *The Technological Impacts on Human Rights*. Tokyo: United Nations University.

Weeramantry, C. G. (ed.) (1991) *Human Rights and Technological Development*. Tokyo: The United Nations University.

Winner, L. (1977) *Autonomous Technology. Technics-out-of Control as a Theme in Political Thought*. Cambridge, Mass., London: MIT Press.

Woodward, J. (1958) *Management and Technology*. London: Her Majesty's Stationery Office.

Club Hierarchy, Social Metering and Context Instruction: Governance Structures in Response to Varying Self-command Capital.

SIEGWART M. LINDENBERG[1]

A major function of management is to set schedules and monitor accomplishments so as to prevent procrastination (George A. Akerlof, *Procrastination and Obedience*, 1991, p. 7).

The family is the most likely place for the individual to learn (or not learn) the rules and norms necessary to overcome the self-control problems (Richard H. Thaler and H. M. Shefrin, *An Economic Theory of Self-control*, 1981, p. 401).

Introduction

The field of organization studies has produced a prominent focal point of analysis: governance structures. Wherever parties enter into a contract, a governance structure is part of the arrangement and the question is: why and how do these governance structures differ?

In the last decade, one could also observe quite another development: work on organizational culture,[2] on the management of meaning,[3] on the quality of working life.[4] This emphasis on culture and meaning is accompanied by a related effort: the pin pricked into heroic leadership, pointing to the importance of little things routinely done. "It is probably true that the conspicuous differences around the world in the quality of bureaucratic performance are due primarily to variance in the competence of the ordinary clerk,

[1]Interuniversity Center for Social Science Theory and Methodology (ICS) and Department of Sociology, University of Groningen, the Netherlands.
[2]See Deal and Kennedy (1982).
[3]See Bouwen (1993).
[4]See Hofmaier (1993).

bureaucrat, and lower manager, and to the effectiveness of routine procedures for dealing with problems at a local level" (March, 1986, p. 23).

The most general link between these heirs of the human relations approach and transaction cost economics (which centers on governance structures) can be forged from the role culture plays for the production of trust and trust for the reduction of transactions costs. This point is a variant of the human relations tradition which calls into question the efficiency of purely bureaucratic organization. In 1970 Brewer summarized cumulating sociological evidence that, quite contrary to what one might expect on the basis of Weber's theory of bureaucratization, there are many organizations in which the style of supervision is in the direction of less strict hierarchical control and less impersonality. This contrary trend held only for some, not for all organization. Why? Brewer (1970) stated two conditions: first, the more complex an organization, and second, the more dangerous or unusual the tasks that are carried out in otherwise isolated units, the more de-bureaucratization. He explained these links by the autonomy that employees need for the execution of complex or dangerous and unusual tasks. Years later, economists sharpened theory on this point by identifying metering problems (Alchian and Demsetz, 1972) and asset specificity (Williamson, 1985) as the major conditions leading to nonbureaucratic supervision. In addition, "style of supervision" was replaced by "governance structure" of the employment relation, with wages removed from individual bargaining, and special grievance/arbitration and internal promotion schemes (Williamson, 1975, 1985).[5]

This was certainly an advance, and yet, in the whole process, the emphasis was more on measures (like hostage exchange) that reduce the need for trust than on an analysis of how trust operates in the governance of incomplete contracts (see Lindenberg, 1990a). Recent theoretical elaborations by Lindenberg (1988), Casson (1991), Raub and Weesie (1991), Coleman (1990, 1993) and others[6] have changed this emphasis. The new theories of trust all recognize the increasing importance of *autonomy* even in labor relations and the ways of building or reinforcing trust as a barrier against the exploitation of that autonomy. The most advanced theoretical problem here is how to create or mobilize a

---

[5]Damage potential in general (with or without asset specificity) was identified as a condition for weak solidarity norms governing the employment relation by Lindenberg (1988).
[6]See also Mitchell and Zaidi (1990).

trust relation strategically without getting all the negative effects of such a relation for doing business (such as mutual obligations that greatly restrict the goals of the business relationship). One can expect more progress along this line of work. However, once this line of research is set out, the following step has to be set: even if the governance structure succeeds in motivating people not to exploit the autonomy given to them, they may not be able to deliver. *Their ability to control themselves may be too weak to make them even approximately a perfect agent of the principal.*

Let me take a simple but realistic example to illustrate this kind of situation. You discover on your desk the confirmed order of a customer that should have been handled a week ago for delivery yesterday. Since you know that an angry customer is more likely to go to the competition than a disappointed but understanding one, you decide that you should call and tell him that there has been an unfortunate mixup and that, alas, the order will be delayed for a week. Because you feel uneasy and embarrassed making this call, you don't make it right away but decide to ring him up later in the day. In the afternoon you feel you are too busy to make the call now and you decide to call the next morning. The next day the cycle repeats itself, until a few days later, the furious customer calls you. What he has to say confirms all your anticipations of what he would say if you did not inform him early on. You lost him as a customer. There is really no surprise involved and you agree that not making such a call was certainly not worth losing the customer. Still, you did it. It is not that you did not care. To the contrary, forgetting his order was very embarrassing to you which made it so painful to call in the first place. What you did not have was the ability to counteract the effect of the uneasiness making the call, which led to the repeated postponement. You knew full well that you should call and you would have reprimanded any employee of yours if he had not called simply because he felt uneasy making the call. In fact, you could not command yourself. Then, of course, there are millions of others who also lack this ability to various degrees. It is a very well recognized phenomenon (see, for example, Ainslie, 1986). In order to bring out the fact that this ability to command oneself is a resource in the contractual relationship, I call it *self-command capital*.

The current conceptualization of the employment relation more or less assumes self-command problems away. Organization is brought about by an explicit or implicit contract which Simon (1951) in a by now classic article called "the employment relation". He assumed that people are indifferent with regard to a class of their own actions. This allows a person to sell the right to somebody to tell him which of these actions he should perform: "If the orders transmitted to him by the organization remain within these limits of acceptance, [the employee] will permit his behavior to be guided by them" (Simon, 1957, p. 116). Thus under certain conditions, I will permit my actions to be guided by the order of others. Williamson also sees the employment contract this way (Williamson, 1985, p. 249). Coleman (1990) goes one step further. Like Simon, he assumes that individuals control their action, but in order to trade this control, I first must have the *right* to control my own actions. The right may not exist at all, or somebody else may hold it (as in slavery). In such cases, the right cannot be traded. Both for Simon and for Coleman, the theory of organization depends on the ability to sell the right to control one's actions. The underlying assumption is that I do control my own actions, so that I can credibly sell this control. What does this require about my own functioning? Is it reasonable to assume that I am so much in control of my own actions that I can decide whether or not to "permit" my actions to be guided by other people's orders, as Simon assumes? According to Elias's famous thesis on the process of civilization, man's control over his own action increases exactly with increasing organization (see Elias, 1982). Thus Elias would concur with Simon and Coleman that at least for "modern" society, one should not worry much about the ability to sell the right to the control of one's actions. Yet, there are also compelling reasons to assume that while Elias was right until much of the nineteenth century, he only looked at centralization of power and did not really analyze the effects of *prosperity* on self command. Could there possibly be generational changes in the ability to control one's own actions? If there are these changes, they would have important consequences for the kinds of governance structures organization have to devise. What kind of structures?

In the following, I will address these questions. I will first describe how self-command capital might be most fruitfully conceptualized. The important result here will be that due to framing, small things can have large consequences, so that "atmospheric" aspects of governance structures can acquire great importance. Then I will deal with the major source of variations in the level of self-command capital: the household. Here, prosperity depresses the incentive for socialization directed at the formation of self-command capital. Finally, I will analyze some of the forms that governance structures take in response to lack of self-command capital. Basically, they consist of three marked deviations from traditional hierarchies: hierarchies that do not issue commands but priorities and deadlines for tasks (club hierarchies); forms of access that enhance *informal* (social) metering of performance, and instruction in order to induce clarity, consensus and commitment with regard to the purpose of activities and plans. For all three, the production of meaning is a necessary ingredient.

Self-Command Capital

Conditions have not been optimal to get the problem of self-command into any prominent place on the agenda of institutional analysis. Ainslie (1986, p. 139) observed that "philosophers and psychologists since Plato have described competing principles of decision-making, usually a lower, impulsive principle and a higher, rational principle . . . but the relationship between these principles has been elusive." Let us call this relationship between conflicting principles of decision-making within the same person, the *problem of self-command*. In the socio-economic sciences, the problem seemed more or less solved long ago. In economics, enlightened self-interest moved into place as the ruler of passions (cf. Hirschman, 1977). In sociology, morality, acquired during socialization, was seen as the conqueror of impulses (Parsons, 1937). While these respective solutions underwent considerable refinement,[7] they did not generate genuine puzzles. Each discipline, in its own way had reason to put this problem on the back burner and thus institutional analysis was not affected by it. Why?

In sociology, institutional analysis depended on the given solution to the problem of self-command. Rules are internalized through socialization; in this way, they govern behavior which, in turn, is automatically coordinated with all other players and thus institutionalized. Fluctuations in this social governance of behavior had to come from one of two sources: either incomplete socialization or conflicting rules (cf. Merton, 1957). As a consequence, what had to be explained was not conformity but deviance and thus conformity to rules was trivialized.

In economics, conformity to rules was systematically divorced from the self-command problem because conformity is a matter of a rational response to given constraints. Lack of conformity is due to a lack of interest alignment (see Lazear, 1981). In this

---

[7]In economics, the problem was eventually flattened into a matter of individual time preference related to interest rates and incorporated into the general trend of formalization in neo-classical economics (see Fisher, 1930; Fishburn and Rubinstein, 1982). In sociology, the role of morality governing impulse has been vastly elaborated and incorporated into the general trend of categorization in structural-functionalist sociology (see Parsons, 1951).

view, the problem of self-command is altogether misconceived in the sense that it stems from an old-fashioned and misguided difference between passions (or impulses) and interests. There is no such difference. Rather, we are dealing with preferences, one of which is a time-related preference for goods available now rather than later. This preference is by and large rational because if I receive money now, it will bear interest and if I receive the same amount later, I will miss out on this interest. The research puzzle then boils down to the question: what is the rate of the time discount? Is it really anywhere related to the interest rate? (see Holcomb and Nelson, 1992). The general trend in this discussion is thus to incorporate apparent self-command problems into the standard analysis and to show that there is really no such problem.

In recent years, there has been one shift away from these trivializing tendencies. It is part of a larger development of convergence in the socio-economic sciences (see Lindenberg, 1990b). While in economics constraints are usually taken as given, a whole new vista opens up if one assumes that individuals also *choose* constraints. Books appeared on multiple selves (Elster, 1986), and in 1990 Buchanan observed that "the *economics of self control* has reached the status of a respectable, if minor, research problem" (Buchanan, 1990, p. 3). Many examples for the constraint seeking behavior come to mind. For instance, in Holland, university teachers receive a certain amount of money from the university for their health insurance. Early in the year, they have to decide when they would like to receive this money, in May or in December. Because of other administrative reasons, the paycheck in December is for most teachers lower than for the other months in the year, and receiving the health insurance money in December would render the December paycheck similar to the ones of all other months. Most teachers decide to receive their health insurance money in December, voluntarily forgoing the interest from May to December. On the other hand, they also cannot spend that money before December and as a consequence wont have to face the possibility of a month with strongly reduced income. In fact, they choose their own constraint. March (1986, p. 26) says similar things about managers:

> Many managers engage in activities designed to manage their own preferences. These activities make little sense from the point of view of a conception of action that assumes administrators know what they want and will want . . . . Ordinary human actors sense that they might come to want something they should not, or that they might make unwise or inappropriate choices under the influence of fleeting but powerful, desires if they do not control the development of preferences or buffer action from preferences.

The idea that people choose their own constraints is very appealing because it brings seemingly irrational behavior back into the fold of rationality. People who opt for delayed payment, do not act irrationally by foregoing the interest voluntarily; rather, they forego the interest as payment for the discipline they receive by the delay. Yet, this picture is misleading. People often do *not* choose or create the constraints necessary for their functioning with minimal regret. In our other example above, a person procrastinated about an important telephone call because he felt uncomfortable making it. He did not manage to create the constraints necessary to *make* him call. While all or most people may be playing self-control games, they are not all equally successful in achieving their goal. What are we to make of this? Can there be ways in which the governance structure can minimize this difference among people or do people simply differ in the degree to which they can act rationally? In that case, not governance structures but selection procedures should solve the problem, although such an assumption of unequal rationality puts considerable strain on any kind of rational choice approach.

Framing and Self-command

Most individuals make decisions at least some of the time that are seriously flawed *in their own eyes* (as well as in the eyes of relevant others). Some of these can be attributed to faulty judgment, as when you trusted somebody whom (with hindsight) you should not have trusted. But many of these decisions have been taken against one's own better judgment.[8] These are problems of self-command. The existence of such problems violates the standard assumption of rational, forward-looking utility maximizing behavior.

Schelling has observed that "tuning in and tuning out perceptual and cognitive and affective characteristics is like choosing which 'individual' will occupy this body . . ." (Schelling, 1984, pp. 95f.). Akerlof has similarly suggested recently that procrastination and other wrong decisions are "due to unwarranted salience of some cost or benefit relative to others" (Akerlof, 1991, p. 3). Yet for both, the possibility that salience changes is introduced side-by-side

---

[8]I would like to avoid the vexing question whether the individual would have to be aware of this mismatch between judgment and decision and if so what this awareness would have to look like. Maybe the best way to circumvent this problem is to stipulate that there is a self-command problem if the individual *can be made aware* of a mismatch between his or her own judgment and the decision (if need be by a trained psychologist).

with the standard model that does not accommodate these changes in salience. Clearly, a theory is needed that integrates possibilities of changing salience with rational choice.

I would like to suggest that recent developments in the theory of framing can help us here.[9] Framing means in this context the structuring of an action situation by *one* particular goal. This is the salient goal and at first blush it is similar to a single maximand in the standard analysis. However, contrary to the standard analysis, the salience can vary, and that has direct behavioral effects. If the salience of a goal decreases, the probability with which the (subjectively) "best" alternative is chosen will drop below unity and the choice probabilities for the second best and subsequent alternatives will increase. It is the influence of other, non-salient goals that make the salience vary. Those that are compatible with the salient goal will increase the salience, and those that are incompatible will decrease it.

An important consequence of framing is that the effect of changes in constraints on behavior is much larger if the constraints pertain to the salient goal than if they pertain to the non-salient goals in the background. For example, if getting things cheap is the salient goal then information on the price of a good will have a larger impact on behavior than when quality is the salient goal (and vice-versa). In this way, it is possible that for example the goal of avoiding social embarrassment (losing social approval) can indeed have an unwarranted salience. When this goal is salient, the influence of incompatible goals (such as to inform the customer) is only indirect and thus muzzled.[10]

When the weighted utility difference between my alternatives is not large and/or the salience is low, the choice probability approaches non-discrimination (i.e., 0.5 in the two alternative case). The closer the choice probability approaches non-discrimination, the more likely that there will be a *frame switch*, i.e., a new salient

---

[9]See Lindenberg (1989).
[10]Expressed algebraically, this framing model looks as follows:

$$P_i = \beta(g_i - U_o) + 1/n \tag{1}$$

where:

P_i=probability of choosing the ith alternative, $(i=1,2...n)$; β=situational salience of the maximand g; g_i=the sum of the utilities of outcomes of the ith alternative, each weighted by the appropriate event probability, $(i=1,2...n)$; $U_o=(1/n)^*\Sigma G_i (i=1,2...n)$, i.e., the average expected utility over all alternatives.

The situational salience is a function of situational background aspects (x_i):

$$\beta = f(x_1, x_2...x_n) \tag{2}$$

goal will replace the old (it will be the goal from the background that discriminates best between alternatives). Such a frame switch also means that the weight of constraints changes: those pertaining to the new frame influence behavior more than before whereas the "old" frame, now in the background, will influence behavior less than before. In addition, the alternatives or their order may have changed. The top alternative under the old frame may now be on the bottom and vice-versa.

One may usefully distinguish three related but analytically distinct self-command problems: procrastination, impatience and addiction. In all three cases, framing effects play a prominent role. Let me take them up in order.

Procrastination. We procrastinate if we keep postponing something of which we are convinced that it should be done. In our example above, an employer kept postponing making a telephone call to one of his customers because he felt uncomfortable relaying the bad news. In terms of framing, this kind of behavior can be explained as follows. The customer has to be called. But does he have to be called right now? It is important to notice that my alternatives are *not:* to call now versus to call later, because that would imply that if I decided against calling now I did choose the alternative calling later. Instead, my set of alternatives is: to call or not to call now. In fact, I have *not* bound myself at all, I just postponed the decision. There is no direct intertemporal decision being made. The salient goal is to inform the customer and that means that the alternative to call is superior to the alternative not to call. But how salient is this goal? The fact that it is possible to call the customer at a later time without great expected loss in outcome allows a related goal in the background to have considerable influence: inform the customer at another time. This background goal lowers the urgency and thereby the salience of the goal "informing the customer." The salience is also lowered by a still stronger goal in the background, viz. to avoid exposing myself to an embarrassing situation. Both influences on the salience add up and are now so strong that my choice probability of "calling now" approaches 0.5 thus inviting a *frame switch.*

What will be the new frame? It will be the strongest contrary goal in the background, in our case the goal to avoid an embarrassing situation. This frame switch creates a completely new action situation: it leads to a *reversal of alternatives,* so that the superior alternative is "not to call now." Every time I consider again calling the customer, the process is repeated with the same outcome: not now. The cycle will be broken if and when the background goal of "inform the customer at another time" is weakened or even vanishes due to the strong expectation that further postponement will lead to considerable imminent loss. When this happens, the urgency (salience) of "informing the customer" will greatly increase and thus the frame switch to "avoid an embarrassing situation" will not take place. In sum, *a procrastinator allows his salient goal to be displaced by an alternative-reversing goal he himself considers to be "minor" by comparison*. In this new frame, information on the embarrassing aspects of the situation will become very prominent, while information on the situation with the customer will recede into the background.

Impatience. When I am willing to forego a larger reward in the future in favor of a smaller reward now, then I am impatient. This is different from procrastination because when I am impatient I do not postpone a decision but choose the "objectively" less attractive alternative. I later reprimand myself for having done so. Except for this element of regret, impatience is identical to what economists mean by time preference. Here we do have an intertemporal choice. How are we to explain impatience in terms of framing?

Assume that my salient goal is to make as much money as I can. If I am now confronted with the choice of say $10 or $20, it is clear that $20 is the superior alternative. However, if somebody informs me that I have to wait a week for the $20 while I can have the $10 right now, what will happen? It is interesting to note that ever since time preference was incorporated into the theory of interest in economics (with Böhm-Bawerk and subsequently Fisher), an *ad hoc* framing theory had been bootlegged into micro-economic analysis: the idea that, as Schumpeter (1954, pp. 928f) put it, "most people do not experience future enjoyments with the same pungent sense of reality as they experience present ones." Here "pungent sense of reality" refers to the things I can do with the good in question and things that may accompany its use. In short, it refers to an influence of goals in the *background* although micro economic analysis does not (yet) recognize explicitly a difference between foreground (salient) and background goals. In any case, the standard time preference assumption really boils down to the idea that *in any intertemporal choice, the influence of background goals is uneven*: for the proximate reward, my imagination of what I can do with them or what goes along with them is more vivid than for the distant rewards. But since these "proximate" goals are incompatible with the present frame, they drag down its salience. For example, the goal of "making as much money as I can" will become less salient by the fact that if I go for as much money as I can, I cannot realize any of the proximate goals. The distant goals are in this respect too vague to compensate this decrease in salience. As a consequence, the probability that $20 will be chosen goes down and the probability that $10 will be chosen goes up. The larger the intertemporal difference between the rewards, *ceteris paribus*, the stronger the relative influence of background goals pertaining to the proximate reward.

The situation can be more extreme. The more the choice probability for the top alternative ($20) approaches 0.5, the more likely that a frame switch will occur. This can happen if the difference in reward between the alternatives is small and/or if the salience is very low (for example because the wait is very long). The new frame will be a goal connected to the proximate (lower) reward,[11] for example buying lunch for a friend in half an hour. Note that *the new goal reverses the order of alternatives*. The $10 will now be chosen with a probability larger than 0.5, phenomenologically indicating strong impatience.[12]

Phenomenologically, this effect expresses itself as impatience if the decision maker identifies myopia as the basis for his decision. It should be distinguished from a situation in which the researcher has misspecified the utility function by having left out an important proximate reward.

Addiction. Most people get hooked on something, be that a person, a kind of situation, a kind of activity, food or drugs. Of course, the degree to which they get hooked varies greatly and only the most severe cases will be clinically identified as addiction. From a

---

[11]It will be the goal that discriminates best between the alternatives.

[12]This framing interpretation of intertemporal choice is quite compatible with the seemingly paradox results of the careful study of Holcomb and Nelson (1992). People seem to have a hyperbolic discount rate, and still they seemed not to react to front-end delays (i.e., having the proximate reward moved backward in time while keeping the interval to the distant reward constant). In the interpretation offered here one would expect results that *appear* to point to a hyperbolic discount rate: given constant interest rates, an increase in the length of time to the future payment will also increase the absolute difference between payoffs. When the interest rate is very high (as in Holcomb and Nelson's case: 1.5% or 3% per day), this increase in difference well outpaces the decrease in salience due to the concreteness effect. In addition, discounting should be disentangled in terms of the goals involved because reaction or non-reaction to front-end delays depends on the question how these delays influence the goals. When there are not many concrete plans (in a laboratory situation), it may well be that the asymmetry in concreteness is similar with different front-end delays.

framing point of view, addiction is a situation in which changing circumstances fail to lower the salience of your present frame as much as you expect them to do. For example, you know that spending too much money in the casino will create great problems for yourself and others and you know that the amount you spend should be sensitive to the magnitude of problems created by spending it. Yet you find that the magnitude of problems fails to lower your salience of gambling. The stability of salience is similar to the inelasticity of demand in the standard analysis. But there may be inelastic demand without regret, for example demand associated with "rational addiction" (Becker and Murphy, 1988). Some people feel so strongly about their hobby that their demand may be quite inelastic with regard to price and other aspects. But they do not necessarily feel that what they do is a mismatch between their decisions and their judgment. People generally know that their present consumption can influence their future demand and they know that once they are addicted, they wish they weren't. The question of non-rational addiction is then: why do they get hooked? How is "non-rational" addiction possible? Let us assume that one of the goals of a person (not yet addicted) is the enjoyment that comes with the consumption of a particular substance or with a particular activity. Let us also assume the person believes that he can get addicted to this enjoyment. The anticipated negative consequences of this possible addiction are not worth the enjoyment to him. When the enjoyment is the salient goal, the negative consequences (in the background) should then lower the salience sufficiently to produce a frame switch. Addiction can only come about if this frame switch consistently fails to occur. Why could it fail to occur? There is a parallel with procrastination. The intertemporal aspect in this situation is not choice but the ability to postpone. The decision is: should I or should I not take this substance? With procrastination, the possibility to postpone the decision lowered the salience and effected a frame switch. Here, the converse is the case. I do not anticipate grave consequences taking the substance one more time. Thus, I can to postpone the decision until next time. This greatly *enhances* the salience of the present frame by neutralizing the effect of negative consequences. No frame switch will occur. The next time, however, the salience has increased somewhat through the onset of addiction, and that makes a frame switch even less likely. Step by step, I get into a situation in which the frame becomes more and more stable and thus increasingly less sensitive to changing circumstances. Again, this explanation of addiction through "gradualism" is not new but it is a framing explanation that had previously been bootlegged into the standard analysis without adapting this analysis to framing effects (by introducing explicitly foreground and background goals).[13]

What constitutes self-command capital with regard to these three forms of problems? As mentioned above, the traditional sociological view, strongly influenced by Durkheim and Freud, was that during child rearing, a personality structure would develop through identification and internalization of norms and values. As a result, a socialized individual has an internal command structure (composed of ego and super ego) that would allow the person to adequately select and perform social roles. By contrast, the view taken here, supported by the recent developments in the study of self control (Schelling, 1984; Ainslie, 1986) is that self-command is a skill in dealing with potential procrastination, impatience and addiction situations. Since these situations are largely governed by framing effects, the skill in question is largely a skill to influence one's own framing. Being attentive to framing effects means that you try to manipulate *small* things in order to prevent (or create, as the case may be) large effects. For example, a person knows that chocolate has bad effects on his skin and general health. Yet, he also knows that the very sight of chocolate makes the wish to eat it so dominant that all other goals are pushed into the background, none of them strong enough to effect a frame switch. The skill here is to manipulate one's surrounding in such a way that one will not be confronted with the sight of chocolate. This does not just mean not buying it. It also means avoiding gatherings where chocolate is offered, informing friends not to bring chocolate as a gift, etc. Similarly, a person may have developed a skill to imagine future benefits or costs so vividly that he can counteract the reality effect of immediate benefits or rewards. In this way, he can increase the salience of an objectively attractive intertemporal choice, or prevent the salience-decreasing effect of the possibility to postpone a decision. Public commitment to a course of action will also increase the salience of that course of action. Similarly, a person develops skills in avoiding some and seeking other activity sequences on the basis of their framing consequences by formulating private rules about them. For instance, "Each day something needs doing most of all. Never begin the day by postponing what needs doing most of all." This rule summarizes the experience that if you postpone even what needs doing most of all, the possibility to postpone will greatly increase in salience for all other decisions as well.

---

[13]See, for example, Akerlof's (1991) explanation of addiction.

The skill to deal with your own procrastination, impatience and addiction situations is self-command capital. It applies to role performance just as much as to novel situations and it is a skill with many facets rather than an inner commander that directs you to conform to expectations. Why would training in this skill differ in social strata and over time? Here the household plays a crucial role and it is to this aspect that we turn next.

The Household

Sharing groups and changes in the home. Self-command capital is built up in the home through socialization. This does not happen without cost. In order to achieve a successful socialization with self-command capital, the parents have to be (a) consistent in their handling of rules and agreements, and (b) they have to be supportive of the child so that it will not develop a strategy of avoiding them (see Rollins and Thomas, 1979). This is a delicate balance between strictness and supportiveness and it is very restricting for the parents. For example, the mother cannot delay bedtime because there is a movie on television she wants to see. Similarly, when the child has transgressed the rule by not saying it would go to a friend's house, the parent has to deal with it even if nobody was inconvenienced by this transgression. When the child did something that really upsets the parents they have to restrain their reaction in order to show that they remain basically supportive. Why would some parents make this kind of effort day in and day out? The answer I would like to give has been worked out in some detail elsewhere. I will summarize it here.[14]

There must be a reason if parents are willing to put in the effort of self-command training: negative externalities of the child's behavior on the parents attributable to lack self-command capital of the child. There are two related kinds of such negative externalities. First, there are those that stem from sharing a home. Second, there are those that stem from the reaction of other people. Let me briefly take up both in order.

Sharing creates positive and negative externalities on the sharing partners. The more the same group of people share in their daily lives, the more they have to come up with rules and norms that emphasize the importance of sharing and that mitigate the negative externalities that come with it. At the same time, their interest in

[14]See Lindenberg (1986, 1991).

the other's conformity to these rules and norms is also higher. For example, a family in which the children have one joint bedroom and there is one living room to be used by everybody, many negative externalities can be generated unless everyone sticks to the rules by keeping the rooms picked up, controlling the noise they generate, refraining from certain activities at certain times, etc. Similarly with bathroom and kitchen use, sharing the television set, etc. Under such circumstances the parents have an incentive to train their children in following rules and norms and to make sure that they can do it on their own without much control and nagging.[15]

When a child is outside the house and behaves badly, it may reflect on the parents. They did not socialize the child properly and thus they meet social disapproval. This does not hold only for the child's public behavior but also for such important decisions that indicate the child's self-command capital. For example, if the child chooses an "easy" occupation or an "easy" partner signifying in fact downward intergenerational mobility, the child seemingly did not choose with an eye to the long-term consequences but was lured by short-term advantages. For this reason, the child's behavior outside the house may also have negative externalities on the parents, motivating the parents well in advance to put effort into building up a stock of self-command capital in the child.

Now let the income of the family rise steadily. What will happen? The economic solution to negative externalities will become more attractive than the socialization solution. The amount of sharing in the family will go down because the extra income will be put into extra bed rooms, bath rooms, television sets, cars, etc. With the extra facilities, the amount of negative externalities will decrease and with it the incentive to put in the effort into self-command training. A nice description of this effect has recently been given by Linda Weltner about mothers and their children's rooms:

> The boy's room looks as if somebody had just thrown a lighted stick of dynamite into it. Or the girl's bedroom looks like the inside of a laundry basket. The bed resembles the bottom of a hamster cage, the floor of the closet is matted with unmatched shoes, there is a wet towel on the hardwood floor .... The bedside table sports a week's worth of rotting banana peel, sour milk, and dry crusts of pizza .... Mother initiates the first skirmish. "How can you stand it?" she asks in her most neutral voice. "Stand what?" the child replies, truly puzzled .... "If it bothers you so much," she says, bristling, "I'll keep my door shut."

---

[15]There is likely to be a lower bound to this relationship. For example, when there is only one room for the family, children may play outside, thus reducing the externalities without the parents' effort in socialization.

Next, Weltner describes the parent's ambivalent reaction:

> Everymom gathers ammunition for the impending confrontation. She fortifies her case with reasons why youngsters should keep their bedrooms clean: because children, as part of a family, must learn to meet community standards . . . because cleaning one's room is a way to learn responsibility . . . . Or she prepares to accept defeat gracefully. She reviews the reasons children have a right to control their own environment . . . . All of a sudden, everymom sees the battlefield on which she stands from a great distance . . . .

And, talking to everymom, Weltner asks: "*Did you whisper, like me, 'I surrender'?*" (Weltner, 1988, pp. 168f). Ask yourself whether your grandmother would have answered: yes.

Simic and Custred (1982, p. 169) observed that "even such venerable ideas as parents' responsibility for the behavior of their children have recently come into question . . .". This fits the consequences that can be expected of the household transformation. When every family around you is in a similar situation of low internal incentives for self-command training, there is little incentive left for the parents to blame each other for their children's lack of self-command. The externalities of children's public behavior on parent will not vanish but they will be strongly reduced, adding to the effect of diminishing externalities in the household. The result is an increasing output of youth who have not been socialized into functioning in hierarchies and into creating large areas of "indifference" for superiors to be filled in. The less the difference in income and security between different strata the stronger this effect for all strata. The same argument explains why at first increasing prosperity in a society will have the opposite effect. At first, some families manage to rise in status due to the generational cumulation of income and education. For them, the public behavior of children (including occupational and partner choice) will have strong externalities on the possibilities of holding on to or improving on the newly acquired status. Later, as more and more families come into this position, and status progress due to generational cumulation slows, the costs of self-command training begin to outweigh the benefits of influencing the public behavior of one's children. Thus, Elias theory of increasing self-control training with increasing civilization only picks up the first part of the impact of prosperity, not the second.

Governance Structures and Self-Command Capital

How can a governance structure do something about self-command problems? Of course, the simplest solution is always to design jobs that require as little self-command as possible. If there is little discretion, there is little occasion for self-command. Also where it is possible to monitor output but pay is unrelated to output, people may ask for performance related pay in order to help them solve their self-command problem. Yet, this option will not hold for most jobs where autonomy is granted. More importantly, as technology changes toward further integration and flexibility, the ratio of the jobs with discretion increases as well[16]. Ironically, this happens just when the ratio of people with a high amount of self-command capital is declining. For these reasons, governance structures will adapt to accommodate rather than eliminate self-command problems.

The classical view of hierarchy is that "each office has a clearly defined sphere of competence in the legal sense" and the office holder "is subject to strict and systematic discipline and control in the conduct of the office" (Weber, 1978, pp. 220f). There are, of course, less extreme views, but by and large, a hierarchy is seen as a layered command structure. Such a structure is based on the presumption of intention-controlled obedience. If you don't do what I say, it is because you don't want to do what I say. Once we admit self-command problems into the hierarchy, intention-controlled obedience becomes questionable. In that case, people are apt to cover up their own "lapses" and fail to allow for such lapses of their subordinates. The larger the self-command problems of the employees, the less a hierarchy can resemble a command structure. Giving up hierarchy in favor of a peer group is one option but it is subject to severe size and homogeneity limitations (see Williamson, 1975, pp. 41ff). What other solution is there? What instruments are available to influence framing effects appropriately? Let us remember that drastic solutions, like close supervision and harsh punishment, are not only expensive, they are also counter-productive for positions with enough autonomy to make lack of self-command capital a problem in the first place. Governance structures are arrangements for managing *relational labor*, with special emphasis on facilitating *ex post* adaptations and on the correspondence of deeds and compensations through internal organization. But for the solution of self-command problems, it is essential that additional instruments are at hand whenever there is a considerable degree of autonomy to be given to the employee. For Williamson, autonomy is given when there is high asset specificity

---

[16]See, for example, Wood (1989). Weiler (1990) points to similar developments and believes that the law will soon adapt to these developments.

(i.e., for the governance structures he calls obligational market and relational team). Lindenberg (1988) suggested to use "damage potential" as the more general condition for autonomy since causes other than asset specificity can create the dependence of management on intelligent effort from the employee (see also Goldberg, 1984). Be that as it may, given a high degree of autonomy of employees the most important of these instruments are:

1. Club hierarchy
2. Social metering
3. Instruction

Club Hierarchy

While the basis for hierarchy is command ("fiat", as Williamson calls it), the problem is that for many jobs considerable discretion has to be granted to the employee and, due to self-command problems, that it is not just a matter of incentive alignment what the employee will do with the autonomy. Given that self-command problems are widespread by now, personnel selection will not be the right answer except with regard to extreme cases (say addiction to gambling or alcohol). While Ford Motor Company still checked on the family situation of its employees in 1913, it abandoned this practice soon after and it has not been used since. The really bad cases can be detected ahead of time and the run of the mill kind of cases are too numerous to try to spot. This of course does not preclude the wisdom of moving to countries where prosperity is high enough to create stability and sharing in the household but not so high that self-command training in the family has already declined. But slowly, we are also running out of those countries. Thus, we will find more and more adaptations to the governance structure in order to deal with self-command problems.

From our framing analysis of self-command problems we know (i) that the possibility to postpone a decision is the major culprit for both procrastination and addiction; and (ii) even a small increase in the definitiveness of deadlines will have an effect. Thus we need hierarchy that prevents postponement. Where it grants autonomy, this hierarchy does not command or issue fiats but *it clearly establishes priorities and it constantly sets deadlines for things that must get done* (no matter how great the discretion about how it got done). Thus, against the idea that hierarchy should be abolished or strongly reduced in order to establish trust which in turn solves all agency problems, it is suggested here that we need a hierarchy exactly where there are trust relations. Only, the hierarchy we need does not command but it generates tasks, it orders these tasks and it times these tasks. It would like to call this kind of task generating structure *club hierarchy* because "club" conveys the style in which people interact with each other, also vertically. Confrontational bargaining blocks are incompatible with such a hierarchy because the legitimacy of the hierarchy itself is couched in functional terms rather than property rights terms (and this will be emphasized by the next two forms of social metering and context instruction). It is thus unlikely that strong union involvement will be found where club hierarchies govern.

Social Metering

One source of self-command problems is a situation in which somebody's performance is not closely monitored so that there is little response to lapses in self-command. There is an extensive discussion in the literature about measurement or "metering" problems of performance, leading to specific forms of governance (see Williamson, 1985). However, there is considerable confusion on this point. One meaning of "metering" is technological separability of performance for the purpose of compensation (Alchian and Demsetz, 1972). Team tasks create nonseparability and thus a decoupling of pay and performance. Another meaning of "metering" is hierarchical control as opposed to autonomy. Whether or not metering is technically possible, it is assumed to lower trust and thus increases transaction costs (see Williamson, 1975, pp. 55f). Conversely, absence of control with the right kind of compensation creates the willingness to perform well. "The worker begins to shirk as soon as it is perceived that the firm does not trust him or her" (Drago and Perlman, 1989, p. 47).

Thus, if the task is nonseparable, we have to trust the worker for technical reasons, but we better trust him or her anyway, even if the metering is technically possible, given we compensate them "fairly". In human resource management circles this view has sometimes led to a direct revival of the old human relations standpoint on this: give workers more responsibility, trust them more and you will increase efficiency. We know from various field experiments on this basis that this standpoint cannot be maintained as it stands (see, for example, Van Hoof and Huiskamp, 1989). It is also known that among the highly educated almost nobody likes a "direct" style of supervision but that for many, the ideal situation is not a "laissez faire" style but a "participatory" style of supervision, as Miller (1967) has shown. In a participatory style, there is a joint discussion before a decision is taken.

These findings fit the point of view developed in this paper. First of all, the likelihood of lack of self-command capital alerts us to the possibility that people do not work better if left alone, trusted, and fairly paid. To the contrary, such a situation may be rife with procrastination and other error-producing framing effects. Secondly, we would not identify metering solely with the measurement of performance for the purpose of compensation or with status-reducing control. Rather, we would look out for metering for the purpose of helping with self-command problems. There are many ways of metering that are neither a basis for payment nor degrading. For example, if we judge the quality of a secretary by the number of letters she types and pay her accordingly, this will interfere with her willingness to answer the telephone, clean up the office, etc. If we count the number of keys she touches on the computer each day, this would be degrading. However, each task she performs can informally be rated by those for whom she performs them. Whether she writes a letter for you, or arranges a meeting, or makes a telephone call, etc., in principle there can be an evaluating feedback on all of these tasks.

What is needed in order to produce performance observation and informal evaluative feedback is an *open communication structure* among all who are affected by each other's performance. Observe that we are not talking about a system of mutual spying and telling. Since we are dealing with framing effects, all we need are relatively small effects to counteract the salience of the (initially) equally small but consequential "deviant" goal. Where people are motivated to initiate talk because of the externalities exerted by their interaction partner, and where it is easy to chat and find out how things are going, where casual contact is normal, where teasing about work related matters is accepted, we get much performance observation and feedback, a combination which I would like to call *social metering*. Observe that social metering is not a style of supervision. It is a context for the *ex post* execution of contracts with considerable emphasis on *lateral* control.

Context Instruction

A key problem with impatience is that distant goals are too vague to balance the effect of proximate goals, so that a preference for the "objectively" inferior alternative is likely. In order to counteract this effect, it is very important to provide as much information as possible on the various aspects of the organization, especially the intended impacts over time. To this end, there are two means. First, *employees can be rotated for training purposes* throughout the organization, especially to departments downstream from where they are supposed to end up. This will help considerably in making important distant goals more concrete. Second, the organization can provide much information on the purpose of various plans and activities. Vaill (1986) calls this *purposing*. He describes it as "continuous stream of action by an organization's formal leadership which have the effect of inducing clarity, consensus, and commitment regarding the organization's basic purposes" (ibid., p. 91). Observe that the importance here is not just being informed about what is going on but being informed about the purpose of what is going on. Management by objective and goal setting techniques form a subset of this activity. But they were suggested as separate instruments, unrelated to the self-command problem and thus also overrated in what they (as the only instruments) could do to improve productivity. In this context of the relational team, Williamson himself only mentions that the firm "will engage in considerable social conditionaing to help assure that employees understand and are dedicated to the purpose of the firm [i.e., context instruction, S.L.], and employees will be provided with considerable job security" (Williamson, 1985, p. 247).

All three instruments support each other, but the strongest impact goes from last to first. Context instruction will furnish the basis on which effective social metering can take place, and effective social metering is needed to fine tune the task priorities and timings issued by the club hierarchy. Very importantly, good context instruction will allow the hierarchy to *legitimize deadlines and priorities functionally* rather than by authority.[17] Legitimation by authority either takes back the autonomy granted before, or it will destroy vertical social metering because people will be careful not to divulge information that may betray their error. For this reason, the punishments for errors and mistakes dealt out by the club hierarchy should be mild. Strong punishment will ruin social metering and will thus increase self-command problems in addition to the possible damage done to trust.[18]

For all three instruments, *culture and the management of meaning* can play an important role. First of all, there are subtle codes that make a hierarchy that does not issue command work. People have

[17]It is interesting in this context to look at a recent study by Heisig (1989) who observed an increase in "responsible autonomy" among highly skilled white-collar workers embedded in structures that come close to my description of club hierarchy, social metering and instruction.
[18]Staw (1981) has also shown that a punitive approach to error can lead to an escalation of commitment to the wrong decision.

to be socialized into this kind of culture. Secondly, social metering is very much dependent on common codes and understandings because it only works if people do not misread the casual interaction as spying or control. Third, context instruction as to the purpose of activities and plans is virtually steeped in management of meaning. However, it should not stand alone without being pegged to the governance problems it is supposed to help solve.

Conclusion

Two important developments with regard to organizations have remained largely unconnected: the new institutionalism with its emphasis on governance structures on the one hand and human resource management with its emphasis on culture, management of meaning and procedure on the other. In this paper, it has been suggested that the current bridge between them, viz. work on the production of trust and its relation to lowering transaction costs and increasing autonomy, is not enough, although it is very important. A second bridge is needed that relates to problems created by lack of self-command capital. It is argued that due to prosperity induced changes in the household, parents' incentive for putting effort into self-command training of their children, has strongly decreased after its long period of increase in Western societies. For this reason, more and more young people enter organizations endowed with little self-command capital and thus not trained in functioning in a hierarchy where they accept commands in return for payment. Ironically, this happens at a time when, for other reasons, autonomy and trust relations are on the increase. Put together, these two tendencies render deficiencies in self-command capital particularly important with regard to productivity because it is exactly in fairly autonomous jobs that lack of self-command capital has the most damaging consequences unless it is compensated by adaptations to the governance structure.

A good part of the paper deals with the question how self-command problems can be squared with rational choice theory. It is suggested that recent developments in the theory of framing offer a good explanation of how self-command problems can occur although people act (situationally) rationally. Because of framing effects, small goals can acquire situationally disproportionate importance. This is possible because actions deemed important (but unpleasant) may nonetheless be postponed and because the instrumental link of future goals to their consequences is weaker than that link for present goals. What needs to be done therefore is to adapt the governance structure in such a way that postponement becomes difficult and the consequences of future goals become more tangible. In special cases where output metering is possible but not implemented, people may ask for performance related pay in order to help them solve their self-command problem. But in most cases where autonomy is granted, this solution will not be available. There are three instruments that I could discern for achieving this: (i) A hierarchy that issues clear priorities and deadlines but not commands. This I call "club hierarchy" because of the relaxed style of vertical interaction. (ii) Massive mutual informal control by people who are tied by externalities. There is a strong emphasis on lateral control here. I call this "social metering". (iii) Each employee must be well informed about the purpose activities and plans of the subunit and the larger organization. This will render future consequences more concrete and it will aid considerably in steering the informal control; and it will allow functional legitimacy to deadlines and priorities rather than legitimacy by authority. There are mainly two ways of achieving this "context instruction": extensive rotating of employees during the training period and "purposing" by a continuous effort of the formal leadership to create clarity, consensus and commitment with regard to the purpose of activities and plans.

Attention to organizational culture and the management of meaning plays a role for all three instruments. The advantage of making the link to governance structure explicit is that we can guard against the unqualified generalizations so well known from the human relational approach. Yes, there should be de-hierarchization, but hierarchy should not go. In some sense, it should become even more visible as a setter of deadlines and priorities. Yes, people should trust each other, but they should also constantly find out about each other if they depend on what the other is doing. Yes, people should be informed about specific goals and plans, but more importantly, they should be informed about the purpose of goals and plans. All this, finally, takes place in conjunction with other features of the governance structure, regarding promotion, pay and conflict resolution.

References

Ainslie, G. (1975) Specious reward: a behavioral theory of impulsiveness and impulsive control. *Psychological Bulletin*, **82** 463–496.
Ainslie, G. (1986) Beyond microeconomics. Conflict among interests in a multiple self as a determinant of value. In *The Multiple Self*, pp. 133–175, edited by J. Elster. Cambridge: Cambridge University Press.

Akerlof, G. A. (1991) Procrastination and obedience. *American Economic Association Papers and Proceedings*, May, 1–19.

Alchian, A. A. and Demsetz, H. (1972) Production, information costs, and economic organization. *American Economic Review*, 62 777–95.

Becker, G. and Murphy, K. M. (1988) A theory of rational addiction. *Journal of Political Economy*, 96 675–700.

Brewer, J. (1970) Organizational patterns of supervision: a study of the de-bureaucratization of authority relations in two business organizations. In *The Sociology of Organizations*, pp. 341–347, edited by O. Grusky and G. A. Miller. New York: Free Press.

Bouwen, R. (1993) Organizational innovation as a social construction: managing meaning in multiple realities. In *Interdisciplinary Perspectives on Organization Studies*, edited by S. Lindenberg and H. Schreuder. Oxford: Pergamon Press.

Buchanan, J. (1990) The domain of constitutional economics. *Constitutional Political Economy*, 1 1–18.

Casson, M. (1991) *The Economics of Business Culture.* Oxford: Clarendon Press.

Coleman, J. S. (1990) *Foundation of Social Theory.* Cambridge, MA: Harvard University Press.

Coleman, J. S. (1993) Properties of rational organization. In *Interdisciplinary Perspectives on Organization Studies*, edited by S. Lindenberg and H. Schreuder. Oxford: Pergamon Press.

Cross, J. G. and Guyer, M. J. (1980) *Social Traps.* Ann Arbor: University of Michigan Press.

Deal, T. and Kennedy, A. (1982) *Corporate Cultures: The Rites and Rituals of Corporate Life.* Reading, MA: Addison-Wesley.

Drago, R. and Perlman, R. (1989) Supervision and high wages as competing incentives: a basis for labour segmentation theory. In *Macroeconomic Issues in Labour Economics*, pp. 41–61, edited by R. Drago and R. Perlman.

Elias, N. (1982) *The History of Manners.* New York: Pantheon.

Elster, J. (ed.) (1986) *The Multiple Self.* Cambridge: Cambridge University Press.

Fishburn, P. and Rubinstein, A. (1982) Time preference. *International Economic Review*, 23 677–694.

Fisher, I. (1930) *The Theory of Interest As Determined By the Impatience to Spend Income and Opportunity to Invest it.* New York: Macmillan.

Goldberg, V. (1984) A relational exchange perspective on the employment relationship. In *Firms, Organization and Labor*, pp. 127–145, edited by F. H. Stephen. New York: St. Martin's Press.

Heisig, U. (1989) *Verantwortung und Vertrauen im Grossbetrieb.* Konstanz: Wisslit Verlag.

Hirschman, Albert O. (1977) *The Passions and the Interests: Political Arguments for Capitalism Before Its Triumph.* Princeton: Princeton University Press.

Hofmaier, B. (1993) The role of dialogue in organizational change programs. In *Interdisciplinary Perspectives on Organization Studies*, edited by S. Lindenberg and H. Schreuder. Oxford: Pergamon Press.

Holcomb, J. H. and Nelson, P. S. (1992) Another experimental look at individual time preference. *Rationality and Society*, 4 199–220.

Lazear, E. (1981) Agency, earnings, profiles, productivity, and hours' restrictions. *American Economic Review*, 71 606–620.

Lindenberg, S. (1986) The paradox of privatization in consumption. In *Paradoxical Effects of Social Behavior. Essays in Honor of Anatol Rapoport*, pp. 297–310, edited by A. Diekmann and P. Mitter. Heidelberg/Wien: Physica-Verlag.

Lindenberg, S. (1988) Contractual relations and weak solidarity: the behavioral basis of restraints on gain-maximization. *Journal of Institutional and Theoretical Economics/ZfgS*, **144** 39–58.

Lindenberg, S. (1989) Choice and culture: the behavioral basis of cultural impact on transactions. In *Social Structure and Culture*, edited by H. Haferkamp. Berlin: de Gruyter.

Lindenberg, S. (1990a) A new push in the theory of organization. In *The New Institutional Economics. Different Approaches to the Economics of Institutions, Special Issue of the Journal of Institutional and Theoretical Economics*, pp. 76–84, edited by E. Furubotn and R. Richter, Vol. 146, 1.

Lindenberg, S. (1990b) *Homo socio-oeconomicus:* the emergence of a general model of man in the social sciences. *Journal of Institutional and Theoretical Economics,* **146** 727–748.

Lindenberg, S. (1991) Social approval, fertility and female labour market behaviour. In *Female Labour Market Behaviour and Fertility: A Rational Choice Approach*, pp. 32–58, edited by J. Siegers, J. de Jong-Gierveld and E. van Imhoff, Berlin/New York: Springer Verlag.

March, J. G. (1986) How we talk and how we act: administrative theory and administrative life. In *Leadership and Organizational Culture*, pp. 18–37, edited by T. J. Sergiovanni and J. E. Corbally. Urbana and Chicago: University of Illinois Press.

Miller, G. A. (1967) Professionals in bureaucracy: alienation among industrial scientists and engineers. *American Sociological Review*, 755–767.

Mitchell, D. J. B. and Zaidi, M. A. (eds.) (1990) *The Economics of Human Resource Management.* Oxford: Basil Blackwell.

Parsons, T. (1937) *The Structure of Social Action.* Glencoe: Free Press.

Parsons, T. (1951) *The Social System.* Glencoe: Free Press.

Rollins, B. C. and Thomas, D. L. (1979) Parental support, power, and control techniques in the socialization of children. In *Contemporary Theories About the Family*, edited by W. R. Burr, R. Hill, F. I. Nye and I. L. Reiss. *Research-based Theories*, Vol. I. New York: Free Press.

Schelling, T. C. (1984) The intimate contest for self-command. In *Choice and Consequences. Perspectives of an Errant Economist*, pp. 57–82, by T. C. Schelling. Cambridge, MA: Harvard University Press.

Schumpeter, A. (1954) *The History of Economic Analysis.* London: Allen & Unwin.

Simic, A. and Custred, G. (1982) Modernity and the American family: a cultural dilemma. *International Journal of Sociology of the Family* **12** 163–172.

Simon, H. (1951) A formal theory of the employment relationship. *Econometrica*, **19** 293–305.

Simon, H. (1957) *Administrative Behavior. A Study of Decision-Making Process in Administrative Organizations*, 2nd ed. New York: The Free Press.

Staw, B. M. (1981) The escalation of commitment. *Academy of Management Journal.*

Thaler, R. H. and Shefrin, H. M. (1981) An economic theory of self-control. *Journal of Political Economy*, **89** 392–406.

Umstot, D. D., Mitchell, T. R. and Bell, C. H. (1978) Goal setting and job enrichment: an integrated approach to job design. *Academy of Management Review*, **3** 867–879.

Vaill, P. B. (1986) The purposing of high-performance systems. In *Leadership and Organizational Culture*, pp. 85–104, edited by T. J. Sergiovanni and J. E. Corbally. Urbana and Chicago: University of Illinois Press.

Van Hoof, J. and Huiskamp, R. J. (1989) New forms of work organization in the Netherlands. In *New Forms of Work Organization in Europe*, pp. 155–173, edited by P. Grootings, B. Gustavsen and C. Hethy. New Brunswick: Transaction Publishers.

Weber, M. (1978) *Economy and Society*, edited by G. Roth and C. Wittich. Berkeley: University of California Press.

Weiler, P. C. (1990) *Governing the Workplace. The Future of Labor and Employment Law*. Cambridge, MA: Harvard University Press.

Weltner, L. (1988) *No Place Like Home: Rooms and Reflections from One Family's Life*. New York: Quill William Morrow.

Williamson, O. E. (1975) *Markets and Hierarchies: Analysis and Anti-Trust Implications*. New York: Free Press.

Williamson, O. E. (1985) *The Economic Institutions of Capitalism*. New York: Free Press.

Wood, S. (ed.) (1989) *The Transformation of Work?* London: Unwin Hyman.

PART IV

Interorganizational Perspectives

Markets, Networks and Control

HARRISON C. WHITE[1]

Any market of significance operates itself and reproduces itself without external planning or auctioneer.[2] It is a social mechanism, which is to say it is an institution and cannot be installed to order, by decree, at least also because it is sustained in part by competing attempts at control. Furthermore, in the longer run a market continues only because and as it is caught up in ties among some larger networks of markets. Call the whole a system an economy or sector of an economy. Such a system supports and is supported by shared terminology and conventions across a population. Such a system entails networks of tangible flows among specific markets.

The general question of this paper is how to conceive of markets effectively within networks of flows and attempts at control which generate and which in turn are generated by and around those markets. Prices and allocations are central to markets and their systems. Also central are flexibilities in choice of whom to deal with and in what particular variety of goods. But then some form of mutually-enforced commitment is also central to sustaining a given market. There are great differences between individual markets in these respects, as there can be major differences among systems.

Two species should be distinguished among individual markets. In exchange markets, ranging from lawn sales or county fairs on through international trade,[3] selling and buying are roles for

[1]Center for the Social Sciences and Department of Sociology Columbia University. *Author's note:* An early version of this paper was also given at a Moscow seminar of young Soviet social scientists. The author is grateful to Seweryn Bialer and Lynn A. Cooper for suggesting changes there, and also to comments from Eric Leifer, Siegwart Lindenberg and Ilan Talmud. I am indebted to the Netherlands Institute for Advanced Study, Wassenaar, for support during the period of preparation for the conference which engendered this volume.
[2]If some auctioneer core is crucial, then that, not the market dress, is the source of control for terms of trade and their evolution.
[3]The range can be extended to cover Coleman's (1990) schoolboys trading cards picturing professional sports players, and the New York Stock Exchange (Baker,

actors rather than positions necessarily fixed with respect to a given sort of product. In this species of markets, the notion of product is labile. A second species, the production market, is the main transducer mechanisms within Western economies. These markets as institutions shape an array of products together with a population of producers as formal organizations. A market is committed to a product. Development paths of markets and networks interact. Exchange markets have generated and nested in mercantile networks for millennia, as portrayed, for example, by Braudel (1982) and Polanyi et al. (1957). Various sorts of partnerships and leagues come to be important actors in such economies. Production markets and networks are also evolved together, along lines sketched, for example, by Bythel (1978) and Kriedte et al. (1981), into the distinctive pattern which we observe today as a manufacturing economy. Each production market ties to other markets in a network of flows, in an input–output network, which can be further dissected into many subsidiary networks of specialized flows.

Just as markets of this second species build up around participation by large producer firms, the networks among these markets embody the actions of producer firms. Yet flows in these networks are subject to pressures from transactions through exchange markets, markets of the first species that are neither localized nor tied down within the input–output network of manufacturing economy. There is a bewildering profusion of levels and locales, as long ago noted by Marshall (1891) and Jevons (1875), such that the species of market and network are sometimes observed as concrete types but sometimes are best seen as analytic abstractions. Control efforts by participants will repeatedly attempt to cross-cut the species.

Current developments in Eastern Europe and elsewhere may be giving rise to new subspecies of markets and networks, and certainly to new configurations and mixes, as, for example, Granick (1972, 1975) and Hamilton and Biggart (1985) have long been suggesting. Fresh ideas are needed in any case to develop for the current Organization of European Economic Cooperation (OEEC) context more adequate theories of markets, networks and their system of organizations and products.

In the following, we begin with phenomenology for networks of markets. Then we turn to individual markets, for which later an

1984), and also New Guinea kula rings (Strathern, 1971). This illustrates the extraordinary scope in exchange markets, which are markets of the episode rather than markets of reproduction.

explicit and testable model is proposed, a model of production markets as a group of peers signalling by a self-reproducing schedule. Finally, among discussion of predictions and conjectures, a central conundrum is identified and a resolution suggested.

Origins and Self-Similarity

A set of actors can become comparable, become peers, through jostling to join in production on comparable terms. They commit by joining together to pump downstream versions of a common product, which are subjected by both themselves and downstream actors to invidious comparison. Children competing in hopscotch or reciting for a teacher, mathematicians in a test for a prize, actors in a play—and manufacturers of recreational aircraft for the U.S. market—are all examples of this basic social formation. The production market is a special case of this social formation, call it the commit interface.

Each production economy is the result of a historical evolution in which market and firm and network and product change together, usually slowly, from a base system of markets in long-distance trade and exchange, markets of the first species. The process began independently many times in Europe, as putting-out systems evolved in tandem with marketing networks. Input–output networks build historically within and into a given economy.

For example, in Florence and other Italian cities of the early Renaissance, production of cloth induced networks for "putting-out" the production of parts of the initial product, such as fustian, and each of these parts could itself become established as the product of a separate market (e.g., Lachmann and Peltersen, 1988). The pattern was heralded earlier in the painful forging of *verlager* and *kaufmann* systems by entrepreneurs in late medieval Europe (Kriedte et al., 1981), in the hinterlands of medieval networks of German cities: early entrepreneurs "put out" raw materials and/or tools cottagers and then "marketed" the resulting production which they collected. And the process was elaborated further in "out-work" patterns of subsequent periods and locales (e.g., Bythell, 1978, on London in the industrial revolution).

Slow change on the surface does not contradict intense social pressures to compete for and to sustain a distinct position. In addition, attempts to assert a new kind of control flair up continuously. Effects of introducing a new technology can partially reroute the input–output networks, and wholly new markets can appear in various ways.

Besides introducing hysteresis and other complexities of analysis, this historicity suggests the possibility of self-similarity. That is, the forms of networks within an industry—itself embracing scores of actual production markets—may resemble the forms of local networks (for example, the *verlager* networks in one sort of cloth among a few cities) and, in turn, both may be homomorphic to input–output networks across a whole industrial sector or national economy.[4] Failing some such cross-level similarity, there is indeed little prospect for effective analysis of economies, and in fact most economic constructs used today rely implicitly on self-similarity.

Products and Production Markets

The producer firms can be seen as pumps expensively committed to spouting continuing flows of products. The set of pumps acting together form the market as superpump in interaction with, and with confidence in, provision of an orderly and continuing social setting with buyers. To the buyers, the array of pumps is a menu of terms of trade. It is this social process which induces a definition of "product" from the common properties of the flows, rather than the product being some pre-existing given.

Thus markets and their products emerge and evolve in a symbiotic process of definition and recognition by suitable clienteles and producers. And here producers typically are large compound actors, firms or other organizations. Equipment and expertise commit them over long terms, as just one "side" to a given market. A product also becomes publicly defined as buyers settle down with the producers across terms of trade.[5] The terms of trade settle into a schedule which becomes the interface between the two sides.

---

[4]Alfred Marshall before 1900 seemed well aware of this. Other levels are required for a full theory of economy: for example, the internal constitution of firms. See Williamson (1975) for one attempt to integrate this level with that of exchange markets. See Eccles and White (1985) for one attempt to integrate the level of firms with that of production markets.

Self-similarity can extend down through persons. Recent surveys of social network analysis construed primarily around individuals can be found in Wellman and Berkowitz (1988), which also contains applications to business at several different scales, which latter are the focus in Burt (1990), and in Mizruchi and Schwartz (1988).

[5]Various of these producers also come to be, simultaneously, members of other production markets (see Baumol et al., 1988). And of course the buyers are in many other markets so that there is an intricate structure of mappings and correspondences required to read input–output networks accurately.

Begin from the individual positions of production firms within a market. For example, in some market for rubber used to manufacture tires,[6] one firm becomes known for producing lower-quality but cheap rubber, another for higher-cost rubber of high durability but low flexibility, and so on. Within a market, each producer is committed for a substantial period, given immobile investment in physical and social machinery. Each producer becomes specialized with a view to maximum net return given the constraints of the structure of competition imposed in that market.

Each producer has established a position on a schedule of terms of trade, in a space with dimensions for producers' volumes and revenues. This schedule is observable from information available to every producer, and it is reproduced by the actions of the "other side" of the market.[7] The producers do not bounce in and out of a market, as they can in the exchange market of economic theory. Each producer is also a consumer of inputs from other markets; so that each market presupposes a continuing network of flows from and among specific other markets (cf. Leontief, 1965). The production economy consists of overlapping networks of procurement and supply among firms in markets (e.g., Corey, 1978).

This view contrasts with and supplements the account of a market as an abstract category that suits the Pure Theory of Exchange (e.g., Newman, 1965; Arrow and Hahn, 1975). Discussions of supply-and-demand also recede into the background, along with money supply and other macro-institutional features. Producers' basic concerns are to hold on to distinctive positions in their markets. They adapt their current outputs to fluctuations in the economy by layoffs and the like without any necessary change in market positions as producers.

Production Network Economies

There are levels in network economies, but they are not discrete hierarchical levels. A given firm may have a position in each of

---

[6]It depends in part on incident and chance—on history—whether the market boundaries are of all tires, or only auto tires, or only in a region, or whether, for example, a separate market develops, permanently or temporarily, around a technological innovation such as radial tires. Or rubber markets may not partition according to end use in vehicles at all.

[7]For simplicity, the "other side" is assumed to be the buyers; but a dual form (White, 1988) of the same model holds when the other side are suppliers of a dominant input, say skilled labor.

several distinct production markets, and the firm may exceed in total size each of the markets it is "in". While there must be at least several firms to structure any given market mechanism, this mechanism usually cannot sustain participation by more than say a score of producers. One can by contrast discriminate hundreds and more markets in a production network.[8]

Terms of trade establish themselves as an interface *within* a given market very differently than do terms of trade *between* markets in production networks. In the latter, entirely different features emerge. Social discipline and the competitive pressures underlying it are no less real, but these pressures are changeable and variegated so that the discipline is of a system within which commitments can be changed. Efforts at control, especially of engrossment of stocks, that is to say of speculation, are important along with strivings for profit from routine mark-ups. Gross profits depend on network possibilities for autonomy and control. Autonomy is possible to the extent there are alternative market sources and destinations for various products as conceived and packaged by a given actor, whereas constraint comes via the actor's lack of alternatives within the established network of markets. Attempts at control can be predicted from reading the converse sides to others' autonomies.

Sense can be made of observations of a production economy only by modeling how all these different attempts fit together over time. This is not easy, since framing of inter-market theory is incompatible with the framing of intra-market theory. One can attempt to stuff the entire picture into one or the other frame. Arrow and Hahn (1973) represent the high-water mark of attempts to make the Pure Theory of Exchange serve as a general theory of a whole economy.[9] Leontief's input–output model is the high-water mark of attempts by economists to stuff an entire economy into the ecological niche suitable to intra-market structure.

A different approach is worth exploring. In this approach we focus on how production markets resemble other social formations, rather than on how they are different. We bring out the abstract parallels between economic and other institutional realms, rather

---

[8]The assertions of my model, like assertions in micro-economic textbooks, require imposition of sharp boundaries upon blurry situations. For example, producers may string out geographically such that the buyers from one producer overlap but do not coincide with buyers of even nearest neighbor producers. The vision of a neat partition among separate markets is an idealization for the purpose of obtaining useable predictions and insights.

[9]A convenient overview of the Pure Theory of Exchange at an intermediate level of technical detail is Newman (1965).

than emphasizing their differences. This amounts to developing a theory of a general social discipline of which one of the species of markets above is a special case. Repeat this for the other species of markets. Then develop and deploy similar theories for still other species of social discipline, whether or not they have a known economic representative. Observations can suggest how such disciplines cumulate and grow into broader social institutions.[10]

Let me rephrase the matter. It aids comprehension to show how the production market, under its particular institutional dress, is an example of a very widespread social formation. This can lead into a formulation of how networks of such markets are special cases of social networks in general. I draw upon models of networks and of control interactions from Burt (1990), which he also applies to systems of other actors besides markets, in order to develop an explanation of aggregate volumes and payments from markets across a production network.

First, I embody my view of the production market in an explicit model, the mathematical formulae and equations for which can be found in White (1988). The main result is that the average price in a production market is arbitrary; only relative prices among producers matter in its construction. The conception behind this model derives from Chamberlin (1933),[11] but its implementation was developed from the mechanism proposed by Spence (1974) for market signalling.

Second, I sketch how one might extend these results so as to embed them in a broader view of an economic system, be that a sector or some more inclusive level. In doing so I shall be guided by sociological theory of how institutional forms in general emerge out of network cumulation. The contrast with extrapolation of the Pure Theory of Exchange to the level of economy should be instructive, as should the contrasts and parallels to the Leontief line.

Terms of Trade in Production

To begin with, in a given market, each producer firm will have a position which is entirely relative to the positions of other producers in that market. So this production market can be conceived as an interface, as terms-of-trade which are a schedule,

---

[10]I offer such a theory elsewhere (White, 1992); here I sketch applications to an economy.

[11]Subsequent microeconomics proved unable to assimilate Chamberlin's seminal analysis of monopolistic competition, and Joan Robinson's parallel discovery (1933), which each brought into focus the vision sketched by Marshall (1891).

say of volume versus price, a schedule in which each producer firm has a distinctive position. This schedule will not reproduce itself unless the specialized product varieties from the various producer firms come to seem to the other side to be equivalent tradeoffs of quality for price at observed total volumes. A handful of producers is sufficient to sustain a market, which cannot support the very large number of producers envisioned in the pure competitive markets of microeconomic textbooks.

The key point is that the terms of trade and the choices of position within this schedule can be estimated by businessmen using ordinary calculations from just the tangible signals that each can garner in the course of business, together with the practical knowledge of one's own cost-of-production schedule. No auctioneer need be hypothesized; instead the practical activities generate the signals needed. Thus the concrete market composes itself as some definite mesh between array of values seen by buyers and array of costs; without such meshing it does not reproduce itself.

Gossip can supply to each producer an estimate of most of the terms achieved by peers. The production market consists of the observable spread of terms of trade being achieved by various producers with their distinctive flows. At the simplest, these terms are revenue for volume shipped.[12] For the market to reproduce itself, each producer must continue to see its pair, revenue and volume, as its optimal choice from the menu of observed terms of trade; only this menu is known to be sustainable by the buyers, who themselves are comparison shopping.

Terms of trade are a commonly observable shape which cues actors into niches by their own preferences which yet are agreeable across the interface. This is an interpolation across revenue and volume pairs observed for the various producers.[13] The terms of trade must be accepted by the purchaser side, which is the arbiter of the competition, the judge of relative performances. The ironic implication is that production markets generate only the relative sizes of differentiated flows, not the aggregate size of flow.

Market outcomes and their correlates. Market stability proves to come from having *unequal* shares held by the different producers, while, sadly for them, cash flows—price less cost—tend to be larger

---

[12]Leave aside for more detailed modeling the line of related products which any given producer may supply.
[13]For illustration see figs. 3.1–3.3 in Leifer and White (1988). The mathematical model is worked out in White (1988).

the more nearly equal are the market shares. Increasing returns to scale, which in microeconomics textbooks bar market formation, can be accommodated by the market mechanism as modeled here.

Supply equals demand as a tautology, each time after the fact. It is the variation among producers in qualities, and the difficulties each confronts in production, that shape the interface which motivates and sets the terms of trade which reproduce themselves. But actors ordinarily do not conceive and relate to higher-order measures like variances, and they may tell stories in stylized terms of supply and demand. The production market mechanism, like any commit interface, must be realized through forms which are perceived and estimated directly in everyday terms.

Control and Network Averages

There is a central conundrum to be resolved: A production market builds itself out of dispersions so that it is variances rather than means of outputs that are controlled. And control is the primary concern in network ties. Yet a network of flows *among* markets must primarily deal with and respond to averages, to what we call "supply and demand".

Control struggles in the network of production markets account for the form for any particular market. No firm likes to depend on a single supplier or a single customer firm or market. So it is hard for firms to survive as isolates, against the pressures from others' desires to have multiple partners for trades. Firms find it necessary to push into a niche among peers in a market, simply in order to gain standing with possible buyers.[14]

Struggles for control and autonomy accompany every tie between markets in the network of a production economy. A market's terms-of-trade schedule can be pushed up or down in these struggles, although the relative positions of producers within the market need not change. The preceding model for a single market leaves arbitrary its exact overall size—in physical volume and in cash flow. It also shows how the sizes of buyer surplus and producer profit, the respective aggregate payoffs for the two sides, follow from the aggregate size, and move in opposite directions with respect to it.

Location in the network determines how much autonomy can

---

[14]This profile of evolution in Western production markets, and their network economies, may suggest leads for conversion of Soviet ones (Podolny, 1990).

accrue to a given market through efforts of producers in it *vis-à-vis* other markets located upstream, downstream and parallel—how much choice it has among other markets for supplying and being supplied with components. Burt has systematically developed this thesis and applied it to interrelations among industries in the U.S. He shows (1983; 1992, ch. 4) that profit margins correlate with network measures of autonomy. If entrepreneurs within a market exploit autonomy and constraint, they increase control and can obtain higher average returns.

Two complementary sorts of regularity can be predicted from Burt's vision. One concerns how individual firms exploit within a market their degree of autonomy across markets. The other regularity is the longer term impact of all these autonomy maneuvers on the relative price levels of different markets. This second regularity can be seen as a new specification or operationalization of actual mechanisms for the Pure Theory of Exchange (Newman, 1965).

The first regularity is exactly that there should be more deviations away from terms-of-trade schedules when more of the producers in a market have high autonomy. There are no such comparative data now available across a population of production markets. But we can rely on self-similarity to argue for a correlation of higher standard deviations in pricing for industrial sectors which have higher degrees of autonomy. Burt has found exactly such to be the case (Burt, 1992).

Average price levels, and thus profits, come from ties between whole markets and not from relative positions of producer firms within a market, which are a profile that shapes only relative prices. But the longer-term effect of the first regularity—the outcomes of individual producer's efforts to exploit autonomy—will tend to move other producers in a given market back into line, or rather into profile, with the achievements of the more autonomous ones.[15] Profits of producers in different markets can be expected to correlate with the objective measures of autonomy in their production network, an autonomy that frees action of executives from external constraints. Substitution is the key in the network of markets. It follows that autonomies and constraints suffered by

---

[15]The more autonomous producers' interests are not served by disappearance of less autonomous peers. The whole point of a market, as discussed before, is to induce custom by having enough similar producers to attract buyers from other markets' substitutable goods—and to reassure such buyers that they are not entering a situation offering no autonomy to them.

neighbor markets also should be taken into account, since they will indirectly influence the autonomy achievable in a given market.

Interfaces

A supplementary goal of this paper is to show how analysis of economies of markets and networks can and should be fitted in as a special case of a more general analysis of social structure. This enriches the latter and ensures the former against divorce from reality, which is a social reality. The component processes of markets can be seen as examples of more general processes with other embodiments more widely familiar in all societies.

In a time when attempts are being made to change whole economies toward a form closer to the Western ones, it is especially instructive to be explicit about how capitalist forms can be understood as particular cases of more general social processes. The aura of magic which at present surrounds "the market" in discussions within formerly state socialist societies should be dissipated. Western economic institutions are robust and effective, but academic economic analysis of them has little correspondence to their realities.[16]

The focus of the study of interfaces, and of markets in particular, should be how separate actors embed into a joint formation and induce a new identity.

Material production of all sorts tends to come from commit interfaces. Here the "receivers" are a distinct set and the context is neither relaxed nor social. The hunting or gathering groups described for tribal contexts (Firth, 1957; Lee, 1979; Rose, 1960; Udy, 1959) are early realizations which have analogues today in sports teams (Leifer, 1990) and in children's games (Fine, 1983; Opie and Opie, 1969). The basic mechanism does not require or presuppose distinct roles among the producers along with explicit cues and assignments. Rather, a spread of performances is induced by attention of producers to differential preferences by the other side, who can turn off their attention (or more tangible payments for production).

Interfaces do not build from a concern with ecology. In shaping structures of importance, it is control projects that compete, and they only peripherally attend to effectiveness of physical work.

---

[16]This is evidenced by the disdain of business executives, both Western and Japanese, for academic micro-economics. The abstract and hypothetical nature of modern micro-economic theory unfortunately contributes to a magical cast of thinking by inexperienced reformers in the Eastern bloc.

Social life is about actors' importance within social settings; so these settings cannot be shaped primarily to effective joint operations on physical settings. As Udy (1970) was among the first to say explicitly, production in the ordinary sense of practical work is difficult to reconcile with the universal tendencies of elaboration and embedding which come with the ongoing process of social structuring.[17]

Asymmetry underlies all the variations of the commit interface. Embedding is built into the form. On one side, individual flows are being induced amid jockeying for relative position, or niche; the other side is (possibly disparate) receivers appropriating the aggregate flow. The flow is always from the one, disaggregate side to the other. The social perceptions that discipline producers into order come from both sides, but behavioral cues to specific niches are on one side only. Producers are choosing what flows to offer. The commit interface presupposed and requires unremitting attention to the flows and the interface by the producers.

Underlying this mechanism is a matching of variances. Producers differ in various combinations of abilities, and so are differentially attractive to receivers. The mechanism sustaining a commit interface continues only if relative recognition of producers can be mapped to their spread on actual productivity. This mapping must emerge and reproduce itself, which happens only when the producer set is arrayed in reward in the same order in which their productions are discriminated. Only if there is variance in abilities across producers, correlated with variance in their receptions, can the commit interface reproduce itself.

Reference group theory long ago came to the view that it was dispersions among actors in rewards, not averages, that drove any organized system. The classic formulation came from the Stouffer (1948) study of World War II military: anticipation over time was equally important with dispersion. Tversky and Kahneman (Kahneman, Slovic and Tversky, 1982), and recently Lindenberg

---

[17]Udy worked out his argument from an extensive cross-cultural canvass of detailed forms of hunting, gathering, agriculture, craft, manufacturing and other contexts for work. The problem of succession to social positions is one major exemplification of this tension between work and the social. Performance in a work team can be seen as dependent on succession, day-by-day, to tasks of work. And the same issue recurs at larger scopes and periods. Solutions of social equations of balance deliver the successors and thereby impinge on technical equations of physical production. Udy's theorem is that the longer and more fully developed the social context of production is, the less effective and efficient the work process: Hunting and gathering, he argues, dominates settled agriculture in efficiency.

(Lindenberg, 1989) have revived this notion. By my different route through study of production markets, I have come to a clipped version of the same general view: species of interfaces disciplined by quality orderings, but only them, survive or not according to, and only to, matchings of variances among the constituent actors.

Industrial production markets of this century are the exemplars of commit interfaces. A production market must induce distinctive flows, at the same time as it renders them comparable, from a to-be-determined set of producers and into the hands of an array of buyers becoming accustomed and committed to that market. Some agreed framing as a linear ordering—which acquires the connotations of a valuation—can provide a scaffolding. Within this scaffolding, dispersions across observed quantities can array in social formations that then prove able to reproduce themselves. "Quality" captures the connotations of the invidious transitive order induced to form this mechanism of commitment. This is the market as interface, the production market induced from quality valuation. Valuations need not find their source in the induction and routing of average flows![18]

Conclusion

A combination of control struggles over time generates the production market as a social category, distinct from the exchange market. The evolution has continued further, as large firms diversify by buying positions in production markets for other products, in an effort to enhance their overall autonomy (Vancil, 1979). But the production market remains the social construction for what "a product" is, overriding engineering and cultural preconceptions.

The commit interface comes in many other varieties than production market, other institutional embodiments. "Star" systems, in entertainment and elsewhere, grow out of interfaces where embedding induces perceptions of events which are greatly exaggerated from the view of actors producing them (Faulkner, 1983). Even where the differentiation or dependence is limited, as among starlets in entertainment, there is the same pressure to generate events sufficient to embed them with a skew distribution of fame despite undetectable differences as judged within the interface. These star systems can be seen as closely analogous to the industrial markets, where some firms or other are forced into leading roles willy-nilly by the enormous social pressures of contention.

---

[18]This is just as the economist Frank Knight long ago intuited (1921).

Competition within any commit interface is about the importance of doing slightly better than your peers who in the larger context are so very similar to oneself. What is not necessarily signified explicitly is the strength of the new joint identity being created by the competition. The interface, in particular the production market, functions as a strong identity. Interjections of manipulations as attempts at control from within, by assembling peers or receivers, find hard going. The equivalency in peer positions subjects insiders to very strong discipline by the comparable others. Effective discipline comes from those similarly located, and thus conversant with the information and perspective the subject brings. Yet interjections by outsiders also find the commit interface difficult to disrupt. The commit interface is robust to both external and internal control projects.

Commit interfaces by their construction do not control for averages, cannot be programmed to yield prespecified flows. Instead commit interfaces build their dynamics around the spread of contributions across the comparable set. The commit interface is best portrayed as a curvature or response across the variation in members' properties. Mutual attention of peers is directed toward jockeying for relative positions which yield each a distinctive niche.

It follows, however, that the commit interface can become a profile subject to higher-level control, conditional on skills in manipulation of multiple rhetorics. A whole new level of sophistication opens up. Only variances and their ratios constrain the shape and positioning of the interface when it is operating autonomously. But rewards, severally and in aggregate, depend upon means, so that there is a latent motivation to try to shift interface in concert. The shift can be accomplished only if the acceptable shapes of profile are retained; so they become envelopes for achieving control. Participants can make systematic use of these facts. For example, Eccles (1985) showed how chief executive officers make use of these interfaces in achieving control over leading subordinates. The executive perspective on markets is to use markets to enhance control within the firm.[19]

Given all these considerations, it is possible to see how networks among markets can come to seem as live actors on their own. The situation is strikingly akin to that in the neural networks of the brain as envisioned in models of parallel distributed processing (McClelland and Rumelhart, 1986). Nonlinearities in synapses, firings of ties, sustain evolution of self-reproducing patterns: what

---

[19]Tendencies toward this have been observed in large Soviet as well as American firms in a recent comparative field study by Vlachoutsicos and Lawrence (1990).

we call memories for brains and faction fights in networks. But these outcomes presuppose the continuation of the substrate of cells and production market interfaces, respectively. An argument can be made that the origin of production firms themselves can be seen as just such nonlinearities or memories in earlier and smaller networks among production interfaces.

References

Arrow, Kenneth J. and Hahn, Frank H. (1971) *General Competitive Analysis*. San Francisco: Holden-Day.

Baumol, William J., Panzar John C. and Willig R. D. (1988) *Contestable Markets and the Theory of Industry Structure*. San Diego, CA: Harcourt Brace Jovanovich.

Baker, Wayne (1984) The social structure of a national securities market. *American Journal of Sociology*, 89 775–811.

Burt, Ronald S. (1983) *Corporate Profits and Cooptation: Networks of Market Constraints and Directorate Ties in the American Economy*. New York: Academic Press.

Burt, Ronald S. (1992) *Structural Holes, The Social Structure of Competition*. Cambridge, MA: Harvard University Press.

Braudel, Ferdinand (1982) *The Wheels of Commerce*. Translated by S. Reynolds. Harper & Row.

Bythell, Duncan (1978) *The Sweated Trades: Outwork in Nineteenth Century Britain*. London: St. Martin's.

Chamberlin, E. H. (1933) *The Theory of Monopolistic Competition*. Cambridge, MA: Harvard University Press.

Coleman, James S. (1990) *Foundations of Social Theory*. Cambridge, MA: Harvard University Press.

Corey, E. Raymond (1978) *Procurement Management*. Boston: CBI.

Dehez, Pierre and Dreze, Jacques (1987) Competitive equilibria with increasing returns. European University Institute, Florence, Working Paper no. 86/243.

Eccles, Robert G. (1981a) Bureaucratic versus craft administration: the relationship of market structure to the construction firm. *Administrative Science Quarterly*, 26 449–469.

Eccles, Robert G. (1981b) *VISA International: The Management Change*. Case 0–482–022, HBS Case Services, Harvard Graduate School of Business Administration, Boston, MA.

Eccles, Robert G. (1981c) The quasifirm in the construction industry. *Journal of Economic Behavior and Organization*, 2 335–57.

Eccles, Robert G. (1985) *The Transfer Pricing Problem: A Theory for Practice*. Lexington, MA: Lexington Books.

Faulkner, Robert R. (1983) *Music on Demand: Composers and Careers in the Hollywood Film Industry*. New Brunswick: Transaction Books.

Fine, Gary A. (1983) *Shared Fantasies: Role Play Games as Social Worlds*. Chicago: University of Chicago Press.

Firth, Raymond (1957) *We, The Tikopia*. London: Allen & Unwin.

Granick, David (1972) *Managerial Comparisons of Four Developed Countries*. Cambridge, MA: MIT Press.

Granick, David (1975) *Enterprise Guidance in Eastern Europe: A Comparison of Four Socialist Economies.* Princeton, NJ: Princeton University Press.

Hamilton, Gary G. and Biggart, Nicole W. (1985) Why people obey. *Sociological Perspectives,* 28 3–28.

Jevons (1875) *Money and the Mechanism of Exchange.* London: Appleton.

Kahneman, D., Slovic, P. and Tversky, A. (eds.) (1982) *Judgment under Uncertainty: Heuristics and Decisions.* Cambridge: Cambridge University Press.

Knight, Frank (1921) *Risk, Uncertainty and Profit.* Cambridge, MA: Houghton Mifflin.

Kriedte, Peter, Medick, Hans and Shlumbohm, Jurgen (1981) *Industrialization Before Industrialisation.* Cambridge: Cambridge University Press.

Lachmann, Richard and Pelterson, Stephen (1988) *Rationality and Structure in the "Failed" Capitalism of Renaissance Italy.* Department of Sociology, University of Wisconsin, Madison.

Lee, Richard B. (1979) *The !Kung San.* Cambridge: Cambridge University Press.

Leifer, Eric M. (1990) Inequality among equals: performance inequalities in league sports. *American Journal of Sociology.*

Leifer, Eric M. and White, Harrison C. (1988) A structural approach to markets. In Mizruchi and Schwartz, eds.

Leontief, Wassily W. (1966) *Input–Output Economics.* New York: Oxford University Press.

Lindenberg, Siegwart (1989) Choice and culture: the behavioral basis of cultural impact on transactions. In *Social Structure and Culture Berlin,* pp. 175–200, edited by Hans Haferkamp. De Gruyter.

Mansfield, Edwin (1975) *Microeconomics: Theory and Applications,* 2nd ed. New York: Norton.

Marshall, Alfred (1891, 1920) *Principles of Economics,* 8th edition. London: Macmillan.

McClelland, James L., Rumelhart, David E. and others (1986) *Parallel Distributed Processing,* Vols. 1 and 2. Cambridge, MA: MIT Press.

Mizruchi, Mark S. and Schwartz, Michael (eds.) (1988) *Intercorporate Relations: The Structural Analysis of Business.* Cambridge University Press.

Newman, Peter (1965) *The Theory of Exchange.* Englewood Cliffs, NJ: Prentice-Hall.

Opie, Peter and Opie, Iona (1969) *Children's Games in Street and Playground: Chasing, Catching, Seeking, Hunting, Racing, Duelling, Exerting, Daring, Guessing, Acting, Pretending.* Oxford: Clarendon Press.

Polanyi, Karl, Arensberg, Conrad M. and Pearson, Harry W. (1957) *Trade and Market in the Early Empires.* Glencoe, IL: Free Press.

Podolny, Joel (1990) *A Sociologically Informed View of the Market.* Harvard University: William James Hall.

Robinson, Joan (1933) *The Economics of Imperfect Competition.* London: Macmillan.

Rose, F. G. G. (1960) *Classification of Kin, Age Structure, and Marriage amongst the Groote Eylandt Aborigines.* Berlin: Akademie-Verlag.

Spence, A. Michael (1974) *Market Signalling.* Cambridge, MA: Harvard University Press.

Stouffer, Samuel A. (1948) *The American Soldier.* Princeton, NJ: Princeton University Press.

Strathern, Andrew (1971) *The Rope of Moka.* Cambridge: Cambridge University Press.

Udy, Stanley (1959) *Organization of Work*. Human Relations Area Files.

Udy, Stanley (1970) *Work in Traditional and Modern Society*. NJ: Prentice-Hall.

Vancil, Richard F. (1979) *Decentralization: Managerial Ambiguity by Design*. Honewood, IL: Dow-Jones.

Vlachoutsicos, C. and Lawrence, Paul (1990) What we don't know about Soviet management. *Harvard Business Review*, pp. 50–64.

Wellman, Barry and Berkowitz, S. D. (eds.) (1988) *Social Structures: A Network Approach*. New York: Cambridge University Press.

White, Harrison C. (1988) Varieties of markets. In Wellman and Berkowitz (eds.), *Social Structures. A Network Approach*. Cambridge: Cambridge University Press.

White, Harrison C. (1992) *Identity and Control*. Princeton: Princeton University Press.

Williamson, Oliver E. (1975) *Market and Hierarchies*. New York: Free Press.

Market Integration

RONALD S. BURT[1]

My topic for this chapter is the question of what holds markets together. I develop a distinction between two approaches to the question and I would like to bring the two approaches more closely together. I present results on the American economy illustrating how the less often used approach can be useful in describing market data typically described only in the first approach. My central goal is to illustrate how the integration question can be studied as a network analysis problem—the same strategy could be used, for example, to study the integration of establishments within a firm, firms within a market, or nations within the world system—and to provide an empirical answer with respect to markets in the American economy. The central conclusion is the identification of the market group as an elementary unit of business integration. A market group contains a set of core markets, a set of satellite markets, and a strong satellite dependence on the core. In contrast to the idea of an enterprise group, structurally analogous to a clique, a market group is stratified into an upper and lower tier of interdependent markets. Within the top tier, core markets tend to be connected by chains (not cycles) of mutual dependence relations. The bulk of the roles among core markets are either mutual dependence dyads or chains of mutual dependence. In their transactions with markets beyond the core, producers are most often in a patron role with a dependent supplier or consumer market. Within the bottom tier of the market group, satellite producers tend to be connected, if at all, by independent, asymmetric dependence relations. When dependence occurs in the satellite group it is most often an isolated, asymmetric relationship. In their transactions beyond the satellite group, producers are most often in a client role, asymmetrically dependent on business in a specific other market.

[1]Professor of Sociology and Business, Columbia University, New York.
Author's note: Work on this chapter was made possible by a Fellowship at the Netherlands Institute for Advanced Study and consulting revenues to Columbia University's Strategy Laboratory. The discussion has been improved in response to comments from Siegwart Lindenberg.

Market Differentiation

The image with which I begin is of a market as a dense point in a network of exchange transactions between markets. From the perspective of economics, this is the image of a sector in input–output economics. Markets are defined by the substitutability of producers within them, two producers operating in the same market to the extent that they similarly draw supplies from the same other sectors of the economy. The analytical concept used to define this metaphor with some formal and empirical rigor in sociology is structural equivalence, resulting in topological images of an economy such as the one presented in Fig. 1 describing markets in the American economy. The displayed markets are the seventy-seven production markets distinguished in the aggregate input–output tables released by the U.S. Department of Commerce in the 1960s through the 1980s. Two markets are close together to the extent that they do similar proportions of business in the same specific other markets. A casual scan of the map in Fig. 1 reveals distinctions between production technologies. The east–west axis is a distinction between markets in the east producing organic goods (e.g., agriculture, petroleum, services) versus markets in the west producing mechanical goods (e.g., motor vehicles, industrial machines). The north–south axis is a distinction between markets in the north using mature technologies (e.g., agriculture, textiles, mechanical engineering) versus markets in the south using new technologies (e.g., aerospace, computers, telecommunications). The map and its connection with input–output economics is discussed in detail elsewhere (e.g., Burt and Carlton, 1989). The point here is that producers are distinguished by their transactions with specific supplier–consumer markets.

Over time, competition drives a division of labor from which new markets emerge in the map. Broad agreement can be found for tracing differentiation to the division of labor driven by the density of contact between market players and the demand for their goods and services (e.g., Burt, 1982, pp. 333ff., for review). Where the demand for the commodity produced in a market is high, profits are good, attracting new entrants. As the number of market producers increases, competition among them intensifies, giving some an incentive to differentiate themselves by specializing in certain of the supplier or consumer transactions defining the market. To the extent that the specialists dominate the transactions in which they are expert, other producers are frozen out. A structural fissure appears in the market between the specialists and the other players, creating a boundary between the old market and a new one defined by the transactions on which the specialists have focused. What

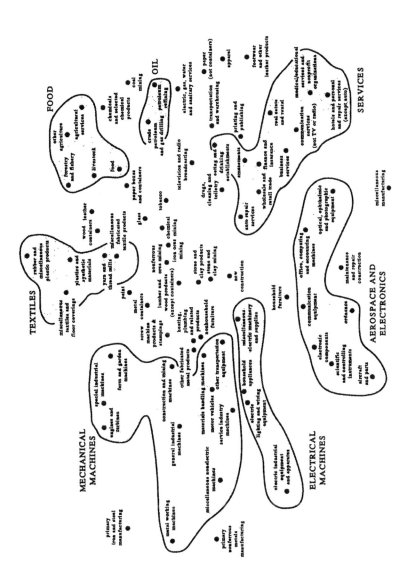

Fig. 1. Market topology map of American economy.

was once a single dot in the market map is now two separate, proximate dots.

In contemporary sociological work on markets, differentiation is driven by social structural models of competition. Network concepts are used to describe structural price mechanisms that define market boundaries and constrained transaction as market parameters. For example, White (1981a, b, 1988; Leifer and White, 1985) uses variations in production price and volume to define market boundaries and stability. I have used transaction networks and concentration ratios to define market boundaries around production roles and constraints on pricing—which then predict relative profit margins across markets and the structure of large firms optimal for individual markets (Burt, 1979, 1980, 1982, ch. 8, 1983, 1988a, 1992; Burt and Carlton, 1989). Leifer (1985) and Burt (1992, ch. 6) provide conceptual bridges between the two approaches. These analyses use the structure of transactions among suppliers, producers and consumers to define the parameters of imperfect competition responsible for the pricing and strategic behavior observed in markets.

Market Integration

Integration is not a central concern in the network models of competition. However, the competitive processes described by the models have implications for the integrative mechanisms that hold markets together. Broadly defined, the integrative mechanisms are two; embedding and dependence.

Embedding concerns relationships created so that producers can conduct a market transaction in a context where they have more control over the transaction. Otherwise distinct markets are integrated by the embedding relations that connect them. This is the more widely studied kind of integrative mechanism, notably in anthropology, economics and sociology. It is the foundation for transaction cost and resource dependence theories of organization. Research questions for the embedding approach ask: (a) how the structure of transactions gives certain players an advantage in negotiating the price of a transaction, creating a market incentive for embedding where players are disadvantaged, (b) how certain kinds of embedding relations provide a favorable context for transacting exchanges, and (c) the extent to which embedding relations occur where there is a market incentive for them.

The *dependence* mechanism concerns the integration inherent in the transactions themselves. Where one market's transaction with another is a substantial proportion of the market's business, producers are dependent on the transaction and thus keenly attentive to the interests of the suppliers or consumers with whom they conduct the transaction. The most notable examples of work on this mechanism come from anthropology and sociology. The central research question for the dependence approach is to identify structures of dependence relations that serve to integrate the markets involved in the relations.

The main contribution of this chapter is oriented toward the second approach. I am concerned with the integration intrinsic to the exchange transactions themselves. But in order to set this second approach into relief I will first describe embedding integration in some detail.

Embedding Integration[2]

Rudiments of embedding integration can be seen in anthropological accounts of markets. To illustrate the point, consider the extreme example of the Kula exchange system among the Trobriand Islanders, described in Malinowski's (1922) classic *Argonauts of the Western Pacific*. The Kula consists of the clockwise circulation of necklace valuables around a ring of islands where necklaces are handed from individual to individual in exchange for armshells which circulate counter clockwise around the same ring of islands. Participation in the Kula creates prestige and obligation relations in much the way Blau (1964) describes social exchange more generally. Details of the exchange and questions raised by subsequent work are succinctly summarized by Leach (1983, pp. 2–5) in preface to a collection of contemporary studies of the phenomenon. The relevant characteristic here is that trade between the islands was normally difficult because of inter-island conflict. The incentive for trade was that different commodities were more often produced on one island than another, copra on one cluster of islands for example and canoes on another. On the occasion of exchanging Kula necklaces and armshells, active economic trade occurs. As Malinowski (1922,

---

[2] I am writing to an audience of colleagues in business, network and organization research, but for the broader audience of sociologists it is important to note that I am using embedding in the relatively narrow sense of its use within my target audience. Focusing particularly on the topic of economic integration, the term has been used more generally to refer to the embedding of economic markets within the broader society. This theme is developed in papers collected in Polanyi et al. (1957, esp. chs. 13 and 14), reflecting themes in Parsons and Smelser's (1956) broad discussion of economic integration. Barber (1977) provides a valuable guide into this work.

p. 83) described it: "The ceremonial exchange of the two articles is the main, the fundamental aspect of the Kula. But associated with it, and done under its cover, we find a great number of secondary activities and features. Thus, side by side with the ritual exchange of armshells and necklaces, the natives carry on ordinary trade, bartering from one island to another a great number of utilities, often unprocurable in the district to which they are being imported, and indispensable there." The point is that people embed economic exchange in social relations of social obligation or authority where desired economic exchange would be otherwise difficult. This is one of the central points in Granovetter's (1985) discussion of market relations being embedded in social relations (his discussion of Geertz's, 1979, rich account of social order in a Moroccan bazaar is particularly relevant here).[3]

Analogous, but more sophisticated, images of embedding integration are available from economic and sociological studies of corporate markets. The greater sophistication of these images can be traced in some part to the more detailed network data available on the transactions defining corporate markets.

Within each of the markets in Fig. 1 are numerous establishments competing with one another. Integration within any one market increases with the extent to which establishments in the market are owned and operated by the same parent corporations. This is usually measured by concentration ratios; the proportion of all market sales that are made by the establishments owned by the four, or eight, largest firms. The higher the proportion is, the more competitive market relations are embedded in, and so replaced by, corporate authority relations.

Across markets, integration by embedding is the same process but the conditions for embedding are better articulated in organization theory. Something (to be elaborated below) about the nature of the buying and selling between two markets gives producers an incentive to embed the transaction in a relationship defined by corporate authority.

Market incentive for embedding. The market incentive for embedding can be traced to the manner in which a transaction is positioned in the social structure of transactions defining markets. From network studies of American markets we know that producers in market i are constrained in negotiating the price of their transactions with

---

[3]See also Benet (1957) on the preservation and explosion of Berber *suq* markets embedded in political and religious institutions.

suppliers or consumers in market j, c_{ij}, to the extent that three conditions occur: (a) the transaction represents a large proportion of producer business, (b) the transaction is coordinated with other transactions of the producer in the sense of extensive business occurring between supplier and consumer markets, and (c) establishments in market j are well organized in large dominant firms. To the extent that these three conditions occur, producers are disadvantaged in negotiating price, traces of which are visible as depressed profit margins (e.g., Burt, 1983, 1988a, 1992, ch. 3) and they have an incentive to move the transaction off the open market and into a corporate hierarchy where they have more control over the negotiation (e.g., Burt, 1983, 1992, ch. 7).[4]

With respect to resource dependence theory, c_{ij} measures the extent to which the resources obtained from market j are a high proportion of producer business and it will be difficult to obtain a favorable price if the business is transacted on the open market. This is dependence in both an actuarial and political sense (see Burt, 1983, pp. 223–235; Pfeffer, 1987, on the connection between resource dependence and the network definition of market constraint). With producers investing in facilities and staff to service their dominant transactional sources of sales and purchases, they face substantial costs in changing those transactions. A condition of dependence develops akin to asset specificity in transaction cost theory (e.g., Williamson, 1989, p. 142), or vulnerability dependence in world system theory (Baldwin, 1980, pp. 491–492).

With respect to transaction cost theory, c_{ij} at minimum captures the small numbers condition. It increases as the number of competitors decreases. However, the uncertainty it captures is not the uncertainty of transaction complexity but the uncertainty of having little control in a transaction: c_{ij} increases as the opportunities for negotiating a favorable price decrease. I maintain

---

[4]For the reader interested in a more precise statement, market constraint is measured as follows (see Burt, 1992, ch. 3, for more detailed discussion): $c_{ij} = [p_{ij} + \Sigma q p_{iq} p q_j] 2 O_j$ $i = q = j$, where p_{ij} is the proportion of producer i business transacted in market j, the bracketed term is the proportion of i's relations that involve market j either directly (p_{ij}) or indirectly ($\Sigma q p_{iq} p q_j$), and O_j is a measure of oligopoly within market j, typically a concentration ratio. The indirect component measures the extent to which market j is prominent in the networks of each other supplier–consumer market, increasing the likelihood of vertical integration across supplier–consumer markets. The bracketed term varies from a minimum of p_{ij}, indicating that market j is completely disconnected from other's in the network, up to a maximum of one, indicating that j is omnipresent in the network. The term is squared to more clearly distinguish supplier–consumer with little presence in the network from those who are omnipresent.

that the latter is the more troubling for producers. It is one thing to have to manage a large volume of information in a transaction. It is another to know that you have little control in negotiating the transaction, however much information is involved. If I add to this the presumption that business partners will exploit producers if they can, then c_{ij} captures the probability of opportunism and information impactedness when it captures the social structural conditions that would make it profitably possible to be opportunistic and manipulate the flow of information.

I take c_{ij} to be an empirically verified measure of transaction cost. I hasten to add that this does not mean that I believe that the market constraint coefficient captures all aspects of transaction cost in Williamson's framework, nor all aspects of resource dependence in Pfeffer and Salancik's framework (e.g., see Pfeffer, 1987, p. 125). It does capture some significant dimension of cost and dependence in both frameworks as described in the preceding paragraphs, and the dimension it captures is empirically verified by the negative association between constraint and profit margins across all kinds of markets. It is formal definition and empirical measure of the extent to which the network structure of economic transactions puts producers in one specific market at a disadvantage in negotiating a transaction with suppliers or consumers in another specific market, where markets can be defined broadly or narrowly. The higher c_{ij} is, the more disadvantaged the producers are on the open market by the lack of structural holes they can exploit to obtain a favorable price.

Coase's equilibrium definition of the firm can now be stated precisely: Begin with the producer's most severely constrained market transaction (maximum c_{ij} for producer i). Evaluate market price versus corporate authority as the mechanism regulating the transaction. If the difference between price and cost under corporate authority would be substantially smaller with suppliers, or substantially greater with consumers, move the transaction into the corporate bureaucracy by creating a suitable organizational tie to the supplier–consumer market. Examples would be purchasing a subsidiary supplier or distributor in the market, adding to the board of directors an officer from a leading firm in the market, creating a joint venture with a firm in the market, etc. Proceed to the next most severely constrained transactions (second largest c_{ij}). Make the same evaluation. Continue down the rank order of market constraints. Where the profit of moving the next class of transactions into the firm equals the profit of conducting them on the open market, stop. The transactions now contained in the firm is optimum for its market.

If the firms in a study population are structured by this logic, there should be evidence to support the following hypothesis: $w_{ij}=f(c_{ij})$, where w_{ij} is a measure of corporate hierarchy relationships between establishments in markets i and j. Without claiming to know the functional form of the association between constraint and corporate ties, I hypothesize that the more constrained producers are in their transactions with suppliers or consumers in market j—in other words, the more disadvantaged they would be in open negotiations under market pricing—the more likely they will have strong corporate ties to market j. As c_{ij} goes up, w_{ij} goes up. Where there is no constraint, there is no market incentive for corporate ties between markets. Where there is moderate constraint, moderate levels of corporate ties are expected. Where constraint is severe, the authority of a corporate hierarchy is expected to be the preferred setting for transacting business.

Evidence on the hypothesis is readily available. Richly detailed evidence is available from case studies describing the few intermarket transactions most significant for a study industry (e.g., Miles, 1982, on the tobacco industry; Stuckey, 1983, on the aluminum industry; Williamson, 1985, pp. 103–123, for review). More systematic evidence is available in Pfeffer and Salancik's demonstration that corporate relations increase with the volume of transactions between markets (e.g., 1978, pp. 157–161) and the subsequent more refined evidence of corporate ties increasing with transaction volume adjusted for supplier–consumer concentration (e.g., MacDonald, 1985, with data on seventy-nine manufacturing industries; Caves and Bradburd, 1988, with data on all Standard & Poor's firms operating in eighty-three industries—excluding transactions under 4% of producer sales; and Burt, 1983, with data on 786 firms operating across 404 transactions defining each of 322 industries). Ziegler (1993) provides analogous evidence on the market basis for interlocking directorates between establishments in aggregate sectors of the German economy.

In sum, to embed constrained transactions in the more easily controlled context of corporate authority, producers build corporate ties of ownership, joint ventures, and the like from their own position in the market topology map to specific other markets with which they have constrained transactions. With respect to markets more generally defined, the embedding relations range from the traditional formal relations of corporate authority, to the social obligation relations of the Kula exchange, to the kinship obligation relations of ethnic enterprise (see Burt, 1992, ch. 7, for more detailed discussion). The result is that integration is predicted within and between separate markets by the extent to which producers have a market incentive to embed specific transactions in a corporate hierarchy. Markets are integrated through strategic expansions of corporate hierarchies.

Dependence Integration

Integration can also be studied directly in terms of aspects intrinsic to being dependent. Integration resides not only in the corporate hierarchies built up to facilitate exchange, but also in the structure of interdependencies among markets. We know that corporate hierarchies expand to embed constrained transactions, and so serve to integrate producers in separate markets. But there is lying below the hierarchies some degree of integration inherent in the structure of the transactions themselves.

Beyond the transaction dyad of producer–consumer or supplier–producer, patterns of dependence relations define integration. Connectedness is the simple structural metaphor in Durkheim's (1893) classic account of the division of labor. Focusing on occupational markets, he describes social evolution from homogenous to heterogeneous production. In advanced society, people in any one market cannot survive without people in certain other markets. The aggregate interdependence of markets integrates people within a single social system.

More sophisticated structural imagery is provided in Levi-Strauss's (1949) analysis of generalized exchange (see Ekeh, 1974, for review). The negotiated exchange between two markets is contingent on negotiations elsewhere. There are cycles of exchange in which the players in market A are dependent on players in market B who are dependent on players in C who close the cycle with their dependence on players in market A. Players in the three markets are integrated within a single system, allowing for imbalance in the transaction between any two markets. This imagery has been productively applied to marriage markets, in Levi-Strauss's (1949) original work, and subsequent elaboration by White (1963) and Boyd (1969, 1980). It has not, to my knowledge, been used to describe the integration of economic exchange markets.

We know that business between broadly defined markets in the American economy is concentrated in a small number of transactions and has been stable at least since the 1960s, judging from the comparable input–output data available since then. To the extent that the bulk of a market's transactions are, and have been, conducted with a small number of certain other markets, then there is integration of a kind in the economy. That stable, focused dependence is a foundation for integration between markets in the sense that producers have a history of dependence on a few other specific markets.

The more interesting integration question concerns the broader structure of the dependence relations between markets. Are they connected in long production chains that weave through the economy integrating markets into a single system? Are they concentrated within separate groups of highly interdependent markets? Do they form a dependence hierarchy in which certain markets occupy top positions forming the core of the economy while other markets occupy positions at the bottom of the hierarchy to define the periphery of the economy? These are empirical questions, easily answered with available data and network analysis techniques, and the questions to be answered here.

Dependence Relations in the American Economy

The potential of studying integration directly in terms of dependence became apparent to me in analyzing the structural holes defining market constraints on producers. The typical producer transaction pattern involves a high proportion of buying and selling with one or two other markets, and very small proportions of business with a large number of other markets (e.g., see the American market hole signatures in Burt, 1992). Buying and selling between markets is concentrated in a small number of transactions. The constraint on producers in their largest transaction, for example, is correlated .98 with the sum of constraint across all of their transactions. This means that a fundamental aspect of market integration is defined by the aggregate structure of those few critical transactions.

The skewed distribution of business across transactions is illustrated in Fig. 2. Markets here correspond to sectors in the aggregate input–output table of the American economy displayed in Fig. 1. For each of the seventy-seven production markets in the table, I have computed the proportion of their business transacted with each other market, including final demands sales to households as the 78th market in the economy and final and intermediate business with government agencies as the 79th market. The transaction variable p_{ij} is the ratio of total dollars of business between markets i and j divided by the total dollars of business exchanged by market i producers with any other market. These proportions are highly stable across the 1963, 1967, 1972 and 1977 input–output tables describing the American economy, so I have averaged p_{ij} across

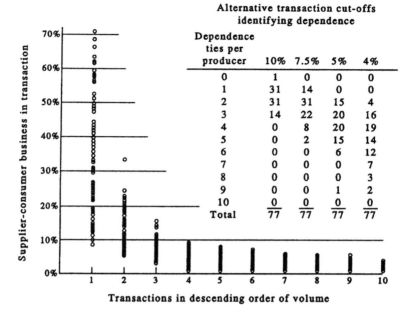

FIG. 2. Identifying dependence relations.

the four tables to get a single estimate of producer *i* dependence on market *j*.[5] This is not dependence in the negotiation sense used to define network constraint and transaction cost, but dependence in the simple sense that producers in the sending market transact a

[5] The transaction stability for these markets is discussed in Burt (1988a) and Burt and Carlton (1989). Since household and government markets are included in a slightly different way here, I checked stability again before pooling over time. Here are the correlations among the proportional trade relations, p_{ij} between pairs of markets in the four years:

1963	1.00			
1967	0.99	1.00		
1972	0.95	0.95	1.00	
1977	0.94	0.95	0.98	1.00

where correlations are computed across the 5852 ordered dyads of seventy-six producer markets *i* transacting business with seventy-seven supplier or consumer markets *j*. Producer markets are ignored as their own supplier or consumers and the household and government markets are not included as producers. The restaurant market is excluded from the correlations because it does not exist as a separate market in the 1960s; however, its transaction pattern is comparably stable between 1972 and 1977. The correlations in the above matrix between the 1960s and 1970s are slightly lower than correlations within each decade because of SIC category redefinitions in 1972 (see Burt, 1988a); all correlations are quite high, however.

large proportion of their business in the receiving market (a familiar measure in resource dependence studies, e.g., Pfeffer and Salancik, 1978, p. 158).

The ten largest transactions for each production market are plotted in Fig. 2. The largest transaction for each market varies from a minimum of 9% of one market's buying and selling, up to a maximum of 71%. The average is 34%. The next transaction is much smaller on average, 13%, and varies over a smaller range of magnitudes. By the fourth transaction, every market is doing less than 10% of their business in the transaction, the average is 5%, and there are some as low as 1%. By the tenth largest transaction, every market is doing less than 4% of their business in the transaction, the average is 2%, and many involve less than 1%.

Looking just at resource flows, producers are dependent on another market when they do a high proportion of their business in the aggregate transaction with the market. The table in Fig. 2 shows how many dependence relations are generated by different cut-offs for the distinction between high and low proportions of business. If the cut-off is set at 10%, then all transactions in the graph over the line at 10% are coded as dependence relations. This contains all but one of the largest transactions for each producer on down to the third largest transaction for fourteen producers. If the cut-off is set at 4%, then all of the largest transactions and almost all of the second largest transactions for each producer are coded as dependence relations. In addition, a large number of very small transactions are coded as dependence relations. For two production markets, dependence occurs in their nine largest transactions. For three production markets, it occurs in their eight largest transactions. I have settled on a cut-off of 7.5% for two reasons. First, it identifies at least one dependence relation for each production market. Second, it does not confuse the high volume relations at the left of the graph with the relatively negligible relations at the right. It preserves the extreme instances of markets highly dependent on a single other market (fourteen of them), and the highest number of dependence relations is five. There are only two markets with this many dependencies. Dropping the cut-off to 5% dramatically increases the number of producers with large numbers of dependence relations. A better approximation to dependence could be obtained by defining cut-offs for each market individually, but the primary dependence in the large transactions to the left of the graph are captured in the simple, global cut-off I have used for this initial analysis. If producers in a market do 7.5% or more of their business with another market, they will be viewed as dependent on business in the other market. To facilitate alternative analyses of these data and their use in sampling transactions for organization research, I have listed the seventy-seven production markets and their dependence relations in an Appendix at the end of the chapter.

Connectivity

The first pass through the data is to trace out the direct and indirect connections among the markets. At minimum, the markets are integrated into a single system to the extent that they are all connected, directly or indirectly. A stronger condition would be to find that there are groups of densely interdependent markets with weak dependence relations between groups. These will be the first of many results highlighting the lack of systemic integration in the American economy.

TABLE 1 *Dependence Path Distances Between Markets*

	Dependence path distance	Path distance with dependence made symmetric
1	184	275
2	236	2124
3	170	2366
4	154	1193
5	94	48
6	80	0
7	64	0
8	38	0
9	30	0
10	12	0
11	4	0
12	1	0
13	0	0
disconnection	4939	0
Total	6006	6006

I know from the data in Fig. 2 is that every market is dependent on business in at least one other market. I know from the frequencies in the 7.5% column of the table in Fig. 2 that there are only 184 transactions coded as dependence relations. There are 6006 transactions that could have been coded as dependence relations (seventy-seven production markets times seventy-eight other markets as potential trade partners), so the density of connections is low. Only 3.1% of the possible connections between markets are dependence relations.

The low aggregate density of dependence relations does not mean that the markets are disconnected from one another. Integration depends on how the few dependence relations are connected to one another. At one extreme, the dependence relations could be concentrated in disconnected cliques of interdependent markets. At the other extreme, the relations could form long chains that weave through the economy connecting markets into a single economic system. There are elements of both extremes in the American economy.

Path distances between markets are presented in Table 1. The path distance from a producer market to another is the number of dependence relations separating the two markets. This is a graph theory measure frequently used in network analysis to locate cliques of interconnected individuals (e.g., Burt, 1982, pp. 25–27, 37–40, for computation and review). The first column of Table 1 contains path distances of the observed dependence relations. A path distance of 1 indicates a transaction in which producers are directly dependent on the reached market. A path distance of 2 means that producers are not directly dependent on the reached market, but are dependent on a market which is in turn dependent on the reached market. The second column of Table 1 contains path distances of dependence relations forced to be symmetric. If producers are dependent on a market or the market is dependent on producers, then the two markets are treated as connected by a dependence relationship.[6]

The lack of disconnected markets in the second column of Table 1 shows that the economy is one large weak component clique. Every market is connected directly or indirectly with every other market in the economy. In the extreme, there are 275 transactions in which one or both markets are dependent on the other. Most markets are connected indirectly by paths through one or two intermediary markets. The longest paths occur forty-eight times between markets connected through four intermediary markets.

If the asymmetry of dependence is preserved, however, the complete integration of the economy disappears. The first column of Table 1 shows that most markets cannot reach one another through any number of intermediary markets. The 184 dependence relations appear as the one-step path distances in the table. The modal connection is an indirect two-step path through one intermediary.

[6]The results in this section were obtained with the general purpose network analysis program, STRUCTURE, first by requesting a search for cliques based on symmetric dependence relations, then by requesting a search for strong component cliques.

The longest completed connection is the path distance of twelve which occurs once between two markets that can only be connected through eleven intermediaries. However, of the 6006 possible connections between markets, most (4939, or 82.2%) cannot be completed through any number of intermediaries.

Still, there are pockets of integration within cliques of interdependent markets. The cliques are displayed in Fig. 3 with their constituent member markets. An arrow from one market to another indicates that the source of the arrow is dependent on the object of the arrow. These are strong component cliques in the sense that every producer in the clique is dependent directly, or indirectly on every other market in the clique.

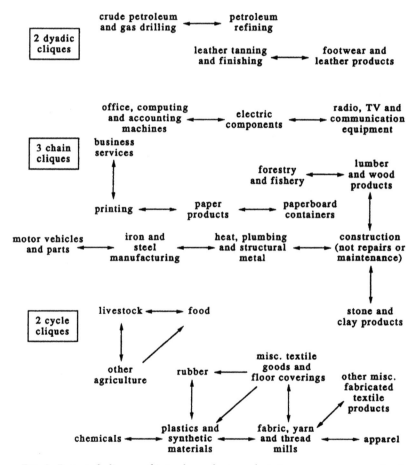

FIG. 3. Detected cliques of interdependent markets (strong components in the network of asymmetric dependence relations).

The detected cliques show three structures. The first two cliques in Fig. 3 are mutually dependent dyads of markets. For example, petroleum refining and drilling are mutually dependent markets.

The next three cliques in Fig. 3 are chains of mutual dependence with no cycles through more than two markets. The first is centered on electronic components, with computers on one side and broadcast and communication equipment on the other side. The second is centered on the paper industry, with paper containers on one side and printing followed by business services on the other side. The third is the most heterogeneous, spanning production activities from forestry through motor vehicles. New construction comes closest to occupying a central position with its mutual dependence on three other markets, but none of the three markets are dependent on one another.

The last two cliques in Fig. 3 show some evidence of cycles. The food clique is composed of the livestock, other agriculture and food industries. Each is substantially dependent on business in the other two. The missing dependence relation from food to other agriculture falls just below the cut-off for dependence (6% of food business). The fabric clique at the bottom of Fig. 3 is the most complex of the detected cliques. The central players in the clique are fabric–yarn–thread mills and firms in plastics and synthetic materials. There are cycles of interdependence among these markets and the markets for rubber products and floor coverings. On the plastics edge of the clique is a mutual dependence with the chemicals industry. On the fabric–yarn–thread mills edge of the clique are mutual dependencies on apparel and other miscellaneous fabricated textile products.

Market Positions

The seven cliques in Fig. 3 are the dense points of interdependence in the economy. There are twenty-eight production markets in these cliques and forty-nine markets outside them. The next question to ask of the data is how the cliques are connected to one another and the forty-nine markets beyond them. Are the seven cliques disconnected centers for a broader circle of related markets surrounding each clique, or do the seven cliques form an interlocked center for the economy around which the forty-nine outsider markets are distributed? Again, there is something of both extremes in the American economy.

The markets are distributed across eight positions forming a dependence hierarchy within the economy. A summary of the economy's aggregate structure is displayed in Fig. 4. Here markets

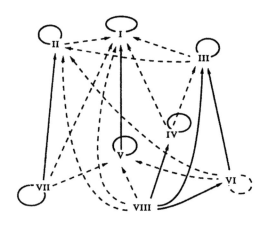

I. Food core
0.95 food
0.94 other agriculture
0.88 livestock
0.84 real estate

II. Distribution core
0.95 paper and allied products
0.93 printing and publishing
0.92 wholesale and retail
0.92 business services
0.86 paperboard containers

III. Manufacturing core
0.98 heating, plumbing and related products
0.97 new construction
0.93 primary iron and steel manufacturing
0.93 stone and clay products
0.93 motor vehicles
0.92 lumber and wood products
0.63 forestry and fishery products

IV. Fabrics
1.00 rubber
1.00 fabric-yarn-thread mills
0.99 misc. textiles and floor coverings
0.98 apparel
0.98 plastics and synthetic materials
0.98 chemicals
0.97 misc. fabricated textile products

V. Food, H&G satellites
1.00 transportation and warehousing
1.00 ordnance
1.00 electric, gas, water and sanitary utilities
1.00 amusements
1.00 scientific and controlling instruments
1.00 aircraft and parts
1.00 petroleum refining
1.00 tobacco
0.99 maintenance and repair construction
0.99 crude petroleum and gas drilling
0.99 household appliances
0.99 misc. manufacturing
0.99 hotels and personal and repair services
0.99 medical/educational services and nonprofits
0.99 restaurants
0.99 agricultural, forestry and fishery services
0.98 footwear and other leather products
0.98 leather

VI. Manufacturing satellites
1.00 materials handling machines
1.00 other fabricated metal products
1.00 misc. nonelectric machines
1.00 auto repair services
1.00 engines and turbines
1.00 coal mining
1.00 electrical industrial equipment
1.00 other transportation equipment
1.00 misc. electrical machines
1.00 construction and mining machines
1.00 nonhousehold furniture
1.00 screw machine products
0.99 metal working machines
0.99 iron ore mining
0.99 electric lighting and wiring equipment
0.99 service industry machines
0.99 general industrial machines
0.99 primary nonferrous metals manufacturing
0.97 household furniture

VII. Distribution satellites
0.98 optical, ophthalmic and photographic equip.
0.98 communications (excluding radio and TV)
0.98 radio and TV broadcasting
0.98 finance and insurance
0.98 radio, TV and communication equipment
0.98 office, computing and accounting equip.
0.97 electronic components

VIII. Periphery
0.99 paints and allied products
0.98 nonferrous ores mining
0.98 farm and garden machines
0.97 special industry machines
0.97 glass
0.96 wood containers
0.96 metal containers
0.94 drugs, cleaning and toilet preparations
0.94 stone and clay mining and quarrying
0.92 chemical and fertilizer mineral mining

Distribution of 184 dependence relations

	I	II	III	IV	V	VI	VII	VIII	H	G
I	6	–	–	–	–	–	–	–	3	–
II	1	8	–	–	–	–	–	–	3	2
III	1	2	12	–	–	–	–	–	2	2
IV	1	–	1	14	–	–	–	–	4	–
V	9	–	–	–	7	–	–	–	12	6
VI	–	1	27	–	2	3	–	–	6	3
VII	1	6	–	–	1	–	4	–	4	3
VIII	5	2	8	5	2	4	–	–	1	–
Total	24	19	48	19	12	7	4	–	35	16

FIG. 4. Positions in dependence hierarchy (positions are structurally equivalent markets, reliability of assignment is given before market name at right, H is households, and G is government).

are grouped into positions in terms of structurally equivalent patterns of dependence. Two markets are put in the same position to the extent that they have similar path distances of dependence relations to each other market in the economy and similar path distances from each other market. The three results presented in Fig. 4 include a sociogram indicating where dependence relations most often occur within and between positions, a tabulation of the 184 dependence relations, and a list of markets assigned to each position with the reliability of assignment.[7]

The positions form a clear hierarchy. The dependence arrows all point up in the sociogram, especially the bold arrows indicating the strongest dependence relations.[8] There are no dependencies in the upper diagonal of the interposition table of dependence relations presented in Fig. 4. There is no market dependent on markets lower in the hierarchy. Dependence occurs within positions or to markets higher in the hierarchy.

More specifically, there are three broad tiers in the hierarchy. Positions I, II and III define the top tier, the core of the economy. There is strong dependence between markets in each position and numerous dependence relations directed at the positions. Position VII defines the bottom tier, the periphery of the economy. No market in the economy is dependent on any of the markets in this bottom tier (column 7 in the Fig. 4 tabulation is blank). The other positions fall into a tier midway between these extremes. They vary in the extent to which they are dependent on one another and others are dependent on them. They are distinct from the top two positions in that they are much less the object of dependence relations and they are distinct from the bottom position in that they are all the object of some dependence relations.

The core positions. The internal differentiation within the top two tiers of the hierarchy requires elaboration beyond the aggregate

[7]The results in this section were obtained with STRUCTURE by requesting a default structural equivalence analysis (e.g., see Burt, 1988b, for a review of structural equivalence measures derived from binary relationship data), then using the ASSISTANT program that accompanies STRUCTURE to explore alternative assignments of markets to positions (e.g., see Gargiulo, 1989). The market reliabilities in Fig. 4 are correlations between structural equivalence distance to an individual market and the aggregate distance to the other markets assigned to its position. The reliabilities are quite high. Accordingly, the eigenvalue measure of aggregate structural equivalence within each position is high. The lowest equivalence occurs within the core positions because of the high volume, and therefore potential variability, of relations coming into the positions. The proportion of structural equivalence variance in distances to the eight positions is; 75%, 76%, 86%, 97%, 97%, 98%, 96% and 90%.

[8]The (8 by 10) table of dependence relation frequencies in Fig. 4 was summarized in a loglinear model. Bold arrows in the sociogram correspond to frequencies generating interaction effects 2.0 or more times the magnitude of their standard error.

results in Fig. 4. The two core positions in the economy are organized around three of the market cliques reported in Fig. 3. To clarify the internal structure of the core positions, Fig. 5 is a sociogram of all dependence relations from markets in the core Positions I, II and III.

The markets in Position I constitute a core built around the production of food. Looking down the list of Position I markets in Fig. 4, you can see the members of the food cycle clique in Fig. 3. Real estate is structurally equivalent with this group and tied to the other agriculture market. The food position lies at the top of the hierarchy in the sense that no market in the position is dependent on any market outside the position (except sales to households).

The markets in Position II constitute a distribution core. The position is anchored on the chain clique that passes through the paper industry. Wholesale and retail trade is structurally equivalent with this group and tied to business services and the paper industry. This group of markets produces the raw materials for packaging commodities and preparing for their distribution. Although these markets are not as frequently the object of dependence relations as other core markets (the food related markets in Position I or the manufacturing related markets in Position III), they are nowhere dependent on another production market except to food. That dependence is based entirely on the business between paper containers and the food industry. The connection displayed at the right of Fig. 5 is asymmetric because the business is a substantial proportion of all paper container business (18%), but a small proportion of all food business (1.4%). The centrality of the distribution position is further established by considering the complete absence of business between markets. There are forty-eight instances of markets having no business with the markets in Position I and fifty-eight instances of no business with markets in Position III. There are only seven instances of no business with the markets in Position II. This is the lowest frequency by far for any of the eight positions. In other words, the distribution core is significant for many more markets than those listed in Fig. 4 as being dependent on distribution business.

The markets in Position III constitute a manufacturing core. Looking down the list of Position III markets in Fig. 4, you can see the members of the chain clique in Fig. 3 that is centered on the new construction industry. The chain involves mutual dependence from forestry and lumber, through new construction and clay products, through the fabricated metal products used in construction, through the steel plants where the raw metal is prepared, on to the motor vehicles. Structural equivalence adds no additional markets to the

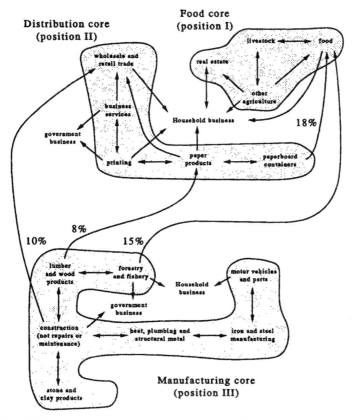

FIG. 5. Differentiation within the core (magnitudes given for dependence relations linking positions).

clique. This position is distinct from the other core positions in having much less dependence on household consumption, different markets dependent on them (discussed below), and the obviously stronger interdependence among themselves. The slight dependence of this position on the other two core positions occurs early in the production chain. There is extensive business between the food industry and the forestry and fishery industry, between lumber and paper products, and between construction and the distribution channels of wholesale and retail trade. The first of these is largely an aggregation problem. If forestry is separated from fishery, forestry remains dependent on lumber, but fishery is strongly dependent on the food industry and would be absorbed into the food position at the top of Fig. 5.

The satellite positions. The internal differentiation of the core sets the stage for differentiation at the next tier of the market hierarchy. These are Positions IV, V, VI and VII in Fig. 4. The positions vary dramatically in external dependence from the relative self-sufficiency of Position IV to the extreme dependence of position VI.

Position IV is the extreme of independence in the economy. The markets in this position are highly dependent on one another, little dependent on other markets, and rarely the object of dependence relations from other markets. The member markets listed in Fig. 4 are exactly the members of the fabrics clique displayed at the bottom of Fig. 3. Almost all dependence relations for the markets in this group occur with another market in the group. There are only two other production markets on which they are dependent. Fertilizer sales to other agriculture (in the food core, Position I) are significant to the chemicals industry, and the sales of seat and panel coverings to the auto industry (in the manufacturing core, Position III) are significant to the other fabricated textiles industry. The remaining external dependencies are all with household consumption through the direct sales by firms in rubber, floor coverings, apparel and other fabricated textiles. The independence of this group is further reinforced by the lack of markets dependent on them. In the Fig. 4 tabulation of dependence relations, notice that the entries under IV are all blank, excluding the large entry for their dependence on one another, and a smaller entry for the dependence of periphery markets.

The other three positions in the middle tier are satellites to the core positions. Each is dependent on its own constituency in the core.

The markets in Position V are dependent on the food core, with a substantial dependence on government and, like the food core markets, on households. The markets in this position have no dependence relations to the other two positions in the core. Here are the petroleum and leather dyad cliques from Fig. 3, amusements, tobacco, household appliances, restaurants, hotels, aircraft and ordnance, medical and educational services.

Position VI is a satellite to the manufacturing core. There are three dependence relations among the nineteen markets in this position versus twenty-seven dependence relations to markets in the manufacturing core. There are no dependence relations to the food core, and only one to the distribution core. Looking down the list of member markets in Fig. 4, you can see production activities associated with the manufacturing core; materials handling machines, miscellaneous nonelectric machines, screw machine products, furniture, and so on.

Position VII is a satellite to the distribution core. The markets in this position are distinct from the distribution core in that they are nowhere the object of dependence relations beyond their own position. They are distinct from the other satellite markets in that most of their own dependence relations occur with the distribution core, Position II. Looking down the list of member markets in Fig. 4, you can see production activities associated with distribution. There is the electronics clique from Fig. 3, expanded by structural equivalence to include broadcasting, communications, photography and finance.

Production axes. At the same time that there are three horizontal tiers in the dependence hierarchy, there are three vertical axes, each anchored on one of the core positions. The generic structural form of each axis has three components; a core position of interdependent markets, a satellite position of sporadically interdependent markets and frequent dependence relations from the satellite to the core. The three axes can be seen in the strong dependence relations marked by bold arrows in Fig. 4. Reconsider Fig. 4, ignoring the dashed lines of weak dependence in the sociogram.

The first production axis revolves around food, households and the government. This axis is composed of the core food group, Position I, and its satellite Position V. The twenty-two production markets listed in Fig. 4 as occupying either of these positions have twenty-two dependence relations to other production markets. All twenty-two relations are to other markets within the axis, with another twenty-one dependence relations to government and household final demand. No market within the food–household– government axis is dependent on a market in the other two production axes.

The second production axis revolves around distribution. The axis is composed of the core distribution group, Position II, and its satellite Position VII. The twelve production markets listed in Fig. 4 as occupying either of these positions have twenty-one dependence relations to other production markets. Of these, eighteen (86%) are to other markets within the axis and three are to markets in the food–household–government axis. Twelve dependence relations go to household and government final demand.

The third production axis revolves around manufacturing. The axis is composed of the core manufacturing group, Position III, the fabrics group in Position IV, the manufacturing satellites in Position VI, and the periphery markets in Position VIII. The forty-three markets listed in Fig. 4 as occupying these four positions have ninety dependence relations to other production markets. Of these, seventy-four (82%) are to other markets within the axis, eleven are to markets in the food–household–government axis and five are to markets in the distribution axis. Sixteen dependence relations go to household and government final demand.

In other words, the American economy is a federation of three quasi-independent production systems. The food–household–government system is the most central of the three with separate distribution and manufacturing systems. Market integration is strongest within each system, focused on a core group, and weak between systems, especially if the dependence on final demand common to all three systems is separated out to highlight dependence between production markets.

Market Roles

I now know the aggregate social structure in which the markets are positioned. What I don't know is how markets enter into their patterns of dependence. This is a question of the roles that producers play within the dependence hierarchy, and those roles turn out to have important implications for the manner in which markets are connected within the market hierarchy. The distribution of roles can be inferred from the structure of the hierarchy, however, the specific roles played by individual markets can vary significantly between markets similarly positioned in the hierarchy.

Illustrative market roles. For example, consider the simple issue of the number of markets on which producers are dependent. From the 7.5% column in Fig. 2, there are fourteen instances of markets dependent on business in a single other market. There are thirty-one markets dependent on two other markets. There are thirty-two markets dependent on three or more other markets. These are three very different circumstances for producers. Where producers are dependent on business in a single other market, they can focus all of their strategic efforts on the one market. Where they are dependent in several different directions, producers are more dependent in the aggregate and strategies have to be, *ceteris paribus*, more complex.

A connection with the dependence hierarchy can be expected simply on the basis of aggregate dependence. Producers at the top of the hierarchy should be less dependent than producers at the bottom. There is a negligible tendency for core markets (Positions I, II and III) to have one rather than multiple dependence relations (0.7 z–score, one-tail $P=.24$) and a negligible tendency for periphery markets (Position VIII) to be dependent on multiple markets (0.9

z–score, P=.18), however, the only significant tendency is for producers in Position V, the food–household–government satellite markets, to have one rather than many markets on which they are dependent (2.2 z–score, P=.01). In the aggregate, there is no association between a market's position in the hierarchy and the distinction between one, two, or many dependencies (15.9 chi–square, 14 df, P=.32). Producer position in the hierarchy is determined by the context in which dependence occurs, or, if you prefer, on who the dependence relation is with. It is not determined by the frequency with which the producer is dependent.

Number of dependence relations is the simplest description of a producer's role in the market hierarchy. More interesting roles can be distinguished when the dependence between producer and supplier–consumer market is considered in the context of relations with a third market. Consumers and suppliers are differentiated into markets that are themselves variably interdependent.

To study integration in terms of these roles, structural equivalence is no longer the optimum vehicle for distinguishing kinds of markets and classes of transactions. Producers are structurally equivalent in Fig. 1 to the extent that they have identical transactions with identical suppliers and consumers. In Fig. 4, producers are structurally equivalent to the extent that they are dependent on, and depended upon by, identical other markets. In contrast, producers are role equivalent to the extent that they have a similar structure of dependence with other markets, regardless of who those markets are.

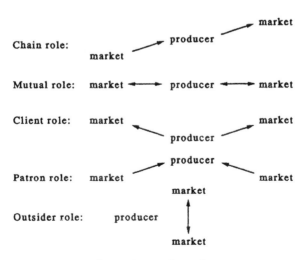

FIG. 6. Illustrative market roles.

Consider Fig. 6. Five illustrative market roles are distinguished as patterns of dependence between a producer and two supplier or consumer markets. This is not a census of all possible roles. I will provide a census later. The roles in Fig. 6 are merely illustrative to orient the discussion. An arrow from one market to another indicates that the source of the arrow is dependent on the object of the arrow.

A *chain role* is presented at the top of Fig. 6. The first market depends on producer business and producers depend on business in a third market. Through vertical integration, producers are expected to develop organizational ties to the third market and expected to be the object of ties from the first market. Markets are integrated through the many links of criss-crossing production chains that weave through the economy. Among American markets, there are seventy-nine instances of the Fig. 6 chain role. The new construction market most often appears in the producer position (fifteen of the seventy-nine). For example, firms in the stone and clay mining and quarrying market (not the stone and clay products market in the lower left of Fig. 5) transact a large proportion of their business with construction firms which in turn transact a large proportion of their business with government agencies. The first step in this chain is the second largest transaction that stone and clay firms have with any other market (20% of their buying and selling). The second step in the chain is the largest transaction for construction firms (31%). Transactions going backwards through the chain are very small, and there is little direct exchange between government agencies and the firms in stone and clay mining and quarrying (all four transactions are less than 2% of the source market's business).

Notice that there is no identification in Fig. 6 of the specific markets with which producers have their transactions. This is a distinguishing feature of role equivalence. Two producers are role equivalent in playing a chain role, for example, to the extent that they are both asymmetrically dependent on one market that is disconnected from another market asymmetrically dependent on the producers.

At one or more points in the production process there can be cycles of exchange in which producers in different markets are mutually dependent on one another's business. In the Fig. 6 *mutual role*, a condition of bilateral vulnerability, producers are only dependent on markets that are dependent on the producers. Collaborative ventures and interorganization ties are expected between establishments in the interdependent markets. Markets are integrated within production cliques. Among American markets, there are seventeen instances of the mutual dependence chain displayed in Fig. 6. These chains hold together the market cliques displayed in Figs. 3 and 5. There are no instances of three markets where each pair is mutually dependent. The closest are the two instances where dependence between the producer's two supplier–consumer markets is asymmetric. In one of the two, for example, livestock firms play the role of producer (displayed in Figs. 3 and 5). The two largest transactions for livestock firms are with the food industry (58%) and other agriculture (23%). Reciprocally, trade with livestock firms is a large proportion of the food industry's business (25%) and a large proportion of the other agriculture business (20%). There is also a considerable volume of business between the food and other agriculture markets, but the markets are not mutually dependent. The business between them is a large proportion of other agriculture business (19%), but a small proportion of all food business (6%).

Turning to the vertical axis of differentiation, the production process can put some producers in a client role and others in a patron role. In the *client role*, producers are everywhere dependent on markets which are not dependent on them. Among American markets, there are fifty-eight instances of the Fig. 6 client role. The nonhousehold furniture market most often appears in the position of producer (seven of the fifty-eight). These are the firms that make office furniture, partitions, drapes and blinds for commercial buildings, and so on. Their most significant client role is played with respect to the steel industry and new construction. The steel they purchase to fabricate furniture is the second largest of their transactions (11%), followed by their sales to firms constructing new buildings (9%). Their business is much less significant from the perspectives of the steel manufacturers and the construction firms (less than 3% for both). On the other side of the transaction, markets in a *patron role* have suppliers and consumer markets dependent on them, while their own dependence is elsewhere. There are 272 instances of the Fig. 6 patron role in the market data to be analyzed. The steel market most often appears in the role of producer (116 of the 272). For example, one of the patron roles connects steel to the firms that manufacture nonhousehold furniture and the firms that mine iron ore. On one side is the just described asymmetric dependence of nonhousehold furniture on steel supplies. On the other is an asymmetric dependence of iron ore firms on sales to steel plants. The transaction between steel plants and iron ore firms is 71% of iron ore business, but only 4% of steel business.

The final role in Fig. 6 is the *outsider*. Producers usually have a handful or fewer of significant supplier–consumer transactions and many transactions that involve little or no business. This means that they are often outsiders to business between other markets. Diversification can create corporate ties between the markets, but there is little resource dependence logic for the ties. Producers in the food industry, for example, have little to do with the transactions between steel firms and ferrous ores mining firms.

The market roles in Fig. 6 describe the local structure of market transactions. The distribution of these local structures across markets characterizes the global integration of the economy. For example, producers in a system characterized by dense cliques of interdependent markets with bridge transactions between the cliques would play three roles; the mutual (with respect to markets in their own clique), the isolate (with respect to markets in other cliques), and with rare frequency the chain (if they were the bridge to another clique). If the system were hierarchically differentiated in terms of center and periphery markets, then producers would play four roles; the mutual (among the center markets), the isolate (among the periphery markets), the client (for periphery producers doing business with the center), and the patron (for center producers doing business with the periphery).[9]

These remarks merely illustrate the idea of market roles. The task for empirical research is to systematically distinguish all possible roles and describe their distribution in an economy. Which roles best characterize the economy? Are roles homogeneous within markets—so that producers in some markets primarily play a client role, for example, while producers in other markets primarily play a patron role—or do producers in each market play a mixture of roles? How are roles interconnected to integrate markets across the economy?

Characteristic market roles. Figure 7 is a census of the thirty-six structures of dependence relations possible among a producer and two other markets. Variation in the producer's interdependence with the two markets occurs across the rows. In the first row, for example, are structures in which there is no dependence between producers and either of the other two markets. In the seventh row are producers mutually dependent with both markets. Variation in the dependence between the other two markets occurs across the columns. Structures in which there is no dependence are listed in

[9]Inferring global structure from the distribution of local structures is best illustrated by the work on network triads in the early 1970s. I have reviewed the development of this work in Burt (1982, pp. 55–60). Davis and Leinhardt's (1972) use of the ranked cluster model nicely illustrates the style of the work.

the first column. Structures of mutual dependence are listed in the second, and asymmetric dependence is listed in the third.

The numbers in parentheses below each triad identification number in Fig. 7 give the frequency with which the structure occurs in the American economy. The most frequent structure is triad 1, in which there are no dependence relations among the three markets ($n=200,894$). At the other extreme, the structure of mutual dependence among any three markets never occurs (triad 17). With

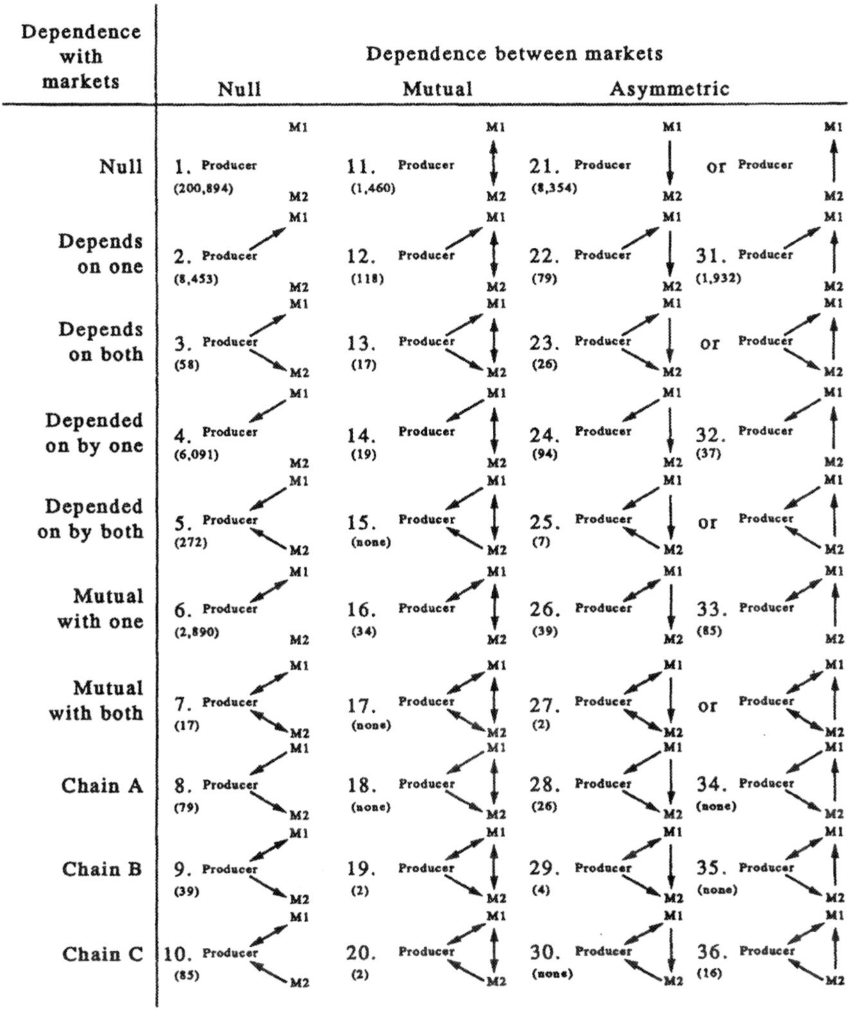

Dependence with markets	Dependence between markets			
	Null	Mutual	Asymmetric	
Null	1. Producer (200,894)	11. Producer (1,460)	21. Producer (8,354)	or Producer
Depends on one	2. Producer (8,453)	12. Producer (118)	22. Producer (79)	31. Producer (1,932)
Depends on both	3. Producer (58)	13. Producer (17)	23. Producer (26)	or Producer
Depended on by one	4. Producer (6,091)	14. Producer (19)	24. Producer (94)	32. Producer (37)
Depended on by both	5. Producer (272)	15. Producer (none)	25. Producer (7)	or Producer
Mutual with one	6. Producer (2,890)	16. Producer (34)	26. Producer (39)	33. Producer (85)
Mutual with both	7. Producer (17)	17. Producer (none)	27. Producer (2)	or Producer
Chain A	8. Producer (79)	18. Producer (none)	28. Producer (26)	34. Producer (none)
Chain B	9. Producer (39)	19. Producer (2)	29. Producer (4)	35. Producer (none)
Chain C	10. Producer (85)	20. Producer (2)	30. Producer (none)	36. Producer (16)

FIG. 7. Census of market roles.

respect to the just discussed example roles, the chain role in Fig. 6 is triad 8 in Fig. 7, the mutual role is triad 7, the client role is triad 3, the patron role is triad 5 and the outsider role is triad 11.

Figure 8 shows that the American markets can be distinguished in terms of four kinds of structures—aggregations of specific triads within the census in Fig. 7. Two triad structures are close together in Fig. 8 to the extent that they tend to characterize the same markets as producers. The four kinds are outsider roles, mutual roles, client roles and patron roles. Knowledge of these results guided my selection of illustrative roles for Fig. 6. Table 2 is a tabulation of the three most frequent triad structures within each of the four kinds.

The most frequently played role is outsider. The outsider roles listed in the first row of Fig. 7 appear in together in the upper left of Fig. 8. Each of the production markets appears as producer in 3003 triads with respect to the other seventy-eight markets as potential suppliers or consumers ($[N-1][N-2]/2$). There are 231,231 triads summed across the seventy-seven production markets. In 91% of these triads, producers play the role of outsider.

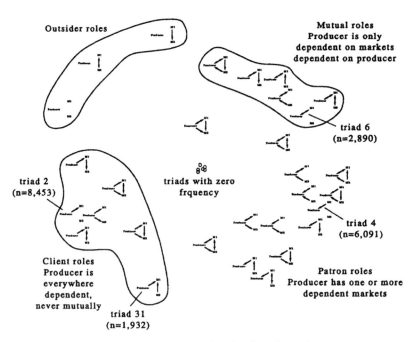

FIG. 8. Distinguishing kinds of market roles.

TABLE 2 Tabulating Kinds of Market Roles

	Frequency	
Outsider roles		(210,708 total, 91.1%)
Triad 1	200,894	
Triad 21	8354	
Triad 11	1460	
Client roles		(10,683 total, 4.6%)
Triad 2	8453	
Triad 31	1932	
Triad 12	118	
Other 4 triads	180	
Patron roles		(6773 total, 2.9%)
Triad 4	6091	
Triad 5	272	
Triad 24	94	
Other 20 triads	316	
Mutual roles		(3067 total, 1.3%)
Triad 6	2890	
Triad 33	85	
Triad 26	39	
Other 4 triads	53	

NOTE: The outsider roles are composed of the triads in row 1 of Fig. 7. The client roles are composed of the triads in rows 2 and 3. The patron roles are composed of the triads in rows 4, 5, 8, 9 and 10. The mutual roles are composed of the triads in rows 6 and 7.

Client roles are the next most frequently observed. They constitute about half of the triads in which producers have some dependence connection with either or both of the other markets (10,683 of 20,523 triads). These roles appear in the lower left of Fig. 8. They put producers in the position of being dependent on one or both of the other markets, neither of which is dependent on the producers. Two triads constitute the bulk of the observed client roles; triad 2 in which the producer is dependent on a single market disconnected from the other market (79% of the client role triads), and triad 31 in which the producer is one of two markets dependent on the third market (18% of the client role triads).

Patron roles are the next most frequently observed. They constitute about a third of the triads in which producers have some dependence connection with either or both of the other markets (6773 of 20,523 triads). These roles appear scattered through the lower right of Fig. 8. They have in common the quality that producers are depended upon by one or both of the other markets. The bulk of the patron roles are triad 4, in which one market is dependent on the producers (90% of the 6773 patron roles).

The remaining 15% of the connections with supplier–consumer markets are mutual roles in which producers are only dependent on markets also dependent on the producers. These roles appear in the upper right of Fig. 8. The bulk of the mutual roles are triad 6 in which the third market is an outsider to the mutual dependence between producers and one of their supplier–consumer markets (94% of the mutual roles).

Emphasis on dyadic dependence. These results emphasize the essentially dyadic nature of dependence. This shows up in three ways. First, note that the clusters of triads into kinds is in terms of the rows of the census in Fig. 7. The outsider roles are row one. The client roles are rows 2 and 3. The mutual roles are rows 6 and 7. The patron roles are the other five rows in the census. The rows in Fig. 6 distinguish conditions of dependence between producers and other markets. The columns distinguish conditions of dependence between the other markets. No distinctions between kinds of roles in Fig. 8 is based on the columns in Fig. 6. In other words, kinds of roles are distinguished by the dependence between producers and other markets—not the dependence between the other markets.

Second, the dyadic nature of dependence is highlighted by the almost complete absence of cycles. A cycle is any closed chain where dependence moves from one market to another, then to the next, then back to the originating market. This only occurs in the 11 triads at the lower right of Fig. 7 (triads 17–20, 27–30 and 34–36). Notice the near-zero frequencies with which these triads occur. The complete mutual cycle, triad 17, never occurs at all. The entire set of eleven cycle triads only occurs fifty-two times among the 20,523 triads connecting producers with supplier–consumer markets. In other words, as illustrated by the structure of the market cliques in Fig. 3 and the structure of the core markets in Fig. 5, integration by dependence is a dyadic phenomenon between pairs of markets in chains rather than sets of markets in cycles.

Third, building on both preceding points, the dependence chains are not responsible for the aggregate organization of markets. There is no cluster of triads in Fig. 8 corresponding to the illustrative chain role in Fig. 6. Its absence is significant. The dependence hierarchy in Fig. 4 shows dependence moving up through levels of the hierarchy and cycling within positions. The fact that the chain of asymmetric dependence occurs so rarely (seventy-nine of triad 8, less than 1% of the 20,523 triads connecting producers with supplier–consumer markets), means that the upward flow of dependence in Fig. 4 is not an upward flow so much as it is a ranking of asymmetric dependence between adjacent levels of the hierarchy. The market in a position dependent on the adjacent higher level of the hierarchy is not the same as the market depended upon by the adjacent lower level of the hierarchy. Dependence moves up from one level to the next, moves through a chain of markets in a position at the higher level, then moves from a different market up to the next level in the hierarchy. Knowing the markets with which producers are structurally equivalent is critical to placing producers in the dependence hierarchy.

The Market Group

The results on market positions and market roles together describe an elementary unit of business integration. I will call this elementary unit a market group. As illustrated in Fig. 9, a market group contains a set of core markets, a set of satellite markets, and a strong satellite dependence on the core. In contrast to the idea of an enterprise group, structurally analogous to a clique, a market group is stratified into an upper and lower tier of interdependent markets with core markets in the upper tier connected by chains (not cycles) of mutual dependence and satellite markets in the lower tier connected, if at all, by independent, asymmetric dependence relations.

The American economy is comprised of three market groups together forming the dependence hierarchy illustrated in Fig. 4.

The highest in the hierarchy is a food–household–government market group which sustains personal and political life. The core tier in this group is anchored on the food industry, Position I, with satellites in Position V. Household and government final demand are not included as member markets in this group, but markets in the group stand out as the most often dependent on that final demand.

The second market group, distribution, produces information to guide the flow of products and the packaging in which the products flow. The core tier in this group is anchored on the chain clique that passes through the paper industry, Position II, with the finance and electronics markets in Position VII as satellites.

The third market group, manufacturing, contains the largest number of markets. This group centers on Position III which is anchored on the chain clique that passes from lumber and stone and clay products, to new construction, to heating, plumbing and structural metal products, to the steel industry, and on to motor vehicles. The fabrics markets in Position IV are a secondary core group. The satellite tier of this market group contains the satellite manufacturing markets in Position VI and the generally peripheral markets in Position VIII. The fabrics markets in Position IV are clearly distinct from the core manufacturing markets in Position III, but they more resemble core markets than satellite markets because of the chained mutual dependence relations within the group and the satellite markets dependent on them beyond the group. In fact, the manufacturing market group can be seen as a cluster of three market groups. The clearest is Position III with satellites in Position VIII. The next is Position IV with satellites in Position VIII. The weakest is Position VI with satellites in Position VIII. These vary in the extent to which they reflect a market group form, but have in common the three relation pattern; weak dependence among the satellite markets, strong dependence among the core markets, and strong asymmetric dependence of the satellite markets on the core markets.

Characteristic roles of core and satellite producers. The characteristic market roles played by core and satellite producers are summarized

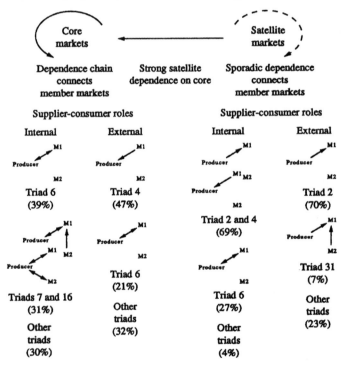

FIG. 9. Market group (Positions I to IV are core markets. Positions V to VIII are satellite markets. Tabulated triads exclude household and government final demand.)

in Fig. 9. Figure 10 is a census of roles among the seventy-seven production markets, showing the extent to which producers in each position in the dependence hierarchy play client, patron, or mutual roles. Roles are tabulated separately for relations within a position versus relations with markets outside the position. The difference between bar height and 100% is the percentage of outsider roles.

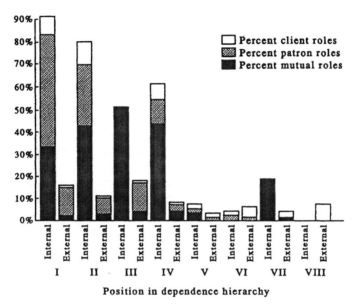

FIG. 10. Market role frequency by position in the dependence hierarchy.

Core markets within each market group tend to be connected by chains of mutual dependence relations. The bulk of the roles among core markets are either mutual dependence dyads (triad 6 in Fig. 9) or chains of mutual dependence (triads 7 and 16). The black areas in the four high bars in Fig. 10 show how well connected core markets are and how often their connections are mutual dependence relations. In their transactions with markets beyond the core, producers are most often in a patron role with a dependent supplier or consumer market (triad 4 in Fig. 9). Half as often, they are in an isolated mutual dependence.

Satellite markets within each market group tend to be connected, if at all, by independent, asymmetric dependence relations. The bars in Fig. 10 describing roles within Positions V through VIII are close to zero, showing how few connections there are within satellite groups. The markets in Position VIII are completely disconnected from one another. When dependence occurs within the satellite group it is most often an isolated, asymmetric relationship (triads 2 and 4 in Fig. 9). Half as often, it is an isolated, mutual relationship. Figure 10 shows that the mutual relations primarily occur in Position VII, the satellite to the distribution core, containing the electronics clique. In their transactions with markets beyond the satellite group, producers are most often in a client role, dependent on a supplier or consumer market (triad 2 in Fig. 9). However, the low height of the bars in Fig. 10 describing the external roles of satellite markets shows that their client dependence on other markets is much less frequent than their disconnection from other markets.

Throughout, market integration is largely a dyadic phenomenon. The aggregate duality is a partnership between subordinate and superior. Markets in the core group are dependent on one another. Markets in the satellite group have in common their dependence on the core markets. Within the aggregate duality, dependence relations in and between the groups are largely dyadic. In Fig. 9, the three markets in each of the most frequent triads are never connected to the other two. Producers are typically connected with only one of the other two markets in a triad. The strongest exception to the dyad rule are the chains of mutual dependence relations among markets in core groups.

Transaction differences for core and satellite producers. Core markets could be viewed as a coalition positioned to exploit the affiliated satellite markets in the sense of negotiating advantageous prices in their transactions with the satellites. Closer study shows this to be true in one sense at the same time that it is untrue in general. The difference is significant for the embedding theories of the firm with which I began the chapter.

In discussing the market incentive for embedding at the beginning of the paper, I described how producer disadvantage in a specific transaction can be measured with the constraint coefficient, c_{ij}. The coefficient increases with the extent to which producers in market i face well organized suppliers or consumers in market j who are strongly connected to other of the producers's key supplier–consumer markets. The empirical validity of the measure lies in its strong negative correlation with profit margins (as aggregate constraint goes up, aggregate producer profit margin goes down) and its positive correlation with interorganization ties (as the constraint on producer negotiation in a specific transaction goes up, the transaction is increasingly likely to be embedded in a corporate hierarchy).

TABLE 3 Core Market Negotiating Advantage

	Mean frequency structural hole roles	Mean level of supplier–consumer constraint
Food–Household–Government		
Core markets		
(Position I, N=4)	21.0	0.053
Satellite markets		
(Position V, N=18)	1.0	0.080
Distribution		
Core markets		
(Position II, N=5)	10.8	0.033
Satellite markets		
(Position VII, N=7)	0.9	0.060
Manufacturing		
Core markets		
(Positions III & IV, N=14)	21.1	0.049
Satellite markets		
(Positions VI & VIII, N=29)	1.9	0.071

NOTE: Positions refer to locations in the dependence hierarchy in Fig. 4, where the markets in each position are listed. The structural hole roles are triads 3, 5, 7, 8, 9 and 10 in Fig. 7. Constraint increases with connections between supplier–consumer markets and concentration within each market.

Table 3 contains results showing the different negotiating positions of producers in core and satellite markets.[10] The first column is the mean frequency with which producers have transactions with disconnected supplier–consumer markets. Six triads in Fig. 7 are roles in which producers have disconnected supplier–consumer markets; triads 3, 5, 7, 8, 9 and 10. The frequencies of these triads are too small to a defining characteristic of the markets, but their relative frequency across markets is significant in light of the known connection between profit margins and disconnected suppliers and consumers. Producers in the core markets clearly have more disconnected suppliers and consumers than do producers in the satellite markets. The second column in Table 3 is the mean level of supplier–consumer constraint aggregated across all of market's supplier–consumer transactions. This value is high to

[10]Here again, transaction measures are averaged across the 1963, 1967, 1972 and 1977 time periods. The constraint coefficients are extremely stable across the four time periods, with correlations very nearly identical to those presented in footnote 4 for business proportions (cf. Burt, 1992, p. 285).

Ronald S. Burt

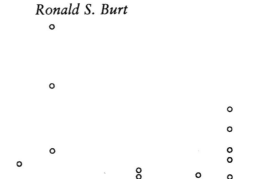

FIG. 11. Supplier-consumer constraint on core and satellite markets (Table 3
identifies the market positions assigned to core and satellite categories and
arrows in the above graph indicate the mean levels of constraint reported in
Table 3.)

the extent that suppliers and consumers are strongly interdependent
and high concentration ratios indicate that they are organized
within large, dominant firms. The results in the second column of
Table 3 show higher levels of constraint on satellite markets. More
specifically, Fig. 11 shows the distribution of constraint around the
mean values in Table 3. In the aggregate, producers in the satellite
markets face a higher level of constraint in their transactions with
suppliers and consumers. This comparison only holds within market
groups. In Fig. 11, the most constrained satellite producer in the
distribution market group is no higher than the most constrained
core producer in the food–household–government market group.
Within each market group, core producers are less constrained than
satellite producers.

It follows that producers in core markets enjoy higher profit
margins. They are less constrained in negotiating transactions with
suppliers and consumers, and that constraint is strongly associated
with profit margins (with t-tests on the order of -3 to -4).

However, holding constant the higher profit margins in nonmanu-
facturing (Burt, 1988a, 1992), the profit margins in core markets
are negligibly higher than the margins in satellite markets (0.7
t-test). There are no significant profit margin differences between

the eight positions in the market hierarchy (0.8 F-test with 7,69 df, $P=.56$).[11]

The contradiction lies in how core and satellite producers are constrained. Core producers face a lower aggregate level of constraint, but it is concentrated in transactions with strong suppliers and consumers in other core markets. Satellite producers face a higher aggregate level of constraint, but it is spread across their transactions with multiple markets.

The point is illustrated in Fig. 12. There are four classes of transactions within a market group, distinguished in the table at the top of Fig. 12. There are transactions within the core and satellite tiers of the market group and transactions between the two tiers, first from the perspective of the core markets and second from the perspective of the satellite markets. The average level of constraint in transactions within each cell of the table in Fig. 12 is presented

		Source of dependence	
		Core market	Satellite market
Dependent market	Core market	Negotiations between strong peers	Empty
	Satellite market	Negotiations between superior and subordinate	Negotiations between peripheral peers

Constraint density across all market groups		Constraint density in food-house-govnmt market group	
.138	.007	.149	.009
.111	.040	.049	.042

Constraint density in distribution market group		Constraint density in manufacturing market group	
.072	.006	.376*	.007
.035	.025	.119	.027

FIG. 12. The four transactions in a market group (*mean of 84 constraints between markets within positions III and IV).

[11]The profit margins used in these results are price–cost margins computed from the four aggregate input–output tables used to compute dependence and constraint. The margin is dollars of value added minus dollars of labor cost, quantity divided by dollars of sales. The data are analyzed in Burt (1992, ch. 3).

in the density tables below it in the figure. The general pattern, repeated within each of the three market groups, can be seen in the density table aggregated across groups.

The most constrained transactions occur between core markets. The average transaction has a .138 constraint coefficient (c_{ij}). This is the cell in which the strongest evidence is to be expected for the embedding theories of the firm. Constraint is strong and focused between mutually dependent markets, providing the clearest incentive for buyer and seller to move the constrained transaction into a corporate hierarchy.

Satellite markets are less constrained on average in their transactions with core markets (.111 mean c_{ij}), and still less constrained in their transactions with one another (.040 mean). The core markets are virtually unconstrained in their transactions with satellite markets. There are no dependence relations at all in the cell labeled "empty" in the table and the mean constraint per transaction is near zero. In other words, the incentive to move the transactions between core and satellite markets into a corporate hierarchy is much stronger for the satellite producers. In the corporate ties embedding these transactions, the partner in the core market can be expected to hold the stronger position.

These results define a sampling frame for studies of corporate embedding ties. Consider Fig. 13. Ninety-five transactions are displayed in the figure. These are the dependence relations within the core positions in each of the three market groups and the dependence relations between satellite and core in each of the three market groups. The specific pairs of markets connected by each transaction are listed in Appendix B with the proportion of business and constraint intensity in each transaction. The proportions of producer business range in Fig. 13 from 7.5%, the cut-off for dependence relations, up to 30% or more. Constraint ranges from zero up to 0.03 or more, the highest levels in the economy. These are the market transactions especially likely to elicit corporate embedding ties according to transaction cost and resource dependence theories of the firm. More specifically, two hypotheses can be advanced from the above discussion.

First, the likelihood of a transaction in Fig. 13 being embedded in a corporate hierarchy, and the strength of the corporate tie, should increase from the lower left to the upper right of the graph. Transactions in the lower left represent a substantial proportion of producer business, but they are conducted with disorganized supplier or consumer markets so producers are not severely constrained in negotiating price. In contrast, the transactions in the upper right of the graph represent larger proportions of producer business

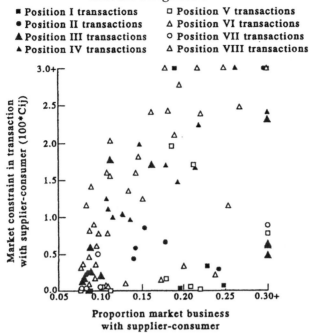

FIG. 13. Sampling frame for studying market group transactions (Transactions between producer and supplier–consumer market are identified by the position of producers in the dependence hierarchy. Solid symbols are transactions between core markets. Hollow symbols are satellite transactions with core markets.)

and are conducted with well organized supplier–consumer markets. Producers have a strong incentive to move these transactions into the more controlled setting of a corporate hierarchy.

Second, asymmetry in the roles played by organizations linked by the corporate ties embedding a transaction should be greater in the hollow symbol transactions in Fig. 13. Transactions within the three market groups can be identified by symbol shape in Fig. 13; squares indicate transactions in the food–household–government market group (Positions I and V), circles indicate distribution transactions (Positions II and VII), and triangles indicate manufacturing transactions. Solid symbols indicate transactions between markets in a core position in a market group. These transactions are more likely to involve mutual dependence between the markets they connect, be the site of severe constraint on producer pricing flexibility, and be interconnected in production chains. Producers, suppliers and consumers connected by these transactions share a strong incentive to move their transactions into the more controlled setting of the corporate hierarchy. Hollow symbols indicate transactions between satellite and core positions in a market group. Dependence and constraint are asymmetric in these transactions. Satellite producers have an incentive to move the transactions into a corporate hierarchy. Core producers have an incentive to keep the transactions on the open market, regulated by competitive market pricing. Accordingly, the kinds of corporate ties used to embed these transactions can be expected to differ in form from the ties that connect producers in core positions, with the core producers having a stronger position in the tie in compensation for their greater advantage on the open market.

Conclusions

I began by distinguishing two mechanisms that integrate markets: strategic embedding of market transactions in corporate hierarchies, and patterns of dependence. I identified 184 transactions between aggregate American markets in which a large proportion of one market's business is concentrated, indicating the dependence of producers in the market on the supplier or consumer market with whom the transaction connects them. The 184 dependence relations are listed in Appendix A to facilitate other network analyses and Appendix B lists the ninety-five dependence relations within market groups to facilitate analyses of the manner in which corporate ties have been developed to manage these key market transactions. I draw three conclusions from my analysis of the relations. Although my analysis of market integration through patterns of dependence is distinct from the more usual analysis of integration through corporate embedding ties, the conclusions of each have implications for the other.

The central conclusion is the identification of the market group as an elementary unit of business integration. As illustrated in Fig. 9, a market group contains a set of core markets, a set of satellite markets, and a strong satellite dependence on the core. In contrast to the idea of an enterprise group, structurally analogous to a clique, a market group is stratified into an upper and lower tier of interdependent markets. Within the top tier, core markets tend to be connected by chains (not cycles) of mutual dependence relations. The bulk of the roles among core markets are either mutual dependence dyads or chains of mutual dependence. In their transactions with markets beyond the core, producers are most often in a patron role with a dependent supplier or consumer market. Within the bottom tier of the market group, satellite producers tend to be connected, if at all, by independent, asymmetric dependence relations. When dependence occurs within the satellite group it is most often an isolated, asymmetric relationship. In their transactions beyond the satellite group, producers are most often in a client role, dependent on a supplier or consumer market.

In the aggregate, core producers have more structurally defined entrepreneurial opportunities to negotiate favorable prices in their transactions with suppliers and consumers—their suppliers and consumers are more likely to operate in disconnected, internally competitive markets—but this doesn't translate into higher profit margins. The contradiction lies in how core and satellite producers are constrained.

Core producers face a lower aggregate level of constraint, but this constraint is concentrated in transactions with strong suppliers and consumers in other core markets. The most constrained transactions occur between core markets. This is the cell of the transaction typology in Fig. 12 in which the strongest evidence is to be expected for the embedding theories of the firm. Constraint is strong and focused between mutually dependent markets, providing the clearest incentive for buyer and seller to move the constrained transaction into a corporate hierarchy.

Satellite producers face a higher aggregate level of constraint, but this constraint is spread across transactions with multiple markets. There is less constraint in the average satellite to core market transaction than there is in the average transaction between core markets. Satellite markets are still less constrained in their average transaction with one another. The core markets are virtually unconstrained in their transactions with satellite markets. There are no dependence relations at all from core to satellite markets and the mean constraint per transaction is near zero. In other words, the incentive to move the transactions between core and satellite markets into a corporate hierarchy is much stronger for the satellite producers. In the corporate ties embedding these transactions, the partner in the core market can be expected to hold the stronger position.

Turning to the substance of the American economy, three parallel market groups are connected to form the eight position dependence hierarchy in Fig. 4.

The highest in the hierarchy is a food–household–government market group which sustains personal and political life. The core tier in this group is anchored on the food industry, Position I, with satellites in Position V. Household and government final demand are not included as member markets in this group, but markets in the group stand out as the most often dependent on that final demand.

The second market group, distribution, produces information to guide the flow of products and the packaging in which the products flow. The core tier in this group is anchored on the chain clique that passes through the paper industry, Position II, with the finance and electronics markets in Position VII as satellites.

The third market group, manufacturing, contains the largest number of markets. This group centers on Position III which is anchored on the chain clique that passes from lumber and stone and clay products, to new construction, to heating, plumbing and structural metal products, to the steel industry, and on to motor vehicles. The fabrics markets in Position IV are a secondary core group. The satellite tier of this market group contains the satellite manufacturing markets in Position VI and the generally peripheral markets in Position VIII. The fabrics markets in Position IV are clearly distinct from the core manufacturing markets in Position III, but they more resemble core markets than satellite markets because of the chained mutual dependence relations within the group and the satellite markets dependent on them beyond the group.

My second conclusion from the analysis is that market integration is largely a dyadic phenomenon. This conclusion greatly increases the legitimacy of case studies of individual transactions, a popular vehicle for transaction cost research. The typology of transactions in Fig. 12 can be a powerful framework for sampling transactions for case studies.

The dyadic nature of market integration shows up in four ways. First, kinds of market roles are distinguished by the dependence between producers and other markets, not the dependence between the other markets. The kinds of market roles I observed using triads of markets could just as well have been detected by studying pairs of markets. Of course, I wouldn't have known this without studying triads. Second, the dyadic nature of dependence is highlighted by the almost complete absence of cycles. As illustrated by the structure of the market cliques in Fig. 3 and the structure of the core markets in Fig. 5, integration is a dyadic phenomenon between pairs of markets in chains rather than sets of markets in cycles. Third, building on both points, the dependence chains are not responsible for the vertical organization of the dependence hierarchy. The dependence hierarchy in Fig. 4 shows dependence moving up through levels of the hierarchy and cycling within positions. The analysis of market roles shows that the upward flow of dependence in Fig. 4 is not a flow through ranked markets so much as it is a dyadic flow between adjacent markets in the hierarchy. The market in a position dependent on the adjacent higher level of the hierarchy is not the same as the market depended upon by the adjacent lower level of the hierarchy. Dependence moves up from one level to the next, moves through a chain of markets in a position at the higher level, then moves from a different market up to the next level in the hierarchy. Fourth, the structure of the market group, the elementary unit of business integration, is a composite of dyadic relations. In the aggregate, the market group is a partnership between subordinate and superior. Markets in the core group are dependent on one another. Markets in the satellite group have in common their dependence on the core markets. Within the aggregate duality, dependence relations in and between the groups are largely dyadic. In Fig. 9, the three markets in each of the most frequent triads are never connected to the other two. Producers are typically connected with only one of the other two markets in a triad. The strongest exception to the dyad rule are the chains of mutual dependence relations among markets in core groups.

My third conclusion from the analysis, building from the first two, is that American markets are not strongly integrated within a single economic system. From the connectivity results, I know that the economy is a completely connected system of interdependent markets but dependence is very unevenly distributed within dense pockets of integration defined by cliques centered on construction, electronics, fabrics, food and paper. From the structural equivalence results, I know that these dense pockets of integration are interlocked in an eight position dependence hierarchy of markets. The hierarchy is less integrated as a single system than it is a set of three parallel market groups. In other words, the economy is a federation of three quasi-independent production systems. The food–household–government market group is the most central of the three with separate distribution and manufacturing market groups. Integration is strongest within each market group, focused on a set of core markets, and weak between market groups, especially if the common dependence on final demand is separated out to highlight dependence between production markets.

These conclusions leave me with two questions. Are other economic systems also reducible to quasi-independent market groups as an elementary unit of business integration? Is the evidence of embedding integration, which up to this point has been used to make inferences about managing constrained transactions in general, contingent on the cell of the Fig. 12 transaction typology from which transactions are sampled? The hypothesis is that the evidence is strongest in the mutual dependence transactions between core markets, while asymmetric corporate ties tend to embed the asymmetric dependence transactions between core and satellite markets.

References

Aldrich, Howard E. and Marsden, Peter V. (1988) Environments and organizations. In *Handbook of Sociology*, pp. 361–392, edited by N. J. Smelser. Beverly Hills: Sage.

Barber, Bernard (1977) Absolutization of the market: some notes on how we got from there to here. In *Markets and Morals*, pp. 15–31, edited by G. Dworkin, G. Bermant and P. G. Brown. Washington, DC: Hemisphere.

Baldwin, David A. (1980) Interdependence and power: a conceptual analysis. *International Organization*, 34 471–506.

Benet, Francisco (1957) Explosive markets: the Berber highlands. In *Trade and Market in Early Empires*, pp. 188–217, edited by K. Polanyi, C. M. Arensberg and H. W. Pearson. New York: Free Press.

Berkowitz, S. D. (1988) Markets and market-areas: some preliminary formulations. In *Structural Sociology*, pp. 261–303, edited by B. Wellman and S. D. Berkowitz. New York: Cambridge University Press.

Blau, Peter M. (1964) *Exchange and Power in Social Life*. New York: Free Press.

Boyd, John P. (1969) The algebra of group kinship. *Journal of Mathematical Psychology*, 6 139–167.

Boyd, John P. (1980) The universal semigroup of relations. *Social Networks*, 2 91–118.

Burt, Ronald S. (1979) A structural theory of interlocking directorates. *Social Networks*, 1 415–435.

Burt, Ronald S. (1980) Autonomy in a social topology. *American Journal of Sociology*, 85 892–925.

Burt, Ronald S. (1982) *Toward a Structural Theory of Action*. New York: Academic Press.

Burt, Ronald S. (1983) *Corporate Profits and Cooptation*. New York: Academic Press.

Burt, Ronald S. (1988a) The stability of American markets. *American Journal of Sociology*, 93 356–395.

Burt, Ronald S. (1988b) Some properties of structural equivalence measures derived from sociometric choice data. *Social Networks*, 10 1–28.

Burt, Ronald S. (1990) Detecting role equivalence. *Social Networks*, 12 83–97.

Burt, Ronald S. (1992) *Structural Holes: The Social Structure of Competition*. Cambridge: Harvard University Press.

Burt, Ronald S. and Carlton, Debbie S. (1989) Another look at the network boundaries of American markets. *American Journal of Sociology*, 94 723–753.

Caves, Richard E. and Bradburd, Ralph M. (1988) The empirical determinants of vertical integration. *Journal of Economic Behavior and Organization*, 9 265–279.

Coase, Ronald H. ((1937) 1952) The nature of the firm. In *Readings in Price Theory*, pp. 331–351, edited by G. J. Stigler and K. E. Boulding. Chicago: Richard D. Irwin.

Davis, James A. and Leinhardt, Samuel (1972) The structure of positive interpersonal relations in small groups. In *Sociological Theories in Progress*, pp. 218–251, edited by J. Berger, M. Zelditch Jr. and B. Anderson. New York: Houghton-Mifflin.

Durkheim, Emile ((1893) 1933) *The Division of Labor in Society*. Translated by G. Simpson. New York: Free Press.

Ekeh, Peter P. (1974) *Social Exchange Theory*. Cambridge: Harvard University Press.

Gargiulo, Martin (1989) Testing equivalence hypotheses with STRUCTURE: a practical example. Unpublished paper, Center for the Social Sciences, Columbia University.

Geertz, Clifford (1979) Suq: the bazaar economy in Sefrou. In *Meaning and Order in Moroccan Society*, pp. 123–313, edited by C. Geertz, H. Geertz and L. Rosen. New York: Cambridge University Press.

Granovetter, Mark S. (1985) Economic action and social structure: the problem of embeddedness. *American Journal of Sociology*, **91** 481–510.

Hamilton, Gary G. and Biggart, Nicole Woolsey (1988) Market, culture and authority: a comparative analysis of management and organization in the Far East. *American Journal of Sociology*, **94** S52–S94.

Hamilton, Gary G., Zeile, William and Kim, Wan-Jin (1990) The network structures of East Asian economies. In *Capitalism in Contrasting Cultures*, pp. 105–129, edited by S. R. Clegg, S. G. Redding and M. Cortner. Berlin: Walter de Greyten.

Holmstrom, Bengt R. and Tirole, Jean (1989) The theory of the firm. In *Handbook of Industrial Organization*, Vol. 1, pp. 61–133, edited by R. Schmalensee and R. Willig. New York: North-Holland.

Leach, Jerry W. (1983) Introduction. In *The Kula: New Perspectives on Massim Exchange*, pp. 1–26. New York: Cambridge University Press.

Leifer, Eric M. (1985) Markets as mechanisms: using a role structure. *Social Forces*, **64** 442–472.

Leifer, Eric M. and White, Harrison C. (1988) A structural approach to markets. In *The Structural Analysis of Business*, edited by M. Schwartz and M. Mizruchi. New York: Cambridge University Press.

Levi-Strauss, Claude ((1949) 1969) *The Elementary Structures of Kinship*. Translated by J. H. Bell, J. R. von Sturmer and R. Needham. Boston: Beacon Press.

MacDonald, James M. (1985) Market exchange or vertical integration: an empirical analysis. *Review of Economics and Statistics*, **67** 327–331.

Malinowski, Bronislaw (1922) *Argonauts of the Western Pacific*. London: George Routledge & Sons.

Miles, Robert H. (1982) *Coffin Nails and Corporate Strategies*. Englewood Cliffs, NJ: Prentice-Hall.

Parsons, Talcott and Smelser, Neil J. (1956) *Economy and Society*. New York: Free Press.

Pfeffer, Jeffrey (1987) Bringing the environment back in: the social context of business strategy. In *The Competitive Challenge: Strategies for Industrial Innovation and Renewal*, pp. 119–135, edited by D. J. Teece. Cambridge, MA: Ballinger.

Pfeffer, Jeffrey and Salancik, Gerald R. (1978) *The External Control of Organizations*. New York: Harper & Row.

Polanyi, Karl, Arensberg, Conrad M. and Pearson, Harry W. (eds.) (1957) *Trade and Market in the Early Empires*. New York: Free Press.

Powell, Walter W. (1990) Neither market nor hierarchy: network forms of organization. In *Research in Organizational Behavior*, Vol. 12, pp. 295–336, edited by B. Staw. Greenwich, CT: JAI.

Stuckey, J. A. (1983) *Vertical Integration and Joint Venture in the Aluminum Industry*. Cambridge: Harvard University Press.

White, Harrison C. (1963) *An Anatomy of Kinship*. Englewood Cliffs, NJ: Prentice-Hall.

Ronald S. Burt

White, Harrison C. (1981a) Where do markets come from? *American Journal of Sociology*, 87 517–547.
White, Harrison C. (1981b) Production markets as induced role structures. In *Sociological Methodology, 1981*, edited by S. L. Leinhardt. San Francisco: Jossey-Bass.
White, Harrison C. (1988) Varieties of markets. In *Structural Sociology*, edited by B. Wellman and S. D. Berkowitz. New York: Cambridge University Press.
Williamson, Oliver E. (1975) *Markets and Hierarchies*. New York: Free Press.
Williamson, Oliver E. (1981) The economics of organization: the transaction cost approach. *American Journal of Sociology*, 87 548–577.
Williamson, Oliver E. (1985) *The Economic Institutions of Capitalism*. New York: Free Press.
Williamson, Oliver E. (1989) Transaction cost economics. In *Handbook of Industrial Organization*, Vol. 1, pp. 135–182, edited by R. Schmalensee and R. Willig. New York: North-Holland.
Ziegler, Rolf (1993) Market structure, ownership, and cooptation: accounting for interlocking directorships. In S. Lindenberg and H. Schreuder (eds.), *Interdisciplinary Perspectives on Organization Studies*, Oxford: Pergamon.

Appendix A. List of Markets and Dependence Relations

(Markets 78 and 79 are Household and Government Final Demand.)

#	Market					
1	Livestock and Livestock Products	2	14			
2	Other Agricultural Products	1	14	71	78	
3	Forestry and Fishery Products	14	20	78	79	
4	Agriculture, Forestry, Fishery Services	1	2	71		
5	Iron and Ferroalloy Ores Mining	37				
6	Nonferrous Metal Ores Mining	27	38			
7	Coal Mining	37	68			
8	Crude Petroleum and Natural Gas Drilling	31	68	71		
9	Stone and Clay Mining and Quarrying	11	12	36		
10	Chemical and Fertilizer Mineral Mining	27				
11	New Construction	20	36	40	69	79
12	Maintenance and Repair Construction	71	79			
13	Ordnance and Accessories	60	79			
14	Food and Kindred Products	1	78			
15	Tobacco Manufactures	2	78			
16	Broad and Narrow Fabrics, Yarn and Thread Mills	17	18	19	28	
17	Miscellaneous Textile Goods and Floor Coverings	16	28	32	78	
18	Apparel	16	78			
19	Miscellaneous Fabricated Textile Products	16	59	78		
20	Lumber and Wood Products (except containers)	3	11	24		
21	Wood Containers	2	14	20	69	
22	Household Furniture	20	78			
23	Other Furniture and Fixtures	11	20	37	78	79
24	Paper and Allied Products (except containers)	25	26	69	78	
25	Paperboard Containers and Boxes	14	24			
26	Printing and Publishing	24	73	78	79	
27	Chemicals and Selected Chemical Products	2	28			
28	Plastics and Synthetic Materials	16	27	32		
29	Drugs, Cleaning, and Toilet Preparations	27	73	78		
30	Paints and Allied Products	11	12	27		
31	Petroleum Refining and Related Industries	8	65	78		
32	Rubber and Miscellaneous Plastic Products	28	78			
33	Leather Tanning and Finishing	14	34			
34	Footwear and Other Leather Products	33	78			
35	Glass and Glass Products	14	59			
36	Stone and Clay Products	11				
37	Primary Iron and Steel Manufacturing	40	59			
38	Primary Nonferrous Metals Manufacturing	11				
39	Metal Containers	14	37			
40	Heating, Plumbing & Structural Metals Products	11	37			
41	Screw Machine Products and Stampings	37	59			
42	Other Fabricated Metal Products	11	37	59		
43	Engines and Turbines	37	59	79		
44	Farm and Garden Machinery	2	37	43	49	
45	Construction and Mining Equipment	37	49			
46	Materials Handling Machinery and Equipment	11	37			
47	Metalworking Machinery and Equipment	37				
48	Special Industry Machinery and Equipment	27	37	49		
49	General Industrial Machinery and Equipment	37				
50	Miscellaneous Machinery (except electrical)	37	59	60		

51	Office, Computing, and Accounting Machines	57	73	79
52	Service Industry Machines	11	53	
53	Electrical Industrial Equipment and Apparatus	37		
54	Household Appliances	78		
55	Electric Lighting and Wiring Equipment	11	78	
56	Radio, TV, and Communication Equipment	57	78	79
57	Electronic Components and Accessories	51	56	
58	Miscellaneous Electrical Machinery & Supplies	38	59	78
59	Motor Vehicles and Equipment	37	78	
60	Aircraft and Parts	79		
61	Other Transportation Equipment	37	78	79
62	Scientific and Controlling Instruments	78	79	
63	Optical, Ophthalmic, and Photographic Equipment	73	78	79
64	Miscellaneous Manufacturing	78		
65	Transportation and Warehousing	78	79	
66	Communications (except radio & TV broadcasting)	69	73	78
67	Radio and TV Broadcasting	73	76	
68	Electric, Gas, Water, and Sanitary Services	78	79	
69	Wholesale and Retail Trade	78		
70	Finance and Insurance	71	73	78
71	Real Estate and Rental	78		
72	Hotels; Personal & Repair Services (except auto)	78		
73	Business Services	26	69	79
74	Eating and Drinking Places	14	78	
75	Automobile Repair and Services	59	69	78
76	Amusements	71	78	
77	Medical/Educational Services & Nonprofit Orgs	78		

Appendix B. List of Key Transactions in Market Groups
(These are the 95 transactions displayed in Fig. 13.)

	Producer	Supplier–Consumer	P_{ij}	$100 * c_{ij}$
Transactions in Position I:				
	1	14	0.5841	0.1334
	2	14	0.1903	0.0410
	1	2	0.2282	0.0034
	2	1	0.2471	0.0007
	14	1	0.1960	0.0004
	2	71	0.0874	0.0001
Transactions in Position II:				
	25	24	0.2963	0.0304
	26	24	0.1534	0.0085
	24	26	0.1781	0.0066
	24	25	0.1420	0.0058
	73	69	0.1396	0.0044
	26	73	0.2411	0.0029
	24	69	0.0849	0.0025
	73	26	0.0825	0.0022

Transactions
in Position III:

3	20	0.3566	0.0230
37	59	0.1121	0.0178
40	37	0.1621	0.0171
36	11	0.4432	0.0064
40	11	0.4339	0.0062
59	37	0.0874	0.0059
20	11	0.3779	0.0047
11	36	0.0883	0.0026
11	40	0.1000	0.0021
37	40	0.0799	0.0017
11	20	0.0776	0.0013
20	3	0.0853	0.0001

Transactions
in Position IV:

28	27	0.2621	0.0326
16	18	0.3448	0.0240
19	16	0.2194	0.0223
17	16	0.1794	0.0170
28	32	0.2147	0.0166
18	16	0.1937	0.0147
17	28	0.1094	0.0111
32	28	0.1267	0.0104
27	28	0.1274	0.0103
16	28	0.1145	0.0100
28	16	0.1360	0.0096
17	32	0.0856	0.0045
16	19	0.0945	0.0036
16	17	0.0788	0.0036

Position V to
Position I
transactions:

74	14	0.1865	0.0196
33	14	0.2122	0.0171
4	2	0.3685	0.0077
15	2	0.1785	0.0017
4	1	0.2082	0.0006
12	71	0.2198	0.0002
8	71	0.1114	0.0001
4	71	0.0870	0.0001
76	71	0.0756	0.0001

Position VI to
Position III
transactions:

5	37	0.7088	0.2315
41	59	0.2484	0.0691
58	59	0.1793	0.0365
45	37	0.2177	0.0350
41	37	0.1822	0.0242
49	37	0.1616	0.0240
7	37	0.1898	0.0210
50	59	0.1121	0.0203

47	37	0.1474	0.0198
46	37	0.1465	0.0181
75	59	0.1078	0.0160
43	37	0.1114	0.0156
43	59	0.0887	0.0141
42	37	0.1336	0.0135
50	37	0.1077	0.0125
42	59	0.0828	0.0116
53	37	0.0866	0.0081
23	37	0.1085	0.0078
61	37	0.0978	0.0077
55	11	0.2373	0.0021
22	20	0.0931	0.0017
46	11	0.1724	0.0015
23	20	0.0770	0.0014
52	11	0.1293	0.0010
23	11	0.0860	0.0009
42	11	0.1060	0.0008
38	11	0.1002	0.0007

Position VII to
Position II
transactions:

67	73	0.4192	0.0088
66	69	0.0967	0.0050
63	73	0.1019	0.0006
51	73	0.0999	0.0006
70	73	0.0821	0.0004
66	73	0.0771	0.0004

Position VIII to
Positions III and IV
transactions:

10	27	0.5123	0.1141
44	37	0.1960	0.0277
9	36	0.2672	0.0247
39	37	0.2212	0.0238
48	37	0.1427	0.0160
30	27	0.1513	0.0125
21	20	0.2532	0.0115
35	59	0.0917	0.0090
6	27	0.0947	0.0061
48	27	0.0789	0.0036
9	11	0.2002	0.0033
29	27	0.0760	0.0031
30	11	0.1089	0.0006

Market Structure, Ownership and Cooptation: Accounting for Interlocking Directorships

ROLF ZIEGLER[1]

Both academic and political interest in interlocking directorships dates back to the beginning of the century. The first large study was carried out in Germany and focused on the relationship between the large German banks and industry (Jeidels, 1905). This topic was taken up in the discussion about the role of "finance capital" (Hilferding, 1910) and the search for "financial interest groups" (Sweezy, 1953). Anti-trust investigations in the United States by the Pujo Committee in 1913 and, more than twenty years later, by the U.S. National Resources Committee (1939) stressed another aspect of interlocks: being potential instruments for collusive behavior among competitors or for control of suppliers and customers, thereby increasing the degree of economic concentration. A third issue came up again with the renewed interest in interlocking directorates after the mid-sixties: Neo-Marxian critiques of the managerialists' thesis of "separation of ownership and control" (Berle and Means, 1932) did not see the significance of interlocks primarily in terms of specific connections between individual firms but rather as a more diffuse set of social relations which result in the maintenance of "class hegemony" (Domhoff, 1967, 1979; Zeitlin, 1974; Useem, 1984).[2]

---

[1]Institute of Sociology, University of Munich. *Author's note*: The research reported here was supported by the Deutsche Forschungsgemeinschaft (Zi 207/3). The data has been collected and analyzed in collaboration with Donald Bender, Hermann Biehler, Michael Braun, Anton Kunz and Frauke Wilkens. Gerhard Arminger made extremely helpful suggestions for the statistical analysis. The larger part of this paper was written while the author was visiting as a Fellow at the Netherlands Institute for Advanced Study in the Humanities and Social Sciences at Wassenaar in 1990.
[2] For a more general discussion of the research on interlocking directorates see: Fennema and Schijf (1979); Koenig, Gogel and Sonquist (1979); Andrews (1982); Glasberg and Schwartz (1983); Scott (1985); DiDonnata et al. (1988).

If one looks at the data used and the analyses made, these studies have dealt with three broad questions about networks of common directorships. The first concentrates on the global structure: What do the networks look like? The task of describing complex structures is not an easy one, but the tools of network analysis developed during the past decades have greatly enhanced our analytical capabilities. However, people have sometimes been seduced to play around with this batch of new tricks giving little thought to the question why a particular descriptive aspect of a network should be considered meaningful. They have often taken the observed morphological properties of the total network as direct evidence of some hypothesized generating process or have directly inferred specific economic and political functions of different types of companies from their location within the structure.[3] But this cannot be assumed without answering the two other questions which are theoretically and analytically more demanding if dealt with in a precise and not merely discursive manner. One is the question of consequences: How do these networks of relations affect behavior and outcomes?[4] The other relates to causes: What accounts for the development and change of the networks? Again these questions are not always completely distinct. Networks or parts of them may be created and maintained in order to bring about certain consequences, though even then intentions and consequences should be kept separate.

It is the third question we want to deal with and we do aim at a complete coverage of the total network of common directorships among the 322 largest German corporations in 1981. To our knowledge this is the first study which tries to account for the occurrence of different types of interlocks among *all* (more than 100,000) *pairs* of companies. This is done in three steps. Firstly, we

---

[3]The following rather typical quotation may illustrate this kind of analysis: "First, the relative connectivity of the network will be employed as an indicator of intercorporate cohesion and interdependence. Second, the centrality of particular corporations will be employed as an indicator of their significance within the system. Finally, an examination of cliques within the network will assess the extent to which specific interest groups have evolved over time" (Mizruchi, 1982, p. 33). Mizruchi, however, is well aware of the fact that "a major problem with studies of interlocking directorates has been the absence of systematic, reliable evidence with which to compare interlocks" (1982, p. 94).

[4]The past two decades have seen considerable growth of scholarly work on how interorganizational relations in general and interlocking directorates specifically facilitate resource acquisition and are the basis for coalitions and collective action (see, e.g., Galaskiewicz, 1979, 1985; Marsden and Lin, 1982; Perrucci and Potter, 1989).

formulate a set of hypotheses about the influence of certain factors on the occurrence of common directorships. Secondly, we describe the definition and measurement of the variables and how the data has been collected. Thirdly, in a multivariate model we estimate the specific effect of each factor on the probability of the occurrence of a common directorship and the goodness of fit to the observed set of interlocks.

Theoretical Framework

It follows from our basic structural-individualistic approach that we are searching for the generating mechanisms of common directorships at the *interorganizational level* (Allen, 1974; Pfeffer and Salancik, 1978). This is not to deny either the impact of more global structural constraints on this process or the fruitfulness of looking at emerging properties of the whole configuration. However, we explicitly reject the idea—probably never seriously supported by anyone, though sometimes metaphorically stated—that the network has been designed and created with the total structure, or at least its important characteristics, in mind.

Our decision to use the dyadic relationship, i.e., each pair of two companies, as the unit of analysis is in a way a compromise to keep the problems both theoretically and analytically tractable. Creating a link between two companies or dissolving it may be an indication of their specific relationship and/or the outcome of their common orientation toward a third party. Putting an executive on the board of one's subsidiary is a clear example for the first case; two firms, asking a politician, an expert or a prestigious token to join their boards illustrates the second. Focusing on the dyadic relationships, therefore, does not mean that we neglect the structure of the wider environment. A specific relationship between two corporations may be defined in terms of their relation to third parties, e.g., being competitors or holding shares in a joint venture. As will become clear in a moment, we took some pains in taking into account these triadic or "*n*-adic" relations at the level of independent variables.

Companies, i.e., *corporate actors*, are assumed to be the main decision-making units. Individuals are either being considered as *agents* of the enterprises or of other corporate actors outside the scope of our study (e.g., trade unions, governmental bureaucracies, employers associations, etc.) or as objects of interest to the corporate actors because they command important resources (e.g., being experts or highly reputed figures). By this assumption we do not want to imply that individual interests are irrelevant but simply that they are too varied and too difficult to assess comprehensively.

In Useem's (1984) terminology, we are exploring the corporate principle of organization of the business community. In this framework, "location is determined not by patrician lineage (as the upper-class principle asserts—R.Z.) but by the individual's responsibilities in the firm and the firm's position in the economy. Coordinates for the latter include such standard dimensions as company size, market power, sector, organizational complexity, source of control, financial performance, and the like" (1984, p. 14). Useem's own analysis is based on the classwide principle which interprets interlocks as the result of an informal cooptation into a leadership cadre which takes responsibility of managing the broadest political affairs of the entire big-business community.

We remain at the *interorganizational level* and hypothesize three groups of factors to be most important in explaining common directorships: markets, corporate size, ownership and monitoring of capital and credit allocation.[5]

Markets

Let us first look at *markets for commodities and services*. Competitors in highly concentrated, oligopolistic markets have an incentive for collusive behavior and may therefore interlock. This should not be an efficient means in highly competitive markets with low concentration where the disincentive to disclose confidential information to a competitor prevents interlocking (Pfeffer and Salancik, 1978, pp. 165f.). As far as buying and selling relationships are concerned, we follow Burt's (1983) argument that firms try to coopt sources of severe market constraint stemming from important uncompetitive suppliers and consumers.

There seems to be a general tendency in many countries that corporations in the *commercial and service sector* are less interlocked than other companies (Stokman et al., 1985, p. 273). Though we do not have a strict theoretical explanation, we included this variable in our analysis. A partial explanation for this effect may be that in market economies the main sources of uncertainty for this type of company are on the demand but not on the supply side of the chain of transactions. Especially with retail trade and services the demand side is probably too "atomistic" to be successfully coopted.

---

[5]A useful source of information about the functioning and recruitment of boards of directors are interviews of executives: see Mace (1971); Witte (1981); Useem (1984); Waldo (1985); Bleicher (1987). We ourselves interviewed forty multiple directors who were members of the boards in 107 of our 330 companies studied (Biehler and Ortmann, 1985).

The functioning of *capital and credit markets* has always been a major explanation for the high degree of interlocking between financial (especially banks) and nonfinancial enterprises (Kotz, 1978; Pennings, 1980, ch. 5; Herman, 1981, ch. 4; Mintz and Schwartz, 1985). Compared with U.S. standards, German industrial companies have very low amounts of equity capital. "Thus, banks and insurance companies are almost the only German sources of outside capital. About 75% of debt capital raised within Germany are provided by banks" (Poensgen, 1980, p. 212). Even without the specific needs for monitoring the process of capital and credit allocation—which we try to measure separately—there are incentives on both sides to establish interlocks. By enhancing the *business scan*, banks get a broader view on the general economic development, and industrial enterprises may draw on this expertise (Useem, 1984, pp. 45f.). Besides banks, insurance companies have become important institutions for accumulating capital and often manage the pension funds of other companies. It is therefore to be expected that they are interlocked both with banks and with nonfinancial enterprises.

Size and capital allocation

Another important factor determining the probability of interlocking is *corporate size*. All studies so far have shown the most interlocked corporations to be the largest and economically most important ones.[6] This tendency seems to be most easily explained by a prestige-seeking and prestige-generating mechanism. Prestige can be accumulated by publicly observed association with others of even higher prestige. Assuming a corporation's status to be dependent on its size, the previously observed correlation (Andrews, 1982, pp. 148ff.) is to be expected for our data as well.

It has sometimes been argued that the size/interlock correlation is an artifact of sheer *board size*. This seems to be a misleading argument as it overlooks the fact that—even within the limits often required by law—the size of the board may itself be a strategic variable. Rather few German companies exhaust the legal possibilities of board size. "For example, seventy percent of companies with common stock at par above DM 20 million provide for only 9 seats (or less) whereas the legal maximum is

---

[6]This finding is so pervasive that we only cite some major works and summary reports: Dooley (1969); Pfeffer (1972); Daems (1977); Pennings (1980); Stokman, Ziegler and Scott (1985).

21" (Poensgen, 1980, p. 214). Partialling out the effect of board size would amount to erroneously controlling for an intervening or dependent variable. Besides, the larger number of interlocks of big companies is predominantly due to a higher accumulation of positions by executives of these companies and not to an enlargement of their boards. In our stepwise regression analysis we therefore introduced board size as the last predictor variable in order to test whether it is able to explain something beyond the other factors.

Information impactedness and the possibility of opportunistic behavior in a situation of uncertainty create the need to monitor *financial participations and crediting.* This need should be the stronger the more is at stake and the less easily transaction-specific investments may be withdrawn (Williamson, 1975, 1985). In a situation of uncertainty, there may be fundamental differences about future events and the adequacy of alternative corporate policies among investors. This creates an additional incentive for capital owners to monitor their investments (Daems, 1978). It is therefore to be expected that the probability of interlocking rises with the size of shareholdings or with a precarious financial status of the loaner (Pennings, 1980).

Ownership, Codetermination and Informal Networks

Mainly for descriptive purposes, we have also included the *type of ownership* in our analysis to find out whether there is any tendency over and above specific financial participations to interlock among or between corporations ultimately controlled by certain categories of owners. There is a specific category for which a theoretical argument may be constructed. The control over the crucial resources of capital and technology which multinationals possess makes them rather independent of local banking and industrial firms. Multinationals will create alliances with their home economy but have less need to ally their foreign subsidiaries with domestic firms.

Workers' representation on the supervisory boards is a peculiar feature of German industrial relations (Witte, 1980a,b; Säcker and Theisen, 1981; Kirsch and Scholl, 1983; Gerum, Steinmann and Fees, 1988). Some variables have therefore been added to explore the influence of *codetermination* on the structure of interlocks.

Finally we have made a very tentative attempt to test the *old-boys-network hypothesis.* It assumes that those people are asked to join the board whom one has come to know as being competent, trustworthy and sharing the same general outlook.

Following our structural-individualistic approach which centers on constraints, we can order our independent variables according to the implied or suspected weight of the constraint *vis-à-vis* other constraints. We thus arrive at a block-recursive "causal" order among our independent variables, i.e., variables in "causally" prior blocks may partially determine those independent variables following in the causal order but not the other way round[7]:

- structure and type of markets (i.e., markets of commodities and services, capital and credit markets, enterprises in commercial or service sector, business scan);
- corporate size;
- capital and credit allocation (i.e., financial participations, crediting);
- ultimate ownership (i.e., intra- and intercategories);
- codetermination;
- informal network (i.e., indirect interlocks);
- board size.

The main hypotheses to be tested with our data have now been stated. There is also an *exploratory aim* concerning the effects of our independent variables: their impact on the direction, strength and reciprocity of direct interlocks. When a primary (executive or non-executive) interlock exists, we may speak of a direction from A to B if an executive of A or someone otherwise primarily affiliated with A is sitting on the supervisory board of B.[8] Interlocks can also vary in strength. There are either multiple interlocks between two companies or there are executives sitting on the managing boards of both companies. The latter is also an indication of a strong relationship, as the explicit consent of both supervisory boards is required by law.

German law proscribes the "crossing of executive interlocks" (*Überkreuzverbot*), i.e., if an executive of A is sitting on the supervisory board of B, an executive of B is not permitted to sit on the supervisory board of A. The philosophy behind this legal requirement is that a supervisory position implies control which is thought to be asymmetrical. However, there may be

---

[7]There may be some questions about this ordering, especially as regards the first two blocks of variables. From an empirical point of view, however, this seems not to be important as there is almost no explained deviance which cannot be uniquely attributed to either market factors or corporate size.

[8]A directed interlock from A to B does not necessarily imply control of B by A. It may also indicate a successful cooptation of A by B. Without further information about the underlying social relationship between the two firms, the "meaning" of the direction of an interlock cannot be determined. However, as we will see later on, in many cases there is information to infer whether it is control or cooptation.

incentives to establish *reciprocal relationships*. One way to reach this aim without violating the *Überkreuzverbot* is to have primary interlocks running in opposite directions, of which at least one is carried by a non-executive, but primarily affiliated director. We will also look at the effects of our independent variables on these kinds of relationships.

Before describing the operationalization of our variables, some basic features of the institutional structure of German industry and banking have to be briefly outlined.

Some Remarks on the Institutional Structure of German Industry and Banking

The German *corporate governance system* is characterized by a *two-tier structure*, being very different from the Anglo-Saxon single-board system (Bleicher and Paul, 1986a, 1986b). In all joint stock companies, direct control of the enterprise is vested in the managing board (*Vorstand*) which is comprised of the corporation's top executives. It is in turn supervised by the *Aufsichtsrat* which cannot include any members of the managing board. The supervisory board can adopt rules requiring its approval for specific types of transactions, but is not otherwise empowered to involve itself in the daily management of the corporation. It appoints the members of the managing board for periods not exceeding five years and can express disapproval of the managing board in its comments to the shareholders on the results of the annual audit.

Though not obliged by law, many companies have adopted a two-tier structure. Nevertheless, 12% of all companies studied had only a managing board, being solely comprised of insiders, i.e., top executives or managing owners.

Historically, only shareholders were represented on the supervisory board. Shortly after World War II, employee representation was introduced by several acts of *codetermination*. For companies with less than 2000 employees, the formula of the Labour Relations Act of 1952 (*Betriebsverfassungsgesetz*) still holds: one-third employee representation and two-thirds shareholders representation. For companies with more than 2000 employees, the Codetermination Act of 1976 (*Mitbestimmungsgesetz*) marked a major change, asking for equal representation of owners and labour on the supervisory board. However, in case of a stalemate, the chairman of the board (who has to be a shareholders' representative) gets an additional vote. Corporations in the mining and steel industries are subject to special regulations (*Montan-Mitbestimmungsgesetz* of 1951) requiring equal representation on the supervisory board with one additional neutral outside member acceptable to both sides. Many codetermined corporations have implemented practices (e.g., entrusting subcommittees with decisional power over important matters or strengthening the influence of the chairman) which limit the impact of these codetermination laws (Gerum, Steinmann and Fees, 1988, pp. 143ff.).

Depending on the number of its employees, the supervisory board of a codetermined corporation has to have twelve, sixteen or twenty members. The majority of the workers' representatives have to be employees of the corporation. Two, respectively three, workers' representatives are nominated by the trade unions and may not be employed by the corporation. It is therefore important to know that the sixteen German *trade unions* are organized by industries, i.e., all employees of a corporation, whether they are blue- or white-collar workers and whatever trade they belong to, form the constituency and are potential members of one and only one of the sixteen trade unions which have combined in the German Federation of Labor (*Deutscher Gewerkschaftsbund*). There is another trade union based on a different organizing principle. The *Deutsche Angestellten Gewerkschaft* is open only to white-collar workers, but from all trades. However, in comparison to the DGB, the DAG is much less important and has little representation on the supervisory boards except in certain sectors because of its smaller size and its very unequal distribution of membership over industries.

There are some institutional characteristics of the German *banking system* which at least partially account for its traditionally important role played in economic development. German banks are predominantly so-called *Universalbanken*, i.e., they are not only taking deposits and offering short-and long-term credit, but also underwriting and trading securities, financing foreign trade, mortgaging and providing other services like investment consulting. Though many banks concentrate their business, the largest ones do not restrict their activities to any special field or region. They also hold shares in nonfinancial corporations, these holdings being concentrated in certain industries, e.g., brewing, cement manufacturing, building, insurance and retail. Another important instrument for exercising influence, which has been hotly debated, is the *Vollmachtstimmrecht*, permitting banks under certain circumstances to vote on behalf of the shares put on deposit. By proxy voting German banks command on the average about seven times as many votes as they own stockholdings (Monopolkommission, 1978, pp. 294ff.).

Compared with other European countries like Austria, Italy or France, the ownership role played by the *public sector* is relatively low (Stokman, Ziegler and Scott, 1985). Fourteen per cent of the companies studied are directly or indirectly owned by federal, state (*Länder*) or local governments. Besides the two big nationalized enterprises, railways and PTT, public ownership is concentrated mainly in utilities and regional banking. Two exceptions should be mentioned, because they belong to the largest industrial enterprises: Volkswagen VAG and the combine VEBA operating in the oil refining and chemical industry. At the time of our study, both corporations had to be considered state-controlled, though the majority of shares was held in dispersed ownership.

Data and Measurement of Variables

We applied the same selection criteria as in a previous comparative research project (Stokman, Ziegler and Scott, 1985, pp. 15ff.). A target of 200 largest legally and economically independent nonfinancial companies was set, using turnover (the monetary value of sales) as a measure of size. In addition some fifty financial enterprises were selected, with total assets for banks and other financials and sum of premium for insurances as yardstick. In a second step, all legally independent companies were added which were majority-controlled by one of the "independent" corporations but larger than the smallest of these. In 1981 this selection comprised 330 corporations. Because of missing data about the composition of boards, we had to discard eight companies. This left 322 corporations to be studied.

Using annual reports, directories and other official sources, data on members of both boards and various items of economic information on the companies was collected. Not all the companies selected, however, were joint stock companies (*Aktiengesellschaft*) and the various partnerships, mutual companies, cooperatives, limited liability companies[9] or corporations under public law were treated in such a way that the principles of selection and classification would approximate to that used for joint stock companies. If only one board existed, it was always classified as managing board. Direct financial participations among the selected companies were coded from the annual reports and from a handbook on shareholdings published annually by *Commerzbank* (1982).

---

[9]This is the preferred legal form for subsidiaries and joint ventures. One of the main reasons for this is the legal right of the parent companies to issue direct orders to the managing board of their subsidiaries (Gerum, Steinmann and Fees, 1988, pp. 152f.).

The Variables

We will now describe the definition of the *independent variables* listed in Table 2 and the additional data which had to be collected. There is no information available on buying and selling among individual firms. *Patterns of market transactions* were therefore inferred from the input–output table of 1972 published by Deutsches Institut für Wirtschaftsforschung, Berlin (Pischner, Staeglin and Wessels, 1975). This table is based on the so-called "institutional principle", i.e., each firm is assigned to exactly one of the fifty-six two-digit sectors according to its most important product supplied. Excluding intra-industry transactions, i.e. blanking out the diagonal cells, we calculated the proportion of all (intersectoral) purchases and sales between any two sectors. A uniform cutting criterion of 7% was used for dichotomizing. Economic concentration was measured by three-firm ratios (Monopolkommission, 1978). A supplying or buying sector was defined as being uncompetitive if the ratio was above 0.30, i.e., if more than 30% of total turnover of an industry was sold by its three largest firms. Our companies were mapped onto the economic sectors of the input–output table according to their most important product supplied (*Umsatzschwerpunkt*). A pair of firms belonging to different sectors was classified as indicating "high constraints" if either sector was an important supplier and/or consumer to the other, i.e., proportion of purchases and/or sales was higher than 7% in either direction, *and* the important supplying (or purchasing) sector was highly concentrated, with its three-firm ratio above 0.30. If not, the pair was classified as showing "low constraints". If both firms belonged to the same sector, a pair was classified as being highly uncompetitive if the concentration ratio was at least 0.20. This procedure follows the general argument of Burt (1983, ch. 2), with some minor modifications (Ziegler, 1982). The cutting points used to dichotomize the variables were empirically determined by discernible "shifts" in the pattern of bivariate relationships with interlock density.

These first four[10] categories were only applied to pairs of nonfinancial enterprises. The next three categories classify pairs of *financials*. We distinguish among banks (*Geschäftsbanken*) offering all the services of a German *Universalbank*, insurances and other financial institutions (e.g., banks specialized in mortgaging, financing export or rendering other specialized services). The last two cat-

[10]The first category of all categorical variables is always used as reference category in the logistic regression model. These codes are listed in the legend at the bottom of Table 2.

egories ("Financials and Nonfinancials") include pairs consisting of a nonfinancial enterprise and either a bank or an insurance—respectively another financial institution. In addition, pairs were classified according to whether none, only one, or both companies were operating in the *commercial and/or service sector*.

By some indirect reasoning we tried to arrive at a measurement for the *business scan* hypothesis. If banks try to get a broad view on the economy, they should not restrict their interlocks to a few industries but spread it over different ones. The probability of an interlock between a bank and a non-bank should therefore *decrease* with the number of corporations of an industry being included in our selection. We distinguished fourteen industries and calculated a variable which tries to measure this effect.

According to the different yardsticks mentioned above, *size-classification* into sextiles was done separately for nonfinancial corporations (volume of sales, *Umsatz*), insurances (sum of premium, *Prämiensumme*) and other financials including banks (assets, *Bilanzsumme*). The lower three sextiles have been lumped together, as preliminary analyses did not show significant differences in degree of interlocking among these "smaller" firms.

If a main size-effect on number of interlocks exists, it is to be expected that large companies are more densely linked among themselves than smaller ones. To test for an *additional* size-dependent *reciprocity effect* we have defined a variable which estimates the effect of "in- or outbreeding" at different size levels.

We did not want to restrict the analyses to effects of direct *shareholding* only. Therefore we traced all indirect financial participations which could be detected among our 322 companies moving beyond the selection (Biehler, 1986). This was a very laborious task and required up to nine steps in some cases. By an iterative procedure using the principle of additive and transitive closure (Rudolph, 1977) we calculated the amount of indirect shareholding between any two firms. Taking into account all direct shareholdings among the selected companies and all one-step financial participations coming in and going out from our selection, we found out whether any two firms were participating in joint ventures and/or whether they were controlled by the same parent(s). However, we did not trace shareholdings abroad, i.e., through foreign-owned companies outside our selection. Besides missing data, this is the only systematic bias in determining indirect financial participations. These different types of financial relationships were then put into a lexicographic order as shown in Table 2. For example, a pair was classified into the category "direct < 25%" if one firm held less than 25% of shares of the other company even if the indirect financial participation amounted to, say, 45%, or if both were controlled by a common parent.

Pairs of firms being financially unrelated were split into three categories: those where both (used as reference category) and those where only one company was majority-controlled by a third corporation, and into those dyads that consisted of two legally and financially unrelated firms. We distinguished between these categories because we expect common directorships to be less frequent among subsidiaries from different financial groupings than among their parents, i.e., interlocking across financial groupings should occur at the top.

As with buying and selling, we do not have information about *crediting*. However, from the annual reports and the directories we know the bank(s) with which a corporation has its accounts (*Bankverbindungen*). One may safely assume that if a bank lends money to a company, the latter will have its accounts with the creditor. Though not completely reliable, a *Bankverbindung* may therefore be used as a (necessary) indicator of an unobserved credit relation.

Ultimate ownership of each company was detected by tracing back financial participations. Seven categories were distinguished: private ownership (including family holdings or foundations), dispersed ownership, federal government, state (*Länder*) or local government, cooperatives, trade unions, and foreign ownership. It must be stressed that with the exception of federal government, these are only categories of ultimate ownership. Usually it does not mean that ultimate control of companies is in the hands of a single person, family or legal party. In very few cases we have to classify a company on the basis of the largest (direct and indirect) minority-shareholding. Five cases had missing data and were classified as privately controlled.

The next two variables try to capture some of the effects of *codetermination*. The first indicates whether both firms are required by law to have workers' representation on their supervisory boards. The second shows whether both companies are organized in the same trade union, i.e., whether their employees belong to the constituency and are potential members of the same union.

The last variable is admittedly a very crude measure of an *informal network*. We reason that one possibility to get to know competent and trustworthy people is meeting them on the boards of third companies. The chances of a direct interlock should therefore be higher if two companies are indirectly linked via a third corporation. However, this was only coded if the two companies were financially unrelated, because one may argue that within financial groupings, knowledge about persons is diffused by many other channels besides board interlocking.

It is now commonplace in interlock research to distinguish different *types of common directorships* as they signify different types of social relations (Stokman, Ziegler and Scott, 1985, pp. 32ff.). We have distinguished six types and analyzed them separately:

- (Primary) *executive interlocks*: the multiple director holds an executive position in the managing board of one of the two companies (or very rarely in both).
- *Primary non-executive interlocks*: executives are formal agents of the companies they represent. However, some multiple directors may be considered to be primarily affiliated with a particular corporation though not holding an executive position at present. By looking at the former careers, ownership status and other relevant information, we inferred in each individual case the primary affiliation of a multiple director who was not an executive, employee representative or union officer.
- *Specialist interlocks*: if a link was created by a person not being executive, primarily affiliated or employed by any company (inside or outside our selection) and if he was not a union officer, he was labeled "specialist". This category includes politicians, civil servants, officers in economic associations, lawyers, scientists and (as a residual category) other experts.
- *Employee interlocks*: the multiple director is a workers' representative employed by one of the two companies.
- *Union interlocks*: the multiple director is a union representative, usually a union officer.
- *Induced interlocks*: these are links between supervisory boards created by multiple directors holding executive positions or being primarily affiliated with any third company inside or outside our selection.

This concludes the description of our main variables. Further information will be given when needed. We are now presenting the empirical results of our analysis.

Empirical Results

Obviously, the independent variables are correlated. To separate the effects and to evaluate the overall goodness of fit, we ran multivariate logistic regressions using GLIM[11] (Baker and Nelder, 1978). The model assumes a dichotomous dependent variable y_i ($i = 1, \ldots, N$; number of observations) to be binomially distributed and linked to a systematic component η_i:

$$P_i := \frac{y_i}{n_i} = \frac{\exp(\eta_i)}{1 + \exp(\eta_i)} + e_i =: \pi_i + e_i \tag{1}$$

[11]GLIM is a very flexible program which has several advantages. There is a high flexibility in specifying a model by defining specific independent variables. One is

e_i is a random error term; n_i equals 1 if each individual observation is used in the analysis.[12] The systematic component η_i is a linear function of the k independent variables x_j which may be continuous or discrete.

$$\eta_i = \sum_{j=1}^{k} \beta_j \cdot x_{ij} \qquad (i = 1,....,N) \tag{2}$$

Positive (negative) values of β_j indicate that the independent variable raises (lowers) the predicted probability π_i. An intuitively more satisfying measure is found if we evaluate the partial derivative of π_i at the average probability π.

$$\frac{\partial \pi_i}{\partial x_{ij}} (\pi_i = \pi) = \pi \cdot (1- \pi) \cdot \beta_j \tag{3}$$

A coefficient α_j defined by:

$$\alpha_j := 1 + (1 - \pi) \cdot \beta_j \tag{4}$$

may be interpreted as the relative increase ($\alpha_j > 1$) or decrease ($\alpha_j < 1$) in the average probability α due to a change in the independent variable x_j.

Traditional log-linear analysis usually overestimates the goodness of fit of the models because it does not measure the fit to the individual data but to the aggregate figures of a cross-classification. With our models it is possible to define a PRE-measure which is strictly comparable to the amount of explained variance in classical regression analysis. The following formula gives the so-called "true deviance" of the baseline model which parallels the total explained variance in regression analysis.

$$D(M_B) = -2N \cdot [p \cdot \ln p + (1 - p) \cdot \ln(1 - p)] \tag{5}$$

not restricted by any kind of hierarchical assumption as in traditional log-linear analysis. The program also takes account of structural or sampling zeroes and automatically calculates the correct degrees of freedom. When some of the parameters cannot be estimated because of perfect multicollinearity, they are declared "aliased". We are analyzing all 103,362 ordered pairs of 322 companies as we want to predict the direction of executive and primary non-executive interlocks too. However, even when undirected interlocks are analyzed the total set of ordered pairs is used. Percentages and coefficients are unaffected by this procedure as are estimates of goodness of fit of models.

[12]However, to save computer time aggregate data may be used as input. n_i then is the number of observations with the same unique combination of values as on the independent variables x_j. Estimates of the coefficients β_j and their standard errors are not affected by these different ways of analyzing the data.

p is the observed proportion and N the sample size. In our case
$N = 103,362$.

Overall Effects

Based on the causal ordering stipulated above, we ran stepwise
logistic regressions. The figures in Table 1 show for each type of
interlock the relative amount of *additionally* explained deviance
which can be attributed specifically to the set of independent
variables entered at a particular step.

TABLE 1 *Occurrence of Executive and Primary, Non-Executive
Interlocks (percentage of explained deviance by sets of
independent variables; N = 103,362)*

	Type of Interlock				
	Executive	Primary non-executive	Specialist	Union	Induced
Structure and type of markets	17.7	34.7	28.5	6.9	9.0
Corporate size	22.4	23.5	16.9	35.7	23.8
Capital and credit allocation	50.9	11.2	9.2	8.1	16.4
Ultimate ownership	5.4	9.9	24.6	31.4	9.0
Codetermination	0.5	6.5	0.4	1.2	6.0
Informal network	1.7	10.0	8.4	1.5	32.2
Board size	1.4	4.3	12.2	15.2	3.6
	100.0	100.0	100.0	100.0	100.0
Total percentage of explained true deviance	39.5	20.6	22.5	31.7	33.9
True deviance $D(M_B)$	(15,219)	(8,567)	(10,065)	(7,107)	(32,902)
Mean percentage of interlocks p	1.40	0.69	0.84	0.56	3.73

To make figures comparable across types of interlocks, percentages are based on the total amount of deviance explained by all variables taken together. This total amount of explained deviance is given at the bottom of the table as a percentage of the "true deviance" calculated by formula (5) using the densities of each partial network (i.e., the mean percentage of interlocks p). The model is obviously able to account rather well for the occurrence of executive interlocks (39.5%), but less so for union (31.7%), specialist (22.5%) and primary non-executive interlocks (20.6%). Nevertheless, this goodness of fit is quite satisfactory taking into account the large number of observations, as these figures are analogous to multiple correlations between 0.45 and 0.63.

For the sake of completeness we have also included the figures for induced interlocks which—with two exceptions—will not be analyzed later on. Most of the 33.9% of explained deviance is due to indirect interlocks. This shows, of course, that part of the indirect interlocks between two firms are created by an executive of a third company sitting on the supervisory boards of both firms, thereby also linking them directly by an induced interlock. Without indirect interlocks the percentage of explained deviance drops to 23.0%.

It may have been noted that "employee interlocks" are not shown in Table 1. Though about 22% of all 5331 persons holding a directorship in any of the selected companies were employee representatives, they created only thirty(!) interlocks, twenty-eight of which coincided with financial participations. Employee interlocks are obviously a very rare exception and confined to combines.

The relative importance of the independent variables varies in a very interesting way among the different types of interlocks. Size contributes roughly the same relative amount to the explanation except with union interlocks, where it is more important because larger companies are more often subject to codetermination laws. Type of ultimate ownership seems to be an important factor over and above specific financial participations in explaining union and specialist interlocks, but less so for primary non-executive links and certainly not for executive interlocks. The latter are predominantly due to the existence of financial participations and/or credit relations. Quite to the contrary, primary non-executive links have little to do with the process of capital and credit allocation, but seem to be shaped by more general market forces. This is a very interesting finding, which indicates that executives as formal agents monitor specific capital and credit allocation while primarily affiliated, non-executive directors take care of more general market constraints. Finally, an informal network seems to be more important for recruiting primarily affiliated non-executives and specialists who may also become known through these indirect contacts.

Effects in Detail

We will now discuss the detailed pattern of effects of the independent variables. Because of space limitations we only show the α-coefficients for executive and primary non-executive interlocks in Table 2, but will present the most important figures for the other types of interlocks in the text.

As said above [see formula (4)], the α-coefficients may be interpreted as the relative change in the average probability π due to the respective independent variable. Effects are always estimated relative to the reference category of a variable which are omitted in Table 2 because they are uniformly set to 1. For instance, intersectoral relations with high constraints raise the average probability of *executive interlocks* 1.4 times. If both firms are operating in the same, low concentrated market, chances of common executive directorships are extremely low ($\alpha = 0.2$), while in high concentrated sectors the average probability does not significantly differ from the baseline category ($\alpha = 1.1$). Operating in the *commercial* or *service sector* drastically reduces the chances of interlocking ($\alpha = 0.3$).

Competitors in low concentrated markets do not only avoid common directorships of their executives but interlocking by other people as well. Chances are usually lower (or do not differ from the reference category) that primarily affiliated non-executive, specialist or union officer interlocks exist between competing firms if market concentration is low. The absence of even induced interlocks ($\alpha = 0.0$; not shown here) indicates that if a third firm is represented on the supervisory boards of two competing companies, care is taken to have this done by two different executives.

Executive interlocking is very pronounced among financials ($\alpha = 1.8$) but avoided among banks ($\alpha = 0.5$). This seems to be at odds with the observed higher than average density of executive interlocks among banks (3.3% as compared with the average density $p = 1.4\%$; figures not shown here). However, *financial participations among banks* act as an intervening mechanism. If they are controlled for—as in Table 2—chances of interlocking are even lower than in the reference category ($\alpha = 0.5$) while the bivariate coefficient is $\alpha = 2.3$ (not shown here). Only when they are financially related do banks tend to interlock through their executives with nonfinancial corporations. When capital

TABLE 2 *Effects of Market Structure on the Occurrence of Common Directorships*

		Executive interlocks	Primary non-executive interlocks
Markets of commodities and services[1]			
Inter-sectoral	High constraint	1.4[c]	2.0[c]
Intra-sectoral	Low concentration	0.2[b]	0.9
	High concentration	1.1	2.7[c]
Capital and credit markets[1]			
Intra-financials	Other financials	1.8[c]	4.2[c]
	Banks	0.5[a]	3.3[c]
	Banks-insurances	1.8[a]	5.4[c]
Financials and	Banks-nonfinancials	1.2	4.4[c]
nonfinancials	Insurances, other financials		
	– nonfinancials	1.0	2.9[c]
Enterprises in commercial or	Only one	0.3[c]	1.4[c]
service sector[2]	Both	0.3[c]	2.3[c]
Business Scan		1.0	1.5[c]
Size of first	4th sextile	1.2[a]	1.1
(second) firm[3]	5th sextile	1.7[c]	1.7[c]
	6th sextile (large)	2.1[c]	1.8[c]
Both firms are[4]	In 1st–4th sextiles	1.4[c]	1.7[c]
	In 5th sextile	0.5[a]	0.9
	In 6th sextile	1.1	1.2
Financial participations[5]	Financially unrelated, one dependent	0.9	1.8[a]
	Financially unrelated, both independent	1.3	2.6[c]
	One joint venture	2.4[c]	3.4[c]
	≥ two joint ventures	2.6[c]	3.3[c]
	Common parent(s)	3.2[c]	3.9[c]
	Indirect <10%	3.5[c]	3.2[c]
	Indirect 10–50%	5.2[c]	2.1
	Direct <25%	5.4[c]	3.4[c]
	Indirect >50%	6.3[c]	–
	Direct ≥25%	8.1[c]	2.6[b]
Crediting[6]	Insurances and their bankers	1.9[b]	0.1
	Nonfinancial corporations and their bankers	2.9[c]	1.7[c]

TABLE 2   *Continued.*

		Executive interlocks locks	Primary non-executive interlocks
Intra-categories[7]	Federal government	2.0[c]	0.7
	State, local government	1.6[b]	1.5[a]
	Cooperatives	2.9[c]	2.5[c]
	Trade unions	0.0[a]	1.6
	Foreign	0.5[b]	0.9
Inter-categories[7]	Public-private	0.0[c]	0.4[c]
	Public-cooperatives, union	0.9	0.3[b]
	Private-cooperatives, union	0.3[c]	0.0[c]
	Cooperatives—unions	1.5	–
	Federal-state, local	0.0[b]	0.4[c]
	Foreign-others	0.1[c]	0.6[c]
Both firms codetermined		1.2[b]	1.6[c]
Both firms are organized in the same union		1.1	0.5[c]
Indirect interlocks present		1.7[c]	2.1[c]
Board size		1.05[c]	1.05[c]

[a] Significant at the 0.05 level (one-tailed test).
[b] Significant at the 0.01 level (one-tailed test).
[c] Significant at the 0.001 level (one-tailed test).
– Unreliable estimate.

Reference categories
[1] Relations among nonfinancial corporations with low inter-sectoral market constraints.
[2] Pairs of corporations both *not* operating in the commercial or service sector.
[3] 1st to 3rd sextile (small firms).
[4] Both firms belong to different size categories.
[5] Pairs of firms being financially unrelated but both dependent.
[6] All other pairs of corporations.
[7] Pairs of corporations both being held in private or dispersed ownership.

and credit relations are controlled for, the coefficient ($\alpha = 1.2$) becomes insignificant.

At first sight, the *business scan* hypothesis does not seem to hold (or our operationalization has low validity) as there is no effect discernible ($\alpha = 1.0$). However, this is not the whole story. If one enters this variable after the market and size factors but before taking financial relations into account, it has a significant effect in the expected direction ($\alpha = 1.3$; not shown here). That could mean that banks spread their financial participations and lending relations (backed by executive interlocks) in such a way that there remains no additional incentive to establish common directorships. Yet the strong effect on primary non-executive interlocks ($\alpha = 1.5$), which is hardly reduced by controlling for financial relations, indicates that there is a definite need for scanning the whole industry, but this job seems to be done not by formal agents but by experienced and loyal former executives.

The coefficients in Table 2 show the effect of *size* to be mono-tonically increasing. The α's reported can be interpreted as the increase (because all are above 1) of the average probability of interlocking if one firm is below median size (i.e., belongs to the reference category of the lower three sextiles) and the other belongs to the 4th, 5th or 6th upper sextile respectively. The expected increase of the average probability between any other sized pair of firms is simply given by $\alpha_i + \alpha_j - 1$; e.g., if one firm is in the 5th and the other in the 6th (largest) sextile the expected increase is $1.7 + 2.1 - 1 = 2.8$.

The "inbreeding coefficients" if both firms are in (approximately) the *same size* category show an interesting pattern. Predicting the probability of interlocking among firms of the same size from the main effects only, we correctly estimate this figure for the largest sextile (as there is "no inbreeding", $\alpha = 1.1$), we overestimate it for the second largest (there is "outbreeding", $\alpha = 0.5$) and we underestimate it for pairs of "smaller" companies (here we observe "inbreeding", $\alpha = 1.4$). This indicates that "medium-sized" enterprises (belonging to the 5th sextile) concentrate more on "vertical" interlocking, while "smaller" companies interlock more horizontally in comparison to what one would expect from their general, size-dependent tendency.

As was to be expected, *financial participations* show extremely strong effects on executive interlockings which increase monotonic-ally from common control of joint ventures ($\alpha = 2.4$) to stronger forms of indirect and direct shareholding ($\alpha = 8.1$). The hypothesis that financial groupings are interlocked by their executives at the top is, however, *not corroborated*: financially unrelated independent companies have a slightly higher but statistically not significant chance of being connected ($\alpha = 1.3$) as compared with two firms from different financial groupings if both are subsidiaries.

As expected, *crediting* and ongoing business relations between banks and insurances or nonfinancial enterprises do significantly raise the probability of interlocking ($\alpha = 1.9$ respectively 2.9).

Over and above specific financial participations, the type of ultimate *ownership* still does have an effect on executive interlocking. Links between different types are usually less or at least not more likely than the average (all statistically significant α-coefficients of "inter-category relations" are close to zero). On the other hand, if both firms are ultimately controlled by federal, state or local government or are cooperatives, they tend to have common executive directorships more frequently than the average. Foreign-owned companies interlock considerably less frequently among themselves ($\alpha = 0.5$) and with other corporations ($\alpha = 0.1$), indicating their high chance of being isolated in the network.

If both firms are *codetermined*, the chances of common executive directorships are slightly higher ($\alpha = 1.2$) while no effect of being organized in the same union on executive interlocks could be detected ($\alpha = 1.1$).

Even after controlling for all other variables, *indirect interlockings* (outside financial groupings!) make direct executive interlocks very likely ($\alpha = 1.7$). Informal cooptation seems to be facilitated by meeting each other on the board of third companies.

Board size still exerts an influence even after all the other structural variables have been controlled for ($\alpha = 1.05$; i.e., one more seat raises the chance of interlocking by 5%). However, board size is not a good single predictor. By itself it explains 7.1% of the true deviance; this figure drops to 1.4%—see Table 1—if the other structural variables (on which—as we argue—it partially depends) have been controlled for.

Coefficients for *primary non-executive interlocks* are also shown in Table 2. In general, they correspond with those for executive common directorships. However, two exceptions should be stressed. Firstly, though usually pushing in the same direction, effects of market factors are always much stronger. Secondly, the probability of primary non-executive interlocks does not increase with the strength of direct or indirect shareholdings. What has been said above can now be stated even more precisely: executives as formal agents monitor specific and strong capital and credit relations while non-executive directors who are primarily affiliated with a company concentrate more on weaker forms of financial relationships and market transactions.

We already noted that *other types of interlocks* by specialists, union officers or even induced links are likely to be absent among strong competitors, i.e., in low concentrated markets. Without presenting the figures in detail, we will briefly discuss further results of our analysis with these other types of relations.

With a few exceptions to be noted, the effects of our independent variables on *specialist interlocks* are quite similar to those on common executive directorships, though market forces, type of ultimate ownership and informal networks seem to be more important while size effects are somewhat less pronounced. Firms belonging to the same financial grouping are more likely to rely on the same specialists, but there is much less variation in the size of the α-coefficients ranging from 1.2 to 3.5 (as compared with a range of 2.4 to 8.1 with executive interlocks). Banks and their debtors do not attract the same specialists ($\alpha = 1.3$, not significant), but they are linked by their executives (Table 2, $\alpha = 2.9$). Finally, pairs of companies both of which are publicly owned are likely to be linked by the same specialists who include politicians and civil servants.

The pattern of α-coefficients for *union officers* corresponds in general with that for executive common directorships, but market variables and weaker forms of financial participations have less influence. On the other hand, size and type of ultimate ownership show stronger effects. That union officers are very likely ($\alpha = 7.5$) to link union-owned companies comes as no surprise, but they also seem to play an important role in linking companies from the public and cooperative sector both with each other and with the privately owned firms and enterprises in dispersed ownership. The hypothesis that officers from one of the sixteen trade unions would be more likely to link companies organized by their union was also corroborated; the chances are raised by 40% ($\alpha = 1.4$).

Though the direction of effects on *induced interlocks* is generally the same as with common executive directorships, their size is usually lower, indicating that they are more likely to be the by-product of other mechanism. That indirect links account for most of the explained deviance—as already mentioned—is substantively uninteresting, but shows that a high proportion of these indirect links is created by the same executive of a third company sitting on the boards of two firms and thereby inducing a link between them. The strongest effect ($\alpha = 4.0$) shows up with two companies being controlled by the same parent(s). This indicates a strong tendency to put the *same* director on the supervisory boards of one's subsidiaries.

Direction, Strength and Reciprocity of Primary Interlocks

So far the effects of our independent variables on the probability of the occurrence of certain types of interlocks have been estimated.

Rolf Ziegler

In this section we will explore the effects of the independent variables on direction, strength and reciprocity of interlocks.

TABLE 3 *Direction of Primary Interlocks (percentage of explained deviance by sets of independent variables;* N = 103,362)

	Type of interlock	
	Executive	Primary, non-executive
Structure and type of markets	26.9	77.7
Corporate size	34.5	7.7
Capital and credit allocation	19.2	5.0
Ultimate ownership	11.8	5.6
Legal status	6.5	3.0
Existence of supervisory board	1.1	1.1
	100.0	100.0
Total percentage of explained true deviance	58.6	39.4
True deviance $D(M_B)$	(1991)	(976)
Number of existing interlocks	1436	704

As can be seen in Table 3, the set of independent variables accounts for 58.6% of the true deviance in the conditional probability of the direction of executive common directorships, but only 39.4% with primary non-executive interlocks. This corresponds to multiple correlations of 0.77 and 0.63, respectively. The *direction of primary non-executive interlocks* seems mainly determined by market factors. The α-coefficients (not being reported here) indicate an extremely strong tendency of non-executives primarily affiliated with banks ($\alpha = 2.0$) and insurances ($\alpha = 3.0$) to sit on the supervisory board of nonfinancials, whereas the opposite hardly ever occurs. Non-executives primarily affiliated with commercial or service companies have a high chance ($\alpha = 1.6$) of being coopted by corporations from other sectors. Among the two top size categories, non-executives are much more likely to be coopted upwards ($\alpha = 1.5$) than the other way round. All other variables had rather low predictive value for the direction of primary non-executive interlocks.

The predictive ability for the *direction of executive interlocks* is more evenly distributed among the sets of independent variables. Without presenting the α-coefficients, we briefly summarize the significant and strongest effects. Executive interlocks are directed from larger to smaller companies, though this size-effect is only significant with very large companies (i.e., among firms in the 4th, 5th and 6th sextile). As one would expect, they run parallel to direct and indirect financial participations; this is true even for smaller amounts of shareholding and not only because the law prohibits an executive of a subsidiary to sit on the supervisory board of its parent. Looking at the executive links between nonfinancials and their banks, an interesting difference was found. If the debt–equity ratio of a nonfinancial enterprise is high, it is almost certain that the bank has its executive sitting on the supervisory board of its debtor ($\alpha = 2.1$). If, however, the debt–equity ratio is low, chances are even that an executive interlock is running in either direction. Finally, odds are much in favor of an executive interlock being directed toward foreign-owned companies ($\alpha = 2.0$), i.e., these foreign subsidiaries coopt executives from domestic corporations if they interlock at all.

Besides its direction, the *strength of an executive interlock* was analyzed. Of all executive interlocks, 16.7% is either multiple or involved executives sitting on the managing boards of both companies. Two kinds of independent variables show a significant effect on the strength of executive interlocking. As to be expected, the (conditional) probability of strong interlocks monotonically increases with the strength of financial participation (from $\alpha = 2.8$ to $\alpha = 7.2$). On the other hand, strong executive interlocks are completely absent between financial and nonfinancial enterprises.

Reciprocal relationships not violating the law against crossing of executive interlocks (*Überkreuzverbot*) are those for which primary interlocks run in the opposite direction and of which at least one is carried by a non-executive, but primarily affiliated, director. Of all primary interlocks, 9.1% is of this reciprocal nature. They are especially prevalent among companies holding several joint ventures, within financial groupings, and among the largest companies, especially if these are independent (and presumably the head of larger combines). It is quite remarkable that this was the only time that the inbreeding coefficient among the largest companies was strong and statistically significant ($\alpha = 2.0$). Reciprocity seems to be a pattern of behavior among companies related by shareholding and among financially independent, very large corporations. It should be noted that reciprocity is completely absent in high constraint and high competitive markets.

Conclusions

This is the first study to try to account for the occurrence of different types of common directorships *among all pairs of firms* in a large network: the 322 largest German corporations in 1981. In line with our basic structural-individualistic approach, we postulated the generating mechanism to be operating at the interorganizational level with companies being conceptualized as corporate actors and executives as their agents. By this we deny neither the impact of structural constraints on individual companies, nor the relevance of individual interests, nor the fruitfulness of looking at the emerging properties of the whole configuration. Structural constraints were captured by carefully defining and measuring a dozen independent variables for each of the 103,362 ordered pairs of firms which constituted the units of analysis.

In a multivariate logistic regression model, the specific effects of market structure, business scan, corporate size, financial participations, credit allocation, type of ultimate ownership, codetermination and informal networks on the probability of the occurrence of various types of interlocks were estimated. In general, the hypotheses have been confirmed and a satisfactory fit with the observed set of interlocks was found. For primary interlocks, the effects of the independent variables on direction, strength and reciprocity of existing links were also determined.

At the end we want to outline two extensions of our analysis and discuss some limitations and directions for future research. Firstly, though generally quite satisfactory, the goodness of fit of our models is far from perfect. If we move from the level of dyadic relations to the total network, the question arises how well we do recover structural aspects of the whole configuration, e.g., the distribution of incoming and outgoing primary interlocks. If our model would perfectly predict interlocking on the dyadic level, all global properties of the total network would simply follow by aggregation because our transformation rules (Lindenberg, 1977; Coleman, 1986) linking micro- and macro-level are partial definitions. However, if the fit is less than perfect at the dyadic, interorganizational level, important features of the global network may not be recovered. Secondly, in our analysis we have only used (inter)organizational characteristics. One could add positional or personal characteristics of the executives, e.g., being chairman or holding shares, or look at the career progression of multiple directors.

There are some obvious limitations of our cross-sectional study to be mentioned. One should measure change of the dependent and independent variables.[13] Ideally one should use event history data

---

[13]The interesting and often cited studies of Omstein (1982) and Palmer (1983) on replacement patterns of accidentally broken ties do not systematically relate these patterns to changes in independent variables.

with time-dependent covariates, but the difficulties of collecting and analyzing such a large data set over an extended time period seem to be prohibitive. Improving on the quality of data is certainly also desirable, though difficult to achieve. Information on buying, selling or lending among individual corporations or about individual instead of categorical ultimate ownership (taking into account kin relations) should raise the predictive power.

Despite these limitations of our analysis, we hope to have demonstrated that it is possible to account for interlocking directorates from an interorganizational perspective. Enterprises have been treated as corporate actors with interests structurally determined primarily by their position in the market and by financial participations. Distinguishing among various types of common directorships enabled us to detect the differential impact of interorganizational relations. Executives as formal agents seem to control and monitor strong interests, while loyal representatives, like former executives, are used for cooptation, interorganizational intelligence and for establishing reciprocal ties proscribed by law.

References

Allen, Michael Patrick (1974) The structure of interorganizational elite cooptation: interlocking corporate directorates. *American Sociological Review*, **39**, 393–406.

Andrews, John Albion Young (1982) The interlocking corporate director: a case study in conceptual confusion. Unpublished Ph.D. dissertation, The University of Chicago.

Baker, R. J. and J. A. Nelder (1978) *The GLIM Release 3. Generalised Linear Interactive Modelling, Program Manual.* Oxford: Numerical Algorithms Group.

Berle, Adolf A. and Gardiner C. Means (1932) *The Modern Corporation and Private Property.* New York: The Macmillan Company.

Biehler, Hermann (1986) Die Kapitalverflechtung zwischen den größten deutschen Unternehmen des Jahres 1981. *Soziale Welt*, **37**, 79–106.

Biehler, Hermann and Rolf Ortmann (1985) Personelle Verbindungen zwischen Unternehmen. Ergebnisse einer Interviewserie bei Vorstands- und Aufsichtsratsmitgliedern großer deutscher Unternehmen. *Die Betriebswirtschaft*, **45** 4–18.

Bleicher, Knut (1987) *Der Aufsichtsrat im Wandel.* Gütersloh: Bertelsmann Stiftung.

Bleicher, Knut and Herbert Paul (1986a) Das amerikanische Board–Modell im Vergleich zur deutschen Vorstands-/Aufsichtsratsverfassung—Stand und Entwicklungstendenzen. *Die Betriebswirtschaft*, **46**, 263–288.

Bleicher, Knut and Herbert Paul (1986b) Corporate governance systems in a multinational environment: who knows what's best? *Management International Review*, **26**, 4–15.

Burt, Ronald S. (1983) *Corporate Profits and Cooptation. Networks of Market Constraints and Directorate Ties in the American Economy.* New York: Academic Press.

Coleman, James S. (1986) Social theory, social research, and a theory of action. *American Journal of Sociology*, 91, 1309–1335.

Commerzbank (1982) *Wer gehört zu wem?* 14th ed. Frankfurt.

Daems, Herman (1977) *Invisible Concentration and Holding Companies. The Case of Belgium.* DBW-Depot 77-2-3. Stuttgart: C. E. Poeschel.

Daems, Herman (1978) *The Holding Company and Corporate Control.* Leiden.

DiDonnata, Donna, Davita Glasberg, Beth Mintz and Michael Schwartz (1988) Theories of corporate interlocks: a social history. In *Research in the Sociology of Organizations*, Vol. 6, edited by Sam Bacharach and Nancy DiTomaso, Greenwich, CT: JAI Press.

Domhoff, G. William (1967) *Who Rules America?* Englewood Cliffs, NJ: Prentice-Hall.

Domhoff, G. William (1979) *The Powers That Be. Processes of Ruling Class Domination in America.* New York: Vintage Books.

Dooley, Peter C. (1969) The interlocking directorate. *American Economic Review*, 59, 314–323.

Fennema, Meindert and Huibert Schijf (1979) Analyzing interlocking directorates: theory and methods. *Social Networks*, 1, 297–332.

Galaskiewicz, Joseph (1979) *Exchange Networks and Community Politics.* Beverly Hills, CA: Sage.

Galaskiewixz, Joseph (1985) Interorganizational relations. *Annual Review of Sociology*, 11, 281–304.

Gerum, Elmar, Horst Steinmann and Werner Fees (1988) *Der mitbestimmte Aufsichtsrat. Eine empirische Untersuchung.* Stuttgart: C. E. Poeschel.

Glasberg, Davita Silfen and Michael Schwartz (1983) Ownership and control of corporations. *Annual Review of Sociology*, 9, 311–332.

Herman, Edward S. (1981) *Corporate Control, Corporate Power.* Cambridge: Cambridge University Press.

Hilferding, Rudolf (1910) *Das Finanzkapital.* Berlin. (Translation 1981, Finance Capital. Boston: Routledge & Kegan Paul).

Jeidels, Otto (1905) *Das Verhältnis der deutschen Großbanken zur Industrie mit besonderer Berücksichtigung der Eisenindustrie.* Leipzig.

Kirsch, Werner and Wolfgang Scholl (1983) Was bringt die Mitbestimmung: Eine Gefährdung der Handlungsfähigkeit und/oder Nutzen für die Arbeitnehmer? *Die Betriebswirtschaft*, 43, 541–562.

Koenig, Thomas, Robert Gogel and John Sonquist (1979) Models of the significance of interlocking corporate directorates. *American Journal of Economics and Sociology*, 38, 173–186.

Kotz, David M. (1978) *Bank Control of Large Corporations in the United States.* Berkeley and Los Angeles, CA: University of California Press.

Lindenberg, Siegwart (1977) Individuelle Effekte, kollektive Phänomene und das Problem der Transformation. In *Probleme der Erklärung sozialen Verhaltens*, edited by Klaus Eichner and Werner Habermehl. Meisenheim: Anton Hain.

Mace, Myles L. (1971) *Directors: Myth and Reality.* Boston: Graduate School of Business Administration, Harvard University.

Marsden, Peter V. and Nan Lin (1982). *Social Structure and Network Analysis.* Beverly Hills, CA: Sage.

Mintz, Beth and Michael Schwartz (1985) *The Power Structure of American Business.* Chicago and London: The University of Chicago Press.

Mizruchi, Mark S. (1982) *The American Corporate Network 1904–1974.* Beverly Hills, CA: Sage.

Monopolkommission (1978) *Fortschreitende Konzentration bei Großunternehmen.* Hauptgutachten 1976/1977. Baden-Baden: Nomos.

Ornstein, Michael D. (1982) Interlocking directorates in Canada: evidence from replacement patterns. *Social Networks,* 4 3–25.

Palmer, Donald (1983) Broken ties: interlocking directorates and intercorporate coordination. *Administrative Science Quarterly,* 28, 40–55.

Pennings, Johannes M. (1980) *Interlocking Directorates. Origins and Consequences of Connections among Organizations' Boards of Directors.* San Francisco: Jossey-Bass.

Perrucci, Robert and Harry R. Potter (eds.) (1989) *Networks of Power. Organizational Actors at the National, Corporate, and Community Levels.* New York: Aldine de Gruyter.

Pfeffer, Jeffrey (1972) Size and composition of corporate boards of directors: the organization and its environment. *Administrative Science Quarterly,* 17, 218–228.

Pfeffer, Jeffrey and Gerald R. Salancik (1978) *The External Control of Organizations.* New York: Harper & Row.

Pischner, Rainer, Rainer Staeglin and Hans Wessels (1975) *Input–Output–Rechnung für die Bundesrepublik Deutschland 1972* (Deutsches Institut für Wirtschaftsforschung: Beiträge zur Strukturforschung, Heft 38). Berlin: Duncker und Humblot.

Poensgen, Otto H. (1980) Between market and hierarchy—the role of interlocking directorates. *Zeitschrift für die gesamte Staatswissenschaft,* 136, 209–225.

Rudolph, Bernd (1977) Der Durchgriffswert von Beteiligungen. *Kredit und Kapital,* 10, 233–265.

Säcker, Franz Jürgen and Manuel René Theisen (1981) Veränderungen der unternehmerischen Leitungsstrukturen durch das Mitbestimmungsrecht? *Mitbestimmung und Effizienz,* pp. 125–166 edited by F. J. Säcker and E. Zander. Stuttgart: Schäffer.

Scott, John (1985) *Corporations, Classes and Capitalism,* 2nd rev. ed. London: Hutchinson.

Stokman, Frans N., Rolf Ziegler and John Scott (eds.) (1985) *Networks of Corporate Power. A Comparative Analysis of Ten Countries.* Cambridge: Polity Press.

Sweezy Paul M. (1953) Interest groups in American economy. In *The Present as History,* edited by P. M. Sweezy. New York: Monthly Review Press.

Useem, Michael (1984) *The Inner Circle. Large Corporations and the Rise of Business Political Activity in the U.S. and U.K.* New York and Oxford: Oxford University Press.

U.S. National Resources Committee (1939) *The Structure of the American Economy.* Washington, DC: Government printing Office.

Waldo, Charles N. 1985) *Boards of Directors. Their Changing Roles, Structure, and Information Needs.* Westport, Conn.: Quorum Books.

Williamson, Oliver E. (1975) *Markets and Hierarchies: Analysis and Antitrust Implications.* New York: The Free Press.

Williamson, Oliver E. (1985) *The Economic Institutions of Capitalism. Firms, Markets, Relational Contracting.* New York: The Free Press.

Witte, Eberhard (1980a) Das Einflußpotential der Arbeitnehmer als Grundlage der Mitbestimmung. Eine empirische Untersuchung. *Die Betriebswirtschaft,* 40 3–26.

Witte, Eberhard (1980b) Der Einfluß der Arbeitnehmer auf die Unternehmenspolitik. Eine empirische Untersuchung. *Die Betriebswirtschaft,* 40, 541–559.

Witte, Eberhard (1981) Die Unabhängigkeit des Vorstandes im Einflußsystem der Unternehmung. *Zeitschrift für betriebswirtschaftliche Forschung,* 33, 273–296.

Zeitlin, Maurice (1974) Corporate ownership and control: the large corporation and the capitalist class. *American Journal of Sociology*, 79, 1073–1119.

Ziegler, Rolf (1982) *Market Structure and Cooptation. Research Report, Mimeo.* München: Ludwig-Maximilians-Universität, Institut für Soziologie.

Interorganizational Democracy

CORNELIS J. LAMMERS[1]

Introduction

When forms or degrees of democracy in organizational decision-making are studied, the analysis is nearly always focused on processes or arrangements taking place *within* rather than *between* organizations. However, in our day and age interorganizational democracy could be(come) an issue as salient, or perhaps even more so, as intra-organizational democracy. The more single organizations loose their autonomy and get enmeshed in interorganizational webs, or become parts of organizations-of-organizations, strategic decisions affecting the fate of our life and work tend to be taken more and more frequently in interorganizational than in intra-organizational contexts.

Therefore, for organized groups which have no institutionalized access to, or find themselves in the minority on, such supra-organizational *fora*, their only chance to get a fair deal is in proceedings firmly based on a set of rules ensuring democratic rights for all organizational actors involved. Moreover, when the scope for intra-organizational democracy diminishes due to these interorganizational entanglements, it matters a great deal for the average organization member not only to have some say in what goes on in his/her organization, but also to have and to hold at least some voice via his/her representatives in the counsels of such interorganizational decision-makers.

The idea of interorganizational democracy and some of its problems are illustrated in the following paper with the aid of a story concerning the establishment of a new European Community (EC) agency. International organizations, one should realize, are a special type of interorganizational (or intermediary) organization in

[1]Department of Sociology, University of Leiden. My thanks go to G. A. M. Hermsen for her assistance in screening some literature for this paper, and to Prof. H. G. Schermers for his readiness to enlighten me on the intricacies of the EC and the EBRD, and to Drs. A. A. Mijs and B. F. van Waarden for their comments on an earlier draft of this paper.

323

so far as they are mandated by a number of (national) state agencies. Since such international intermediaries on the whole receive much wider publicity than national ones, they provide the sociologist with a rich source of readily available data on their dynamics and dealings!

A Prime Minister is Concerned

In a TV interview (Friday, May 18, 1990), the Dutch Prime Minister Lubbers expressed his deep concern about the democratic quality of decision-making in the European Community (EC). He told his audience that the Great Powers of the EC, especially France and the UK, had made a deal in Washington—during a meeting of the seven main industrial nations of the Western world (Canada, Japan, the US and the "big four" of the EC: France, the FRG, Italy and the UK)—concerning the location and the presidency of a new institution, the EBRD.

EBRD stands for the "European Bank for Reconstruction and Development" founded and financed by forty-two countries plus the EC. The bank in question aims at aiding the nations of Eastern Europe to reform and revitalize their economies. Of course, the seat of this bank and the incumbency of its top position were hotly contested prizes among the nations participating in the project. Given its tasks and given that the EC countries had undertaken to furnish 51% of its funds, it was agreed at an earlier stage that the EBRD should be located within the borders of the European Community and directed by a citizen of an EC nation. Not surprisingly, the Dutch could imagine no better place than Amsterdam for such an institution and no better man to head it than our former Minister of Financial Affairs Ruding!

These issues were to be (and have meanwhile been) settled formally in a constituent assembly on May 29 by representatives of the forty-two participating member states and the EC. Before that, the EC's Council of Ministers had to give its final consent to the European Commission to commit the EC as such to the project and to contribute 3% of the funding capital for the EBRD.

Now, to come back to the sorrows of our prime minister. Apparently he had expected that proposals about the seat and the head of the EBRD would be agreed upon among the twelve EC countries in conjunction with decision-making concerning EC participation in the EBRD. It also became clear that Mr. Lubbers's protests could be interpreted as threats that the seven "small" EC countries (Belgium, Denmark, Greece, Luxembourg, The Netherlands, Portugal and Spain) would block the decision concerning EC participation in the EBRD if the "big four" would be unwilling to compromise.[2]

Turning to the content of his concerns, Mr. Lubbers criticized the facts (1) that the "big four" in the EC were about to confront the "small seven" with a *fait accompli*, and (2) that they (the big four) came to see eye to eye on this issue as part of a deal with other non-EC nations in a non-EC setting outside Europe.

The UK and France had, with the connivance of West Germany and Italy, fixed London as the preferred location for the European Bank for Reconstruction and Development, and chosen Jacques Attali, advisor of President Mitterand of France, as the prime candidate for its presidency. In doing so the "big four" of the EC had in the eyes of Mr. Lubbers—and many other observers in the "small" EC countries as well—ignored the wishes and interests of the "small seven". Adding insult to injury, the big ones had come to this agreement and made it public prematurely in Washington DC at the end of a meeting with non-EC countries, ostensibly about non-EC matters.

In other words, the Dutch Prime Minister denounced the course of events as "undemocratic" because of a violation of two norms supposedly applicable in this case:

(1) Since in an international organization all member states have more or less equal rights, Great Powers should not lord it over smaller ones.
(2) In an international organization all crucial decisions—including those on a joint policy with respect to an issue pending in another international organization—should be taken according to the rules in the proper setting.

Later reports made it clear that the Dutch opposition, supported only weakly by the Belgians and even more weakly by the other "small" nations, came to nothing. In the end, the forty-three EBRD members, their votes weighted according to their shares in the capital of the bank, did accept London as its seat and Attali as its head.

One final bit of information: strictures made by the Dutch Prime Minister on Friday were duly reported in the Dutch press on the following Saturday. However, his appeal to the value of democracy by calling the maneuvers of France and Great Britain "undemocratic" and by expressing his anxiety about the "democratic quality of Europe", was not mentioned, at least

[2]Since there are twelve EC states, and since this story is about the "big four" and the "small seven", I should explain that the twelfth (missing) nation is Ireland which at the time was chairing the EC's Council of Ministers and therefore remained "neutral" in the conflict.

not in the newspapers I examined (NRC/Handelsblad, Trouw, Volkskrant).

This case provides us with ample opportunity to introduce the concept of "interorganizational democracy", and to discuss some of the problems and intricacies it refers to.

Organizational and Interorganizational Democracy

"Organizational democracy", says Heller in his Foreword to the first volume of the International Yearbook of Organizational Democracy, "is meant to describe a considerable variety of inter-personal and/or structural arrangements which link organizational decision-making to the interests and influence of employees at various levels. This approach means that organizational democracy can exist in places that do not have political democracy as defined in most Western countries. At the same time, organizational democracy is compatible with individual ownership of the means of production" (Heller, 1983, p. xxxvi).

This delineation of organizational democracy can serve very well likewise for the description and analysis of similar arrangements— and, I would add, also similar *processes!*—linking *inter*organizational decision-making to the interests and influence of the organizational participants in such arrangements and processes. However, let us turn for a somewhat more precise definition of the meaning of the concept of organizational democracy to the work of Katz and Kahn (1966, pp. 212–213). They contrast a democratic model of organization with the usual hierarchical one by singling out three main features:

1. An organization is democratic if there is a separation between legislative and executive power, and to the extent to which the legislative subsystem includes the entire membership of the organization.
2. An organization is democratic if the assembled membership, or their representatives, possess veto power. Whereas in a hierarchical organization the ultimate authority resides at the top, in a democratic one the rank and file—or their delegates—have the final say over policy issues.
3. An organization is democratic if the assembled membership, or their representatives, have the right to decide about the selection, tenure, and dismissal of executive officers, especially the top ones.

The three criteria identified by Katz and Kahn can perhaps be summarized in the statement that organizations by and large are more democratic, the more channels and chances their common members have to—directly or indirectly—influence or (co)determine the major policies and decisions of their organizations.

Obviously, a truly democratic organization where government is conducted—as Katz and Kahn (1966, p. 213) put it—"by the active and expressed consent of the governed", is an ideal realized in the modern world only to some extent and/or in some respects in the practice of voluntary associations, cooperatives, self-managed enterprises in Yugoslavia, Kibbutzim in Israel, etc. Likewise, hierarchically designed organizations vary a great deal in the extent to which the rank and file, or those who represent them, have some say in the decision-making of higher echelons and/or get a chance to prohibit, retard or twist the implementation of decisions of their higher ups. It follows that organizational democracy—or for that matter organizational oligarchy—should be regarded not as an attribute, but as a variable, or rather as a set of variables.

The same goes for interorganizational democracy[3] which refers to the degree of participation or (co)determination with respect to strategic decisions by the constituents of an interorganizational network. One can distinguish various types of more or less organized complexes of organizations, but let me simplify matters by applying the concept of interorganizational democracy here only to intermediary organizations of the representative variety. Local coordination councils, federations of trade unions, of business interest organizations, of sportsclubs, and also national or international professional associations, intergovernmental agencies or councils, have in common that they are "designed and maintained by one or more organizational mandators to interlink (sets of) organizations" (Lammers, 1988, p. 439). In so far as (one of) their main function(s) is to promote the interests of the mandators *vis-à-vis* other organizations, they can be called "representative intermediaries" (in contradistinction to the "control type" of intermediary; for example, a regulatory agency).

The representative intermediary is constituted by organizational mandators who—usually via an assembly, a congress or whatever other body of representatives—hold the ultimate legislative and veto powers and also the right to appoint and dismiss the top executives. Therefore, such "second degree" organizations can be modeled in similar fashions as "first degree" ones after the democratic ideal as formulated by Katz and Kahn. Consequently, participants or observers—like the Dutch Prime Minister and other critics of the ways in which M. Mitterand and Ms. Thatcher prepared the

[3]The concept of "interorganizational democracy" was, to the best of my knowledge, used for the first time in an empirical analysis by Mijs (1987, p. 59). Of course, the phenomena referred to are already treated in earlier studies (for example, about union democracy: Lipset, Trow and Coleman, 1956; Edelstein and Warner, 1975), in so far as the organizations focused upon were federations of local or regional units.

way for decisions as to the seat and head of the EBRD—can meaningfully preach and/or practice "second degree" organizational democracy.

Referring to organizational democracy at the level of intermediary organizations, it makes sense to use the term "interorganizational democracy" to emphasize the salient fact that in this instance "the people" (who are supposed to rule in a democracy) are not natural persons, but organizational actors.[4]

One Organization, One Vote?

Practically all representative intermediaries wrestle with the problem of how to cope with inequalities between their mandator organizations. Should all member organizations have equal rights, regardless of their size or resources? Or should their rights be weighed according to the number of people they represent, or in proportion to the means they invest in their joint enterprise? Of course, in polities or organizations professing political or organizational democracy, the "one man, one vote" principle was and is not universally adhered to either. The "natural persons" who live, work, or recreate in communities or associations differ a great deal also and some of these differences are generally assumed to have implications for their democratic competence, i.e., their abilities to judge, to vote and/or to be a candidate for office. The inequalities in question, however, are usually taken care of by considering democratic rights as attributes. By enfranchising only certain classes of people (for example: adults or men only, or only those who have been a member or employee for a designated time), or by differentiating certain rights of participation or (co)determination according to categories of decisions, intergroup variance in democratic competence is artificially maximized and institutionalized, while intragroup variance in democratic competence is officially ignored.

In the case of interorganizational democracy, dissimilarities between organizational actors apparently are not so easily coped with in this manner. Proceedings in federations, peak associations, national unions or parties, or in similar intermediary organizations, often exhibit an implicit or explicit supposition that democratic

---

[4]An organizational actor is pretty much the same kind of actor whom Coleman (1982) designates as the "corporate actor". However, I rather use the adjective "organizational" than "corporate" to avoid the impression that such an actor has to be a judicial person or a "corporation" in the sense of an incorporated enterprise.

rights, at least to some extent and with an eye to certain decisions, ought to be scaled according to the "weight" of the members. Inequalities between organizational actors are thought to entitle them to different degrees of rights for two reasons. First of all, if democracy stands for "rule by the people", then it appears logical that democratic rights of organizational actors in the setting of an intermediary should be commensurate with the number of people each actor represents. Moreover, member organizations with ample resources will inevitably have to contribute much more money, services or officers to the common endeavor than their poorer fellow members. The more duties members have to undertake, so the reasoning goes, the more rights they can claim.

In other words, in interorganizational arrangements of a somewhat democratic nature, rights to nominate candidates, to vote in elections, to approve or disapprove policy proposals, etc., are not always treated as attributes, but also conceived of as variables. Therefore, the principle of "weighted rights" can coexist, or conflict, with the principle of "equal rights" of members.

As to the "logic" of the latter principle, the following can be surmised. Interorganizational forms of cooperation are usually tenuous, since the organizational actors tend to retain their exit options as long as possible. A representative intermediary in general, however, is very keen on encompassing *all* organizations in its domain, or anyway in keeping on board as many subsets as possible of organizations which can be presented as "representative" of a great variety of relevant, relatively homogeneous, subclasses of their membership. Thus, an intermediary is always on the alert not to loose members belonging to a particular group of organizations, such as the class of medium or small ones, even if the group threatening to secede constitutes only an insignificant minority in terms of people represented or contributions made.

Consequently, the equal rights principle (one organization, one vote) is frequently incorporated in the statutes of representative intermediaries as the sole basis of representation, or in combination with the weighted rights principle. There is "strength in numbers" not only of individual, but also of organizational, actors involved. In this vein, Business Interest Associations (see, for example, Van Waarden, 1989, ch. 8; De Vroom, 1990, ch. 9) know either only equal voting rights, or only rights according to the number of employees of the member firms,[5] or they combine both principles.

---

[5]To weigh the rights of member organizations, other indices may also be used such as: total amount of wages, size of turnover.

In the last case, sometimes qualified majorities are required for strategic issues (so as to forestall the eventuality that small firms can outvote the big ones), or certain positions on the executive board are reserved for the big top firms of the industry. Inequalities between member organizations can furthermore be taken care of by a differentiation of voting procedures for different categories of decision (some categories to be dealt with by weighted, others by "simple" voting), or a system of "double voting" (i.e., voting first according to the "one organization, one vote" norm and subsequently according to a system of weighted voting; a proposal is endorsed only if it receives a majority both times).

Likewise, in international organizations one finds various arrangements to reconcile the two principles (see, for example, Jacobson, 1984, pp. 86–89). In addition to similar provisions as the ones mentioned, there occur rules of unanimity, veto rights for some very powerful members (like in the UN Security Council). In the case of the EBRD described above, the Dutch Prime Minister, by stressing the "equal rights" of all EC members regardless of their weight, in all likelihood tried to invoke the unanimity rule which obtains—or obtained—in the EC for very important decisions. Although Mr. Lubbers recognized that the statutes of the new bank stipulated decision-making according to a weighted rights norm, he appealed to his counterparts in the hope that they be so "wise" as to apply the equal rights norm instead.

Democracy, as recognized already by de Tocqueville (1963, pp. 149 ff.), can easily foster the tyranny by a majority, unless the priciple "abide by majority decisions" is supplemented by the principle "respect the rights of minorities". Minorities will accept majority decisions in the long run as legitimate only as long as their wishes and interests are sufficiently taken into account. On the other hand, majorities will tread warily with respect to minority rights only if the minorities in question abide by majority decisions. Similarly, in the case of organizational politics, the observance of minority, as well as majority, rights is crucial for the viability of democratic procedures (Dahl, 1985, pp. 27–31).

In the case of interorganizational decision-making, I surmise that if the equal rights principle is rigorously observed, the "big" partners will feel to be the "minority" whose "rights" ought to be protected, while in the case of procedures designed solely according to the weighted rights principle, the "small" partners will be convinced that their rights as a "minority" are in jeopardy. In other words, a well-balanced interorganizational democracy requires some sort of reconciliation of both principles.

Interorganizational Oligarchy

Oligarchy, according to Michels (1925, pp. 370–371), is endemic in all democratically constituted organizations: "die Organisation ist die Mutter der Herrschaft der Gewählten über die Wähler, der Beauftragten über die Auftraggeber, der Delegierten über die Delegierenden" (organization generates the domination of constituents by their delegates). If one considers organizational actors as the electorate of an interorganizational organization, the concept of oligarchy can be applied in a meaningful way to "second (or higher) degree" organizations as well as to "first degree" ones. Then the problem is posed in how far elected officers in representative intermediaries can achieve a measure of autonomy from and/or ascendancy over their mandators.

Of course, if the officers in such a second degree organization usurp power, they may do so to make their intermediary agency less dependent on—and thus more powerful over—its member organizations. However, at the interorganizational level one can encounter another form of oligarchization which originates not so much from efforts by officers of the intermediary to aggrandize their central agency, but rather from the tendency of officers to use the intermediary on behalf of their own (member) organizations. Obviously, both forms of oligarchization may serve the personal interests of the officers of the central agency in question, but there is a difference. In the first case they expect to benefit from a strong intermediary which becomes more powerful *vis-à-vis* the mandators in general, whereas in the second case they hope to be rewarded by the organizations they represent for furthering their special interests. In the following section I will limit the discussion to this second form of oligarchization, since it is a typically "second degree" phenomenon.

Given the fact that organizational actors enter into interorganizational relations nearly always with an eye towards certain gains—or in order to avoid certain losses—the supposition is warranted that in "second (or higher) degree" organizations, even more than "first degree" ones, officers will be on the look-out for policies and practices beneficial to their own organizations.

Moreover, it stands to reason that in such intermediaries, representatives of member organizations are, in comparison with individual members of a democratic organization, on the whole less likely to blame their officers for catering to sectional interests. After all, if the joint endeavour is oriented to the pursuit of interests anyway, the boundaries between "common" interests and special interests of one's own (class of) organization(s) tend to be hazy, if distinguishable at all. Therefore, the norms and values of the sector or organizational field in question will in all likelihood condone efforts on the part of officers to get the better part of the intermediary's output for their own organizations.

Nevertheless, even if participants in the intermediary think there is "no harm in trying" (by officers to bias decision-making in favor of the interests of their own organizations), they may object to "trying too hard", "trying too often", or "trying on the sly". For example, in an international organization like the EC efforts by the "big four" to secure top executive posts or seats of new institutions may in general be considered as quite normal, even by the small powers. The case of the EBRD, presented at the beginning of this paper, however, could be the instance of a violation of the taboo on "trying too often". Mr. Lubbers and other advocates of the cause of the "small seven" may have felt that similar attempts by the "big four" to have their interests prevail had regularly occurred—and met with success!—in recent years. This time, therefore, Mr. Lubbers and others may have concluded that the "big four" really had gone too far: if the dominant elite of the EC made a habit of settling such issues among themselves, there was a real danger that they were going to form a sort of oligarchic "directorate" within the EC.

The fact that the Dutch journalists did not report our prime minister's references to the threats to democracy, but tended to interpret the whole affair as one of the usual EC power games about spoils, is an indication that they were not convinced of the authenticity of his moral indignation. In general, of course, it is hard to know to what extent politicians—or, for that matter, representatives of other organizational actors—appeal to mores because they themselves really believe therein, or because they assume that their constituents or adversaries believe in such norms or values. However that may be, the case illustrates that democratic norms—either in their own right and/or to legitimize certain interests—do play a role in settings of this kind as an antidote to oligarchic tendencies.

To take up again the topic of the two principles of democratic rights, one could easily imagine that oligarchic tendencies—in the form of a certain preponderance of the representatives of large member organizations—emerge more often in cases where the formal structure of the intermediary is based strictly on the "one organization, one vote" rule than in cases where weighted rights form the exclusive guiding principle. Some evidence in support of this hypothesis can be found in studies of Business Interest Associations (Van Waarden, 1989, ch. 8; De Vroom, 1990, ch. 9). In the Dutch construction industry as well as in the food and pharmaceutical sectors, big firms were definitely overrepresented in the executive boards of the intermediary organizations that serve the economic, technical, social and political interests of the enterprises concerned. Interviews with functionaries of the organizations studied revealed that this "overrepresentation" more often than not resulted from deliberate policy or well-known custom. Most people involved in the affairs of such intermediaries, it was said, realize it to be of crucial interest that the big firms in the industry will remain committed to the common cause and continue to contribute funds, expertise, capable officers, etc., to keep the intermediary viable and effective.

This brings us to the point that the self-interest of the richer or more powerful members does not necessarily conflict with the interests of the "rest". According to Olson (1971, p. 29), among a relatively small group of firms there is even "a systematic tendency for 'exploitation' of the great by the small!" Even if the rich profit more from certain measures than the poor do, the net balance for the poor can still be modestly positive! However bad oligarchic tendencies are in the light of the value of democracy, such practices may be quite functional for the organization in question and its members, rich and poor. In fact, as Michels already pointed out, the drive towards efficiency and effectiveness is quite often one of the main forces which give rise to oligarchy.

Although oligarchic tendencies in intermediaries are not always necessarily disadvantageous for less well-off members, this should not blind us to the fact that dependency relations between organizations can and frequently do entail extreme forms of power inequality. Lehman (1975) refers to "Interorganizational Empires" and "Corporation-Guided Fields" as types of interorganizational networks in which one member organization, or an intermediary (of the control type), dominates and often exploits other organizations participating in the network. In the case of the "Corporation-Guided Field" the dominant elite does not only consist of elected officers, but also—or even mainly—of bureaucrats.

Oligarchization and bureaucratization, and again this is a theme already quite prominent in the writings of Michels, often go hand in hand. In interorganizational organizations the distinction between elected officers and employed bureaucrats gets easily blurred if functionaries of member organizations become officers of their intermediary and/or if they aspire to become (better paid, or more powerful) functionaries in the intermediary.

An interesting case of this nature is described by Mijs (1987, pp. 165–249) in a study about the laborious formation of a merger between fourteen specialized institutions for non-residential mental health care which took place in Amsterdam from about 1964 until 1983. Most of the institutions in question were either associations or foundations, each headed by an elected or coopted board of volunteers. These institutions established an interorganizational association (the Amsterdam Association for Non-Residential Mental Health Care) to develop among one another the designs for a small number of integrated institutions and to negotiate with government agencies the conditions for the new organizations to be recognized and subsidized. In the end it turned out that the professional managers of the larger member institutions took the lead and succeeded—via positions in an advisory committee of the Amsterdam Association—to work out a set-up satisfactory to most of the parties involved. The key figures became, not surprisingly, the new managers of the five new institutions providing integrated non-residential mental health care in Amsterdam.

Discussion

Interorganizational democracy deserves further investigation by social scientists because it is at the same time a highly relevant as well as a very interesting field of study. Let me mention just a few possible lines of further inquiry.

In the first place, what are the connections between intra-and interorganizational democracy? Although the idea of organizational democracy in the last decade lost some of the appeal it had in the late sixties, early seventies, the *practice* of participation and codetermination in organizations—as evinced by research in many Western countries—did not noticeably decline (Lammers and Széll, 1989). What of it as a condition for, or offshoot from, interorganizational democracy?

In the introduction to this paper I pointed out that the scope for internal democracy tends to shrink due to the growth of interorganizational intertwinements. Therefore, for organization members and their representatives it becomes more crucial to obtain information, and have some influence, on what transpires in the decision-making world of those superordinate organizations on which their organization depends. Of course, such indirect access to higher levels is practicable and meaningful for rank and file organizational members only if there is a fair measure of intra- and interorganizational democracy. Consequently, forms of interorganizational democracy do not only depend on intra-organizational democracy for support at the grass roots level, I surmise, but are important as well as potential reinforcements of intra-organizational democracy.

Another fruitful subject matter for further research would be the origin of interorganizational democracy. When autonomous organizations (or nations) join forces and form interorganizational (international) bodies, the constituting agents, one would guess, will endow such second degree organizations with a more or less democratic constitution if they themselves are founded on such principles. One reason for such a supposition would be the circumstance that the architects of such superorganizational constructs themselves would believe in the value of democratic governance and/or in the necessity to legitimize their initiative in terms of democratic values to which they believe their constituents to adhere. However, what about the curious fact that also many heads of non-democratic organizations—for example—, entrepreneurs or managers—when coaligning with each other to generate strength by unity, adopt strictly democratic rules of the game for their overarching association?

Mijs (1987) views democratic rules of the interorganizational game as a rather natural outgrowth of the institutionalization of relations between—officially at least—autonomous organizations. It is in the interest of the less well endowed organizational actors involved to stick to the belief that all partners have equal rights and that the affairs of their joint endeavor ought to be conducted in a democratic manner. Given then the prevalence of some sort of democratic ethos among the "lower" and "middle classes" of the organizational participants—and probably also among the public at large—it is expedient for the "upper class" organizational actors also to honor the democratic etiquette. What way is a better way than the democratic way to legitimize binding decisions for the collectivity in the eyes of those inside or outside the organization who are affected by such decisions?

Therefore, the democratic character of intermediary organizations could very well be a factor in their viability and effectiveness (Mijs, 1987, p. 59). This might be true, particularly for Western interstate intermediaries, since in these cases the participating governments are usually pledged to see to it that democratic procedures will be observed.

This brings me, as a more general point, to the role of norms and beliefs in interorganizational negotiations and decision-making. Take, for example, the deal between representatives of the Great Powers to which Mr. Lubbers took exception and which formed the starting point of our story. What practices promoting what interests by officers in what positions are deemed admissible by what categories of participants or observers? In addition, one could try to find out how effective such norms are, what sanctions they entail, and under what conditions they change.

In international organizations, one suspects, to arrive at some tacit agreements concerning the informal rules of the interorganizational game will be more difficult than in comparable national organizations. In the latter case, participants can rely on their experience in similar interorganizational settings in their country. If national cultures furnish a common core of expectations and norms to be observed in such cases, trust relations and common understandings will develop more easily and sooner in a new national than in a new international intermediary organization.

References

Coleman, James S. (1982) *The Asymmetric Society*. Syracuse, NY: Syracuse University Press.

Dahl, Robert (1985) *A Preface to Economic Democracy*. Berkeley/Los Angeles: University of California Press.

Edelstein, J. David and Malcolm Warner (1975) *Comparative Union Democracy. Organisation and Opposition in British and American Unions*. London: Allen & Unwin.

Heller, Frank A. (1983) Foreword. In *International Yearbook of Organizational Democracy*, Vol. I, *Organizational Democracy and Political Processes*, edited by Colin Crouch and Frank A. Heller. New York: Wiley & Sons.

Jacobson,Harold K. (1984) *Networks of Interdependence. International Organizations and the Global System*, 2nd ed. New York: Alfred A. Knopf.

Katz, Daniel and Robert L. Kahn (1966) *The Social Psychology of Organizations*. New York: Wiley & Sons.

Lammers, Cornelis J. (1988) The interorganizational control of an occupied country. *Administrative Science Quarterly*, 33, 438–458.

Lammers, Cornelis J. and György Széll (1989) *International Handbook of Participation in Organizations*, Vol. I, *Organizational Democracy: Taking Stock*. Oxford: Oxford University Press.

Lehman, Edward W. (1975) *Coordinating Health Care. Explorations in Interorganizational Relations*. London: Sage.

Lipset, Seymour Martin, Martin Trow and James Coleman (1956) *Union Democracy. The Inside Politics of the International Typographical Union*. Glencoe, Ill.: The Free Press.

Michels, Robert (1925) *Zur Soziologie des Parteiwesens in der modernen Demokratie. Untersuchungen über die oligarchischen Tendenzen des Gruppenlebens*, 2e Auflage. Stuttgart: Alfred Kröner (original edition: 1910).

Mijs, A. A. (1987) *Het ontstaan van de Riagg's in Amsterdam. Een sociologische studie naar de vorming en ontwikkeling van interorganisationele verbanden in de gezondheidszorg*. Lisse: Swets & Zeitlinger.

Olson, Mancur (1971) *The Logic of Collective Action. Public Goods and the Theory of Groups*. Cambridge, Mass.: Harvard University Press (original edition: 1965).

Tocqueville, Alexis de (1963) *De la démocratie en Amérique*. Paris: Union générale d'éditions (original edition: 1835).

Vroom, B. de (1900) *Verenigde Fabrikanten. Ondernemersverenigingen van de voedingsen geneesmiddelen-industrie.* Groningen: Wolters/Noordhoff.

Waarden, Frans van (1989) *Organisatiemacht van belangenverenigingen. De ondernemersorganisaties in de bouwnijverheid als voorbeeld.* Amersfoort: Acco.

Author Index

Subject Index

347

Printed in the United Kingdom
by Lightning Source UK Ltd.
124502UK00001B/217/A